THE
BOOK OF
GAMES

THE BOOK OF GAMES

general editor
Peter Arnold

Exeter Books

NEW YORK

First published in USA 1985
by Exeter Books
Distributed by Bookthrift
Exeter is a trademark of Simon & Schuster, Inc.
Bookthrift is a registered trademark of Simon & Schuster,
Inc. New York, New York

Copyright © Newnes Books, a Division of The Hamlyn
Publishing Group Limited 1985

ISBN 0-671-07732-5
Printed in Italy.
Typeset by Gee Graphics Limited London

CONTENTS

GAMBLING GAMES

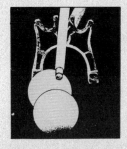

PHYSICAL GAMES

CREDITS AND ACKNOWLEDGEMENTS

WRITERS

Peter Arnold, the General Editor, is a freelance writer and author of numerous books of sports, games and leisure activities, including one described as the 'best history of gambling'. **Paul Richmond** is the *nom de plume* of a consultant on indoor games, puzzles and competitions. **Paul Langfield** has written books and contributed to others on Chess and Draughts. **Francis Roads** was President of the British Go Association from 1971 to 1975, is Editor of the BGA Newsletter, and an advocate of the game in the media. He is a 3-dan player and captained the European team in Tokyo in 1982. **John Fairbairn** is a journalist and translator specialising in Japanese. He has published ten books on Oriental games and through his concern that they should be presented accurately to Western audiences – not to mention his own proficiency in the games – he has become an unrivalled authority in the field. **Matthew Macfadyen** was a Civil Servant who decided occasional painting and decorating combined with games playing to a high level offered a more attractive life-style. At the card table, he is particularly interested in Skat and games with the Tarot pack; he is also currently the European Go Champion. **Mark Wildman** was English Boys and Youth champion at both Snooker and Billiards, and is currently a leading Snooker professional and television commentator. In 1984 he became World Billiards Champion. **Ron Law** is Editor of the magazine *Play Pool* and a contributor on Pool to *Cue World*. **Marion Swan** is the *nom de plume* of a sports graduate and all round sportswoman with a particular involvement in Table Tennis.

DESIGNERS
Design Editor: **Christopher Pow**
Designer: **Karel Feuerstein**
Assistant Designer: **Mei Lim**

ARTISTS
The artwork was prepared by **Karel Feuerstein**, assisted by **Mei Lim**.

PHOTOGRAPHY
Special photography was supplied by **Peter Loughran** (chapter openers), **David Wingar** (Table Tennis) and **M. Athar Chaudhry** (Snooker and Billiards). Leading players **Philip Bradbury** (Table Tennis) and **Mark Wildman** (Snooker and Billiards) did the modelling.

Other pictures were supplied by:

ALDUS ARCHIVE, LONDON 31, 197 (MIKE BUSSELLE); THE BRIDGEMAN ART LIBRARY, LONDON 14, 79, 123 (MUSÉE DES BEAUX ARTS, ROUEN), 128 (WOLVERHAMPTON ART GALLERY), 130, 145, 152 (VICTORIA & ALBERT MUSEUM), 167 (VICTORIA & ALBERT MUSEUM), 171 (TOWNELEY HALL ART GALLERY AND MUSEUM, BURNLEY); PHOTO BULLOZ, PARIS 23; CAMERAPIX HUTCHISON LIBRARY, LONDON 27, 53, 61; MARY EVANS PICTURE LIBRARY, LONDON 32, 33, 57, 77, 155 BOTTOM, 163, 198-9, 202-3; SALLY & RICHARD GREENHILL, LONDON 86 BOTTOM, 87; MICHAEL HOLFORD, LOUGHTON 29; MANSELL COLLECTION, LONDON 17, 21, 37, 39, 81, 89 LEFT, 197, 119, 121, 133, 139, 148, 149, 155 TOP, 161, 179 BOTTOM, 181, 186, 192, 193 TOP, 193 BOTTOM, 201; DAVID MUSCROFT, SHEFFIELD 211 TOP, 211 BOTTOM, 215, 219, 223, 227, 230, 231 TOP, 231 BOTTOM, 233, 239; NEWNES BOOKS 78, 86 TOP, 92, 126; NEWNES BOOK, M. ATHAR CHAUDHRY 209, 210 TOP, 210 BOTTOM LEFT, 210 BOTTOM RIGHT, 212 (ALL SIX), 213 TOP, 213 BOTTOM, 214, 216 TOP, 216 CENTRE, 216 BOTTOM, 221 (ALL FIVE), 222 LEFT, 222 CENTRE, 222 RIGHT, 224 TOP, 224 BOTTOM, 226 TOP LEFT, 226 BOTTOM LEFT, 226 RIGHT; NEWNES BOOKS, PETER LOUGHRAN 10-11, 18-19, 34-5, 42-3, 54-5, 62-3, 70-1, 74-5, 82-3, 90-1, 100-1, 156-7, 204-5, 206-7, 234-5, 242-3; NEWNES BOOK, MICHAEL PLOMER TITLE PAGES, CONTENTS PAGES; NEWNES BOOKS, DAVID WINGAR 247 BOTTOM, 248 (ALL FIVE), 250 LEFT, 250 RIGHT, 251 LEFT, 251 RIGHT, 252 LEFT, 252 RIGHT, 253 LEFT, 253 RIGHT, 254; THE PHOTO SOURCE/COLOUR LIBRARY INTERNATIONAL, LONDON 162; SPECTRUM COLOUR LIBRARY, LONDON 15, 194 TOP, 194 BOTTOM, 195, 200; SYNDICATION INTERNATIONAL, LONDON 59, 89 RIGHT, 175, 179 TOP, 247 TOP; ZEFA (U.K.), LONDON 50.

JACKET ILLUSTRATIONS: NEWNES BOOKS, MICHAEL PLOMER (FRONT) AND PETER LOUGHRAN (BACK).

ASSISTANCE
The Publishers wish to thank the following who kindly provided assistance:
Harrods Ltd, Knightsbridge, London, SW1, for lending the collection of games photographed on the jacket; **Jon James** and **Steve Parker**, of the **Virgin Games Centre**, 22 Oxford Street, London, W1N 9FL, for lending games for photography inside the book; **David Vine**, for lending from his collection the print on page 70-71; **R. Somerville of Edinburgh**, 82 Canongate, The Royal Mile, Edinburgh, EH8 8BZ, mail order playing card suppliers, for supplying the Tarot pack used in the artwork; **Waddingtons Playing Card Co. Ltd**, Wakefield Road, Leeds, LS10 3TP, for supplying cards and allowing them to be used in artwork; **Ashford Table Tennis Centre**, Woodthorpe Road, Ashford, Middlesex, for providing their tables and premises for photography: **The Shogi Association Ltd.**, PO Box 77, Bromley, Kent, for equipment and artwork references.

Associations who kindly supplied sets of official rules in which they own the copyright, and from whom full copies of rules can be obtained are:
The Billiards and Snooker Control Council, Coronet House, Queen Street, Leeds, LS1 2TN; **The English Pool Association** (General Secretary: K. Woodward, 90 Wayneflete, Road, Headington Oxford); **The English Table Tennis Association**, 21 Claremont, Hastings, East Sussex, TN34 1HA (the rules are the copyright of the **International Table Tennis Federation**, 53 London Road, St. Leonards-on-Sea, East Sussex, TN37 6AY); **The British Darts Organisation**, 2 Pages Lane, Muswell Hill, London N10 1PS.

INTRODUCTON

The games in this book were chosen from the thousands eligible for no better reason than that they were considered by the editor and contributors to be games worth playing.

They are presented in four sections. The first section, Table Games, includes some, like Chess (in its western, Chinese and Japanese forms) and Go, which a player can study for a lifetime without exploring all the possibilities in them. Others, like some domino and dice games, while not devoid of skill, are much less demanding.

The section on Card Games also offers a range, from Bridge, with its vast literature, to, perhaps, Casino or German Whist, although even these simpler games can be played well or badly. This section includes games for one (patience in the UK, solitaire in the USA), and games regarded as the best for two, three, four or more players, including one using the Tarot pack.

The Gambling Games section includes games of all kinds which are either of pure chance, like Boule or Hoggenheimer, or which would lose their point without betting, such as Poker.

Games played indoors which involve more physical effort and co-ordination than laying a card or rolling a die are included in the section called, for want of a better description, Physical Games. These include the widespread Table Tennis (92 nations contested the 1985 World Championships), to the more parochial, but not less keenly played and followed, Snooker, Pool, Billiards and Darts.

This final section in particular contains pointers on playing well, and throughout the book the object has been to describe the games in such a way as to indicate where skill and judgement play their part, and where appropriate there are few a paragraphs on strategy.

It is thereby hoped that readers learning new games will obtain the best from them, and that articles on games readers already know will still be found of interest.

PDA

TABLE GAMES

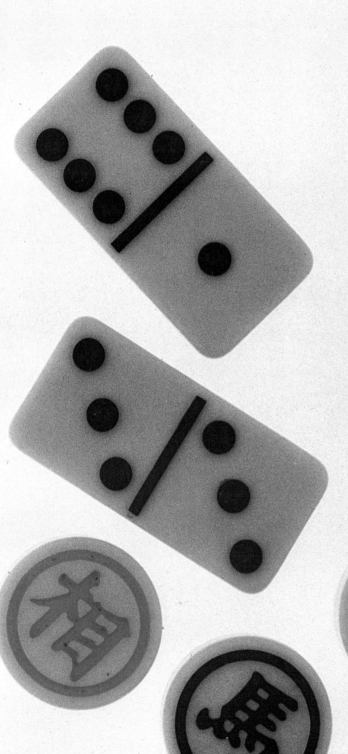

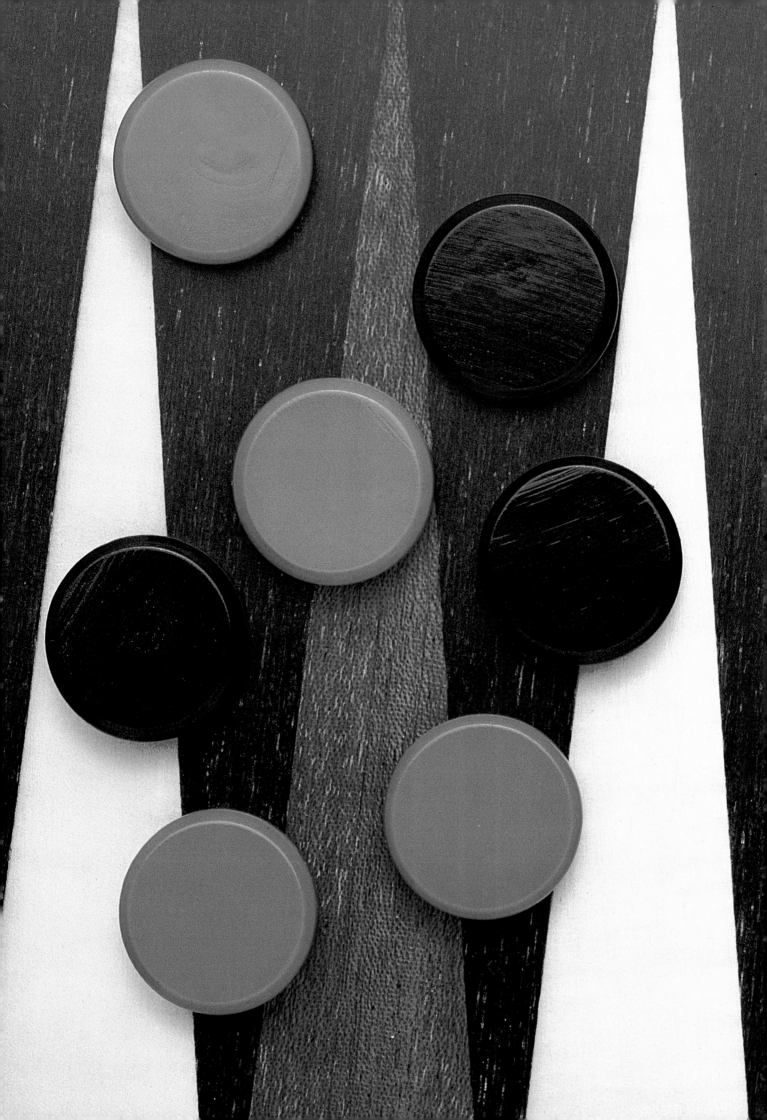

BACKGAMMON

Backgammon, or a game much like it, has been played for many ages. Its origins are pre-Roman and it has long since been a favourite café pastime in the lands that border the eastern Mediterranean where it is found in several forms. The game, then known as Tables, was popular in Europe during the 17th and 18th centuries and has enjoyed bursts of popularity since.

BACKGAMMON HAS MUCH to commend it. It is simple, fast, skilful, and at the same time includes a fair element of chance so that even the beginner can sometimes beat the expert. Backgammon has always been a gambling game and is much played in gaming establishments all over the world, but this does not prevent it from being an excellent social game also, and because a game takes on average no more than 20 minutes, it can be played more casually than the time-demanding Bridge or Chess.

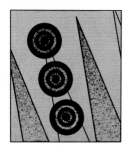

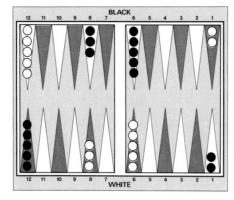

Figure 2 The starting position.

Preliminaries

Backgammon is a game for two players although more can take part (see Chouette). It is played on a backgammon board which often comes in the form of a hinged box that opens out with a raised perimeter and a central partition, known as the bar, which divides the board into two. Within the two halves, a total of 24 saw-tooth 'points' are regularly marked in two alternating and contrasting colours, usually selected from red, black, white, green and buff. Colouring is simply to assist counting.

The board is placed between the players, and one half, conventionally that nearest the light source, is termed the home board or inner table, the other is called the outer table. The six points nearest the player in each half are named after him, so one refers to White's inner table (or home board), White's outer table, and similarly for Black. A backgammon board is illustrated in Figure 1 with the points numbered for reference.

Each player begins the game with 15 tablemen (more commonly simply 'men' or 'stones') distributed on the board in the starting position shown in Figure 2. Notice that two or more men of each player occupy one point in each of the four tables.

Play

The men are moved round the board according to the throws of two dice. The object of each player is to be the first to get all his own men off the board. One player (White in Figure 2) moves his men counter-clockwise, the other clockwise. Men are taken off ('borne off'), subject to certain conditions, when they pass the first point in the player's inner table. Once removed from the board the men are dead and take no further part in the play.

Figure 3 shows direction of movement keyed to Figure 2. Notice that each player has two men, known as runners, on the opponent's first point. These will have to make the full circuit of the board before they can be borne off. At the other extreme, each player starts with five men in his own inner table, just a few points away from home. Movement from point to point corresponds to the spots on the dice thrown by the player. The bar is ignored in counting, and a man on an end point (12) of the opponent's outer table passes to the point opposite on the player's outer table and continues its march round the board.

The game is started by both players rolling a die into their right-hand tables (it is customary at all times to throw

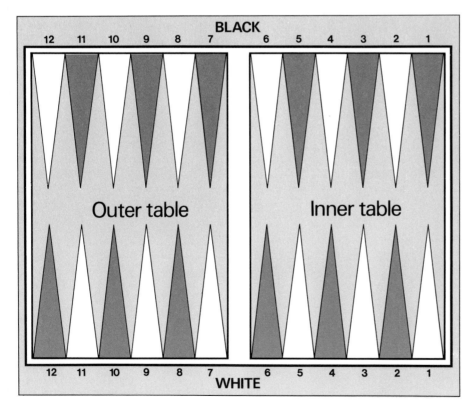

Figure 1 A Backgammon board, outer table to the left, inner table to the right.

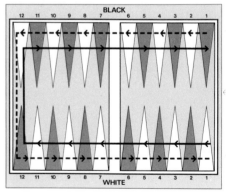

Figure 3 White moves counter-clockwise; Black clockwise.

dice into the half-board on your right). Highest wins (if equal, roll again) and the winner moves the total shown by the two dice. Thus if Black rolled 3 and White rolled 5, White would start and move a total of a 8 points.

Players move only their own men but are always free to choose which men, subject to certain restrictions. Further a player can elect, again subject to certain restrictions, to move two men, each man the number of points indicated on one of the dice, or to move one man the

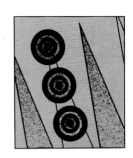

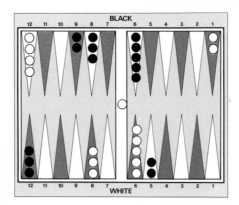

Figure 4 White to play

sum of the dice. Thus White, in the case above, could move one man 3 points and another man 5 points or he could move one man 8 points. A player who is able to move must do so: he cannot elect to pass.

The principal restriction on movement is that any point which is occupied by two or more of the opponent's men cannot be alighted on. Again in the example, White might choose to move one of his runners from B(Black)1 to B4 (3 points) but he could not move the other because B6 is occupied. There is no restriction on passing over an occupied point, nor is there any restriction on the number of men on a point (you stack them if they get overcrowded).

Still with the example, White could move a runner the sum of the two dice (8) because B9 is free. When a man is moved in this way, it must be able to alight on the point indicated by one of the dice. In other words, the chosen man in effect makes two moves. Here, the move to B9 is admissible because White could have 'landed' at B4 *en route*. If this point had been controlled by Black, then a roll of 5:3 would not allow White to move either runner even though B9 is open.

Blot

A point that is occupied by only one man is called a 'blot', and that man is captured if landed on by an opposing man. A man 'hit' in this way is sent to (put on) the bar. Notice that to hit a blot, the point must be landed on, not passed over during the course of a move. It follows that only men of one colour may occupy a point at any one time – men of opposite colours can never share the same point. As you can see (Figure 2), there is no blot in the starting position.

Captured men re-enter the game at the player's 1–point and thus have to complete a full circuit of the board before they can be borne off.

A player may not move any man that is on the board so long as he has a man on the bar: all men on the bar must be re-entered first. If a player is unable to re-enter a man because the point(s)

indicated by the dice are blocked, the player forfeits his turn. Similarly, if a player, though without a man on the bar, has no legal move on the board, he misses his play. It often happens that only one of the dice can be used, while the other is forfeit.

Doublet

About once every six throws a player will roll a double – the same value on both dice. This is called a doublet in backgammon and it permits the player to move four times the value shown. Thus, if fortune smiles with a 6:6, the player moves a total of 24 points which can be made with different men or combined. Thus, if a doublet is thrown, one, two, three or four men may be moved.

With a throw of 6:6, a player who had a man on the bar could re-enter it and move it all the way round to his 1–point provided that the intermediate points (B6, B12, W7) were open to him.

Returning to our initial dice roll, White, instead of advancing a runner, might have elected to move a man B12 to W5, but by so doing he would have created a dangerous blot. There are 36 possible combinations of two dice, and of these one quarter would allow Black to hit the blot on W5 with one of his runners on W1.

Suppose then Black had the good fortune to throw a doublet – 4:4. He at once hits the blot with one of his runners and sends the white man to the bar. However, it would be unwise to separate the runners, leaving them vulnerable, since White, on his next turn, would probably be able to re-enter his man from the bar and perhaps utilise the other dice count to return the compliment and hit a Black blot. So Black moves his second runner up to W5, thereby 'securing the point'. But he rolled a doublet and so still has two 4–point moves to make. His best play would be to move two men from W12 to B9, leaving White no target. This position is shown in Figure 4. Make sure you understand this before proceeding.

Bearing off

No man may be borne off until all of a player's men are in his inner table. A man is considered to have been borne off if it can be notionally moved one point beyond the player's 1–point; thus a man on the 5–point is borne off with a roll of 5. If, during the process of bearing off, a player's man is sent to the bar, no further men may be borne off until the man on the bar has been re-entered and brought round to the inner table. Men once borne off are dead and take no further part in the game. Bearing off is optional. If the player has a move within his home board he can make it instead of taking off a man.

An example of bearing off is demonstrated in Figure 5. Here, both players

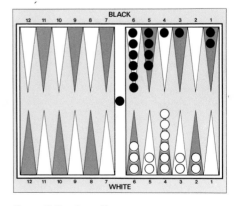

Figure 5 Bearing off.

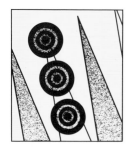

have amassed their men in their respective home boards. White can begin to bear off but Black cannot because he still has a man on the bar.

Supposing it is White's turn and he throws a 6:6 which gives him moves of 6,6,6,6. He must bear off the three men on his 6–point. He is now left with a single move of 6 points which he cannot execute. If the move were entirely within the board, then it would be forfeited. But in bearing off one is obliged, in these circumstances, to make the next highest move. In this case, White must bear off one of the men on his 5–point, exposing the other.

If all White's remaining men had been grouped, say, on his 1–point, then one of these would have been removed.

Now Black has a 3 to 1 chance of entering his man from the bar. His ideal roll would be 5:1, when he would enter to hit White's blot and secure his 3–point so as to offer no target to the white man now on the bar.

Scoring

The game ends when one player has borne off all his men. If he does so before his opponent has borne off any, and while the opponent still has at least one man in the player's home board or on the bar, he scores a backgammon, or triple game. If the opponent has not borne off a man but has no man in the player's home board or on the bar, the player scores a gammon, or double game. If the opponent has borne off one or more men, the player scores a single game.

Doubling die

The cubic doubling die is a modern invention that has transformed backgammon as a gambling game. The die has progressive multiples of 2 on its six faces: 2,4,8,16,32,64. Its use is by agreement between the players. At the start of a game, the die is placed beside the board or on the bar, 64 uppermost.

At each turn, and before rolling the dice, a player has the option of picking up the doubling die and placing it by his opponent, 2 uppermost, saying 'Double', though the statement is not essential. This action proposes to double the ultimate score (stake) of the game. The receiver can accept or decline. If he declines, he in effect resigns, the game ends and the player doubling is credited with a single game. If the double is accepted, the game continues with the score (stake) doubled. Thereafter the second player may pick up the doubling die at any turn, and before rolling the dice, place it in front of his opponent with the 4 uppermost, again proposing to double the score (stake), and so on. Observe that the same player can never double twice in succession – the right alternates. It is possible, at least in theory, for a game to be played with the maximum increment and to be concluded with a backgammon for settlement at 192 times the stake!

Backgammon players painted by Dirk Hals (1591-1656) (Alan Jacobs Gallery, London).

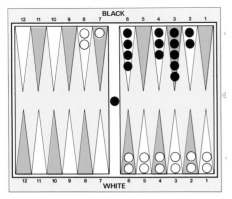

Figure 6 A closed board.

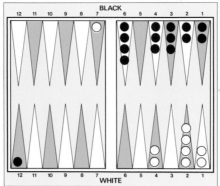

Figure 7 A critical moment.

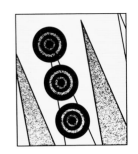

The doubling die adds spice to the game and introduces new skills. Foresight and calculation are called for: if the odds are one-sided, a double will be declined. A weakness inherent in the use of the die is that the stronger player will be tempted to double at the beginning of the game so that the weaker player, if he wants to play at all, must accept increased stakes.

Prime

If a player succeeds in making six consecutive points, he has achieved a prime. The significance of a prime is that the opponent's men cannot pass it since the highest dice roll is a 6. Men trapped behind a prime must mark time until the player chooses to break it. A prime in one's own home board, which is known as a closed board, can be devastating. Look at Figure 6. Black is poised to bear off – except for that man on the bar which cannot re-enter on account of White's prime. It would now be pointless for Black to roll the dice until the prime is broken.

White will try to retain the prime as long as possible. He will bring his three men round from Black's outer board and will then start to bear off; his priority being for him to avoid leaving a blot for Black to hit when re-entering the man from the bar. Even should he be hit, he would have a good chance of passing successfully through Black's home board.

The position in Figure 7 could have arisen from Figure 6. White succeeded in bearing off six men before he was forced to expose a man which was hit by Black. White was able to re-enter at once and Black, instead of hurrying his straggler, chose to make his 1–point. The two re-entered men now face each other in a critical encounter.

It is White's turn, and fortune gives him a 6:1 which means that he can hit the black man and advance to W11 or

he can decline the capture by playing to W11, reversing the order of the moves. If he hits the blot, White has a chance of a gammon or even a backgammon – but he stands an excellent chance, too, of being hit again with the prospect of himself facing a closed board. On the other hand, if he passes Black, the game is safely won. If the doubling die were in use, White might elect to hit the blot

Above Modern players taking advantage of the climate to play outdoors in Greece.

and double, tempting Black. This is an illustration of the kind of decisions that have to be taken in Backgammon, which despite superficial appearances, is a game controlled by the players rather than the dice.

Strategy

Backgammon games are sometimes classified according to the strategy employed. This is often governed by the opening dice rolls. Two of the commonest types of games, and also the simplest to identify, are the running game and the back game. In the running game, one or both players advance their runners early, probably because of favourable dice rolls. Blocks and blots are subordinated in the race to get one's men round the board. The influence of the dice is enhanced at the expense of the skill element. An early throw of 6:6 is a great inducement to play a running game.

A back game calls for much greater skill and is usually forced on the players by circumstance rather than choice, perhaps as a result of repeated hits and counter hits. The back game is characterized by one, sometimes both players retaining at least two men and perhaps several more that have been re-entered, in the opponent's home board with the aim of hitting unguarded men as the adversary is bearing off – an expansion of the ideas exemplified in Figures 6 and 7 above.

The trouble with a back game is that if it goes wrong, as it often does, then

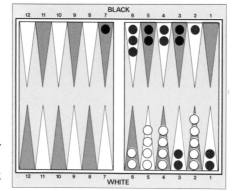

Figure 8 The late stages of a typical back game.

the penalty could well be a gammon or backgammon.

A position arising from a typical back game by Black is illustrated in Figure 8. Notice that Black has made two points in White's inner table, a common strategy in a back game.

Other types of game are more complex but basically they are blocking games – on the one hand, the player endeavours to get his men safely round to his home board; on the other he attempts to thwart his opponent doing the same by setting up blocks; that is, by securing a number of points adjacent to one another to impede the advance of the opponent's men. The perfect block is the prime but even that, to be effective, must be in or near the home board and a prime cannot be held for long since it requires the immobility of all but three of one's force, and sooner rather than later they will have to be moving on.

There are a number of key points which it is an advantage to hold; principally the bar point (7) but also the adjacent 8–point and the 5–point and 4–point within the home board.

It is poor strategy to occupy the 1-, 2- and 3–points until preparing to bear off, since here the blocks do not constitute an effective barrier as they can be easily jumped. The men are better employed further back.

Looked at statistically, and assuming no hazards are encountered, dice throws totalling a minimum of 167 points are needed to bear off all men from the starting position. Since the value of the average dice roll (two dice) is just over 8, the requirement is met on average in about 20 turns. That is of course in theory and takes no account of men being sent to the bar or the effect of blocks, which frequently force a player to forgo his move entitlement because points he needs to occupy are closed to him. This is where blocks score: if you can take full advantage of your turns and your opponent cannot because of your blocks, then the law of averages determines that you will bear off first because you will need less turns to do so.

Blots can be two-edged. If your opponent has brought a runner round into his inner board where you hit it, then he has been set back in effect two or three turns, but if you send a man to the bar from your home board, it is only moved back a few points – the equivalent of perhaps half a dice roll, not a serious setback. What is more, the hit may be returned when the man re-enters and the damage to you will be more serious because your man is close to bearing off.

Opening plays

An insight into Backgammon strategy may be gained from examining the recommended opening moves for the first player. Surprisingly, the experts are not unanimous; alternatives are argued for many rolls. These disputed plays are indicated below with an asterisk. Where there is no asterisk, the play given is favoured by all experts.

6:5 B1–B12
6:4 B1–B11*
6:3 B1–B7 B12–W10*
6:2 B1–B7 B12–W11*
6:1 W8–W7 B12–W7
5:4 B12–W8 B12–W9
5:3 B12–W8 B12–W10*
5:2 B12–W8 B12–W11
5:1 B12–W8 B1–B2*
4:3 B12–W9 B12–W10
4:2 W8–W4 W6–W4
4:1 B12–W9 B1–B2*
3:2 B12–W10 B12–W11*
3:1 W8–W5 W6–W5
2:1 B12–W11 B1–B2*

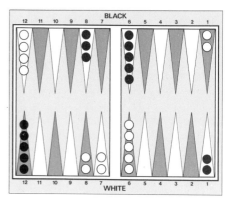

Figure 9 A good start for White.

Good players never lose sight of the odds. There is nothing difficult about these but they demand mental agility – Backgammon is a fast game and it is considered a discourtesy to ponder plays. You need to know the odds against a number coming up, the chances of having a blot hit, probability of being able to bear off in a certain number of throws, and of being able to enter a man from the bar, and so on.

One calculation frequently necessary where a game is closely fought is applied when all the men of both sides have passed each other. Now it is a simple matter of who gets there first and, if you are gambling, it is a good time to consider a double. Figure 10

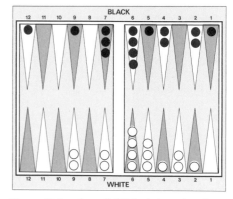

Figure 10 Bearing off: White is just ahead.

illustrates such an occasion. The calculation is quite easy: you simply add up the numbers of the occupied points, multiplying as necessary if more than one man occupies a point. For example, White has two men on his 9–point and

these must be moved 2 × 9 = 18 points to bear off. Thus White's requirement is one less than Black's (83–84), and if it were White's turn, he would be tempted to double if the die lay with him – the first throw, worth an average of 8 remember, would give him a 9 point advantage – roughly 10% ahead of Black.

Finally, a golden rule if you are playing with the doubling cube: decline a double if the odds are 3–1 or worse against you, otherwise accept. Apart from the game odds, you will then hold the powerful doubling option.

Chouette

Chouette is a system that allows three or more to play Backgammon. All players roll a die with repeat rolls as necessary to break ties. Highest score is 'man in the box' with the other players competing against him under a captain (second highest roll). Other players are ranked in the order of their rolls, any new players joining the game later being entered at the bottom.

Each game is between the man in the box and the captain assisted by his partners. The team advises the captain who makes all decisions except when the man in the box doubles, when the team members make individual decisions whether or not to accept. If the captain refuses a double, the highest-ranking player who accepts takes over the captaincy and the deposed captain is relegated to the foot of the team. Any team member who refuses a double drops out and can no longer offer advice in that game.

If the man in the box wins the game, he stays there, the captain is sent to the bottom of the team and the next game starts with the highest-ranking player as the new captain. If the team wins, the captain takes over as man in the box and the senior-ranking team member becomes captain while the man in the box goes to the bottom of the team. Scores are settled individually.

Acey-Deucy

This is a version popularised by the U.S. Navy. The game starts with an

An early engraving showing Backgammon: the game is nearly over.

empty board. On his turn, a player is free to enter a man through the opponent's 1–point in the same manner in which a man is entered from the bar in Backgammon, or he can make a move on the board, otherwise the usual rules of Backgammon apply. There is one additional feature; the rolling of a 2:1 (hence the name) confers a big bonus. The player first moves 2:1 in the normal way, then chooses any doublet he wishes and plays these moves as well after which, for good measure, he has another turn. If the next roll is also a 2:1, then the sequence is repeated. Luck can obviously play a big part in Acey-Deucy but there is additional skill in controlling entry: a man held back is invulnerable and can strike a blot as the opponent is poised to bear off.

Moultezim

In this Turkish game, the home boards are in diagonally opposite corners and both players move in the same direc-

tion. To start, all 15 men are stacked on the opponent's 12-point. There are no blots, a single man controlling a point; however, a player may not control more than four points in his outer board. Each player must move his first man round into his own outer board before he is free to move as he pleases.

Plakato

This is a Greek version, sometimes called Mahbousa. Players start with all their men on their opponent's 1–point so that every man must be moved a complete circuit of the board. The only other difference from regular Backgammon is that when a blot is hit, the captured man is not removed to the bar (which is not used in the game) but is instead imprisoned. It cannot be moved until the opponent's man moves away; meanwhile the point is safe for the captor who may, if he wishes, add further men to the point.

CHESS

The origin of chess is to be found in a game first played in Northern India during the 5th century. Called Chaturanga the board was set up for four players and each moved in turn depending on the throw of a die. As the years went by the dice were discarded. The game was then arranged for two players and the result was now a test of skill only.

THE PIECES USED in Chess have remained much the same since the game was for four, and this explains why a player today has two each of the Bishops, Knights and Rooks. In the original game the pieces used were symbols of the four divisions which comprise an army – chariots, ele-phants, horsemen and foot soldiers.

Ambassadors and traders took the game firstly to Persia, then following the Arab invasion of that country, to North Africa. Before long traders had taken it to Italy, and the invasion of Spain by the Moors paved the way for chess to travel north into Europe. Not

until the eleventh century invasion of England by the Normans did chess reach the English Court and it soon became popular among the upper classes.

With the advent of the Renaissance came certain changes in the rules of the game and modern chess was born. It had been usual for Pawns to move forward one square at a time but now it was agreed that any Pawn being moved for the first time could leap forward two squares. This was to speed up a rather slow game. The chief change was the rule governing the movement of the Queen. She now had new powers conferred upon her and could be moved as far across the board as the player wished and could move in any direction. The only other changes came much later and related to a special move called castling, which will be described below.

The modern rules of chess have been set out by F.I.D.E., the International Chess Federation.

Learning to Play

Chess does have a reputation for being a very difficult game to learn and play and is widely thought of as a pastime for intellectuals. This is not the case, as is clear when one considers how many children of six or seven years old play the game. Some patience is needed in learning the moves and in understanding the notation. This is soon rewarded when one starts to play the game.

Aim of the Game

The aim of the game is to trap one's opponent's king. This can be done in a number of different ways and is known as checkmate or mate. If a King is threatened and could be taken prisoner in the player's next move, this is known as a check.

The Board

A chessboard has sixty-four alternate black and white squares or light and dark coloured squares. When setting up the pieces for the start of a game always ensure that there is a white square in the right hand corner of the board for each player.

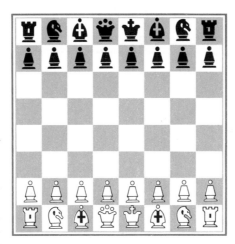

Figure 1

Figure 1 shows the position of the Pawns and pieces before a game starts. The rows of squares which go from a player's back row to his opponent's back row are the files. The rows of squares which run from left to right across the board are the ranks. As will be seen later some pieces may be moved across the diagonals – that is across the corners of the squares.

Note that the Queens always start the game on a square of their own colour – White Queen on a white square and Black Queen on a black square. This means that Queens face each other in the same file as do the Kings. Note that in the figures showing movement of the pieces, examples of check and checkmate etc., all pieces have been removed from the board except those needed for demonstration. In an actual game there may be other pieces all over the board.

Movement of the pieces

Unlike draughts (checkers), the pieces in chess do not all have the same rules governing their movement. Players move only one piece at a time except in a special move called castling which will be explained later. Players move alternately and the player with the White pieces always starts a game. The decision as to who plays White is decided by lottery and it is customary before play begins for one of the players to conceal in his hands one White and one Black pawn. He offers his clenched fists to his opponent who chooses a hand and plays the colour which is revealed when that hand is opened.

All Pawns are governed by the same rules. If moved, a Pawn always moves forward in its own file except when it makes a capture. A Pawn moves only one square at a time except when moved for the first time. In this case the player has the right to move it forward two squares. For reasons which will be discussed later it is usual for players to open a game with centre Pawns, either the Pawn in front of the King or the one in front of the Queen. If a Pawn meets another in the same file it is blocked and cannot be moved until a capture has been made. Pawns capture diagonally one square forward.

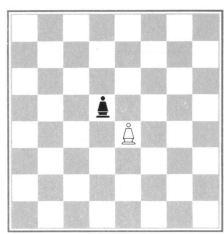

Figure 2

Figure 2 shows a White Pawn which has been moved two squares forward in White's opening move. Instead of blocking this with the Pawn he has in the same file Black has moved a Pawn two squares forward in an adjacent file. White's next move could be to caputre the Black Pawn by moving onto the square it occupies and removing the Black Pawn from the board. The more of your opponent's pieces you can capture the weaker become his forces and the more likely you are to achieve a checkmate.

Look at Figure 1 again. On each player's back row are pieces to be identified. From left to right on White's back row there is a Rook (children often refer to them as castles), a Knight, a Bishop, a Queen and a King, another Bishop, Knight and Rook. Different

The checkmate – all except the loser shows some amusement at his discomfiture.

colour. They do not, of course, capture the pieces they leap over. Figure 6 shows the moves that Knights can make.

The King is the most important piece on the board but it is far from being the strongest. Limited in its move to one square in any one move it can however use a file, a rank or a diagonal. Figure 7 shows the squares to which the White and Black Kings can move from the squares they occupy in this particular

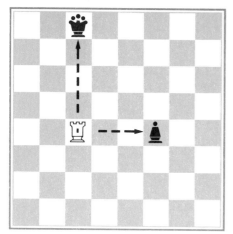

Figure 3

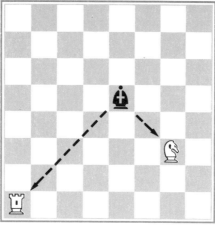

Figure 4

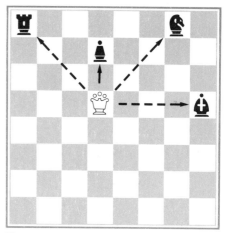

Figure 5

rules apply to the movement of these pieces but they all capture in exactly the same way as Pawns – that is they occupy the square of an opponent's piece and the captured piece is removed from the board.

First of all the Rooks. These pieces are confined to files and ranks but they can be moved as far across the board as the player wishes. They can never be moved across the diagonals.

Look at Figure 3. The White Rook shown here can capture either the Black Queen or the Black Pawn if it is White's turn to move.

Now the Bishops. These are confined entirely to the diagonals. One Bishop starts on white squares and the other on black squares. Because they use diagonals they remain on the colour they start on throughout the game unless they are

captured and are removed from the board. Figure 4 shows a Black Bishop that can capture either the White Knight or the White Rook if it is Black's turn to move.

The Queen is the strongest piece on the board. She is allowed the same long diagonal move as the Bishop and can also use either a rank or file. In Figure 5 the White Queen can capture either the Black Knight, the Black Pawn, the Black Bishop or the Black Rook.

The Knights have a move quite different from any other piece. They go two squares up or down a file and then one square to left or right in a rank, or two squares along a rank and one square up or down a file. This L shaped move means that the knights are slow moving but they do have the advantage that they can leap over other pieces of either

Figure 6

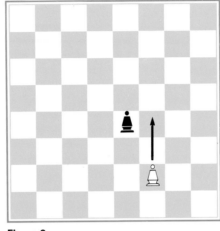

Figure 9

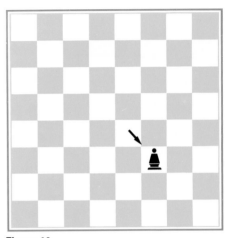

Figure 10

illustration. Like all the other pieces, Kings capture by moving onto the square of an opponent's piece. Kings must never move into check. Look at Figure 8. The Black King cannot capture the White Queen because it would be moving into check from the White Rook. The two Kings must never occupy adjoining squares though the square that separates them need not be vacant.

Pawn promotion

A Pawn might not be very powerful at the start of a game, but is potentially as powerful as any piece on the board. This is because a Pawn which reaches the eighth rank can be promoted to any other piece, except, of course, a King.

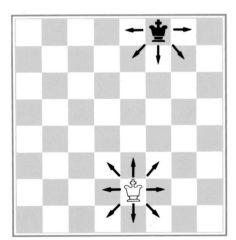

Figure 7

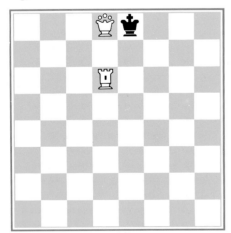

Figure 8

Usually such a Pawn is promoted to Queen, but not necessarily, and there are situations when it is better to promote to another piece.

If a player wishes to promote a Pawn to Queen, and his Queen has already been captured, then it is easy to exchange one for the other. However, if his Queen is still on the board, so that in effect he has two Queens, then some improvisation will be necessary. In the absence of a duplicate set of chessmen, perhaps the Pawn could be stood upon a Rook to represent a Queen.

Special Moves

There are two special moves a beginner must learn before he can play a game of chess.

When a Pawn is moved for the first time it may be moved two places forward. In the original game, Chaturanga, only a one square move was allowed. If a Pawn is moved two squares to avoid capture by moving into the same rank as a hostile Pawn it can be taken on the square it would have occupied if it had moved only one square forward. Look at Figure 9. If White Pawn is moved forward two squares and draws up alongside the Black Pawn then Black Pawn can capture it on the square indicated in Figure 10. This is known as capturing 'en passant'. The capturing move must be made in the player's next move. He cannot move another piece and then return to the Pawn that moved to escape capture.

The other special move is called 'castling'. The object of this move is to bring a powerful piece, the Rook, towards the centre of the board where it is more useful and, at the same time, to move the King to a safer square. Castling can be performed only once by either player in any one game. It is the only time two pieces are moved in any one move. Figure 11 shows the move for White on the King's side and for Black on the Queen's side. Figure 12

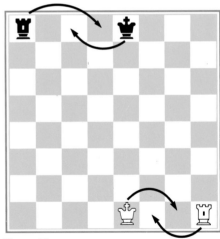

Figure 11

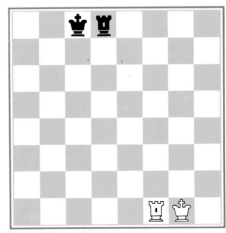

Figure 12

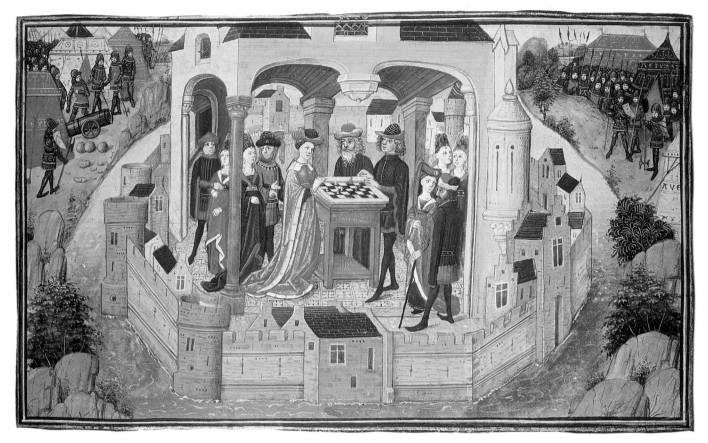

Above Chess players from a book 'Histoire du Grand Alexandre' by Jean Vauquelin, 1460.

shows the position of the pieces after each player has castled. Note that the King is always moved two squares towards the side of the board and the Rook is then placed on the other side of the King. If you castle on the King's side there is always one vacant square in the corner. If you castle on the Queen's side, as Black has in this example, then there will be two vacant squares in the back rank corner. Players usually aim to castle by about the tenth move, though a game can take place without either player castling.

It is also possible to play chess without knowing either of the systems of Notation but all players will benefit from learning both.

Notation – Reading or Recording a Game

Until quite recently all English books on chess used what is known as the Descriptive or English Notation. The other system is called Algebraic. Most English readers prefer the Descriptive system but the International Chess Federation decreed that as from 1 January 1981 only Algebraic Notation would be acceptable at International Chess Tournaments. The result of this has been that chess writers have tended to drop Descriptive in favour of Algebraic. However, so many readers have pro-

tested that some chess correspondents to newspapers have reverted to Descriptive. Nearly all books published in the past in both the U.K. and the U.S.A. have used Descriptive so it will pay the reader to learn this shorthand. On the other hand, Algebraic is taking over and eventually all books will no doubt use this system.

In fact both methods of recording games are very simple and in a matter of minutes most people find they can master both.

Descriptive Notation

Figure 13 (A) shows a numbered board. This is numbered for Descriptive Notation. Each file is numbered 1 to 8 for each of the pieces on the back row. Looking at it from left to right we have the Queen Rook file, the Queen Knight file, the Queen Bishop file, the Queen file and then the King file. It goes on to the King Bishop file, the King Knight file and finally the King Rook file.

The abbreviations are as follows:–

K	=	King
Q	=	Queen
KB	=	King's Bishop
QB	=	Queen's Bishop
KN (or KKt) =		King's Knight
QN (or QKt) =		Queen's Knight
KR	=	King's Rook
QR	=	Queen's Rook

The board also has the numbers for Black and, as the diagram shows, White's No. 1 square in each file is Black's No.8 and vice versa. The movement of a Pawn or Piece is given as the identity of the piece, the square it moves from and the square it moves to.

Other symbols that are used are as follows:–

–	moves to
x	indicates a capture
ch	check
O.O.	castles on King's side
O.O.O.	castles on Queen's side
!	a good move
?	a poor move

Algebraic Notation

This is a rather less complicated method of reading or recording games. It is also a far more logical approach to Notation. Basically it is the map reference system, as shown in Figure 13(B). The files are all identified with the letters of the alphabet from a to h. The ranks are

KR1 / QR8	KN1 / QN8	KB1 / QB8	Q1 / Q8	K1 / K8	QB1 / KB8	QN1 / KN8	QR1 / KR8
KR2 / QR7	KN2 / QN7	KB2 / QB7	Q2 / Q7	K2 / K7	QB2 / KB7	QN2 / KN7	QR2 / KR7
KR3 / QR6	KN3 / QN6	KB3 / QB6	Q3 / Q6	K3 / K6	QB3 / KB6	QN3 / KN6	QR3 / KR6
KR4 / QR5	KN4 / QN5	KB4 / QB5	Q4 / Q5	K4 / K5	QB4 / KB5	QN4 / KN5	QR4 / KR5
KR5 / QR4	KN5 / QN4	KB5 / QB4	Q5 / Q4	K5 / K4	QB5 / KB4	QN5 / KN4	QR5 / KR4
KR6 / QR3	KN6 / QN3	KB6 / QB3	Q6 / Q3	K6 / K3	QB6 / KB3	QN6 / KN3	QR6 / KR3
KR7 / QR2	KN7 / QN2	KB7 / QB2	Q7 / Q2	K7 / K2	QB7 / KB2	QN7 / KN2	QR7 / KR2
KR8 / QR1	KN8 / QN1	KB8 / QB1	Q8 / Q1	K8 / K1	QB8 / KB1	QN8 / KN1	QR8 / KR1

Figure 13(A) Descriptive Notation.

numbered from 1 to 8 starting at White's back row. Each square therefore has the same reference for each player. Pieces are identified as in Descriptive Notation, but pawns are not identified. Here is an opening in both Notations:

Descriptive		Algebraic	
White	Black	White	Black
1) P–K4	P–K4	1) e2–e4	e7–e5
2) N–KB3	N–QB3	2) N–f3	N–c6
3) B–B4	N–B3	3) B–c4	N–f6

It is usual to abbreviate as much as possible. If only one Bishop can move to a certain square there is no need to identify it as, say King's Bishop (KB). In Algebraic Notation it is sufficient for White to write his first move as simply e4 because this Pawn is the only one that can reach this square at the start of a game, but to help beginners the opening moves are set out in full in the examples which follow later.

Value of the Pieces

A slow moving Pawn is obviously less valuable than a piece which can sweep across the board to make a capture. Experts have therefore worked out a system of points giving the following value to Pawns and pieces.

Pawn	1 point
Bishop	3 points
Knight	3 points
Rook	5 points
Queen	9 points

It is not possible to give a point value to a King. It is confined to a one square move though it can use ranks, files or diagonals. On the other hand if you lose your King you lose the game. In other words he is your most valuable piece but also a weak piece.

From this it is clear that to capture a Pawn with a Knight and then lose the Knight to one of your opponent's Pawns is not a good move.

The Queen is the strongest and therefore most valuable piece because of its mobility. Players should always keep an eye on their Queens and try to avoid putting this piece *'en prise'*, which simply means in a position from which it can be captured.

Rooks have more mobility than either Knights or Bishops but are less powerful than Queens.

Bishops and Knights have more or less the same value but much depends on where they happen to be situated on the board at any particular time.

Much the same applies to Pawns. A Pawn which can put your opponent's King in check without being captured is far more valuable than the one point it has at the start of a game.

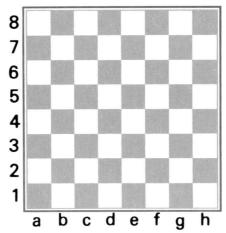

Figure 13(B) Algebraic Notation.

It is worth keeping in mind the value of the pieces so that in any exchange you do not capture a minor piece only to lose a more valuable piece.

Check and Checkmate

When a King can be captured in a player's next move he is in check and it is usual for the player making the move to say 'check'. The King must now be moved to a safe square or the attacking piece must be captured and removed from the board. A third way of getting out of check is to interpose a piece between the attacking piece and the King. A player must never move his own King into check.

If the King under attack cannot get out of check he is checkmated and that is the end of the game.

Figures 14-16 show a simple check and checkmate with two White Rooks against a lone Black King. Black King is not in check in Figure 14 but it is White's turn and the arrow shows his best move. In Figure 15 Black King is in check from White Rook and must move. He has no alternative but to go to the back rank otherwise he would be moving into check from the other

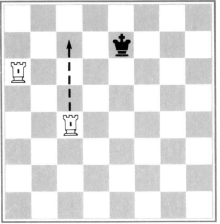

Figure 14

Figure 17

Figure 15

Figure 18

Figure 19

White Rook. Figure 16 shows White's last move. It is checkmate.

Another simple checkmate is shown in Figures 17-18. This time it is a White King attacked by Black Knight and Queen. It is Black's turn to move and he goes Q–KN2 mate as shown in Figure 18. White King cannot capture the Queen because he would be moving into check from Black Knight. The move in Algebraic Notation is Q–g2 mate.

Figure 16

A Pawn, if supported by other pieces, can achieve checkmate. Look at Figure 19. Black King is not in check but it is White's turn to move. He goes P–N7 ch (g6–g7) as shown in Figure 20. Black King cannot capture the attacking Pawn because this would mean moving into check from the Rook Pawn. He cannot move to R7 because the White Bishop attacks this square. It is checkmate from a Pawn (Figure 20). The only flight square which appears to be available to Black King is, in fact, attacked by White's Bishop.

Openings

According to experts the first four moves in a chess opening can be played in 197,299 ways! The player with the White pieces has the option of 20 different moves as his first. He can move a Pawn one square forward which gives him a choice of eight, or two squares forward giving him sixteen possible first moves. The only other pieces that can be used to start a game are the Knights and each has a choice of two squares to leap to giving the player a further four possible first moves.

Most games start with a centre Pawn opening. Pieces placed in the centre of the board command more squares than those at the side. It is also usual for Black to block White's first Pawn move as will be seen from the examples given here of well established openings.

The most popular and widely used of all is known as the Ruy Lopez which acquired its name from a 16th century chess playing Spanish priest. He was one of the earliest chess players to write

Figure 20

a book on the subject. Here it is in both Notations.

	Descriptive		*Algebraic*	
	White	Black	White	Black
1)	P–K4	P–K4	e2–e4	e7–e5
2)	N–KB3	N–QB3	N–f3	N–c6
3)	B–N5		B–b5	

Figure 21 shows the position at this stage. Note that White can castle in his next move. Black Knight can be taken but need not move to escape capture because his Queen's Pawn or Knight's Pawn could take the Bishop.

Another frequently used opening is called the Sicilian Defence. Here's how it goes and again the reader can choose which Notation to follow:

	Descriptive		*Algebraic*	
	White	Black	White	Black
1)	P–K4	P–QB4	e2–e4	c7–c5
2)	N–KB3	P–K3	N–f3	e7–e6
3)	P–Q4	PxP	d2–d4	c5xd4
4)	NxP	N–KB3	Nxd4	N–f6
5)	N–QB3	P–KN3	N–c3	g7–g6

After the first five moves each player has captured a Pawn leaving the position fairly equal with opportunities for each player to mount an attack.

There are many different openings and players do well to study and memorize some of them.

Popular with beginners is the Four Knights' Game. This begins as follows:

	Descriptive		*Algebraic*	
	White	Black	White	Black
1)	P–K4	P–K4	e2–e4	e7–e5
2)	N–KB3	N–QB3	N–f3	N–c6
3)	N–B3	N–B3	N–c3	N–f6
4)	B–N5	B–N5	B–b5	B–b4
5)	0–0	0–0	0–0	0–0
6)	P–Q3	BxN	d2–d3	Bxc3
7)	PxB	P–Q3	b2xc3	d7–d6

By the seventh move both players have castled – and all experts advise early castling – and each has captured a minor piece. Bishops and Knights are of equal value. From now on the game may develop in a number of different ways. Figure 22 shows the position after the seventh move.

Figure 21

Figure 22

An interesting opening not much used by beginners and therefore worth some attention is what is known as the English Opening. This is how it goes:

	Descriptive		*Algebraic*	
	White	Black	White	Black
1)	P–QB4	P–K4	c2–c4	e7–e5
2)	N–QB3	N–KB3	N–c3	N–f6
3)	N–B3	N–B3	N–f3	N–c6
4)	P–Q4	P–K5	d2–d4	e5–e4

This is a variation of the four Knight's opening. Black has the opportunity to capture White's Queen Pawn but instead moves on to threaten White's Knight. Figure 23 shows the position then the opening proceeds as follows:

	Descriptive			*Algebraic*	
	White	Black	White		Black
5)	N–Q2	NxP	N–d2		Nxd4
6)	N(Q2)xPNxN	N(Q2)xe4Nxe4			
7)	NxN	B–N5ch	Nxe4		B–b4ch

Each player has captured a hostile Knight and Pawn. White is now in check. The opening continues:

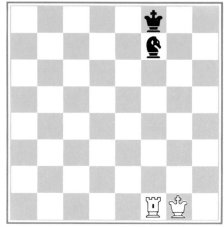

Figure 23

Figure 24

	Descriptive		*Algebraic*	
	White	Black	White	Black
8)	B–Q2	BxBch	B–d2	Bxd2ch
9)	QxB	N–K3	Qxd2	N–e6

The captures are still equal and the game can continue in a number of different ways.

Middle Game

Strategy and tactics are involved in every game. Strategy implies the overall planning of your attack on either the hostile King or Queen. Tactics are merely the movement of pieces to the best advantage in any particular situation. Once a game is under way the player should look for certain opportunities to set traps for his opponent and keep a wary eye on the board to make sure he does not fall into any himself.

A piece that is pinned is not only vulnerable but is immobilized. A piece is pinned when it should not or must not be moved. Look at Figure 24. Here the Black Knight is pinned because to

Men playing chess in Syria.

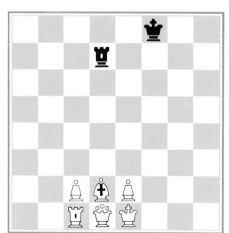

Figure 25

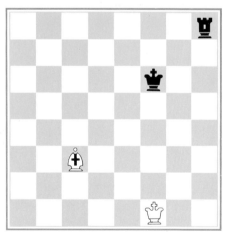

Figure 26

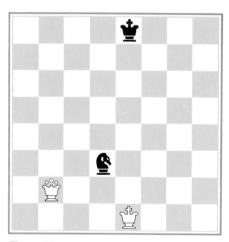

Figure 27

move it would expose Black King to check from the White Rook. In Figure 25 the White Bishop is pinned though of course the player may move it if he wishes. Move White Bishop and White Queen is lost to the Black Rook.

Look out for skewers. This is where an attacking piece aims to capture a piece which is actually beyond the piece first attacked. Figure 26 shows the Black King put in check by a White Bishop. The King must move so then the Bishop captures the Black Rook.

Now for a particularly deadly form of attack. Beware of forks from your opponent and, of course, seek opportunities to fork his pieces. A fork is a double attack. Look at Figure 27. Here is the most deadly fork of all! Black Knight has moved to a square from which he attacks White's King and Queen. White must move his King and then Black captures the White Queen.

Figure 28 shows a potential fork. If White Bishop captures Black Pawn he will fork Black King and Rook. King must move. Black Rook is then captured by White Bishop.

Players sometimes find opportunities to gain material by what is known as a Discovered Check. This occurs when a piece is moved to reveal a check from another piece. In Figure 29 there is now a chance for Black to achieve a capture, a Discovered Check and indeed a Double Check. Black Bishop moves to

27

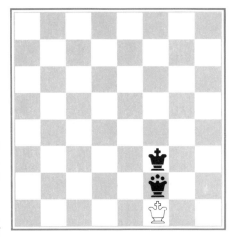

Figure 30

Figure 31

capture the White Pawn and, at the same time, put White King in check. There is also a Discovered Check from Black Rook.

End Game

A game can end in a number of

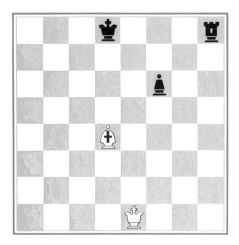

Figure 28

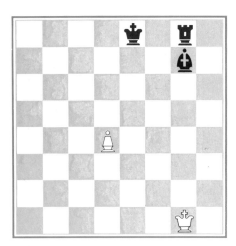

Figure 29

different ways. Players hope for a checkmate but if the captures they each make reduce each other's forces so that neither can effect a mate then a Draw should be agreed.

The minimum requirements to effect a mate are 1) King and Queen. 2) King and Rook. 3) King and two Bishops. 4) King, Bishop and Knight. 5) Queen and Knight. 6) Queen and Bishop.

A player can evade checkmate if his opponent has only 1) King and one Bishop. 2) King and two Knights. Obviously a King and one Knight cannot force checkmate.

Figure 30 shows a mate from King and Queen. White King cannot capture Black Queen because there must always be a square between the two Kings though this need not be vacant. Figure 31 shows a mate in which White Rook traps the Black King but only with the assistance of White King.

Now for a checkmate from a King and two Bishops. Look at Figure 32. One Bishop has just put the King in check and he is forced into a corner. The Bishop on the black diagonals has moved to give checkmate. There is no flight square. Black King is trapped.

Draws and Stalemate

Finally it must be said that players of equal strength are more than likely to end a game in a Draw. There can be several reasons for this. Firstly if neither player has strong enough material on the board to effect a checkmate it is a waste of time to continue playing. A Draw is then agreed.

Perpetual check can result in a Draw. If a player makes the same moves three times either player can claim a Draw.

There is also Stalemate which forces a Draw on the players. If a player has sufficient strength to checkmate he will be careful to avoid a Stalemate. On the other hand if he cannot win the game he will welcome a position which gives him a Draw rather than a lost game.

A Stalemate comes about if a player

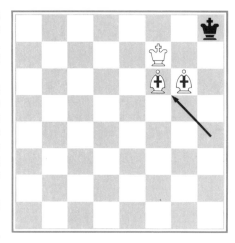

Figure 32

finds that the only piece he can move is his King – he may have blocked Pawns or a piece that is pinned – then he must move the King. If the King is already in check and to move it is to move it into check then that, of course, is checkmate. But suppose that the King is not in check but the only square or squares available to him are already attacked which would mean moving into check, then the King cannot be moved. The player cannot play. That is a Stalemate.

Computers

There are any number of computers to challenge the serious chess player. They can all be set at different levels of play from beginner up to what seems like playing against Bobby Fischer. The player who has only just learned how to play may find it difficult to beat the computer, even when it is set at 0 or 1, whichever is beginner level. The ordinary home computer from the cheapest to the most advanced and most expensive usually has a chess 'program' available in what they call the software. The advantage of playing against this sort of

computer is that the player does not have to move any pieces but merely to key in his moves and watch the computer make his reply on the television screen.

There are however many chess computers which are designed to do nothing else but play chess. With these it is necessary to move pieces on a board according to the instructions the player gives the computer and the computer's reply. In all cases the Notation is Algebraic.

There is no quicker way of improving one's game than by playing regularly against a computer. There is, however, one snag when playing against any computer at its highest levels. It does take a very long time to reply to the moves the player makes. In some cases the computer will take half an hour to reply or even longer. But its answer is always the best move that could possibly be made!

Chess Summary – A Quick Guide

Algebraic Notation
The only system of recording games now acceptable by F.I.D.E. at International Tournaments. Ranks are numbered 1-8 from White's back row and files are identified with the letters a to h. Pieces but not Pawns are referred to by initials. Knights are identified by the letter N.

Back Row
This is the rank nearest to each player and on which the major and minor pieces are placed.

Bishops
Each player has two Bishops. White's King Bishop is confined to white squares and his Queen Bishop to black squares. For the player with the Black pieces it is the other way round. Bishops are confined to diagonals. They can never use ranks or files. Bishops can be moved backwards or forwards across the board provided the

diagonal used is clear. They capture by occupying the square of an opponent's piece which in the same move is removed from the board.

Board
This has 64 squares alternately white and black (or light coloured and dark coloured). A player should always ensure that there is a white square in the right hand corner of his back rank. The board is the same as that used for draughts (checkers).

Capture
All chess pieces including Pawns take hostile pieces in the same way. They move to the square occupied by a hostile piece and that piece is removed from the board.

Picture from a manuscript in Alfonso's library, El Escorial, near Madrid, Spain, showing Moors playing chess.

Castling
A special move that either player may make once in any game. The King is moved two squares towards the side of the board and the Rook is then placed on the other side of the King giving it a more central position. A player may castle only if the squares between them are unoccupied. A King must not pass through check – that is the piece must not pass a square under attack from a hostile piece. When a King-side castle has been moved there is a single vacant square in the corner. If a player castles on the Queen's side of the board there will be two vacant squares in the corner. A player may not castle if his King is in check or if either his King or his Rook have already been moved.

Check
A piece is in check when a hostile piece is moved to a square from which it can capture in the next move. When a King is put in check the player making the move usually says 'check' and the King must either move to a flight square, interpose a piece to block the check or capture the piece making the attack.

Check, Discovered
It sometimes happens that when a player moves a piece it is then revealed that the enemy King is in check from another piece. This is a Discovered Check.

Check, Double
If a piece is moved to check the hostile King and there is a Discovered Check from another piece this is a Double Check. The King must get out of check from both attackers.

Checkmate
If a King is put in check and cannot escape then that is checkmate and the game is over. Most players who see a checkmate coming and realise there is no escape, resign.

Clock, Chess
Special clocks are available for Match and Tournament play. Two clocks are assembled in one unit and when the game begins White's clock is started. As soon as he has made his move he presses a button on his side of the clock which then stops his but starts his opponent's clock. Black then moves and presses his button and so on. If there is a time limit for a game a player can see if he is taking too long to make his moves.

Development
To attack the enemy King a player must move his pieces out to positions of advantage. It is a mistake to keep pushing Pawns forward without bringing out Knights and Bishops.

Descriptive Notation
This is sometimes called the English Notation and, in the past, was widely used in English-speaking nations and Spain. It is now being phased out but it has been used in so many books and articles that readers do well to understand it. The files are identified by the initials of the pieces on each player's back row. The ranks for each player are numbered 1-8 so that White's K1 is Black's K8.

Diagonals
Moving a piece in a straight line across the corners of the squares is to use a diagonal. Bishops are confined to diagonals and Queens have the option of using them. A Pawn captures across a one square diagonal.

Draws
When neither player has sufficient strength to achieve a checkmate it is usual for them to agree a Draw. If a player makes the same move three times a Draw can be claimed. If after 50 moves no Pawn has been moved and no piece captured a Draw can be claimed by either player – a most unlikely event.

En prise
A piece is *en prise* when it is threatened by a hostile piece and can be captured in the opponent's next move.

Exchange
A player who captures one piece only to lose a more valuable piece has had a bad exchange. Swop a Knight for a Knight or Bishop but not for a Queen. Beginners often resist equal exchanges and soon find their whole game is defensive and that they cannot mount an attack.

Files
The sequence of squares in a straight line between the player and his opponent.

Files, Open
Any file which is not obstructed by Pawns and in which there is a Rook giving support.

Forced Move
When there is no alternative to making a certain move this is called a Forced Move.

Fork
A move which gives the player the option of capturing either of two different hostile pieces. A Knight fork on King and Queen may force the King to move and then the Knight can capture the Queen.

Gambit
A Gambit is when a Pawn or piece is deliberately put *en prise* in the expectation that a later advantage can be obtained after the loss of that piece.

Interpose
To interpose is to place a piece between the King and any piece putting the King in check.

Kings
A King is limited in his movement to one square but he can use ranks, files or diagonals. A King can capture by moving onto the square of a hostile piece provided he does not move into check. There must always be one square between the two Kings – they must not occupy adjacent squares.

King's side
This refers to all squares on the King's side of the board. For White this means the 32 squares on the right hand side of the board and for Black those on the left.

Knights
If moved the Knight makes an L-shaped move: two squares in one direction and then one square to the side. He moves from one corner of a six-square rectangle to the opposite corner. The Knight can move over squares that are occupied by pieces of either colour.

Mate
See Checkmate.

Middle Game
Any moves after the developing moves of the opening are described as the middle game. This is the main battle leading to the end game and either checkmate, a resignation or a draw.

Notation
There are two systems of recording or reading games. Descriptive Notation is being phased out and Algebraic Notation universally accepted. Readers do well to understand both because there is so much literature available in both systems.

An early 'Treatise on Chess', an undated Persian manuscript.

Openings

There are 20 possible first moves for the player with the White pieces. Two squares forward with any one of eight Pawns or one square forward. The Knights can leap to a choice of two squares. Beginners do well to open with a centre Pawn. The following six to twelve moves tend to follow one or other of a number of known sequences. Openings have acquired names mostly based on players who made them popular.

Pawns

Pawns are limited to a move forward one square at a time except when moved for the first time, when they may be moved two squares forward in their own files. Pawns capture diagonally one square forward. A Pawn can put a King in check.

Pawns, Blocked

When a Pawn is advanced and meets a hostile Pawn in the same file it is blocked and cannot be moved until there has been a capture or it can capture in an adjoining file.

Pawns, Doubled

When a player has two of his own Pawns in the same file, he has doubled Pawns. So far as possible this should be avoided.

Pawns, Passed

A Pawn which has a clear run along a file without being threatened by hostile Pawns in adjacent files is a passed Pawn.

Pieces

Strictly speaking, only those chessmen in a players back row when he starts a game are pieces. Pawns are often referred to separately as Pawns. Queens and Rooks are major pieces and Bishops and Knights are minor pieces.

Pin

When a piece cannot or should not be moved it is pinned. If a Knight stands in a file before his King and a hostile Rook moves into that file the Knight is pinned because to move it would put the King in check, and players may not put their own King in check.

Promotion

When a Pawn reaches the opponent's back rank it is entitled to be promoted. In almost every case the player chooses to exchange it for a Queen.

Medieval chess players.

Queen's side

This refers to all the 32 squares on the Queen's side of the board.

Ranks

There are the lines of squares which go from left to right across the board.

Rooks

Second only to the Queen in strength, the Rooks are confined to ranks and files. They can be moved as far across the board as the player decides provided the rank or file is clear.

Sacrifice

A player may move a piece to a square from which it can be captured but this may lead to an overall stronger position. This is a planned sacrifice.

Skewer

An attack on a piece which can be moved to safety only to reveal the real quarry is known as a skewer. A King in front of his Queen may be put in check and when he is moved to a flight square the Queen is seized.

Stalemate

If a King is not in check and is the only piece a player can move when it is his turn, and if it can only be moved into check, then this is a stalemate and the game is a Draw.

Touched Piece

The rule in chess is that if a player actually touches a piece he must move it. Players should never ask opponents if they may change their minds. Touch and Move is the rule.

White, who plays?

The decision as to who plays White is decided by lottery. Either player holds a Pawn of each colour in his hands and offers his clenched fists to his opponent. Whichever fist the opponent points to reveals the colour he must play in their first game. In subsequent games they change over each time.

A Complete Game

Here is a complete game to play out on your own board. The opening is called the Sicilian Defence.

Descriptive		*Algebraic*	
White	Black	White	Black
1) P–K4	P–QB4	1) e2–e4	c7–c5
2) N–KB3	P–K3	2) N–f3	e7–e6
3) P–Q4	PxP	3) d2–d4	c5xd4
4) NxP	P–QR3	4) Nxd4	a7–a6
5) N–QB3	N–QB3	5) N–c3	N–c6
6) B–K3	N–B3	6) B–e3	N–f6
7) B–Q3	P–Q4	7) B–d3	d7–d5

At this stage the position for each player is more or less equal. Each has captured a Pawn and if you study the pieces on the board every Pawn and piece is protected except White's Knight Pawns (Figure 33). On the other hand White has got his Bishops out and both are near the centre of the board. The game now continues:

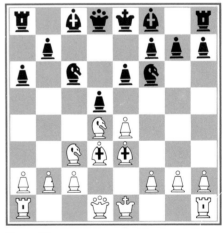

Figure 33

8) PxP	PxP	8) e4xd5	e6xd5
9) 0–0	B–Q3	9) 0–0	B–d6
10) NxN	PxN	10) Nxc6	b7xc6
11) B–Q4	0–0	11) B–d4	0–0

White's re-positioning of his Bishop to give more active play leaves this piece unprotected (Figure 34).

12) Q–B3	B–K3	12) Q–f3	B–e6
13) KR–K1	P–B4	13) R–eI	c6–c5
14) BxN	QxB	14) Bxf6	Qxf6

Now there is the chance to exchange Queens. Beginners who have discovered the strength of Queens usually resist this.

15) QxQ	PxQ	15) Qxf6	g7xf6
16) QR–Q1	KR–Q1	16) QR–d1	KR–d8
17) B–K2	QR–N1	17) B–e2	QR–b8

This move by Black creates a slight Queen side weakness for White:

18) P–QN3	P–B5	18) b2–b3	c5–c4
19) NxP	BxN	19) Nxd5	Bxd5
20) RxB	BxPch	20) Rxd5	Bxh2ch
21) KxB	RxR	21) Kxh2	Rxd5

An 1850 chess player from a painting 'Les Francais' by Paul Gavarni.

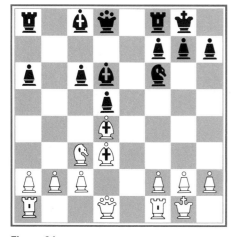

Figure 34

In terms of point value Black now leads. He has captured a Queen, a Rook, two Knights, a Bishop and three Pawns. Total value of captures is 26 points. White has taken a Queen, two Bishops, two Knights and three Pawns. Total value of White's captures: 24 points.

22) BxP	R–Q7	22) Bxc4	R–d2
23) BxP	RxQBP	23) Bxa6	Rxc2
24) R–K2?	RxR	24) R–e2?	Rxe2

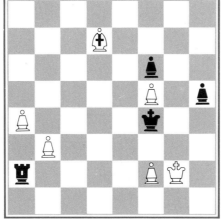

Figure 35

| 25) BxR | R–Q1! | 25) Bxe2 | R–d8! |
| 26) P–R4 | R–Q7 | 26) a2–a4 | R–d2 |

Add up the point value of the captures now. Black's captures equal 32 and White's 31. Neither player appears to have any real positional advantage.

| 27) B–B4 | R–R7 | 27) B–c4 | R–a2 |
| 28) K–N3 | K–B1 | 28) K–g3 | K–f8 |

Both players bring their Kings into play and towards the centre of the board. It is hard to see why Black made his 27th move, R–R7.

| 29) K–B3 | K–K2 | 29) K–f3 | K–e7 |
| 30) P–KN4 | P–B4! | 30) g2–g4 | f6–f5 |

White wants to get his King to the Queen's side of the board to support the progress of his Pawns. Black's Pawn move is good. If White captures it Black has a passed Pawn in the Rook file.

31) PxP	P–B3	31) g4xf5	f7–f6
32) B–N8	P–R3	32) B–g8	h7–h6
33) K–N3	K–Q3	33) K–g3	K–d6

White now has to stop the passed Pawn and can no longer cross the board with his King.

| 34) K–B3? | R–R8 | 34) K–f3? | R–a1 |
| 35) K–N2 | K–K4 | 35) K–g2 | K–e5 |

White King is still waiting for the Black passed Pawn. Black King moves to attack the White Bishop Pawn.

36) B–K6	K–B5	36) B–e6	K–f4
37) B–Q7	R–QN8	37) B–d7	R–b1
38) B–K6	R–N7	38) B–e6	R–b2
39) B–B4	R–R7	39) B–c4	R–a2

White's position now begins to look pretty hopeless. He has four Pawns to Black's two but they are not well placed. Black has a Rook against White's Bishop.

| 40) B–K6 | P–R4 | 40) B–e6 | h6–h5 |
| 41) B–Q7 and resigns |

The last move (Figure 35) was a sealed move that was never actually played because the player resigned instead of returning to the game. The White pieces were played by World Chess Champion Boris Spassky and the Black pieces by Bobby Fischer. This was the last game they played in the 1972 World Championship Match and the one that gave Fischer the crown.

If the game had proceeded to a checkmate it is interesting to speculate how Fischer would have forced this. If he had moved his Rook to the third rank his passed Pawn could not only have put the White King in check but was then a possible Queen. White had four moves of his Rook Pawn to Queen it. Why did Spassky resign?

DOMINO GAMES

Dominoes are of Chinese origin and have an ancient history. Many different sets are used in different parts of the world.

THE STANDARD PACK used in Britain and the U.S.A. (domino sets are termed 'packs') is the Double–6, so-called because the highest domino in the set is the 6:6 (double–six). This pack is of European origin and dates from the 18th century. Figure 1 illustrates the 28 tiles that make up the pack. (Individual dominoes are known as tiles or stones, sometimes bones.) Double–9 packs (55 tiles) and Double–12 packs (91 tiles) are to be found in some regions. These packs have the twin virtues of permitting more players to take part and more sophisticated games to be played but their use is not widespread.

Each domino is divided into halves, each half having a number of spots (called 'pips') or none ('blank'). A tile that bears identical halves (for example, 4:4, 0:0) is known as a double. All other tiles are called singles.

Tiles are classed in suits of which

Figure 1 The complete double-6 pack.

there are seven, named after the numbers 1 to 6 and the blank. Each suit consists of seven tiles, making up all possible combinations of the suit number. All single dominoes belong simultaneously to two suits, corresponding to their pip values; thus a 5:2 tile belongs to both the 5 and 2 suits. Doubles belong only to a single suit. Notice that there is no duplication in the Double-6 pack.

Dominoes are not a game but game tools, like playing cards. There are a large number of domino games for one or more players, but four is the ideal number for most games.

Those described here are among the most popular games using the Double-6 pack. There are no universally accepted rules for any game and regional differences are quite usual. Often these affect the number of tiles drawn by each player; sometimes they are only concerned with technicalities, such as the method used to decide pairings or who begins. The accepted practice is to play the house rules – the host is legislator.

Block

When people talk of playing a game of dominoes in Britain they are usually referring to Block, the most common game with the Double-6 pack.

Block is best as a game for four players in partnerships. Partners sit opposite each other round a table on which the dominoes are placed face down and shuffled.

Each player draws five, six or seven tiles at random (the number is agreed beforehand) and examines them. The experts hold the dominoes in the palm of the hand and put them back on the table, face down in front of them, when not in use. This picking up and putting down is performed in a single movement and requires practice; alternatively, stand the tiles on end on the table, faces towards you so that their identities are screened from the other players.

The object of the game is to be the first player to dispose of all tiles in hand to the table. The player with the highest double (the 6:6 if all tiles are drawn)

starts and places it face up on the table. Play is clockwise, and the second player now puts down any single that matches the starter. For example, the 6:5 or the 6:0. This second tile is played at right angles to, and abutting the first. If the second player has no 6-suit tile, he is unable to play and 'knocks' – he raps the table and his turn ends. A player may not knock if he holds a matching tile – it is compulsory to play if able to do so.

Suppose the second player put down a 6:5. There are now two tiles on the table and these constitute the 'leg'. In Block, only the two ends of the leg are 'open'; that is, may be played against. The third player may now place a tile to match the 5 or, if he so chooses, the 6 at the other end of the leg. Suppose he holds the 6:1 and elects to play it. At the end of his turn, the leg would appear as shown in Figure 2.

Figure 2 The leg after turn 3.

Now the open ends are 5 and 1 and the fourth player must play to match one of these. If a double is played, it is placed at right angles to the matching tile.

The leg may be bent at any time. The purpose of this is to keep the dominoes within a manageable area, or at least to stop them falling off the table. The action in no way alters the game. An example of how the above game might

appear after a dozen plays is shown in Figure 3.

The game ends either when one player goes out ('domino') or no further play is possible (all players knock in turn). The player who goes domino scores the sum of the pips on his opponents' remaining tiles. In a partnership game, the sum of the remaining pips on one side are subtracted from the remaining pips on the other to give the game score; thus it is possible for a player to go domino but his side lose the hand because his partner has a higher pip count than the opponents combined. In the case where all players knock, then the player with the lowest pip count scores the sum of his opponents' pip counts less his own, while in a partnership game the sum of the two sides are compared and the lower-scoring side scores the margin between them. After the initial draw, unless there are four players and each draws seven tiles, there are likely to be 'sleepers' in the 'boneyard' – that is, tiles face down on the table that cannot be used. Sleepers can add zest to a game as the players try to deduce their identities.

Strategy There is more strategy in Block than might be suggested by the simple rules. The main objectives, which are often in conflict, are to go out as soon as possible (but not, in a partnership game, if this leaves partner with a ruinous pip count); to minimise possible penalties by playing out high suit tiles, also doubles, since the opportunities for playing these are half those of singles; to ensure one is not blocked on the next play; and simultaneously to hinder the opponents from attaining these same objectives. Clearly, the abil-

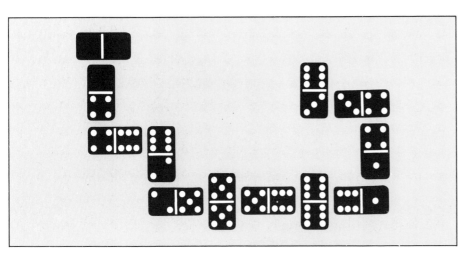

Figure 3 A Block game in progress.

A game of dominoes sketched in 1883. A cribbage board is being used to score.

ity to deduce the hands of the other players, together with the sleepers, is a big advantage.

Muggins

There is a family of domino games in which points are earned during play as well as at the end. The best-known members of the family – the most widely played in the U.S.A. – are Muggins, All Fives and Five-up, three games which differ only in minor details and are often confused.

Preparation is as for Block. Two, three or four players (best in partnership) take part and draw respectively seven, six or five tiles at the start. There are two objects. The first is to amass the highest score by playing tiles such that the pips on the exposed tiles at the two ends of the leg sum to 5 or a multiple of 5. One point is earned for every 5 pips; thus if the two ends sum to 20 – only possible using the doubles 6:6 and 4:4 – 4 points are scored. Notice that all the pips of an exposed double are counted. The second object is to go out. Remaining pips are totalled by the other players as in Block, but in Muggins the winner(s) score 1 point for every five pips that the scores differ. Numbers are rounded up to the next multiple of five. As an example, in a partnership game A goes out and his partner C has a pip count of 7 remaining. The pip count of B and D sums to 18. C's count is deducted, leaving 11, which is rounded up to the next highest multiple – 15. A and C score 3 points in addition to those scored by both sides during play. A game is commonly to 61 points.

Holder of the highest double plays first by placing the tile face up on the table. If this is the 5:5, he (or his side) scores 2 points 'for 10'. Thereafter play is similar to Block, each player in turn matching an open end of the leg. If unable to play, a player must draw from the boneyard until he gets a tile that can be played. This is then matched and the turn ends. When the boneyard is exhausted, players knock, as in Block.

Figure 4 Early stages of a game of Muggins.

If a player omits to claim points to which he is entitled during play, any other player can score the points by calling 'Muggins!' Figure 4 shows the early stages of a game of Muggins. If the next player has any of the tiles 5:5, 5:0 and 0:0, he can score. He is free to play any other matching tile (for example, 0:1 or 5:2) but in this case would not score since the two ends of the leg would not then sum to 5 or a multiple of 5.

Five-up

Muggins can be played with 'spinners', when it is more usually known as Five-up. A spinner is a double from which it is permitted to extend in four directions. This may only be done if the double has first been extended at right angles in both directions in the normal way. The two ends of the double may then be matched to form new ends, though for scoring purposes the ends of the double are not considered as ends themselves. The use of spinners makes

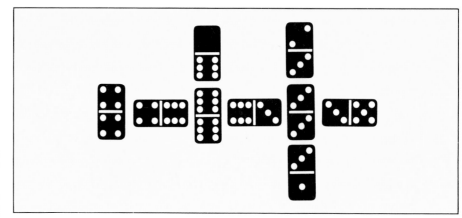

Figure 5 A game of Five-up in progress: open ends total 16.

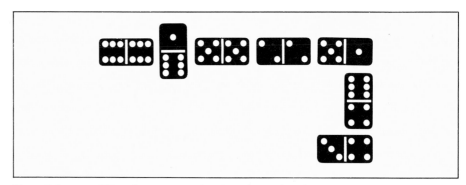

Figure 6 A game of Matador: two matadors have been played.

Muggins a much more interesting game since all ends are totalled after each play in assessing the score.

Figure 5 shows a game in progress in which there are five open ends totalling 16. Notice that although the 6:6 can be extended downwards by matching a 6–suit tile, the open 6 of the tile does not count for scoring purposes. Also note that the next play against the 4:4 must be to the left, not up or down.

In this position, there are 19 tiles either held by the players or in the boneyard – and any one of them can be played here. Seven are scoring tiles: for example, the 0:1 might be played. However, if this were placed against the blank then the sum of the ends would be 8+1+2+5+1=17 – no score! Better to play the 0:1 against the 1 when the ends would sum to 15 for a score of 3.

All-Threes and Fives-and-Threes

Two other games, played to the same general rules as Muggins or Five-up, are All-Threes, when both table and hand scores are counted in multiples of three rather than five, and Fives-and-Threes. In the latter game, multiples of five and three both count when played to the leg; thus a pip count of 15 would yield 8 points – 3 for fives and 5 for threes.

Lowest double is the starter. The player (or side) who goes out scores 1 point; game is 31 or 61. A cribbage board is commonly used for scoring.

In the U.S.A., the winning player (or side) of a hand scores the difference in pip count and game is 251 points.

Sniff

This is another game of the Muggins family. Two, three or four (who play in partnerships) can take part, drawing respectively seven, six or five tiles.

First player is agreed by lot, and the starter may be any domino. The first double on table, which may or may not be the starter, is Sniff. Sniff is a spinner, but as in Five-up, the long sides must be matched before the ends can be played against. However, all open sides of the spinner are included in the pip count at the end of each turn when 5 points is earned by the player for five and for every multiple of five. All other doubles are played as usual at right angles to the leg but are not spinners.

If a player is unable to play, he draws from the boneyard but no more than twice: if neither tile permits a match, that player's turn ends.

At the close of a hand, the player (or side) with the lowest remainder count scores the opponents' total remainder count (not the difference) rounded up to the nearest 5 points. Game is 250.

Strategy Scoring on table is the main aim of the Muggins games. Where no score is possible, play so that the ends of the leg match suits you hold. Conceal whether a play is from choice or necessity. The longer the leg, the more information is available to you – use it. Near the end of a hand it is frequently possible to deduce other players' holdings.

Matador

Matador, also called Russian Dominoes, is a quite different game from Block or Muggins. Again, two, three or four players (four play as individuals) draw seven, six or five tiles respectively. First player puts down any domino as starter. Thereafter the leg is extended not by matching but by making the two half-tiles joined sum to seven pips. Doubles are played as singles in a straight line; thus if the starter is 3:3, then any tile of the 4-suit, including the 4:4, may be played against it.

Four tiles are known as matadors; these are the three that sum to seven (6:1, 5:2, 4:3) and the double-blank. Matadors are wild tiles and may be played against either end of the leg regardless of pip count. A matador may be played with the line of play, or across it like a double in other games. If it is laid with the line of play, the exposed half-tile alone can be joined; if it is played across the line of play (the player is free to choose) then the pip count of the half-tile subsequently played against it may be added to either half-tile of the matador.

Figure 6 shows a hand in progress. Notice that one matador (the 6:1) has been placed across the line of play against the 5:5. The 6:6 has been played

subsequently to join with the 1-pip half-tile of the matador for the count of seven. A second matador (the 4:3) has been laid in the line of play so that only the 3-spot is open.

Notice that in joining to a matador, the 'rule of seven' applies. Matadors may be played against one another.

A player is never obliged to play a matador. If he cannot make a join according to the rule of seven, he draws from the boneyard until he can join. When the boneyard is exhausted, the player passes even if he holds a matador unless of course he elects to play it. When one player is void of tiles or all players pass in turn, the hand ends. The player who goes out scores the total of his opponents' remaining pips, matadors scoring like other tiles. If all players pass, then the player with the lowest pip count scores the difference between his own and the sum of his opponents' pips. Game is 101 points.

Strategy The blanks hold the key to the game since a blank cannot be joined (because the two half-tiles can never sum to seven) except by a matador. There are only four matadors against six blank singles in the pack, and one of the matadors (the double-blank) cannot be played against anyway except by another matador. Thus quite early on one end of the leg may be blocked. If you hold the last matador (unless it is the 0:0) it may be dangerous to pass since all other players may then pass. If you hold a low-scoring hand, it may be wise to stitch up both ends of the leg as soon as all matadors are played in order to win on the remainder count.

Excitement during a pub game in 1823 – enough to make a man spill the ale.

GHinot. Pub June 29, 1823 by G Humphry 24 St James St & 74 New Bond Street   WH Sr

"Well done partner- take another   (The Game of)   Six's all; & —
Chalk for us, !   Domino's!   — my Dab, !"

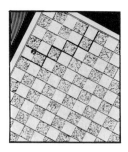

HALMA

HALMA WAS INVENTED in the 19th century. It is for two or four players and is played on a board of 256 squares, in each corner of which heavy lines enclose sections of 13 squares. In two diagonally opposite corners additional heavy lines enclose an extra six squares (Figure 1).

These enclosures are called camps – the camps of 13 squares being used when there are four players and those of 19 squares when there are two players. Four players can play either as individuals or as two teams.

There are four sets of pieces, each set being of a different colour. Two sets contain 19 pieces and are used when there are two players. At the start of the games these are placed on the board in

move to an adjacent vacant square in any direction, along a file or column or diagonally, as illustrated in Figure 3.

The *hop* is a move whereby a piece may hop over any other piece on an adjacent square to a vacant square beyond.

The piece hopped over can be one's own, one's partner's or an opposing piece. Again the move can be in any direction. A piece may make several such hops in one move (but a step and a hop cannot be combined in one move). A piece may change direction during a multiple hop, an example of which is illustrated in Figure 4.

Hopping is not compulsory. There is no capturing, and pieces hopped over remain on the board.

Strategy Halma is a race game, and clearly pieces can move across the board quicker in hops, particularly multiple hops, than in steps. The formation of 'ladders' for hopping will allow pieces to advance several squares at a turn. Of course, since pieces can hop over both friendly and opposing pieces, such ladders can equally well be used by opposing pieces coming in the opposite direction. This becomes an asset in partnership play, in that partners can form ladders to help each other. Players should attempt to form ladders more suitable for themselves than their opponents, and attempt to block opponents' ladders.

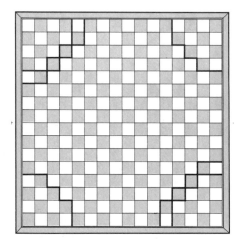

Figure 1 The board.

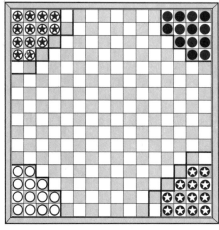

Figure 2 Set up for four players.

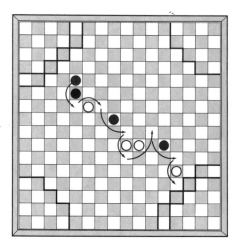

Figure 4 The multiple hop.

the opposite camps of 19 squares.

The other two sets contain 13 pieces each. All four sets are used when there are four players, the game starting with 13 pieces in each of the four smaller camps as illustrated in Figure 2.

The object of the game is to move all of one's pieces from the starting camp to that diagonally opposite. The first player to do so wins. In partnership play (the partners sit opposite each other) the first pair to transfer both sets of pieces wins.

Players move one piece in each turn, and the turn passes clockwise. There are two ways to move. The *step* is a

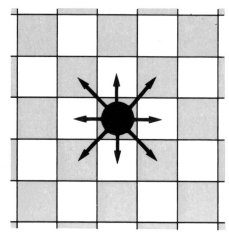

Figure 3 The step.

Hex

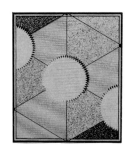

HEX IS A TWENTIETH CENTURY game claimed to have been invented independently in both Denmark and the U.S.A. It is played on an 11 × 11 rhombus-shaped grid ruled into equilateral triangles as shown in Figure 1. Play takes place on the points of intersection, as in Go. It is convenient to play with Go stones, but failing these any sets of differently coloured counters will do as well. Isometric drafting paper is a good starting point for the board. You will have gathered that manufactured sets are hard to find.

Play starts with the board empty. Black moves first by placing a stone on any point. White then plays on any unoccupied point, and so play continues alternately. Once played, stones are not moved about.

The object of the game is for a player to build a connected chain of stones between the two edges of the board marked with his colour. Figure 2 shows an example of such a winning chain of white stones. The chain may turn and twist, or be linked to redundant stones. So long as you can get from a point on one white edge to a point on the other by a path of adjacent white stones White has won.

A moment's thought will show that this game is not just a race. If White has a winning chain it effectively prevents Black from having one. There are no drawn games in Hex.

The four corner points (A1, K1, A11, and K11) are common to both players. Either may use them as the end of a winning chain.

There is a mathematical existence proof of a winning strategy for Black. The strategy has yet to be found, but Black does have a great advantage, especially if he plays his opening move on F6, the centre point. This feature can be used to handicap the more experienced player, by his taking White. Alternatively, the game can be made more even by banning Black from playing F6 as his opening move, or from several of the central points.

One elementary tactical point is illustrated by the black stones at E3 and F4. These make a so-called "double connec-

tion". If White plays at either F3 or E4, Black can connect by playing on the other. Furthermore E3 is securely connected to the edge. If White tries to intercept at F1 Black plays at D2 or G2. You will infer that opening moves in Hex are of vital importance, and that as in Go it pays not to play your stones too close together to start with.

There is no special reason for playing on an 11 × 11 board. Larger boards may well eventually come into use. There exists another version of the game played on a triangular board. In this version the objective is to link all three sides of the board. Some players prefer a board drawn as a tesselation of hexagons, playing inside the hexagons instead of on the points.

This game will appeal to players who prefer a game which depends on over-the-board ability rather than on studying books – there are virtually no books to study on Hex. No doubt it will attract the attention of programmers ere long.

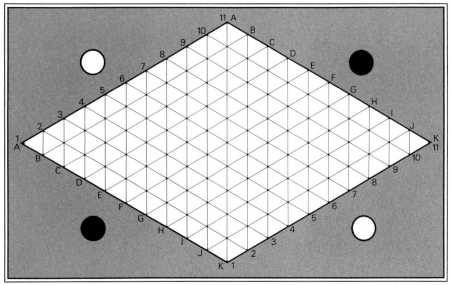

Figure 1 The grid for Hex.

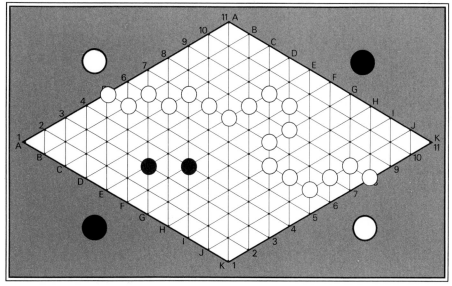

Figure 2 A winning chain for White.

CHINESE CHESS

In 1975 the Red Chinese government, deciding that Chinese chess was a 'good thing', published 487,000 copies of the official rules. Xiangqi, as they called it, thus joined weiqi (go) and western chess in a triumvirate of board games blessed with government patronage in China.

OF THE THREE games receiving Government support in China, it is Chinese chess that remains, as it has been for centuries, the game that most attracts popular support. Indeed, the Chinese outside the mainland, left to their own devices, have been running tournaments and international matches for decades, and have produced an immense amount of literature.

Western players have found it to be a first-rate game too, but unlike Japanese chess it suffers here from having no presiding body for the West and from a lack of literature in English. These handicaps, perhaps temporary, should not be allowed to mask the inherent

excellence of the game, especially for those who enjoy fast-moving and broad-ranging tactical fights where good technique is important, for Chinese chess is the kung fu of board games.

The board and pieces

There are regrettably few westernised sets for Chinese chess, but Chinese sets are available very cheaply from games shops or Chinese emporiums. The typical set consists of 32 uniformly sized discs, on one side of which is written the name of the piece in Chinese, and a paper board. The underside of the discs is not used and can easily be marked with English names. That is the type of set that will be assumed here.

Figure 1 Typical pieces.

Figure 1 shows typical pieces. One side's pieces are marked in red and the other in black, blue or whatever – but the two sides are always called Red and Black.

The board is a grid of nine by ten lines with the vertical lines being interrupted in the centre to create a clear row called the river (Figure 2). The portions marked X are the palaces of the respective kings.

The pieces are placed on the intersecting points in Chinese chess and some intersections, usually those representing the starting points of the pawns and cannons, are marked as shown.

There is usually some Chinese writing on the board: it can all be ignored.

Each player starts with one king, two guards, two bishops, two knights, two rooks, two cannons and five pawns. Note that none of these terms is standard for there is no accepted terminology for the game in the West. The practice adopted here, following the successful example of those who introduced Japanese chess to the West, will be to use, where possible, names com-

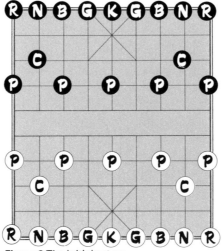

Figure 2 The board.

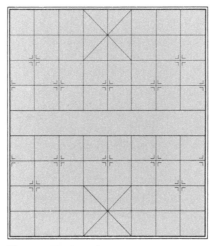

Figure 3 The initial set-up.

mon to the chess family and, in the case of the notation, a system that looks western but which has an underlying affinity to the Chinese system, so that players can more readily have access to game scores in the original language.

But, for reference, other terms used are: king – general, governor; guard – minister, mandarin, counsellor, councillor, officer, queen; bishop – elephant, assistant, militiaman, premier; knight – horse, cavalry; rook – chariot; cannon – ballista, catapult, artillery; pawn – soldier, foot-soldier, infantryman.

How the pieces move

The pieces start in the positions shown in Figure 3. We shall assume here that Red plays first and moves up the board.

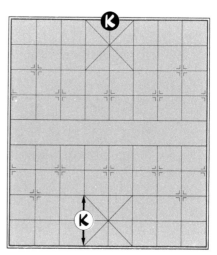

Figure 4 The king move.

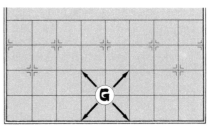

Figure 5 The guard move.

The king (K), capture of which is the ultimate goal of the game, has a very restricted move. It can go one step horizontally or vertically and only within the palace. Nor is a king allowed to be on a file (column of points) directly facing the opposing king. In Figure 4, therefore, the red king can move to only two points, as shown, and it cannot move to the centre point of the palace (it could if the enemy king was shifted one point to the right or if there was any other piece on the centre file between the two kings).

The guard (G) is also confined to the palace. It can move only one step diagonally, so that there are only five points it can ever occupy (Figure 5).

The bishop (B) also moves diagonally, but it must always move two steps. It is also highly restricted in movement, because it cannot jump over other pieces, of either colour (when blocked by another piece it is said to be blinded), nor can it cross the river (Figure 6).

The knight (N) moves in the familiar fashion of chess knights, one step in a straight line then one step diagonally onwards in the same general direction (Figure 7a). However, it cannot jump, so that if there is a piece of either colour on the point covered by the first (straight) step, it cannot move at all in that direction (Figure 7b). In that case it is said to be hobbled. But the knight

A: The bishop move.
B: This bishop cannot move.

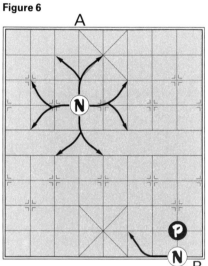

Figure 6

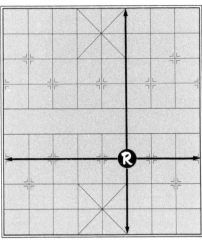

Figure 8 The rook move.

Move restrictions
Since capture of the king ends the game, any move that threatens such a capture – called a check – has to be attended to immediately. A player is not allowed to leave his king in check, or to move so that his king is in check.

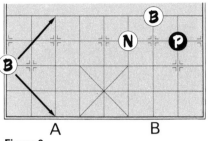

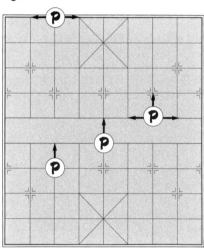

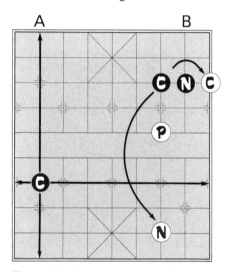

Figure 7 A: The knight move.
B: This knight has only one move.

Figure 9 The pawn moves.

Figure 10 A: The cannon move when not capturing. B: when capturing.

can go anywhere on the board.

The rook (R) is exactly like the chess rook: it moves any number of points along one vertical or horizontal line so long as its path is unobstructed (Figure 8). It cannot jump but it ranges over the whole board.

The pawn (P) moves one step forward so long as it is on its own side of the river, but once it has crossed the river it can move one step in any of three directions: forward, left or right (Figure 9). Obviously, once it reaches the back row it can move only sideways. This change of move by the pawn is the only promotion in Chinese chess.

All the pieces mentioned so far can go to a vacant square or to a square occupied by an enemy piece. In the latter case the enemy piece is captured. It is removed and plays no further part in the game.

The final piece, the cannon (C), is exceptional. It trundles along like a rook if it goes to a vacant square, taking up position as it were, but to capture it has to be cranked up on a gun mount or

support so that the missile can be lobbed onto the enemy piece. This support is simply any intervening piece of either colour on one of the lines along which the cannon would normally move. Capture is thus made in effect by jumping over the support to the point occupied by the enemy piece. The cannon can jump over only one support piece and can move this way only when it captures, but there is no restriction on how long or short the jump is, or on the distance of the support from the cannon or captured piece. Both when moving and capturing the cannon can go to any part of the board. Figure 10a shows the cannon move and 10b shows some captures.

If a player's king is in check and he is unable to move anywhere to get out of check, he is said to be checkmated. In Figure 11a the red king is in check, but it can escape by capturing the pawn. In 11b, however, the black king cannot escape and so is checkmated. The checkmated side loses.

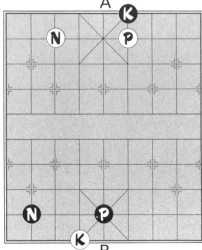

Figure 11 A: Check but not checkmate.
B: Checkmate.

If a player's king is not in check but he is unable to make any move, or only one that leaves his king in check, he is stalemated. In Figure 12, for example, the black king is not in check but moving forward would be check from the pawn and the centre file is barred because of the rule prohibiting facing kings, and Black has no other pieces he can move. This is stalemate, but it is not a draw as in western chess. In Chinese chess the stalemated player loses (and stalemate is also much more common).

Draws are possible, however, either by agreement or when, because of lack of pieces, neither player can force a win.

There are also some rather complicated rules prohibiting certain types of repetitive moves. These will be mentioned in more detail later, but the basic principle to be remembered is that where both players choose, without compulsion, to repeat moves, a game is drawn; but where repetition of moves occurs because one side is being forced to respond to a threat (e.g. check, threat of mate or capture), the attacker must stop repeating his moves or forfeit the game.

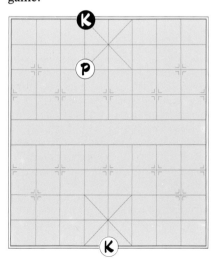

Figure 12 Stalemate: Black loses.

Notation

In the absence of a standard western notation, the method of describing moves here will be based on the Chinese system.

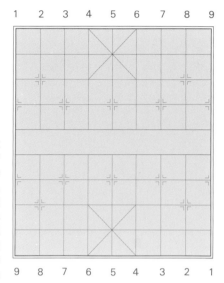

Figure 13 The numbered files.

The files are numbered 1 to 9 from right to left at both ends of the board (Figure 13). The ranks (rows) are unmarked.

Any move forward (diagonally or straight) from the viewpoint of the player is described by "+" and any move back (diagonally or straight) by "−". Any move sideways is denoted "=".

Then if the move is from one file to another the move is described using the format:

Piece moving/"from" file/
how moving/"to" file,

so that, for example, the two possible guard moves in the initial position are G4+5 and G6+5.

But if the move is all on the same file the format is:

Piece moving/"from" file/
how moving/number of ranks moved.

In the initial position, therefore, the only possible king move is K5+1.

The file numbers given are always those of the player making the move, whichever side of the river the move is made. This cross-numbering may seem cumbersome but it has advantages when talking about the openings.

In cases of ambiguity, where there are two similar pieces on the same file, they are distinguished as upper (U) and lower (L), from the standpoint of the player moving, e.g. UR1+4.

As an optional feature for us in the West, captures can be noted by adding "x" and checks by adding "ch".

This system will give access to the Chinese literature once a few characters have been learnt, but it also has the merit of conforming, along with the piece names, to a system recommended

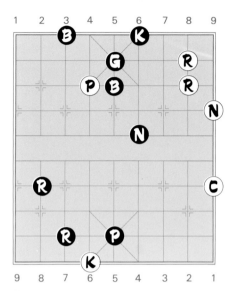

Figure 14 Endgame study.

by the Kowloon Chinese Chess Association of Hong Kong (except that they use "V" for "=") and to a similar system (using "0" instead of "=") adopted in mainland China.

The endgame study in Figure 14 will illustrate use of the notation. It is Red to play and win (Black is threatening checkmate with R3=4).

1) UR2+1 ch   K6+1
2) R2+1 ch   K6+1
3) UR2=4 ch   G5−6 x
4) R2−1 ch   K6−1
5) R2=4 ch   K6=5
   (If Black captures with K6+1: N1+
   2 ch, K6−1; C1+5 checkmate)
6) P6+1 ch   K5−1
7) R4+2 xch   K5=6 x
8) N1+2 ch   K6=5
9) P6+1 ch   K5+1
10) C1+5 checkmate (Figure 15)

The openings

There is a large body of opening analysis, some of it going back centuries. The basic principles are, however, fairly straightforward.

Whoever plays first (usually Red) has a significant advantage, and to keep that initiative Red will normally try to maintain a strong attacking posture. Black can either submit to defence or take up an attacking posture of his own. Attack, defence and counter-attack are the words that dominate Chinese game commentaries and so the first consideration should be to understand what they mean here.

Each player's forces are split in an obvious way between attack and defence in that the guards and bishops cannot leave their own area and are thus

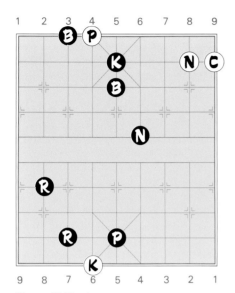

Figure 15 Checkmate.

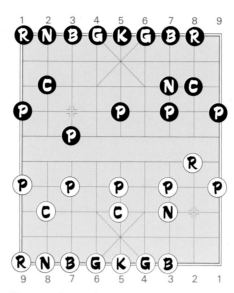

Figure 17 Centre Cannon and Patrolling Rook opening.

Staggered Cannons, answering C2=5 with C2=5.

The middle game

The middle game, the period when pieces come into contact and exchanges are made, can begin very early in Chinese chess. It is usually characterised by enormous tactical complexity, with multiple exchanges being offered

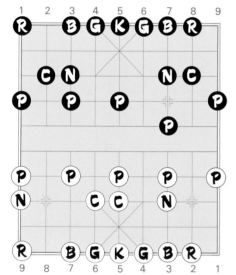

Figure 16 The 5 and 6-file Cannons opening.

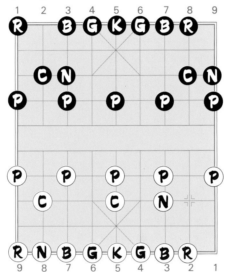

Figure 18 Single Knight Defence.

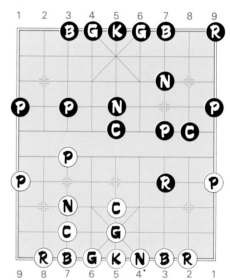

Figure 19 A typical middle game.

useful only for defence. Pawns cannot move backwards and so perforce have to attack. The long-ranging rooks, cannons and knights obviously can serve attacking roles, and in the opening that is their main function, but they can defend when necessary.

The cannons tend to dominate the disposition of the attacking forces, not least because in the early stages there are plenty of pieces to act as a support, and the obvious target is the centre files. The most important opening systems for the attacking side are, in fact, named according to the positions taken up by the cannons and nearly always the first move is Centre Cannon (C2=5 or C8=5).

They are generally sub-divided to what the other cannon does or how the rooks operate.

Figure 16 shows a popular formation

(for Red) called the 5 and 6-file Cannons, for example, and Figure 17 is an example involving a rook. It is called the Centre Cannon and Patrolling Rook opening, the rook being said to patrol the river. Cannons can also be used on patrol, and both rooks and cannons can cross the river.

Black clearly has to respond to what Red is doing but he has a considerable choice of opening systems too. The most commonly used is the Cavalry Screen, that is N2+3 and N8+7, which is seen in Figure 16. It is so powerful that Red sometimes uses it instead. Another common deployment based on knights is the Single Knight Defence of Figure 18.

These last two systems are mainly defensive, but if Black wishes to be aggressive he can play Opposing Cannons, answering C2=5 with C8=5, or

and counter-offered and all sorts of hidden attacks and defences of individual pieces emerging. Yet it would be wrong to assume that gain or loss of pieces (material) is the criterion by which the various exchanges are to be judged. Material is important, more important than in Japanese chess but less so than in western chess, but Chinese players put huge emphasis on two other aspects: keeping or seizing the initiative (and they study many techniques to achieve this) and getting the right combination of pieces for the endgame.

Although the kaleidoscope of exchanges of a typical middle game may seem to be concerned only with rooks, cannons and knights, very often it is the gain or loss of a guard or bishop that determines the true course of a game. A cannon tends to be stronger late in the

47

game if the opponent has lost a guard and so a player may then prefer to have a cannon rather than a knight. But the loss of a bishop often means pulling a knight back to cover for it – a knight would then be preferred to a cannon.

Rooks generally are regarded as the strongest pieces, but if the opponent has lost both a guard and a bishop it may be better to prefer knights to rooks. And so on. One obvious gain, getting a pawn across the river, is not normally regarded very highly. It is only when two or three such pawns can act in concert that they are specially prized. It should be noted, too, that pawns are frequently advanced or even sacrificed early in the game to free knights behind them.

Figure 19 gives a simple example of middle-game play in which Red exploits a weakness on Black's centre file (he has no guard or bishop there) to force him into an inferior position.

1) R2+5 x   N7+8 x
2) R8+5   P3+1
3) R8=7 x   R7=5

Typical confusion. This rook move invites the knight to take it but whether the knight takes or not, the red cannon on the centre file is blocked so that Black can now threaten N5+3 x (that move was not possible before the rook move because otherwise Black was in check from the cannon). In addition the two cannons are now able to capture each other. Red's rook is also threatening a cannon and bishop.

In these circumstances Black's threats to capture an edge pawn or to send his 7-file pawn over the river are trifles.

4) C5+3 ch   N5+3 x
5) N7+5 x   N3+5
6) C5=2 x   R9=8
7) C2–4

The two cannons are more desirable in this position than Black's rook because the presence of all the guards and bishops in Red's camp to act as supports retains their power – cannons normally lose power as the game progresses and pieces disappear.

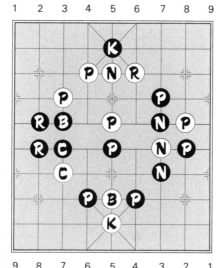

Figure 20 Flashing Diamond.

The endgame

A huge amount of the Chinese literature on the game is devoted to the endgame. Apart from being able to calculate how to win in a given position, a player has to know which positions are likely to be wins and which are draws.

One has to know, for example, that K+N versus K is a win, as is K+N versus K+G but K+N versus K+B is a draw. Similarly, K+P versus K+B is a draw normally, but K+P+P versus K+B is a win. At a more complex level, K+C+B+P should beat K+G+B+B. Even this is nowhere near the limit: how about K+R+R versus K+N+P+P+B+B+G+G? This is a win for the former, but only provided he can take the offensive.

Naturally, irrespective of what the theory might be, skill and experience matter most of all, and since a beginner can be expected to have neither, it may be more interesting here to look at another popular facet of endgame play, the artificial study. Figure 20 is a recent problem by Zhu Hezhou called the Flashing Diamond. Red to play and win.

The solution is: (All Red's moves are checks) (1) P6+1, K5=4 x; (2) R4+1, K4+1; (3) P7=6, K4=5 x; (4) P5+1, LN3–5 x; (5) P6=5 x, K5=4; (6) P5=6, K4=5; (7) P6+1, K5=4 x; (8) N3+4, K4=5; (9) N4–6, K5=4; (10) C7=6, P5=4; (11) R4–1, K4–1; (12) N6+4, K4=5; (13) R4+2, K5+1; (14) R4=5, K5=6; (15) C6=4, N7=6; (16) R5=4, K6=5; (17) N4+3, K5–1; (18) R4–1, K5–1; (19) R4=6 checkmate.

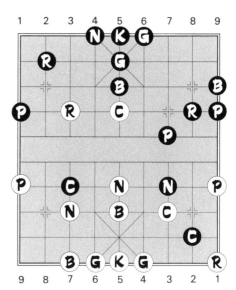

Figure 21 Position after 20) B3+5.

Illustrative game

Two games of very contrasting type will be given. Both were played in the San Chu Championship (which is tantamount to the championship of Central China) in Wuhan in 1984. Comments to the first game are based on those given by the loser in the journal *Beifang Qiyi*, from which it will be apparent that western and Chinese chess players have a lot in common in how they write about the game. The tournament structure is similar too. (Japanese chess is utterly different in both respects).

Game 1

Red: Hu Ronghua (Shanghai) Black: Li Laiqun (Hebei)

5 and 6-file Cannons versus Cavalry Screen

1) C2=5   N8+7
2) N2+3   P7+1
3) C8=6   N2+3
4) R1=2   R9=8
5) N8+7   R1=2
6) R9=8   C8+4

Correct. A similar advance by the other cannon looks possible but if Black plays C2+4 he suffers R2+6, N7+6; P7+1, B7+5; R2=4, N6+7; N7+6 (that is, Red gets a good, coordinated attack).

7) R8+6   G4+5

Black plays here a variation called the Advanced Guard. The alternative was the Flying Bishop, B3+5 which is followed by P7+1, G4+5; G4+5 and Red retains the initiative. With the Advanced Guard, however, Black would answer P7+1 with C8=5 and then Red's C5+4 is met by N3+5, so it

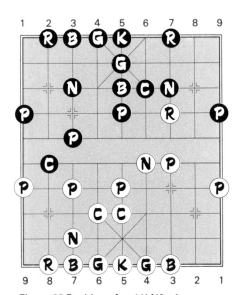

Figure 22 Position after 11) N3+4.

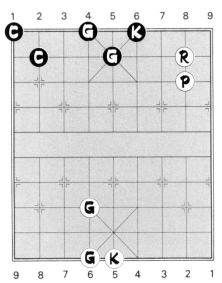

Figure 23 Repetitive checks: illegal.

reverts to a Centre Cannon game.

8) R8=7   N3−4
9) R7=8   B3+5

Red has taken profit by capturing the pawn but has had to waste a move in doing it. This indicates that Red is looking for a slow-paced game.

10) P5+1   R2+1

Red's P5+1 is a good move because he has a positional advantage. Hu is good at psychological warfare, creating positions where the opponent has to make awkward decisions about how to continue. Black opted for R2+1 here with a view to a possible exchange of rooks, knowing that he is safe because he has completed his defensive preparations with the guard and bishop moves.

11) C5+1   C8+2
12) C6=5   C2=3
13) R8=7   N7+6
14) R7−2   R8+3
15) UC5+3   N6−4
16) R7+2   N4+5
17) N3+5   N5+7

After the game Hu said N3+5 should have been G4+5 then Red can maintain his attacking posture. But later analysis showed that Black can counterattack with R2+5.

18) LC5−3   B7+9
19) R2=1   C3+4
20) B3+5   (Figure 21)

This is the critical point. Black should now play R2=4 and then three variations may be considered:
(1) C5=3, C8=4; UC3+3 ch, B9−7; R7=2, R4+5 and Black, through the sacrifice of material, gets a strong

attack;
(2) R7−3, R8=5 and then Red has no way to stop C8=4 or C8−2, both leading to a strong attack;
(3) G4+5, R4+5; C5=3, R8+3 and Black has a big positional advantage, having exploited Red's slow development.

But under time pressure (time limits are normally 30 moves in 1½ hours and 15 moves in 30 minutes thereafter), Black went wrong.

20) . . .   C8=4
21) R7−3   R8=5
22) R7=6   C4=8
23) G4+5   N4+3
24) R6=7   C8−6
25) N5+7   C8=7

Under time pressure Black elected to go for a win rather than a draw and he did indeed still have chances. But with this move he has lost his best chance to fight. He should have played N7−5; R7=2, C8=6; LN7+6, N3+4; R2=5, C6+3.

26) R7=4   R2+3
27) LN7+5   N7−8
28) C3=4   P7+1
29) R4+5   P7=6
30) N5+4   C7=6
31) R4=2   P6+1
32) N4+6   P6+1

Many players pointed out after the game that this should be R2=3; C4+5, G5+6; N6+7, K5=4 and Black is in no danger.

33) N6−8   N8+6
34) R2−4   N6+5
35) B7+5   N3+2
36) G5+4   R5+4 ch

37) G6+5   R5=3
38) R1=2   B5+7
39) LR2+3   C6=5 ch
40) G5+6   R3+2 ch
41) K5+1   R3−1 ch
42) K5−1   N2−3

Better would be N2+3; UR2=6, N3+4; R6=4, R3−1. Note that Black is not permitted to go on checking with the rook.

43) LR2=8   N3+5 ch
44) K5=4   C5=6 ch
45) K4=5   C6=5 ch
46) K5=4   N5+3
47) R8+2   N3−4
48) N7+6   R3+1 ch
49) K4+1   R3−1 ch
50) K4−1   R3−5
51) R8+4 ch   N4−3
52) R8−3   R3+6 ch
53) K4+1   C5=6 ch
54) K4=5   R3−1 ch
55) K5−1   R3−6
56) R2=7   R3=5 ch
57) G4−5

Black resigned here. He has no attack left and Red's two rooks and knight are just too strong on Black's denuded right flank (Black could not play 56 . . . R3+3 because of N6+4 ch for then G5+6 would be illegal: facing kings).
Game 2
Apart from stating that it is rather complicated this game needs no comment, but it illustrates well a common type of game in Chinese chess. The winner was the same player who won the previous, completely contrasting, game. Black's opening, characterised by his second and third moves, is a counter-offensive rather than a defence, but it is difficult to use except for the best players.
Red: Huang Yong (Hobei) Black: Hu Ronghua (Shanghai)
5 and 6-file Cannons versus Siege Knight
(1) C2=5, N2+3; (2) N2+3, C8=6; (3) R1=2, N8+7 (this knight is intended not for defence but to lay siege, if possible, to the enemy palace); (4) P3+1, P3+1; (5) N8+9, B7+5; (6) C8=6, R1=2; (7) R9=8, C2+4; (8) N9−7, C2−1; (9) R2+6, G6+5; (10)

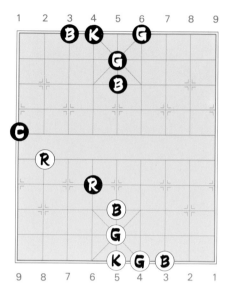

Figure 24 Repetitive mating checks: illegal.

Figure 25 Repetitive attacks: illegal.

R2=3, R9=7; (11) N3+4 (Figure 22), C6+7; (12) K5=4, C2−2; (13) C6+4, P5+1; (14) C6+1, C2=6 ch; (15) R3=4, R2+9; (16) C6=3, R2=3; (17) C3=7, R3=4 ch; (18) N7−5, R7+5; (19) B3+1, R7+1; (20) N4+3, R7=8; (21) C5=3, R8+1; (22) C3−1, R8=5; (23) C3−1, R5=9; (24) N3−2, R9+2; (25) R4=3, R9−3; (26) R3=2, R9=7; (27) C3+2, R7=8; (28) C3=5, R8+3 ch; (29) K4+1, R4−1 ch; (30) C5−1, R8−1 ch; (31) Resigns.

Special rules

As mentioned earlier, there are some special rules concerning repetitions of moves. The official rules published in Peking specifically prohibit the following types of repetition (basically those where only one player compels the other to play in a certain way):

(1) Repetitive checks by one player. E.g. in Figure 23, after R2+1, K6+1, R2−1, K6−1 Red is not allowed to start repeating with R2+1.

(2) Repetitive threats of checkmate next move by one player. E.g. in Figure 24, after N3−5 (threatening R1+3 mate), K4=5; N5+3 (again threatening R1+3 mate), K5=4; N3−5, K4=5 Red is not allowed to continue with N5+3.

(3) Combinations of repetitive checks and repetitive threats of checkmate next move

(4) Repetitive attacks – a player is not allowed to attack one of the opponent's unprotected pieces (he is thus forced to defend it) repeatedly in the same or a similar manner (except with a pawn or king – see below). In Figure 25, after R8=9, C1=2; R9=8, C2=1 Red must vary: R8=9 would lose. But see under draws (8) to (11) below.

(5) Combinations of repetitive checks and repetitive attacks.

(6) Combinations of repetitive checks and repetitive threats to capture an enemy piece after a discovered

Chinese players in Whangpoo Park, Shanghai, playing Chinese Chess.

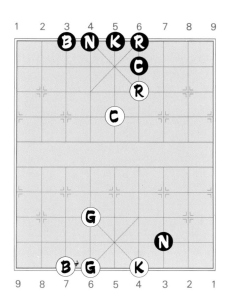

Figure 26 Alternating repetitive attacks: drawn.

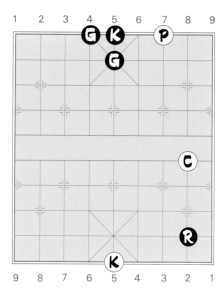

Figure 27 Repetitive chasing when forced: drawn.

check (a check given by a piece not moving but exposed by the piece that does move).

If, however, the following types of repetition occur (basically those where both players repeat voluntarily) the game is a draw:

(1) Repetitive blocking, where a threat is repeatedly made but repeatedly blocked by interposing a piece in the same or similar fashion.

(2) Repetitive chasing, where one side chases the same enemy piece which is protected but keeps running.

(3) Repetitive offers of exchanges, where one player offers the same or similar exchanges and the opponent repeatedly declines them.

(4) Repetitive offers of a sacrifice, where one player keeps offering the same piece in order to achieve a greater gain (e.g. checkmate) and the opponent keeps refusing it.

(5) A combination of repetitive checks and repetitive blocking, providing the checking player is not making a check prohibited as above.

(6) Alternating repetitive checks, e.g. in Figure 26 the game is drawn after R4=5 ch, C6=5 ch; R5=4 ch, C5=6 ch.

(7) Similar cases to (6) but involving double checks.

(8) Repetitive chasing of unprotected pieces where the repetition can be regarded as forced, e.g. Figure 27: after C2=7 Black can play R8=3; C7=2, R3=8, which would normally be illegal, because these are the only moves he has to stop checkmate.

(9) Repetitive chasing of unprotected

pieces by both players alternately. Note: In (8) and (9), if one player varies the other must too.

(10) Repeated attacks on an unprotected enemy piece by a pawn or a king, unless the pawn is attacking (checking) the enemy king.

Despite this lengthy list there are quite a few positions difficult to interpret. The rules give extensive guidance on this but the decision is that of a tournament controller (or as agreed by the players).

Where to get more information

There are no good primers in English but reasonably extensive information on the openings can be found in *A Manual of Chinese Chess* by W.H. Wilkinson (Shanghai, 1893) and for those reading French, *Traité d'échecs chinois* by C. Guermeur (Paris, 1979) is useful but very out of date.

There is abundant Chinese literature. Much can be gleaned from this by knowing the characters in Figure 28.

Figure 28 The Chinese pieces. Slight variation in the calligraphy may be found in some sets, the left portion varying according to Red or Black (a legacy of the days when pieces were not coloured and the two sides were distinguished in this way – notice the rook differs from that at the top of the page). Simplified versions will be seen in modern Chinese books. The characters needed to read the notation there are:

進 or 进 or 上 for +	前 or 上 for U	一 1	四 4	七 7
退 or 下 for −	后 or 下 for L	二 2	五 5	八 8
平 for =		三 3	六 6	九 9

Figure 28

MANCALA

Mancala has often been called the national game of Africa. There is evidence from temple carvings that the game was played in the Egypt of the Pharaohs at least 3,000 years ago and to-day it is widespread over the continent as well as in the Levant, many parts of the East and throughout the Caribbean.

THE MANCALA PLAYING BOARD is sometimes elaborately carved from wood in the local tradition; more often it is crudely made, and often scratched on rock or simply marked on the ground. The men are commonly pebbles ('stones') but any small objects may be used: pulses, seeds, shells or beads.

Mancala is not one game, but at least two hundred games linked by a fundamental play system. The games vary in the board arrangements and rule details and are generally regional in distribution with indigenous names.

Essentially, Mancala is a board game for two or more players (two are best) in which stones are initially distributed in cells arranged in lines on a board and are redistributed during play according to certain rules, with the object of winning the opponent's stones.

Mancala sets are available in games' shops but a board can be simply drawn on a sheet of paper and dried peas or coffee beans used as stones.

Two widely-played and distinct Mancala games are Ayo and Oware, both of West African origin.

Ayo

Ayo ('I play') is a two-player game. The board consists of two lines each of six cups with a larger cup at each end, these being used as stores for captured stones. At the start, the board is placed width-ways between the players and four stones are dropped into each of the twelve central cups (Figure 1).

The first player lifts all four stones from any cup on his side of the board and distributes them one by one in an anti-clockwise direction, the first stone in the cup adjacent to the one vacated. This is called 'sowing'. Sowing requires: (1) the cup chosen must be one of the six nearest the player; (2) the cup must be emptied; (3) sowing must start at the cup immediately to the right of the one emptied or, if it is the end cup in the row, the cup opposite it in the opponent's row; (4) one stone, and only one, must be sown into each cup in turn – no cup can be 'jumped'. Later in a game when a lifted cup may have a larger number of stones in it, the board may be circuited during a sowing. In this case, the cup that was emptied must be passed over – it is always left empty at the end of a turn.

Play alternates, each player on his turn emptying one of his cups and sowing the contents. When the last stone of a sowing is dropped in a cup on the opponent's side of the board that contains either one or two stones (after the sowing, two or three), these stones are captured and are removed to the player's store. If the penultimate cup also contains two or three stones (including in each case the one sown) and is also on the opponent's side of the

board, then these stones are captured too, and so on provided the sequence is unbroken. Notice that a player may never capture stones on his own side of the board.

Ayo is not a ruthless game. There are two rules that favour the losing player. It is forbidden to empty all the opponent's cups, even if otherwise entitled, if, in so doing, he is deprived of the opportunity to play on his next turn. Further, if an opponent is left with no stones in any of his cups, the player must empty a cup that permits at least one stone to rest in the opponent's cups at the end of the turn.

If neither of these concessions is possible, the player takes up all the stones remaining on his side of the board and adds them to his store when the game ends. The game can also be ended by consent when the two forces are so reduced that further play seems pointless. In this case, the players pick up the stones on their respective sides and add them to their stores. The player with the most stones at the end is the winner. If, during the course of a game, one player accumulates 25 or more stones in his store he has clearly won the game and there is no point in continuing play.

A game of Ayo in progress is shown in Figure 2. White, to play, wisely picks up the stones in cup B and distributes them, one per cup, in the sequence C-D-E-F-a-b-c-d-e-f. Because there are now 3 stones in f, these are captured by White; the stones in e,d and c are also captured by White, but not the stones in a because the sequence is broken by the 4 stones in b. White by his play has gained 11 prisoners. The board at the start of Black's turn is shown in Figure 3.

Strategy Mancala games are games of pure skill. Choice is limited – at most a player has six possible sowings on his turn – but great foresight is needed to appreciate the ultimate consequences of a play.

If, at the start of your turn, you have a cup that is vulnerable (because it has either one or two stones in it) you may be able to avoid loss by adopting one of

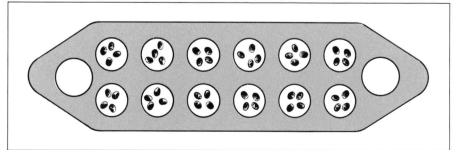

Figure 1 The starting position for Ayo.

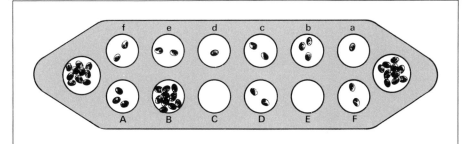

Figure 2 A game of Ayo in progress: White to play.

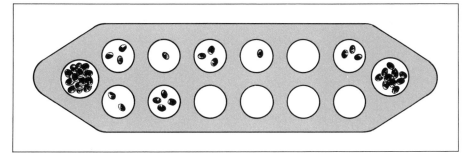

Figure 3 A game of Ayo in progress: Black to play.

three possible measures: (1) emptying the cup and sowing the stone(s); (2) if the threatened cup contains two stones, emptying a preceeding cup so that, during sowing, a stone is added to the threatened cup; (3) choosing a cup to sow from that will result in the adding of a stone to the opponent's cup that threatens yours, thereby ensuring that a sowing will overshoot.

Oware

Oware is ideally played by two but there are three-, four- and six-player versions. The board is the same as that used for Ayo and the starting position – 48 stones distributed equally into the 12 cups – is identical.

Players in turn empty any cup on their own side of the board and sow the stones from it as in Ayo. Now comes the change. In Oware, if there are one, two, or more than three stones in the last cup of a sowing before the final stone is dropped, these are picked up and added to the stone in hand and a new sowing is made moving, as usual, anti-clockwise. Sowings continue in this manner until the last stone of a sowing is dropped into an empty cup or one that contains exactly three stones (four after the sowing). In either event this ends the turn, except that in the latter case the player lifts the four stones and places them in his store regardless of which side the last cup is on. If, during the course of sowing, any cup to which a stone has been added contains exactly four stones (unless it is the last cup – see above), the player on whose side of the board the cup lies picks up the stones at the end of the sowing and adds them to his store.

The same concessions as in Ayo are made to a player who is otherwise unable to move. The game ends when one player has captured the majority of stones, or when no further play is possible or when the forces are so reduced that further play seems pointless.

Strategy Aim to build up cups of two or three stones on your side of the board. Stones on your side are fairly safe, so for preference capture stones on the opponent's side.

A roadside game of Mancala in Syria.

DRAUGHTS

Draughts, or Checkers as it is called in the U.S.A., is an ancient game, the origins of which are somewhat obscure. There are records of the game being played in Britain during the 16th century though the rules were not quite the same as those used today. Not until about 1800 did the modern game become accepted in Europe.

THERE ARE VARIATIONS to the standard game of draughts and these will be discussed later. The basic game is played on a board having 64 squares, 32 of which are white – or light coloured – and the other 32 are black or dark coloured. All play takes place on the black squares. The board should be so placed that each player has a white square in the right-hand corner. This is exactly the same as for chess.

Each player has 12 men and these are round discs which he places on the black squares of his three back rows, as in Figure 1.

Black always makes the first move.

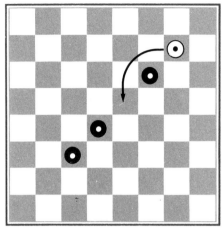

Figure 2

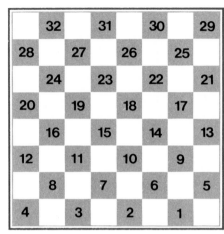

Figure 4

The movement of men is confined to the black diagonal rows. Except when capturing, a man moves only one square at a time. The players continue to move alternately. Captures are made by hopping over a hostile piece or pieces and this can only be done if there is a vacant

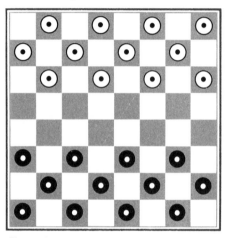

Figure 1

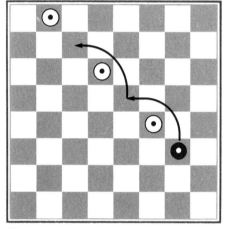

Figure 3

square beyond the piece being taken. A piece making captures may continue to move for as long as there are enemy pieces to hop over. The capturing piece may change direction, while continuing to go forwards. Figure 2 shows White capturing one Black man. He cannot go further than this because there is no vacant square immediately beyond the next black piece. Figure 3 shows a black piece capturing two white men. It is important to capture every man you can in any one move or your opponent is entitled to 'huff' you. This allows him to remove from the board your piece that could have made the capture. He must do it immediately – if he makes his move without huffing the opportunity is lost. The huff does not count as a move, and the player who has called the huff then makes his own move as normal. Alternatively, he can insist that you capture the piece that was threatened and take back the move you have just made.

Before play starts one of the players holds a piece of each colour in his clenched fists and offers them to his opponent. Whichever fist is pointed to or touched is opened to reveal the

colour the opponent must play in the first game. Thereafter in any subsequent games the players change colours.

The object of the game is twofold:
1) a player aims to capture as many of his opponent's men as possible and
2) he aims to immobilize his opponent's pieces.

Whichever player first achieves a position in which his opponent cannot move is the winner.

The pieces must always be moved forward towards the opponent's back row. Any man which can reach this back row is immediately turned into a King. This is done by placing another disc of the same colour on top of the successful man.

A King can be moved backwards or forwards across the board but is, of course, still confined to the diagonals. Like ordinary pieces the King is confined to a move of one square at a time except when capturing, and the same rule applies about the vacant square on the other side of any man to be captured. A King can change direction (forwards and backwards) when capturing two or more pieces.

A game of draughts can be recorded and the system of notation is very simple. The black squares are numbered from 1 to 32 starting at the bottom right-hand corner of the squares being used by the player who has the black pieces. The numbers progress from right to left in each rank (see Figure 4). Chess diagrams always show the black pieces starting at the top and white at the bottom. For draughts it is the other way round.

Occasionally a player may find that more than one of his men can make a capture. Provided that he uses one of these pieces to take a hostile man he cannot be 'huffed' for failing to capture with the other piece.

It is obvious that pieces moved towards the centre of the board have better chances of capturing than those advanced to the sides. Centre men cover more squares in two directions. Men moved to the sides of the board are far more limited.

Here is an opening played by two beginners and shows some of the pitfalls to avoid:
(1) 10–15, 21–17 (2) 7–10, 23–19
(3) 11–16

Black can capture on his next move. The game proceeds:
(3) . . . 24–20 (4) 8–11

Black should have played 16–23 instead of 8–11 so he can now be huffed.

This is an example of an opening from two experienced players:
(1) 11–15, 23–19 (2) 8–11, 22–17
(3) 4–8, 17–13 (4) 15–18, 24–20

Neither player can capture yet. Black's moves have been towards the centre and he is backing up his attack leaving no vacant square beyond a piece. White has been making defensive moves to the side of the board. Now the game goes on:

(5) 11–15, 28–24 (6) 8–11, 26-23
(7) 9–14, 31–26 (8) 6–9 . . .

Here is the first move giving White a chance to capture. If he had ignored this he could have been 'huffed'. The game continues:
(8) . . . 13–6 (9) 2–9, 26–22
(10) 1–6, 22–17 (11) 18–22, 25–18
(12) 15–22 and so on.

This game ended in a draw and is a good example of first-class play by both White and Black. Each player has only sacrificed a piece when he can equalize by a capture of his own. Each has backed up his men to avoid losses.

In friendly games players do not, as a rule, take long to make a move but in competition play the rule is that a player must move within five minutes. If he does not, his opponent may call 'Time'

and if the player then fails to move within one minute he loses the game.

Some players – particularly children – prefer to play on the white squares. There is no reason why all play should not take place on white but the board should be turned before the pieces are set up and there should be a black square in each player's right-hand corner. There must always be a man in his left-hand corner square.

There are a number of variations on the standard game and all, except Polish Draughts, are played on a 64 square board using 12 White and 12 Black men. Here are some of the variations.

Spanish Draughts

The board should be so placed that there is a black square in each player's

right-hand corner. The pieces are then set up as for the standard game using the black squares. Movement of men is also governed by the same rules as in the ordinary game – that is one square at a time except when capturing and always forward on the black diagonals.

Movement of the King in Spanish Draughts is different. A King is made in the usual way. Any piece which reaches an opponent's back row is crowned by placing another man on top of it. It remains on the square on which it was crowned until it is the player's next move.

Drawing by J.L. Gerome of Albanians playing Draughts, 1896.

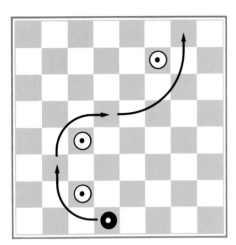

Figure 5

The King has what is called the 'long move' if desired. In other words it can be moved across the board as far as the player wishes provided the diagonal it uses is clear and it captures in the usual way. That is to say a King hops over a hostile piece and lands on a vacant square beyond that piece. As in the standard game a King can move in any direction and, if capturing, it can change direction. Figure 5 shows a black King capturing three white men. Note that this capture includes the 'long move' – there are two vacant squares between the last two men captured.

German Draughts

This game is played with the board in the conventional position and the pieces are set up as for the standard game. As in Spanish Draughts the Kings are entitled to the 'long move' and can be moved backwards or forwards but keeping to black diagonals.

The ordinary men, however, are governed by slightly different rules. They move forward one square at a time as in standard Draughts, but they can, when capturing, move backwards or forwards as required. They are crowned in the normal way when reaching the back row, except that if a man reaches the back row by capturing, and can capture a further piece or pieces by moving backwards, he must do so, and is not crowned.

If there is a choice of moving men

that can capture the player must make the move that captures the most men in one move.

Losing Draughts

This game reverses the normal order of things. Instead of capturing as many of the opponent's pieces as possible, the player deliberately tries to lose as many of his own pieces as he can. Capturing is compulsory.

The board is set up as for the standard game (Figure 1) and pieces are moved in the conventional way along diagonals. Each move is one square only except when capturing. The winner is the player who can no longer move or who loses all his men.

Russian Draughts

The board is set up as for standard Draughts and much the same rules apply to Russian Draughts as apply to German Draughts. The main difference is that a player is not compelled to make the maximum captures possible but may make any legal move he chooses. Kings however are governed by different rules. As in the standard game a man becomes a King on reaching his opponent's back row where he is immediately crowned and can then, in the same move, go on to make any possible captures. The King has the long move, of course.

Italian Draughts

As in the Spanish game the board should be turned so that each player has a black square in his back rank right-hand corner. Movement of the men is the same as in the standard game – one square diagonally forward on the black squares. Any man reaching the opponent's back rank is made a King and remains on that square until the player's next move. A King has the long move and captures in the usual way, that is by hopping over a hostile piece and landing on a vacant square. It is compulsory to take the maximum pieces available, and, where otherwise equal, to take with a King rather than a single piece. Kings in the Italian game cannot be captured by a single piece.

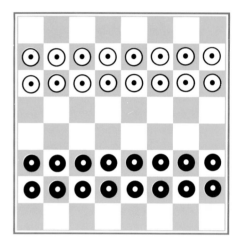

Figure 6

Turkish Draughts

This game differs considerably from the other variations described. The board is the conventional draughts or chessboard. It does not matter which way round the board is placed. Each player has 16 men instead of the conventional 12. These are placed on the second and third ranks as in Figure 6. The pieces move one square at a time but use the ranks and files and not the diagonals and do not move backwards. They also move forward or to the side when capturing, which is by the usual manner, by hopping over an enemy man to an empty square beyond. The maximum number of captures must be made. All squares of the board can be used.

Kings are made in the conventional way when a player places one of his men on his opponent's back rank. These remain on the square where they are crowned until the player's next move. Kings have the long move and can go as far as the player decides to make a capture provided the rank or file is free of men. Captured men are removed immediately in multiple moves, which sometimes enables additional captures previously impossible.

Polish Draughts

This is the only game not played on the conventional 64 squares board. A board having 100 is needed (10 x 10) and these are not easily obtainable except on the

Continent where the game is popular. A board of 50 white and 50 black squares can be made easily out of cardboard.

Each player has twenty men and these are arranged on the four back rows of the board (see Figure 7). Play takes place on the black squares only and the board is so arranged that each player has a white square in the bottom right-hand corner as for standard Draughts. Movement of the pieces is across the black diagonals and players move alternately one square at a time. The decision as to who plays black is decided by one player holding a piece of each colour in his hands and letting his opponent choose. When the chosen fist is opened it reveals the colour the opponent must play. Pieces can capture either forwards or backwards and this is done in the normal way by hopping a man over the piece to be captured and

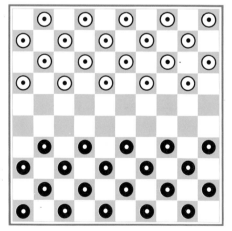

Figure 7

placing it on the vacant square beyond. Any piece reaching an opponent's back rank is crowned a Queen. This does not apply if the piece reaches the back rank

Africans playing Draughts on the main street of Wawa, Nigeria.

by a capture and there are other men the piece can capture. Because every piece can move forward and backward it must continue to make the maximum captures and is not crowned. The powers of the Queen in Polish Draughts are the same as a King in Spanish Draughts. The Queen has the long move and can advance as many squares as the player chooses provided these are not occupied. If both a hostile Queen and an ordinary man are open to capture the player must take the Queen. If a Queen makes a number of captures in one move the men taken should be left on their squares until the move is completed. Then they are removed from the board. 'Huffing' does not apply in Polish Draughts.

59

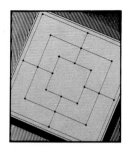

NINE MEN'S MORRIS

Nine Men's Morris, also known as Merelles or Mill, is a game of alignment, a sophisticated relation of the trivial noughts-and-crosses or tic-tac-toe. It is the most popular of the morris games which can claim a great antiquity.

GAME BOARDS, evidently for morris games, were carved on the temples at Thebes, in Upper Egypt, over three milleniums ago, while in the present millenium boards were cut into the furniture of Westminster Abbey and a number of provincial cathedrals, testifying to the game's popularity in medieval England.

The board is square and is made up of 24 points at the intersection of the

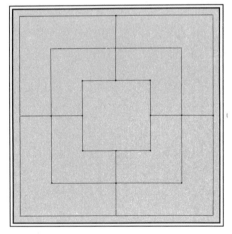

Figure 1

lines, Figure 1. Two players each have nine men, distinctively coloured. The men can be of any regular shape or size – counters can be used if desired.

The game starts with the board empty when the first player puts one of his men on any point. The second player on his turn similarly places a man on any vacant point. Play continues like this with the object of achieving a mill – three men of one's own colour in a row on adjacent points. When a player completes a mill he pounds (captures) any one of his opponent's men that does not itself form part of a mill, and removes it from play. If all the opponent's men are in mills, then the player is free to take any man without restriction, although some circles do not permit this, so that a player who forms a

mill when all his opponent's men are in mills, forfeits the right to capture. The turn then passes.

When all men have been entered (less those already pounded), the next phase begins. Play continues to alternate, but now each player in turn moves one of his men to an adjacent vacant point along any line, at his choice. Again, the object is to form a mill, when an opponent's man is captured, as in the first phase. It is permissible to break a mill by moving a man away and then to reform the mill on the next turn to claim another victim. If a player is unable to move, the second player continues to do so until the first player is free to move again, when the turn passes.

The third phase is reached when one player is reduced to three men. When this occurs, the three men become rovers – the player is free to move a man to any vacant point and is not restricted to moving to an adjacent point. When one player is reduced to two men he has lost, and the game is over.

Opinion is divided on the merits and demerits of the rover rule. On the one hand, the introduction of rovers puts fresh life into a one-sided game and also introduces some novel strategy. Also, without the rover rule, it is quite likely that one player will gain the ascendency early on; and, in the nature of the game, this advantage is then likely to accelerate until the second player is overrun. On the other hand, rovers are arguably too powerful, so that unless the opposition has at least seven or eight men remaining, and favourably deployed at that, the rover player actually has the advantage: he can easily set up double threats so that the course of the game is likely to be that the players will eventually face each other with three men each.

All the men are then rovers, and under these circumstances the player

who has the initiative will probably win – and this is likely to be the player who was first reduced to three men. The rover rule is believed to be historically a recent innovation. Many players do not allow it, preferring to extend the second phase until one player is reduced to two men and so loses.

A game in progress is shown in Figure 2. The points have been lettered for the convenience of recording moves.

Black, whose turn it is, ignores White's threatened mill and plays at X. White completes the mill at E and elects to take off Black X. Black plays again at X and now White cannot meet the double threat so plays at B, threatening

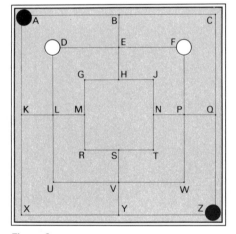

Figure 2

H. Black goes to K, making the mill AKX, and takes off White B (if he takes D,E or F, White completes a mill at once). Now White plays Y to stop the mill XYZ. Black counters with C and again has a double threat (Figure 3). Black will come out of the first phase with a one-man advantage but White will be better placed for phase 2.

Strategy

Nine Men's Morris is not as difficult as it may appear, due to the board's symmetry and because the eight points on the innermost square can be considered identical to those on the outermost – the board turned inside-out as it were. The actual different opening moves are therefore only four: a corner point and a centre point on the out-

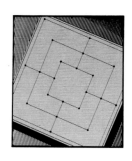

Nine Men's Morris can be played with simple equipment, as shown by these men in Bahrain.

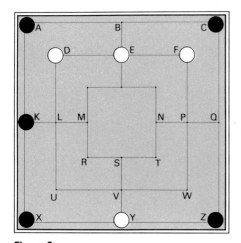

Figure 3

ermost (or innermost) square and a corner point and a centre point on the intermediate square.

The initiative is important: thus the first move (Black starts as a rule) is a considerable, and perhaps theoretically decisive, advantage. In the game above, White tried to wrest the initiative early. If, for example, Black on his third play had destroyed White's threatened mill by playing at E, White might have continued with U, threatening L, and if Black blocked with L, a White attack with W would ensure White the first mill anyway. In the game, Black's play at X temporarily ceded the initiative with the intention of recovering it on the next play. This is a common ploy.

In the rover game, draws are common. In this version, a good guideline

for the player with the most pieces is not to reduce the opponent to three men (which then become rovers) unless he is at least five men ahead or is sure of making a mill subsequently and so forcing the win. Notice that it is obligatory to remove a man after forming a mill – one cannot decline to do so.

There are basically two types of move: the attack, which threatens to make a mill, and the defence, which is played to prevent the opponent making a mill. Sometimes a defensive move proves to be an attacking move as well, when the initiative changes sides. As in many abstract games, it is usually favourable to group your men where possible rather than allow them to be scattered round the board.

Go

"Is it like chess?" is a question often asked by people who have never heard of Go. Go is a board game of pure skill for two players, and that is where any similarity with chess ends. For one thing, it is far older than chess, 4,000 years old according to some historians.

IN THOSE COUNTRIES where it is a traditional game, namely China, Japan, Korea and Taiwan, Go is taken far more seriously than is chess or any similar game in any Western country. Some indication of its popularity is that in Japan there are over 500 professional players, some of them very wealthy. In recent years Western games players have been discovering for themselves the reasons for this fanatical following.

Go is played on a rectangular board ruled with a grid of vertical and horizontal lines. Figure 1 shows a full-sized board suitable for tournament or club play. The dimensions of the grid are 45 × 42 cm. The nine dots, known as "star

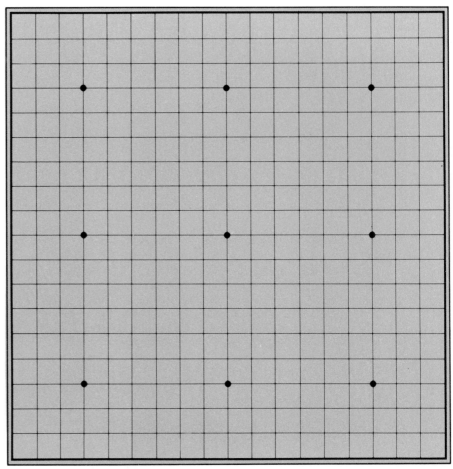

Figure 1 A full-sized Go board.

points", serve not only for orientation, but are relevant to the built-in handicapping system which is an attractive feature of Go.

Beginners and less experienced players are recommended to use smaller boards ruled with 13 × 13 or 9 × 9 lines. The remainder of the Figures in this article use the 9 × 9 board.

For play the two players have a theoretically limitless supply of "stones", coloured black and white respectively. Traditional stones are bi-convex in shape, and made (expensively) from slate and clam shell, or (more cheaply) from glass or plastic. It is usual for 181 black and 180 white stones to be supplied – i.e. enough to cover the board. Games shops supply both traditional oriental and Western cardboard-and-plastic Go sets; it is also a fairly simple matter to construct your own set, using counters or buttons etc. for stones.

To understand the object of the game it is best to start at the end. Figure 2 shows the position at the end of a game between two middle-ranking players. You will notice that play takes place on the intersections of the lines, and not on the squares as in many Western games. Both players have surrounded some empty space with their stones – to do this is the object of the game. In the upper left corner White has surrounded nine points (remember to count the points along the edge of the board and in the corner) and in the lower right he has six, totalling fifteen. Black has thirteen points (six upper right, seven lower left) so White wins this game by two points.

Surrounded areas of empty points are known as territory. It is important to note that it is *unoccupied* points that count; the points your stones are actually on are of no value at all towards territory.

Another important aspect is that every point on the board is either part of a black or white territory or is occupied by a black or white stone. This is how you know that the game has come to an end, and that is the time to count territories and see who has won. There

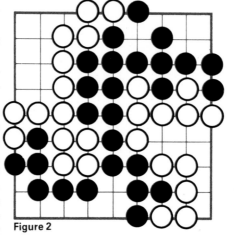

Figure 2

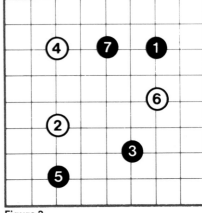

Figure 3

is no additional credit in winning by a large number of points; a margin of one point is enough.

Now let us go back to the start of this game. Play starts with the board empty. Black plays first by placing a stone on any unoccupied point on the board. White then does the same, and so play continues with the players alternately placing stones on the board until the end of the game is reached. There are two restrictions governing where stones may be placed – these will be described later. Once played, stones are not moved about. It is possible for stones to

be captured, in which case they are removed from the board – the way to do this will also be explained later.

The first seven moves are shown in Figure 3. You will notice that all the moves except Black 5 are on the third line from the edge. It has been found that stones placed on the third line are at the optimum distance to make full use of the corners and edges of the board helping to surround territory.

If you compare Figure 3 with Figure 2 you can see that even at this early stage the shapes of the final territories are becoming apparent.

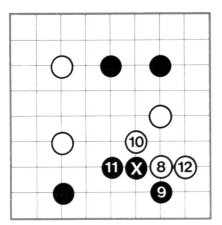

Figure 4

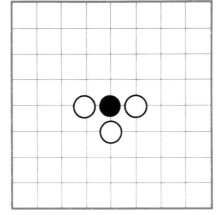

Figure 6

black armies. A stone is needed at 'a' or 'b' to connect them together.

Captured stones are retained by the capturing player as "prisoners" until the end of the game. He is then allowed to add one point to his territory score

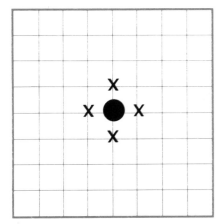

Figure 5

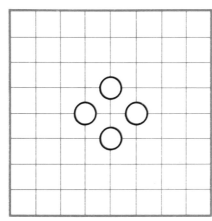

Figure 7

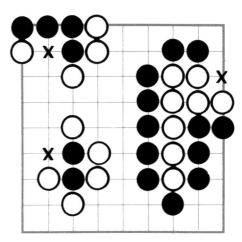

Figure 9

Figure 4 shows moves 8 – 12. A tactical encounter has broken out in the lower right corner. To understand it we must digress to explain captures.

The four points horizontally and vertically adjacent to a stone are called its "liberties". The four liberties of the black stone in Figure 5 are marked with an 'x'. If White is able to occupy all four of Black's liberties, the black stone will be captured and immediately removed from the board. Figure 6 shows three of the four liberties occupied. It is thus subject to capture on the next move if White is able to occupy the fourth liberty. Figure 7 shows the position after White has occupied the fourth liberty and made the capture.

Stones of the same colour connect together along their liberties to form single units or "armies". Figure 8 shows some examples. Armies can only be captured *en masse* – the stones cannot be surrounded and captured one at a time.

Figure 9 shows all the armies in Figure 8 with all their liberties except one occupied by enemy stones. The last liberties are marked 'x'. Go players use the Japanese term 'atari' to describe this situation – it is similar to the chess term

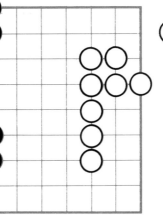

Figure 8

"*en prise*". Note that stones on the very edge of the board tend to be rather short of liberties.

In Figure 10 we see the positions that result if the last liberties are occupied and the armies removed from the board. It is important to note that a point diagonally adjacent to a stone is not one of its liberties. Stones do not connect together diagonally, neither is it necessary to occupy diagonally adjacent points when making a capture. For example Figure 11 shows two separate

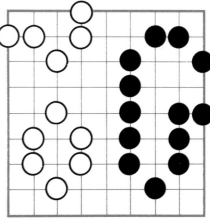

Figure 10

for each stone captured. In the particular game we are looking at no captures were made.

Returning now to Figure 4, Black noticed that after White 10 his stone marked 'x' was already down to two liberties, i.e. half way to being captured. Rather than allow it to become any weaker he connected another stone at '11', which also helped to surround territory on the lower edge. Similar thoughts were in White's mind as he connected '12' to '8'.

Black 13 in Figure 12 is a threat to advance into White's left-side territory, and at the same time prevents White from connecting his left-and right-side positions together. White 16 reduces another black stone to only two liber-

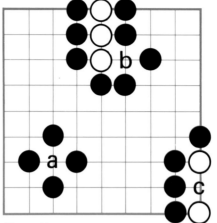

Figure 13

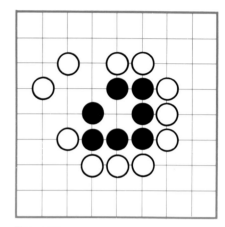

Figure 16

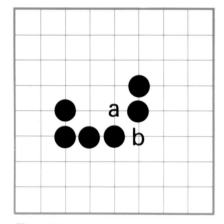

Figure 11

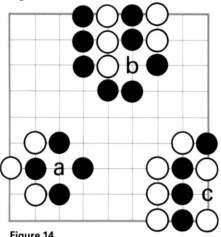

Figure 14

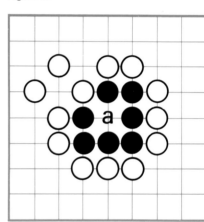

Figure 17

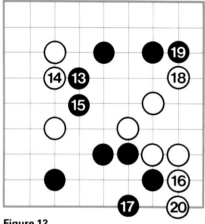

Figure 12

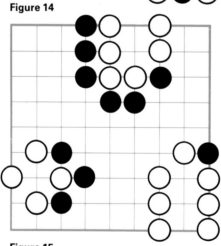

Figure 15

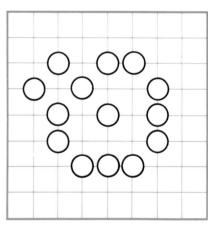

Figure 18

ties, and Black 17 is one way to defend it. Then with 18 – 20 White makes a little territory on the right while somewhat reducing Black's territorial prospects. But White has another purpose with these moves as well, and to explain it we digress again to explain the "suicide rule".

The rule states simply that it is illegal to play so as to leave one of your own stones or armies with no liberty. Thus for example in Figure 13 'a', 'b' and 'c' would all be illegal moves for White. 'a' would place a single stone where it would have no liberty; 'b' would occupy

the last liberty of the three-stone army, leaving a four-stone army with no liberty; and 'c' would join two stones into a three-stone army with no liberty.

However, if such a move has the effect of capturing one or more enemy stones, then it is deemed to create new liberties for the stone or army concerned and is allowed. Figure 14 shows how, with the addition of some stones, the moves which were illegal in Figure 13 would become legal because they now make a capture. Figure 15 shows the positions that would be left after such captures.

It is hard at first to see why one might want to break the suicide rule anyway, but it becomes relevant in situations such as that shown in Figure 16. White is attempting to surround and capture a black army which has an internal space. Including the internal liberty White has now three more liberties to occupy, but the play which finally captures the army *must be on the internal liberty*. To play there any sooner would infringe the suicide rule. Figure 17 shows the position after the two outside liberties have been filled in. Now White may play at 'a' and capture the army (Figure 18).

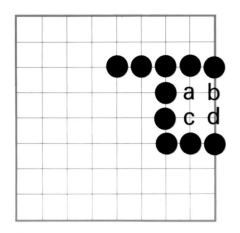

Figure 19

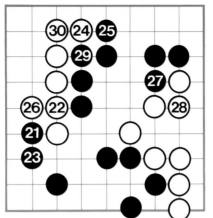

Figure 21

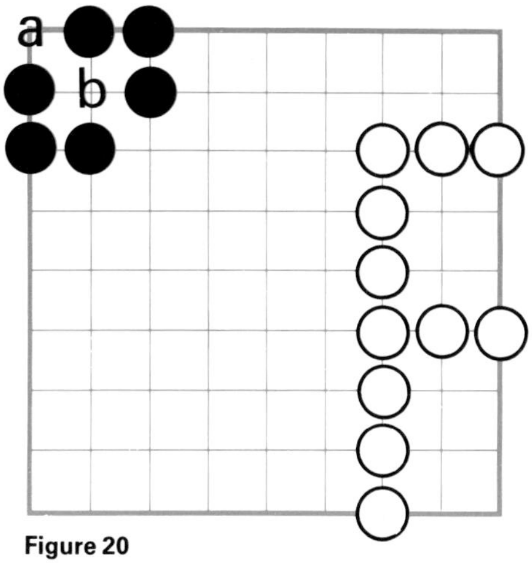

he were to play at 1 in Diagram 22 for example. Black could play at 2, and now extending at 3 does White no good at all. White's two stones are doomed – even if White plays at 'a' he is still in 'atari'. Worse still, the white stones in

Figure 20

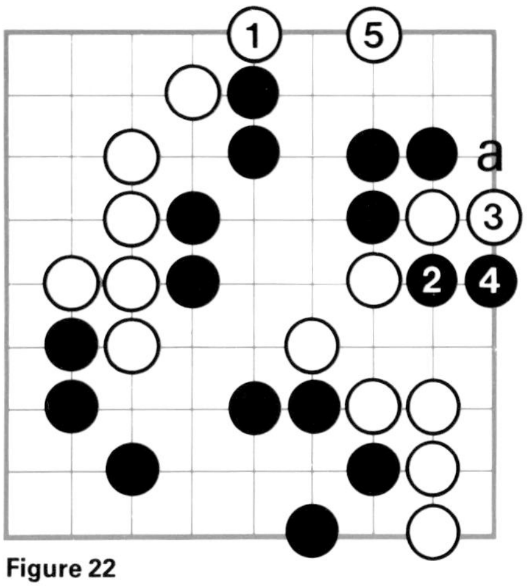

Figure 22

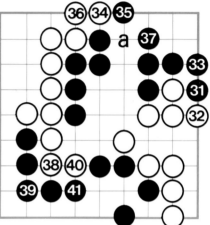

Figure 23

Figure 19 shows an army with a large internal space. It would be legal, though not necessarily wise, for White to play on three of the four liberties marked 'a', 'b', 'c' and 'd' before filling in all the outside liberties. But the play which finally makes the capture must once again be within the internal space – otherwise at some time or other White would have made a four-stone army ('a', 'b', 'c' and 'd') that had no liberty.

A most important corollary of this rule is that when an army or any group of stones can make two separate internal spaces, then that group of stones is permanently safe from capture. Figure 20 shows two groups that are invulnerable in this way. Even if White were to occupy all the external liberties of the black group, to make a capture he needs to be able to play on both 'a' and 'b' at the same time, clearly impossible.

The white group has internal spaces of more than one point but the principle is the same. Black may occupy all the external liberties and some of the internal ones if he wishes, but to capture the group he needs a move inside both the internal spaces at the same time, which he can never make. Such a permanently safe group is said to have "two eyes" and to be "alive".

Groups which surround a large territory can be reasonably sure of being able to divide it in two in the event of an attack, but when the territory is small the ability to divide it in two becomes critical. This is what was in White's mind in Figure 12. After Black 13 and 15 he can no longer link the right side stones to the safer ones on the left, but after the moves up to 20 he is sure of a large enough internal space to divide into two eyes in the event of an attack.

Black 21 in Figure 21 takes advantage of the weakness that he created in White's left side territory when he played 15 in Figure 12. White 22 is necessary to stop Black from playing there. After 23 Black threatens a further advance into the white territory, but rather then defend immediately White makes a counterthreat to advance into the upper right black territory with 24. Black decides to answer this threat at 25, so White has time to go back and defend at 26. Such exchanges are common in Go. Threats are often better met with counterthreats than with straightforward defence.

Black 27 once again reduces a white stone to only two liberties, and it is worth noting what would happen if White failed to defend at 28. Suppose

the lower right corner no longer have enough space to make two eyes, and cannot escape eventual capture.

White can now advance to 5 on the upper edge, but this in no way makes up for his loss in the other corner. So it is well worth White's defending at 28 in Figure 21 to avoid such a loss, and 29 and 30 have a similar thought.

Throughout the moves on Figure 21 Black has held the initiative, or "sente". (This letter is a Japanese term often used by Go players.) He has now run out of useful threats against White, and in Figure 23 it is White who holds "sente". In three separate areas of the board he is able slightly to press back Black's frontier and to force him to make defensive moves. Black 37 is needed to prevent White from playing at 'a'.

White 42 in Figure 24 threatens a move at 43, so Black defends there. White 44 puts one black stone into "atari", so Black defends it at 45. The moves 46 – 48 are the last that affect the final score.

The points marked 'a' – 'e' are neutral points. It is impossible for either player to surround any of them. It might look as if White can surround 'c', but if for example he plays at 'b',

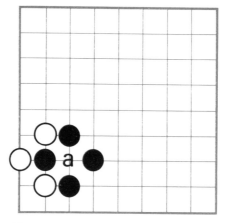

Figure 26

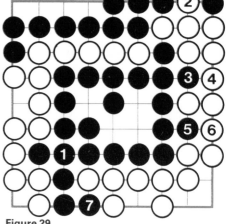

Figure 29

Black will play at 'a' and White must play at 'c' to prevent Black from capturing 42. As it happens Black gets to 'b' first, and the moves in Figure 25 are by way of a formality – they do not affect the result.

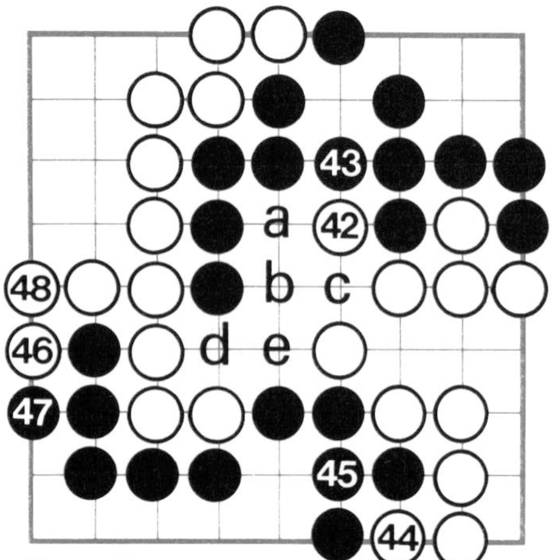

Figure 24

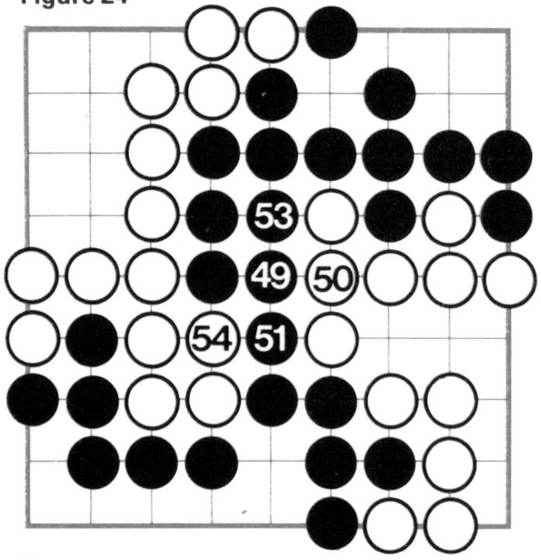

Figure 27

Figure 25

Figure 28

Now we have reached the position shown in Figure 2. Neither player wishes to play any more moves. If either player did play again, he would have to play either on one of his own points of territory, or inside his opponent's territory. In the former case he decreases his own score by a point; in the latter he presents his opponent with a stone which can be captured. Neither option is attractive, so after White 48 Black would say "I pass". White would say the same for the same reason, and the game is then formally at an end.

It was mentioned above that there are

two restrictions on where a stone may be played. The "suicide rule" has already been explained. It is now time to explain the other, the so-called "Ko rule". Figure 26 repeats a position shown in Figure 14. If White captures at 'a' (it is not suicide, because it makes a capture) we have the position in Figure 27. What now if Black recaptures at 'b'? This leads straight back to Figure 26. This exchange could go on for ever, were it not for the Ko rule, "Ko" being a Japanese word signifying "eternity".

The rule states that a player may not

leave on the board a position identical with that left by his last move. The effect of this rule is that while White may capture at 'a' in Figure 26, Black must wait at least one move before recapturing at 'b' in Figure 27. He must first play a move elsewhere, which gives White the chance to end the Ko situation by connecting his stones together at 'b' if he wishes. If he chooses not to, but plays elsewhere himself, Black may then recapture at 'b'. This repeats the position locally, but over the board as a whole at least two more stones have been played. Therefore the game still progresses even if this exchange does keep going back and forth.

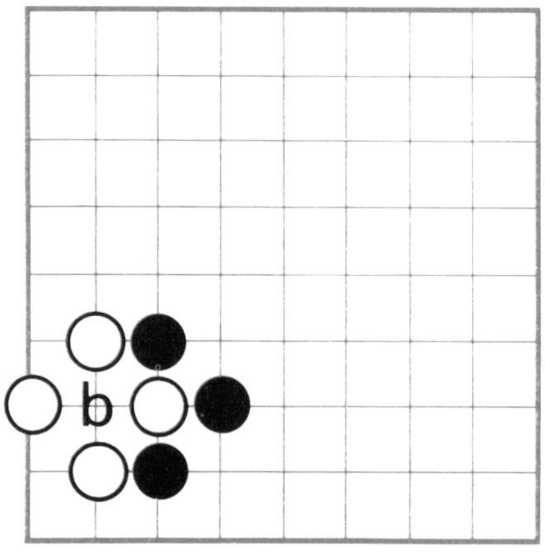

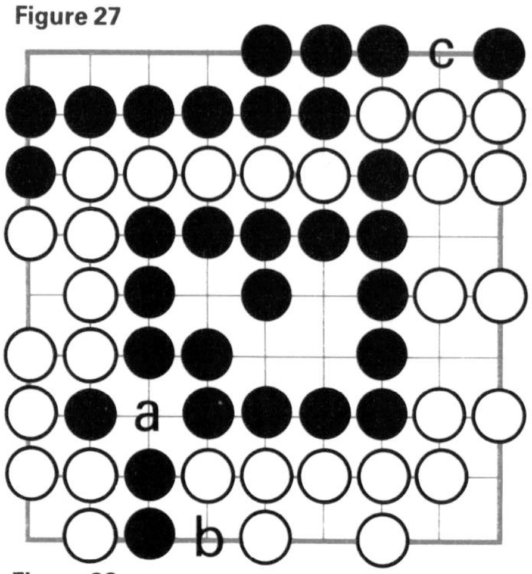

In many Ko positions the fate of only one stone is at stake. As it then requires two moves to capture and keep only one stone, it is a rather unprofitable tactic, and would normally be left until near the end of the game. But sometimes more than one stone's fate depends upon the Ko. Figure 28 shows another game that is nearly finished. If White were able to capture at 'a' and then play another move at 'b' he would gain six points – three for captured stones and another three for territory (the points that the captured stones had been occupying.) This would tilt the balance of territory in White's favour.

White is also threatening to capture a black stone by playing at 'c', thereby gaining two more points. It is Black's move. Where should he play, at 'a' or 'c'?

Your first guess might be 'a', as six points are at stake there rather than the two at 'c'. If Black plays at 'a' the game will proceed to the end as in Figure 29. Black and White will score eight points each (remember White gets an extra point for the captured stone) so the result is a tied score.

If Black saves his threatened stone as in Figure 30 the game proceeds rather

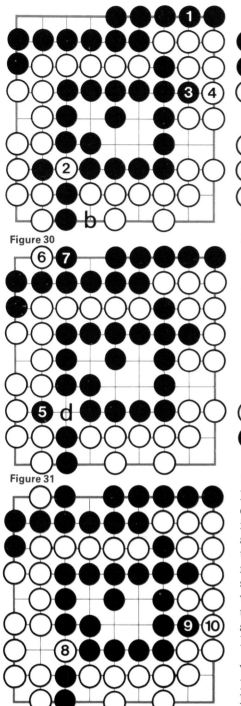

Figure 30

Figure 31

Figure 32

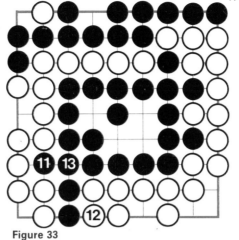

Figure 33

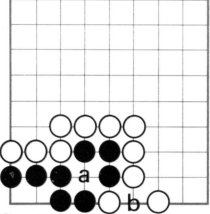

Figure 34

one for the white stone left stranded inside his upper territory, and two for stones captured in the Ko, totalling ten, so he wins by two.

An exchange such as moves 2 – 13 is called a "Ko fight". Threats such as moves 3, 6, and 9 are known as "Ko threats", and the Ko fight will usually be won by the player with more available. One of the skills of Go is to play in such a way as to leave yourself with as many Ko threats as possible while denying them to the opponent, just in case a Ko should arise.

Figure 34 shows a Ko position on the side. White is threatening to capture part of the group at 'a'. Black needs to capture at 'b' and then connect at the point from which the stone has been taken in order to make two eyes. Kos can also occur in the corner.

Did you notice that when counting the territory in Figure 33 it was assumed that the lone White stone in the upper left corner would be removed at the end of the game and counted as a prisoner, without actually having all its liberties occupied? When it is clear to both players that a particular stone or stones are left in a hopeless position, with no prospect either of making two eyes or of being connected to an already safe group, it is customary *at the end of the game only* for such stones to be removed as prisoners, without necessarily having all their liberties occupied. This is not a rule of the game, only a custom, and it tends to worry beginners. Surely if White refuses to surrender his stone without Black's filling in its last liberty, cannot Black be forced to fill in another point within his own territory?

The reason why this is not so is illustrated in Figure 35, which shows a rather improbable end position to another game. White's five-stone army in the upper left corner is completely cut off from the other white stones and cannot even make one eye, let alone two. Black has a single stone cut off at the bottom of White's large central territory. At the end of the game experienced players would remove these stones as prisoners. Black would

he now needs a threat compelling enough to prevent Black from connecting at 'd' on his next move. He has such a threat at 6. If Black fails to answer at 7 then White will play there himself next move. Black can capture these two stones if he chooses, but he will have no way to divide his space into two. His upper edge group will be unable to avoid eventual capture, and winning the Ko will be no compensation.

After the addition of moves 6 and 7 White is permitted to recapture in the Ko with 8 in Figure 32. Now it is again Black's turn to find a suitable threat, which he does at 9, threatening to cut off and capture eight white stones. White must answer at 10, so Black recaptures in the Ko once again with 11 in Figure 33.

But now White has no more threats. There is nowhere he can play that will induce Black to play anywhere other than at 13 on his next move. All he can do is play at 12 and force Black to play where he was going to play anyway.

There are no neutral points to fill, so the game is now over. White ends with six points of territory plus two for stones captured in the Ko totalling eight. Black has four points of territory in the centre, three on the upper edge,

differently. White tries capturing in the Ko with 2. Black is not allowed to recapture immediately, so instead he threatens to capture five of White's stones with 3. If White gives up ten points in this way he will lose the game regardless of the outcome of the Ko. He must therefore connect at 4 rather than playing at 'b' and finishing off the Ko.

Now however Black is allowed to recapture in the Ko at 5 in Figure 31. This does not repeat the position, because of the addition of 3 and 4 in Figure 30. If White still hopes eventually to end the Ko in his own favour

then score 21 points, 16 for territory and five for prisoners, and White 20, 19 for territory and one prisoner.

Suppose White refuses to allow Black to remove these stones, and insists on his filling the five remaining liberties, marked 'x' in the Figure. In this case he would not say "I pass", and the game

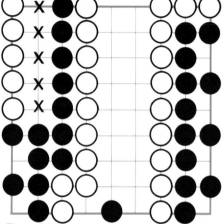

Figure 35

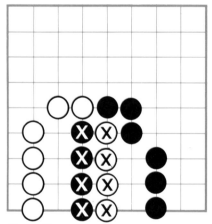

Figure 36

would have to continue. Black proceeds to fill the five liberties, but where is White to put his stones meanwhile? He can only play them within his own territory, thereby reducing his own score by one point for each point by which Black fills in his own territory. Perhaps White will use three of his five moves to take off the lone black stone. It makes no difference – the final score remains one point to Black's advantage so long as both players keep putting stones on the board.

So the golden rule is "when in doubt, play it out". If you can't agree on whether the game is finished, or whether particular stones should be removed or not, or who owns which points of territory, just keep playing stones on the board until the issue is in no doubt.

Stones in a hopeless position as explained above are usually described as "dead". One pointer to the end of the game is that every stone on the board is either dead or part of an invulnerable

group. To have the ability to make two eyes is one way for a group to be invulnerable, but there is another way, which will now be explained.

On Figure 36 the two armies marked 'x' are both cut off from friendly stones, and neither has room to make eyes. (Remember there are no connections along diagonals.) The only way either army can evade capture is by capturing the other one. Go players use the Japanese word "semeai" to describe this situation. It frequently occurs in games,

70

Japanese print of around 1860 depicting a scene from one of the Kabuki plays, in which Go featured regularly. Here the irate husband has failed to notice his wife's lover hiding somewhat inadequately under the Go table and holding the Go stones.

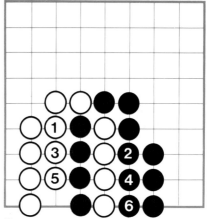

Figure 37

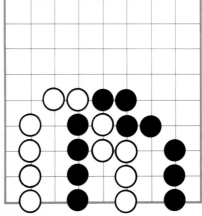

Figure 38

leading to tense and exciting situations.

The black army has four liberties but the white one only three. If White attacks at 1 in Figure 37, Black responds by filling in one of White's liberties, and the race to fill liberties ends with a victory for Black who captures the white stones with move 6.

In an actual game both players would know that the white stones, having one fewer liberty, were doomed from the start. White would keep these moves in reserve as Ko threats. If Black started

with two or more extra liberties then White doesn't even have Ko threats. If the liberties are equal then whoever plays first eventually captures the other.

In Figure 38 the groups involved in the semeai now have two common internal liberties as well as three and four external ones respectively. Figure 39 shows how the game might proceed with a similar sequence to that of Figure 37, but after White 7 Black is stuck for a move. If he plays on either 'a' or 'b' White will play on the other and cap-

ture him. The same is true for White; he neither can play at 'a' or 'b' without being captured himself on the next move. So neither player will choose to play here again, and the stones will be left as they are until the end of the game.

This situation is known by the Japanese word "seki", and it is the second way of making a group invulnerable as mentioned above. A rule of the game provides that no territory involved in a seki counts towards the

final score.

Whether or not a seki can be made is influenced by relative numbers of common and external liberties, and by the posession by either or both armies of a single eye. This would be a fruitful area for the reader's own investigation.

You now have enough information to play Go as a beginner. To become skilful you would need to play against experienced players and to study Go literature. Considering that Go has yet to become a majority interest in the West Go players are rather well served with books. The Ishi Press, Tokyo, publishes a series of books in English to take you from beginner to master level, and there is a handful of books from English and American publishers.

There is room here for just a couple of examples of the sort of tactics that you might not discover for yourself without reading a beginners' book on Go. The position in Figure 40 occurs quite frequently. Clearly Black can capture a stone by playing at 'a'. The question is, can White rescue his stone by playing at 'a' himself?

Figure 41 shows what will happen if White persists in trying to rescue his stone. His growing army can never gain more than one extra liberty by adding on a stone, and eventually . . .

. . . because of the shortage of liberties at the edge of the board, disaster ensues in Figure 42 with the loss of twelve stones, and almost certainly, the game. White shoud never have tried to rescue his single stone in the first place; it was dead already. This attack is normally referred to as a "ladder", because the shape of the stones reminds the Japanese of a ladder or staircase.

What happens if there is a white stone in the path of the ladder as in Figure 43? Figure 44 shows that Black cannot now make a ladder attack. After 12 White captures at 'a', threatening a further capture at 'b' as well as moves like 'c', which places two stones in atari at once. This is a terrible position for Black.

Another fruitful area for the reader to investigate is on exactly which points the friendly stone needs to be to spoil

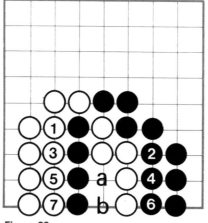

Figure 39

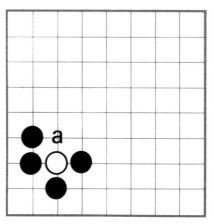

Figure 40

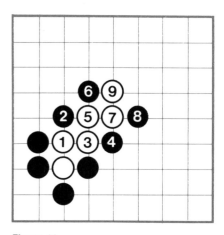

Figure 41

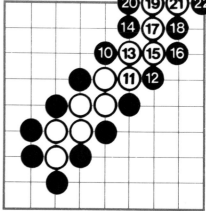

Figure 42

the ladder attack, and what happens if there is an enemy stone in the ladder's path. You will soon discover why problems based on ladders can be quite advanced!

Figure 45 shows another tactical ploy – that of deliberately sacrificing a stone to make a larger gain – the proverbial sprat to catch a mackerel. Where would you play, as White?

Probably not at 1 in Figure 46, because your stone can be immediately captured with Black 2. But that is in fact the best move, because after White 3 in Figure 47 five black stones are in atari. It is no good Black's connecting at 'a' – then he has seven stones in atari which White can capture by playing at 'b'. Worse still, White is now threatening to sacrifice a second stone at 'c'. Black could capture it, but would then be unable to make two eyes, and his stones would be dead. So after White 1 Black should play at 'c' straight away and put up with losing his five stones. If White fails to play at 1 in Figure 46 Black plays there himself, securing all his stones, and making five points of territory including two eyes.

These two examples show you the sort of tactical skills you can learn from

books, but to practise them you need to play against strong players. Most Western countries now have national Go associations. At the time of writing about 50 active clubs are affiliated to the British Go Association, so British players have a fair chance of finding one wherever they live.

There is no need to feel shy about attending a Go club as a beginner. Most clubs are only too pleased to welcome newcomers and to teach them as much as possible, and there is also the handicapping system to ease the path of the new player.

All serious Go players have a grade. The system is similar to that used in Judo, although they don't wear coloured belts. A "dan" player (black belt in Judo) is a master player – at the time of writing there are getting on for 100 of these in Britain. 1-dan is the lowest master ranking: the strongest British players are 6-dans.

Weaker players have "kyu" gradings. With these, 1-kyu is the strongest. A player who has just learnt the rules is about 35-kyu. Advance to about 20-kyu is usually a matter of a few weeks, but the stronger you become the slower progress is.

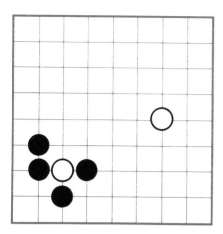

Figure 43

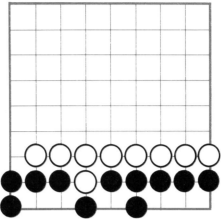

Figure 45

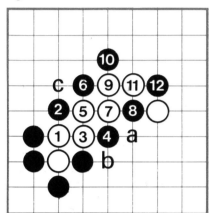

Figure 44

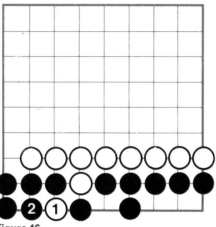

Figure 46

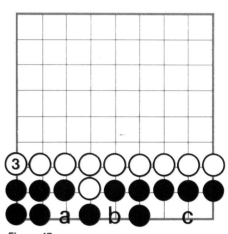

Figure 47

4) Always play the most valuable move. Don't gain one point here when you could gain two points there.

5) Don't play good stones after bad trying to rescue dead stones.

6) Use stones efficiently – never use two

When two players play on the full board (see Figure 1) the weaker player plays up to nine stones on certain of the star points before play starts. The number played is equal to the difference in grade. If both players are correctly graded, this initial start for the weaker player results in both players having an equal chance of winning.

Handicaps on the 13 x 13 and 9 x 9 boards can accommodate differences in strength much greater than nine grades.

Finally, here is a summary of some basic principles of good play:

1) In the opening, control corners first, then sides, lastly centre.

2) Spread stones thinly at first.

3) Don't assume that your best move is near to your opponent's last move. Look at the whole board.

when one will do.

7) Never play inside secure territory, your own or your opponent's. You lose one point whenever you do.

8) If stuck for a move, visualise your opponent's best move. Your own may be at or near the same point.

9) The more liberties a group has, the harder it is to attack. Therefore, keep enemy stones separated, and make sure your own can be easily linked together.

10) Decide whether the tactic you are planning retains or loses the initiative (sente). If you are surrendering it, make sure you gain something tangible in return.

11) Don't play moves *only* because they keep sente. You may be wasting Ko threats.

Noboru Hosokawa (right) and Matthew Macfadyen (left), the British and European Champion, winner and runner-up respectively in the 1984 British Open Go Championship at the London Intervarsity Club, Covent Garden.

DICE GAMES

Dice are the oldest gaming implements known. Today's cubes have their ancestry in bones – flat bones which could land on one of two sides, and the ankle bones of cloven-footed animals like sheep which have four distinct faces.

Hundreds of games can be played with modern dice, some requiring only one die, others several. Some of the best are included here – there are others in the section on gambling games.

The first game, Liar Dice, requires a set of poker dice, which are widely available. The other games require varying numbers of conventional dice.

LIAR DICE IS A VERY ENTERTAINING GAME for about 5 – 10 players. In theory any number from two upwards can play, but much of the fun is lost with small numbers, and with large numbers you have a long wait for your turn.

The only essential equipment is a

table around which the players sit, and a set of poker dice. Some players like a cup or similar to conceal the dice, but experienced players usually manage with hands alone.

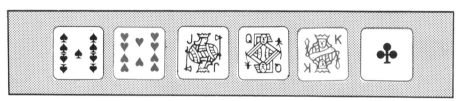

Figure 1 The six faces on each die of a set of Liar Dice.

Poker dice (Figure 1) bear symbols representing 9, 10, J, Q, K, and A of some card suit or other – suits are of no significance. The possible combinations of dice rolls rank in a similar way to poker hands. If you are not familiar with the principle, see page 171. Flushes and straights are not used in Liar Dice, so combinations possible are, in descending order of rank; Five of a kind, Four of a kind, Full House, Three of a kind, Two pairs, One pair, Ace high, etc. Ranking of the various rolls within one of these combinations is determined exactly as in poker.

We will imagine a number of players, A, B, C, etc sitting clockwise around the table. A is chosen to play first. He must roll all five dice, usually without showing them. He must then declare to player B what he claims to have rolled, e.g. "Two jacks, two tens and an ace." Player B must decide whether to accept this call or not. If he says "No," or sometimes "Liar!", then player A exposes the dice. If he has in fact rolled what he declared or a combination which outranks what he declared, then player B loses one life. If Player A's actual roll was of lower rank than what he declared, he himself loses one life.

If player B decides to accept A's call he says "Yes", and the dice are passed to him concealed. He may now roll all, some or none of the dice. He must declare honestly how many he is rolling; the usual formula is "Rolling three", "Rolling all five", "Rolling none", etc. He must then declare to player C a combination which outranks that which was declared to him by player A,

whether he has succeeded in rolling it or not. Player C now says "Yes" or "No", and play continues clockwise around the table until eventually a player says "No" to the preceding call, the dice are exposed, and a life is lost. Then another round is started by the player to the left of the one that lost a life. He must begin by rolling all five dice.

It is usual to play with three lives per player. When a player has lost all three lives he drops out. When only one player is left he is the winner. An optional feature is the "dog's life"; the first player to lose all three lives is awarded one extra life.

Although it is usual to conceal all the dice before, during, and after rolling, a player may choose to expose any or all of the dice at any of those three stages, if he thinks it will help to confuse the opponents. Attempts deliberately to mislead by variations in tone of voice, tempo, facial expression etc. are all part of the game.

Unlike poker players, Liar Dice experts are not usually well versed in the mathematical probabilities of the game – indeed players who always play to the odds are rather easy to beat. More important are the abilities to bluff and to play unsystematically. Liar Dice represents the triumph of Psychology over Mathematics.

Yacht

Yacht is a 'category' game, of which some others follow. Five dice are needed and any number may play. A score sheet is required, ruled up as shown in Figure 2. Players throw one die to determine who goes first – lowest starts. The turn then goes clockwise, with each player having up to three throws at each turn. After the first throw, he may set aside any dice he may wish to keep, and rethrow the remainder. He can then do this a second time, but after his third throw the five dice represent his score for the turn. He then decides into which category on the score-sheet to enter his score.

The categories and scores are as follows:

Yacht (five of a kind): scores 50
Big Straight (2, 3, 4, 5, 6): scores 30
Little Straight (1, 2, 3, 4, 5): scores 30
Four of a Kind: scores the pip value of all five dice, e.g. 4, 4, 4, 4, 2 scores 18
Full House (three of one kind, two of another): scores the pip value of all five dice, e.g. 3, 3, 3, 5, 5 scores 19
Choice (any five dice of no specific pattern): scores the pip value of all five

	JAMES	IAN	CHRIS	CAROL
YACHT				
BIG STRAIGHT				
LITTLE STRAIGHT				
FOUR OF A KIND				
FULL HOUSE				
CHOICE				
SIXES				
FIVES				
FOURS				
THREES				
TWOS				
ACES				
TOTAL				

Figure 2 Score sheet for Yacht.

dice, e.g. 3, 3, 5, 5, 6 scores 22
Sixes: scores six points for every 6 thrown
Fives: scores five points for every 5 thrown, and so on down to *aces*.

Play ends after twelve rounds, when each player must have entered a score

for each category, even if the score for a category is nothing, as will often be the case. Once a score is entered in a category it must remain there, and cannot be moved to another category or superseded by a higher score thrown later. For instance, if a player throws 3, 3, 3, 3, 2 and already has his categories *Four of a Kind* and *Threes* filled, he must enter the score elsewhere, perhaps in *Choice* (only 14, a poor score) or *Twos* (only 2, a poor score). However, the maximum score for *Twos* is only 10, so not much is lost if the score is entered here. Players often, in fact, enter awkward throws in the *Aces* or *Twos* category, even if it means scoring 0, as the maximum scores in these categories are low.

In practice, a player will take account of the categories he has already filled when choosing which dice to rethrow on his turn. For example, a player with only *Little Straight* and *Threes* left to fill, and throwing, say, four 4s would be unlucky – it would be pointless to keep them, and he should rethrow all four. *Strategy* Players should attempt to score the big scores near the top of the score sheet. Should 2,3,4,5 show among the five dice first thrown, it pays to throw the odd die twice more in an attempt to score *Big Straight* or *Little Straight*, as the chance of throwing either a 1 or 6 in two throws is good – 55 per cent. However, 2,4,5,6 showing is less good – the chance of throwing a 3 by rethrowing the remaining die twice is only 31 per cent. It might be better to keep the 6 and try for a big score in the *Choice* category.

A player with a triplet on the first throw will usually keep it and rethrow the other two dice, attempting *Yacht* or *Four of a Kind*. Near the end of the game a player might 'lose' a poor throw in the Yacht category (the 50 for *Yacht* is rarely scored) to keep another category open for a better chance of a score.

Dice players in an English bawdy house around 1620.

Double Cameroon

Double Cameroon is a category game which uses ten dice. The player throws all ten, and then, as in *Yacht*, has two further throws in which to rethrow any dice he wishes. At the end of his turn the player must divide his ten dice into two groups of five and enter each group into one of the categories.

The scoresheet is shown in Figure 3.

	ADELE	SEAN	DAVE	HUGH
FIVE OF A KIND				
LARGE CAMEROON				
LITTE CAMEROON				
FULL HOUSE				
SIXES				
FIVES				
FOURS				
THREES				
TWOS				
ACES				
TOTAL				

Figure 3 Score sheet for Double Cameroon.

The scores for each category are as follows:
Five of a Kind: scores 50
Large Cameroon (2,3,4,5,6): scores 30
Little Cameroon (1,2,3,4,5): scores 21
Full House, Sixes, Fives, Fours, Threes, Twos and *Aces* score as in Yacht.

There being ten categories, the dice pass round among the players five times.

General

General is another category game, played in the same manner as Yacht, and also with five dice.

Figure 4 shows the score-sheet. In this instance scores have been entered against some categories as if a game were in progress.

A major difference to Yacht is that the score in the first four categories is

	KATE	JEAN	PETE	LORNA
SMALL GENERAL	60			
FOUR OF A KIND		40		
FULL HOUSE		30		30
STRAIGHT	20		20	
SIXES		18	18	24
FIVES	15		15	
FOURS	12			
THREES				
TWOS				
ACES		0	0	3
TOTAL				

Figure 4 Score sheet for General.

higher if the category is thrown on the first throw.

The scores for each category are as follows:
Big General is five of a kind made on the first throw of any turn. It is not on the score sheet as it wins the game immediately. It is very rare, the chance of throwing it on any particular turn being 1 in 1,296

Small General is five of a kind made on the second or third throw. It scores 60
Four of a Kind: scores 45 on the first throw, 40 on the second or third
Full House: scores 35 on the first throw, 30 on the second or third
Straight (either 1,2,3,4,5 or 2,3,4,5,6): scores 25 on the first throw, 20 on the second or third
Sixes, Fives, Fours, Threes, Twos and Aces are scored as in Yacht.

In *Straight* an Ace is 'half-wild', i.e. it can be counted as a 2 or 6 (but not as 3,4 or 5). Thus 1,3,4,5,6 and 1,1,3,4,5 are *straights*. Notice there is only one category for *Straight* – not two as in Yacht.

If a player throws *Four of a Kind* on the first throw, but rethrows the odd die in an attempt to score *Small General*, and fails, he scores only 40 for his *Four of a Kind*, as it is regarded as being scored in three throws.

Shut the Box

Shut the Box is one of those games which has attractive equipment, but which can be played as easily with just two dice and pencil and paper.

The game is traditionally played on a rectangular wooden tray with built up sides, and lined with felt so as not to harm the dice (see Figure 5). Along one side of the tray are nine boxes, numbered 1 to 9, each with a sliding lid, so that each box can be either open or shut, i.e. the number can be in view or hidden.

When a player begins his turn, all the boxes are open. He throws the two dice, and adds their values. He can then close any number of boxes which add up to the same total. For example, should he throw 5 and 3, total 8, he can shut boxes 5 and 3, or 6 and 2, or 4, 3 and 1, and so on. He then throws the dice again, and shuts any appropriate boxes that are still open. When a player has shut boxes 7, 8 and 9, he can, if he wishes, continue to throw with only one die. He continues throwing until the total thrown cannot be matched against any combination remaining open. The turn then ends and the boxes still open represent the player's score.

When all players have had their turn, the player with the lowest score wins.

The game can easily be scored by ruling up nine boxes on a piece of paper, of such a size that the numbers in them can be conveniently covered by counters of coins. Or the numbers 1 to 9 can be written down for each player and crossed out as appropriate.

Strategy A player should close as few boxes as possible on a throw. For example it is better on a throw of 9 to close the 9 box rather than, say 5 and 4, or 2, 3 and 4. The more boxes open the more totals can be made to match the next throw.

The decision to throw one die instead of two must be considered carefully. If, for instance, the boxes open are 1,2,3,4,5 and 6, throwing one die would be certain to close a box, but the choice should still be to throw two, as any total thrown can be accomodated. Even if only the boxes 3,5,6 are open which gives an even chance of closing one with one die, it is much better to throw two dice, as the chances of closing either one or two are considerably better than even.

Crag

Crag is a category game which differs from Yacht and General in that only three dice are used. The principle is the same as in those two games, but only

Figure 5 An attractive Shut the Box tray, with dice.

'The Dice Players', an early 16th century painting by Georges de la Tour.

	JACK	JULIE	KIT	TREVOR
CRAG				
THIRTEEN				
HIGH STRAIGHT				
LOW STRAIGHT				
EVEN STRAIGHT				
ODD STRAIGHT				
THREE OF A KIND				
SIXES				
FIVES				
FOURS				
THREES				
TWOS				
ACES				
TOTAL				

Figure 6 Score sheet for Crag.

one rethrow is allowed on each turn. The score sheet is shown in Figure 6.

The scores for each category are as follows:

Crag is a total of 13 which includes a pair (e.g. 6,6,1 or 5,5,3) and scores 50

Thirteen is any three dice totalling 13 and scores 26. If *Crag* is thrown and the category is already filled, the throw can be entered in *Thirteen*

Three of a Kind: scores 25

High Straight (4,5,6), *Low Straight* (1,2,3), *Even Straight* (2,4,6) and *Odd Straight* (1,3,5) all score 20.

Sixes, Fives, Fours, Threes, Twos and *Aces* score as in Yacht.

Dix Mille

Dix Mille is a French game, as its name implies. Its name also suggests its object, which is to score 10,000 points. Six dice are used, with pencil and paper to score.

A single die is thrown by all the players to determine the order of play. The lowest throws first, thereafter the turn passes clockwise.

On his turn a player throws all six dice, removes from them a scoring die or a scoring combination of dice (see below) and rethrows the remainder. He continues thus, removing the scoring die or dice each time, until he makes a throw in which he does not score, when his turn ends. If his turn ends thus, he does not score at all for that complete

turn. However, a player may stop at any time after a scoring throw (with one or two exceptions, as noted below), when his score for that turn is added to his total.

When a player has scored with all six dice, and they are thus removed, he may continue his turn by picking up the six dice and resuming as if beginning his turn again.

The scoring table is as follows:

Single die: 1 scores 100 points, 5 scores 50 points

Three of a kind: Three 1s scores 1,000 points, three of any other number scores 100 × the number (i.e. three 3s scores 300)

Three pairs: scores 1,500 points. Six of a kind, or four of a kind plus a pair, can count as three pairs (but see *Disaster* below)

Straight (1,2,3,4,5,6): scores 3,000 points

Disaster: Four or more 2s wipe out a player's complete score – not just the score for that turn.

A player who scores *Three pairs* or a *Straight* (notice that these combinations can be scored only with all six dice) *must* roll the six dice again – with these scoring combinations he cannot elect to end his turn. Notice, however, that if he throws six of a kind, he need not count the throw as *Three pairs* – he can, if he prefers, count it as *Three of a Kind* twice, which enables him to end his turn if he wishes.

A player who has removed five dice and is reduced to one die only, is allowed two throws to score with it. If he succeeds he scores a 500-point bonus. If he then continues his turn and is reduced to one die again, and with his two chances succeeds in scoring again, he scores a 1,000-point bonus, and throughout that turn, every time he succeeds in scoring with one final die, he scores a bonus which increases by 500 points each time.

A player must score on every throw to continue his turn, but need not take every scoring die in any particular throw. For example, should he have four dice remaining and throw 2,2,2,5, he could score 200 for *Three of a Kind*

and 50 for the 5, but he might prefer to score the 200 only and retain the final die. With two throws in which to throw 1 or 5 with it, he has a good chance of scoring a bonus of 500 points.

It is customary for a player to announce his score and accumulated score for a turn after each throw (e.g. '100 for the 1 makes 500').

All players must have the same number of turns so a player reaching 10,000 might opt to continue in order to increase his score further, especially if players to follow are themselves close to 10,000. Figures 7 and 8 show two theoretical turns to illustrate the scoring system – they are not suggested as good play.

Strategy The main skill lies in knowing when to be satisfied with a score and to end a turn. This, of course, is coloured by the scores of the opponents – a player well ahead might choose to consolidate without risking

too much, while a player well behind will have to keep going in an attempt to make a big score.

It is surprising, given the difficulties of throwing the scoring combinations, that it is odds-on scoring with any throw, no matter how many dice are to be thrown. The odds in favour of scoring with one or two dice, however, are only 5 to 4, whereas with three they are twice as good, with four better than 4 to 1, five better than 7 to 1 and all six better than 12 to 1.

Should a player throw 3,4,4,4,5,6, therefore, he might consider taking the *Three of a Kind* (400 points) but not the 5 (for another 50 points), as he has twice as good a chance of scoring on his next throw with three dice as he would have with two. The advantage of only taking one scoring die, when throwing, say 5,5 with two, has already been discussed, but the accumulated score of the turn will influence the decision here. A

THROW	SCORE	ACCUMULATED SCORE
1	3000	3000
2	100	3100
3	50	3150
4	700	3850
5	1500	5350
6	50	5400
7	0	0

SCORE FOR TURN : 0

Figure 7 A highly promising turn at Dix Mille which built up a big score and unluckily crashed.

THROW	SCORE	ACCUMULATED SCORE
1	100	100
2	100	200
3	150	350
4	—	350
5	600	950
6	400	1,350
7	100	1450
8	50	1500
9	—	1500
10	1050	2550
11	250	2800
12	100	2900

RETIRES, SCORE FOR TURN : 2900

Figure 8 A more gradual accumulation of a good score at Dix Mille which was allowed to stand.

player with a large accumulated score will be less likely to risk it by throwing one die again than a player with a small score for whom the prospect of a bonus will be more attractive.

The dangers of dice addiction. A caricature by Thomas Renton, 1790.

Drop Dead

Drop Dead requires five dice and a pencil and paper to score. Each player throws a single die to decide the order of play – lowest goes first.

The first player throws the five dice, and if no 5s or 2s appear, he scores the total thrown. However, if a 5 or 2 appears, he scores nothing for the throw, puts aside the die or dice showing 5 or 2 and rethrows the remainder. Again he scores the total should there not be a 5 or 2; otherwise he proceeds as before. He keeps rethrowing his dice until all have been eliminated, when he is said to have 'dropped dead'. His score is noted and the dice are passed to the next player.

Figure 9 shows a specimen turn, where the player rethrew seven times before his dice were eliminated.

A player who scores with five dice on his first throw is on the way to a good

THROW		SCORE	ACCUMULATED SCORE
1		0	0
2		12	12
3		0	12
4		0	12
5		9	21
6		0	21
7		1	22
8		3	25
9		0	25

Figure 9 A specimen turn at Drop Dead.

score – the chances are less than one in seven of avoiding both 5 and 2 with five dice. Even with only two dice the chances are slightly against scoring. A player might not score until there were only one or two dice left, but then might run up a reasonable score – anything over 25 has a chance.

The player with the highest score wins. For a longer game the dice might be passed round so that each player has three or perhaps five turns.

Pig

One die and a pencil and paper to score are all that is required for the very simple game of Pig. Players throw for turn, the lowest throwing first, with the turn passing clockwise.

In his turn, a player may throw the die as often as he wishes, adding together his scores. When he decides to stop, his score is entered against his name on the score sheet and the turn passes to the next player. However, should he throw a 1, his turn ends and he scores nothing for that particular turn. The first player to reach 101 wins.
Variation The game can be played with two dice. A player throwing a 1 with either die loses his score for the turn, unless he throws double-1, when he scores 25 for the turn irrespective of how many he had accumulated on previous throws in that turn. There is a bonus for throwing any other double – the score for the throw is doubled, i.e. double-2 counts as eight points, double-3 as twelve etc.
Strategy The only decision to be made is when to be satisfied with a score. Whereas a score of 50 can sometimes be run up on one turn, any score above 15 is reasonable.

The state of the overall score will sometimes dictate how long a player should continue to throw. If a long way behind, with other players about to reach 101, a player will need to keep throwing and risk throwing a 1.

Chicago

Two dice and a score-card are all that is necessary for Chicago. It is a simple game for any number of players, and depends entirely on luck, so it is suitable for even very young children. There are eleven rounds to play. In the first round, each player throws the dice in turn, attempting to score a total of 2 (i.e. double-1). Players who succeed score two points; other totals fail to score.

On the second round each player attempts to throw 3 (i.e. 2 and 1), and if successful scores three points. The games proceeds through each round, with the number required to be thrown increasing by one each time, until on the final round the players are attempting to score 12 (double-6).

It will be noticed that most scores are made on the totals around 7, this being the easiest to score with two dice, but as twelve points are available on the last round, most players continue to have a chance to the end.

MAH JONG

Mah Jong has always been imbued with an aura of romance, partly because of its oriental origins and partly on account of its elaborate formalities, colourful pieces and terms.

THE TRUTH about Mah Jong is that its romantic associations conceal a basically simple game. The game is about 100 years old (though its rules are borrowed from early Chinese games), and its play structure is similar to the uncomplicated card game, rummy. A cynic once said that there are as many sets of rules for Mah Jong as there are players, and indeed Mah Jong has never regained the popularity it enjoyed when the game blossomed in the West during the 1920s. Mah Jong is at its roots a simple gambling game which has long been an addiction amongst Chinese communities. In attempts to make the game more acceptable to Western tastes, the rules were elaborated to the point of absurdity and this, together with the introduction of contract bridge at that time, led to the eclipse of Mah Jong, although it retained a small following in the United States. Only recently is the

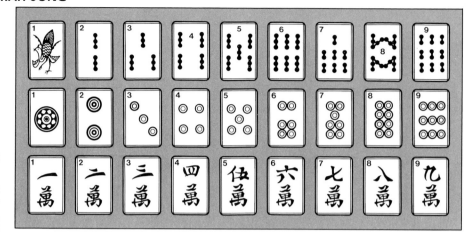

Figure 1 The three suits, (from top) bamboos, circles and characters.

game again being played to any extent in Europe.

There are three main play systems, the Chinese, which has many variations, the Japanese and the American, these last two with codified rules. All three systems use basically the same equipment, the differences between them being reflected in the 'special hands', the use of bonus tiles, and the method of scoring. The Chinese game is described here.

Mah Jong sets are freely available but are not cheap. Since a seductive element of the game is the tactile pleasure of handling the tiles, it is recommended to buy the best set one can afford. If cost is the main criterion, the game can also be played with a pack of Mah Jong cards, sold in Chinese emporiums and supermarkets.

A mah jong set comprises 144 tiles (described below), four racks for the players to keep their tiles on, tallies for scoring, a wind indicator and dice. Tiles used to be made of ivory or bone, often backed with bamboo, but nowadays they are almost invariably made of plastic.

Mah jong tiles are grouped into three suits with the addition of honour and bonus tiles. The suits are circles, bamboos and characters. The circles represent cash (small Chinese coins with a hole in the middle); the bamboos, strings of cash (it is easy to see how these have become transformed into lengths of bamboo); and the characters, cash in multiples of 10,000 denoted by ideographs (Chinese symbols). Each suit has nine values, usually marked 1 to 9 in arabic numerals. There are four tiles of each value, making 36 tiles in each suit or 108 in all three suits. The three suits are illustrated in Figure 1.

The 1 of bamboos is a rice-bird, or sometimes a bamboo shoot, otherwise the tiles are regular in appearance. The 1s and 9s of each suit are known as terminals and rank higher than the other tiles in the suits, which are known as simples.

Mah jong tiles are engraved, usually by hand, and the design is coloured.

These colourings are partly conventional and partly reflect the whims of the manufacturer. Amongst the suit tiles, however, the 2,3,4,6 and 8 of bamboos are always green and this has a bearing on the game.

The honour tiles are dragons and winds. There are three dragons, called Red, White and Green. The red and green dragons are always represented in their respective colours. The white dragon is a blank tile. In many sets there are additional blank tiles intended as

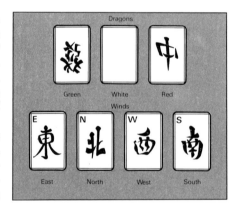

Figure 2 The honour tiles.

replacements for pieces that are damaged or lost; they are not extra white dragons! There are, predictably, four winds: East, South, North and West. East wind takes precedence. The seven honour tiles are shown in Figure 2. There are four of each kind, like the suit tiles, making 28 in all.

Honour tiles and terminals are often referred to as major tiles. In addition to suit and honour tiles, a mah jong set usually includes eight bonus tiles representing flowers and the seasons. These tiles carry highly individual designs and are most attractive. They are not used in play but, as their name implies, they carry a bonus for the holder. They are not used in the Japanese game nor in some Chinese variants. It is not always easy to identify the stylized designs which are, however, helpfully num-

Figure 3 The bonus tiles.

bered consecutively in red (the seasons) and in blue or green (flowers).

Seasons	Flowers
(1) Spring	(1) Plum
(2) Summer	(2) Orchid
(3) Autumn	(3) Chrysanthemum
(4) Winter	(4) Bamboo

A typical set of bonus tiles is illustrated in Figure 3.

The tallies are thin, flat lengths of plastic. There are four values, shown in Figure 4. In older sets the tallies are in bone or ivory and have different markings.

The dice supplied are likely to have the 1-spot and the 4-spot coloured red.

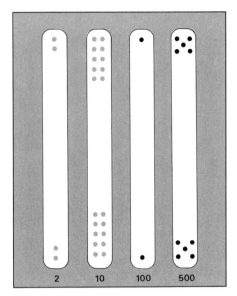

Figure 4 Tallies.

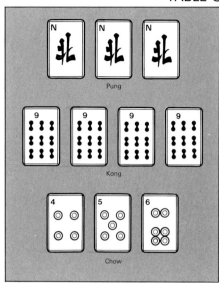

Figure 5 The three types of set.

This is traditional and has no significance. Most sets also have wind discs, one for each wind, for choice of seats, together with a box (the Tong box) in which the wind of the round is displayed, or a double disc, which serves the same purpose. This can be compared with a trump indicator at whist.

Preliminaries

Mah Jong is best as a game for four players and cannot be recommended for other numbers. The four-player game is described here. Everyone plays for himself – there are no partnerships.

Each player assumes the identity of a wind, either by agreement or by lot; for example, by drawing wind discs. East is the dominant wind and the player of East is leader for the first round. Seating does not follow the compass points in Mah Jong, the positions of East and West being reversed so that East has South on his right and North on his left.

The tiles, including bonus tiles, are now shuffled ('washed') face down on the table ('the twittering of the sparrows'), a procedure in which East does not take part, and players then build the tiles into four walls, each 18 tiles long, the tiles placed lengthways against one another, and two tiles high, and the players then push the walls together to form a square – the Great Wall of China.

East throws the dice to determine who shall break the wall. The sum of the two dice are counted anti-clockwise round the table by East, counting himself as 1, South 2 and so on, as many times round as is necessary. If, for

example, a total of 7 is shown on the dice, West breaks the wall. The player so designated now throws the dice (it is practice to throw them within the wall) to determine where the wall will be broken. The dice are again totalled and are added to East's previous total, and the player counts the appropriate number of tiles along his wall, starting at the right end. For this purpose, each stack of two counts as one. If the count exceeds 18, the player will turn the corner onto his left-hand neighbour's wall.

The player then removes the stack indicated by the throws and places the two tiles on top of the wall right of the breach. (Here, as throughout the game, there are formalities to be observed but since they have no bearing on the play they have been ignored for the sake of simplicity.) The player then detaches the last seven stacks of tiles, with the two tiles removed from the wall on top, from the right-hand wall. These 16 tiles are known as the kong box or dead wall, and are used solely to provide replacement tiles ('loose tiles') during play (see below). A broken wall, with the kong box separated, is illustrated in Figure 5.

Starting at the left of the breach (the 'live wall'), four tiles are drawn by each player in turn, starting with East, until all players have 12 tiles. East then draws a pair of tiles and the other players one each in turn. Tiles are placed on the racks and examined. They should of course be concealed from the other players.

The basic aim of the game is to collect four sets, each of three or four tiles, and a pair. The first player to achieve this announces 'mah jong' when the game ends and the hands are scored.

There are three types of sets: the pung, the kong and the chow. These are respectively three tiles of the same kind, four of the same kind and a run of three – for example, 2,3,4 of circles. Pungs and kongs can be suit or honour tiles but a chow can only be of suit tiles. The sets are arranged in Figure 6 and a mah-jong hand is shown in Figure 7.

Play

Players in turn, starting with East, declare any bonus tiles they hold by placing them face-up on the table in front of them and drawing replacement tiles from the kong box. If at this stage, or at any later time during play, a bonus tile is drawn from the wall it is immediately declared and replaced with a loose tile. East now declares any kong he holds and places the tiles on the table, the two end tiles face downwards to show that the kong was 'concealed' (from hand) and draws a loose tile from the kong box for every kong declared. The other players do likewise in turn. East then discards any tile from his hand, placing it face up within the square and announcing it ('three bamboos', 'white dragon'). If any player wants the discard to complete a pung or a kong, or for mah jong, which always takes precedence over any other call, he announces it, picks up the tile and places the set in front of him. The tiles must be face up to indicate that the set is 'exposed'; that is, it includes a discard.

The player then discards and the turn passes to the player on his right. Thus, if West claimed East's discard it would then be North's turn, South having missed out.

If no player wants the discard for a pung, kong or mah jong, then the next player (South) may claim the tile to complete a chow which is then exposed and the turn passes to West. Notice that only the player on the right of the player

Figure 6 A broken wall, with a kong box in the centre and the live wall to the left.

Figure 7 A mah jong hand: four sets and a pair.

discarding may claim the tile to complete a chow, and then only if it has not been previously claimed; also, a discard may never be picked up except to complete a set or to go mah jong. A discard must be claimed before further play. Thereafter it is 'dead' though remaining ·on view throughout the game.

When a discard is unclaimed, the next player takes the first tile from the live wall. If this is a bonus tile or completes a kong, it is declared and a loose tile is taken from the kong box to replace it. The purpose of drawing a loose tile when a kong or bonus tile is declared is to balance the number of tiles held in hand since mah jong requires four sets and a pair. A player could go mah jong with a maximum of 18 tiles (four kongs and a pair), bonus

Figure 6

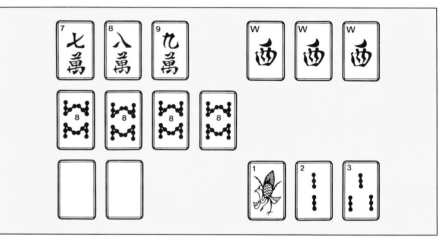

Figure 7

Chinese mah jong players.

Cluttered but attractive Chinese interior with mah jong in progress

tiles not counting, and a minimum of 14, since the player who goes mah jong does not discard. A player who has an exposed pung may convert it into an exposed kong by drawing the fourth tile from the wall (when a loose tile is drawn, as usual) but not by claiming a discard because no set may contain more than one discard. A player who holds a concealed pung does not declare it unless he converts it into a concealed or exposed kong.

If a player requires only one tile to go mah jong he is said to be 'fishing' and must announce this. A player who is fishing has prior claim on any discard even to complete a chow or a pair though of course he may draw the desired tile from the wall.

A player who is fishing may 'rob the kong'. If another player has an exposed pung and adds to it a fourth tile that he has drawn from the wall to complete the kong, the player who is fishing may claim it – he robs the kong. In the example hand in Figure 8, the holder is fishing. Any of the tiles 3,4,5,6,7 bamboos would yield mah jong.

Special Hands

In addition to a mah jong hand of four sets and a pair, there are a number of special hands on which a player may also go mah jong. There is much dispute over the admissability of special hands which have grown absurdly in number. The Chinese game recognizes only a few. It is recommended that the following special hands are allowed.

Imperial Jade Pungs or kongs of green tiles (the green dragons, 2s, 3s, 4s, 6s, 8s of bamboos) only, plus a pair.

Heads and Tails Pungs and kongs of terminals only, plus any pair.

Wriggly Snake One tile of each wind plus a complete suit, one of the suit tiles paired.

Gates of Heaven A pung of 1s, a pung of 9s, plus one each of tiles 2-8, any one value being paired, all tiles being of the same suit.

Thirteen Grades of Imperial Treasure One each of the 13 major tiles with any one of them paired.

Gathering the Plum Blossom from the Roof A player who is fishing goes out with the 5 circles drawn from the wall.

Three Great Scholars A set of each of the dragons, another pung or kong, and any pair.

All Symbols A hand (four sets and a pair) composed entirely of honour tiles.

Four Joys in Full A set of each of the winds plus any pair.

Catching the Moon from the Bottom of the Sea A player who goes mah jong with the 1 circle if it is the last tile of the live wall.

Heaven's Blessing East holds a mah jong after any loose tiles for kongs or bonus tiles have been drawn but before he discards.

Earth's Blessing Any player who similarly goes mah jong with East's first discard.

87

Scoring

This is rather elaborate and many consider it the most unsatisfactory feature of the game. Each player scores his hand according to the tables of values given below. The player who went mah jong is first paid by the other players in turn who then settle between themselves according to the differences between their respective scores, at all times East paying or receiving double. Thus it is possible for a player who did not go mah jong to score better than one who did. This highlights the underlying aim of the game, apart from the basic one of going mah jong – to make the best score.

It is possible to achieve some astronomical scores at mah jong, so it is practical for the players to agree a limit beforehand, particularly if the game is played for stakes. The scoring of special hands is linked to this figure – for example, a limit hand scores the number of points that has been agreed as the limit. A good figure is 1,000 points.

If East goes mah jong or there is a wash-out, players retain their identities for the next game, otherwise the player who was South becomes East and the other players are renamed in sequence (West becomes South, etc.). The prevailing wind or wind of the round starts with East and changes with every game regardless of seating arrangements. The prevailing wind is indicated by a wind disc.

The score of each player is made up of a basic score doubled for each double earned.

Example Score

The lower box shows the hands at the end of a game to demonstrate scoring. Wind of round: South. North went mah jong; the other three players were fishing.

Scoring Table

Basic Score

Pairs

Dragons	2 points
Player's wind	2 points
Prevailing wind	2 points
Player's wind if prevailing wind	4 points

Sets

Pung (exposed):

Honours or terminals	4 points
Simples	2 points

Kong (exposed):

Honours or terminals	16 points
Simples	8 points
Pung or kong (concealed):	double above points

Bonus tiles

Flower or season	4 points

Player going mah jong

Going mah jong	10 points
Final tile from wall	2 points
Mah jong with only possible tile	2 points

Doubles

One double of basic score for each of following:

Mah jong hand only

All chows
No chows
All sets concealed
One-suit hand (one suit and honour tiles only)
Robbing the kong

All hands

Pung or kong of following:
Dragons
Player's wind
Prevailing wind
Player's flower and season (pair)
Set of flowers (4)
Set of seasons (4)

Special Hands

A limit

East			South		
Exposed kong: East wind	16 pts		Exposed pung: West wind	4 pts	
Concealed pungs: 5 circles	4 pts		Chows: 1,2,3 bamboos	0 pts	
4 bamboos	4 pts		4,5,6 bamboos	0 pts	
Chow: 4,5,6, circles	0 pts		Pair of white dragons	2 pts	
2 circles	0 pts		Pair South wind		
Bonus tiles: 1 flowers	4 pts		(wind of round)	4 pts	
Total:	28 pts		Bonus tiles:		
One double (kong)	*56 points*		2 flowers 4 seasons	8 pts	
			Total:	18 pts	
West			Doubles – nil	*18 points*	
Concealed kong: 1 circles	32 pts				
Concealed pung: red dragons	8pts		**North**		
Chows: 7,8,9 bamboos	0 pts		Exposed kong: 3 circles	8 pts	
2,3,4 characters	0 pts		Concealed pung: 9 circles	8 pts	
7 circles	0 pts		Exposed pung: 2 circles	2 pts	
Bonus tiles: 3 flowers			Chow: 6,7,8 circles	0 pts	
3 seasons	8 pts		Pair: North wind	2 pts	
Total:	48 pts		Bonus tiles: nil		
Two doubles			Going mah jong:	10 pts	
(pung and players's			Total:	30 pts	
flower and season)	*192 points*		One double (one-suit)	*60 points*	

Left Mah Jong being played in the West at the end of the Second World War.

Above Work in a Hong Kong factory where ivory Mah Jong pieces are carved.

Note: The flowers and seasons, numbered respectively 1 to 4 in each case, correspond respectively to East, South, West and North. Thus Autumn is West's season etc.

North collects his total score in tallies from South and West, and double his total score from East. Notice that the scores of his opponents are ignored and that he pays no-one. Thus his profit on the hand is 240 points.

East collects 76 from South (the difference between their scores, dou-bled for East) while West gets 174 from South (difference between their scores) and 272 from East (difference between their scores, doubled) for a total of 446 points. Although North went mah jong, West gained most points on the hand.

Strategy

Common sense plays a big part in Mah Jong strategy. Every discard gives information, and unlike rummy and similar card games, the discards are permanently on view so that as the game progresses more and more information becomes available. Use this to assess the chances of drawing a particular tile from the wall and also to build up a picture of the opponents' hands. Similarly, absence of certain tiles amongst the discards might suggest that at least one player is holding them.

Do not attempt a special hand unless you pick up seven or eight tiles towards it at the start. With a bad hand, aim at an early mah jong even if it means making non-scoring chows (some players limit a mah jong hand to one chow – an optional rule which must be agreed at the beginning).

Unwanted major tiles should be discarded early; later there is more chance that they will be picked up and so contribute to opponents' scores.

Psychology has a role: obviously you should attempt to conceal the make-up of your hand even at times by deliberately discarding a useful tile. Frightening someone to go mah jong early to minimize your losses is often a wise ploy.

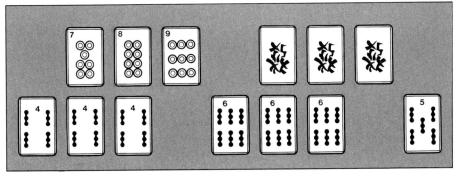

Figure 8 A fishing hand.

89

SHOGI

Of all the varieties of chess, Japanese chess — or shogi — is probably the most fun to play badly. Yet for those who play well it is undoubtedly the most lucrative, for in Japan it has the kind of following and media coverage we are more likely to associate with golf in the West.

I T IS ONLY RECENTLY that shogi has become established in the West, but through the efforts of The Shogi Association there are now players in most countries and a substantial amount of literature in English.

The features of shogi that have found most favour with those westerners who have embraced it are the tactical rich-ness due to the fact that captured pieces are never out of the game but can be re-entered anywhere on the board, the virtual lack of draws, and the relative unimportance (compared to western chess) of learning opening moves.

It is not necessary to learn the Japanese inscriptions on the pieces, as western sets can be used.

Japanese shogi pieces.

The board and pieces

There is a city in Japan — Tendo — that specialises in making shogi equipment: streets are named after shogi pieces and the skyline is dominated by a huge replica of a king. The level of craftsmanship is so high that auction-room prices bat no eyelids. Yet, for all that, the equipment is utterly simple.

The board, for example, is a plain grid of nine by nine squares.

The pieces are all the same colour, material (usually wood or plastic) and shape, Figure 1, distinguished only by size and inscription. The more important pieces are larger but the principal way of telling one piece from another is simply by reading its name, for that is all the inscription is. In Japanese sets this is obviously in Japanese, and these are the sets many westerners prefer to use. But there are westernised sets available and the description of the game below is based on that produced by The Shogi Association.

Figure 1A Japanese shogi pieces.

Figure 1B Western shogi pieces.

The pieces for each side are identical; they have to be, so that when captured they can be re-used by the capturing side. Each player shows which pieces are his by pointing them away from himself (thus the writing on his own pieces is the right way up for him and he reads his opponent's pieces upside down).

Each player normally starts with 20 pieces each: one king, one rook, one bishop, two golds, two silvers, two knights, two lances and nine pawns. This is how an even game starts. In handicap play, which is a prevalent and popular form of the game even at professional level, one side starts with fewer pieces.

All these pieces except the king and golds can achieve promotion, and so they have their promoted ranks written on the reverse side. When a piece is promoted it is simply turned over.

An optional extra piece of equipment is a small stand for each player which he places at his right-hand side of the board. On this he places any pieces he has captured so that they are clearly in view of both players and ready for re-use.

How the pieces move

The players, conventionally referred to as Black and White even though the pieces are not coloured, make alternate moves, attempting ultimately to capture the opponent's king.

On his turn a player can either:
1) move one of his pieces on the board,

according to its power of move, to a vacant square or to a square occupied by an enemy piece (in the latter case he captures and removes the enemy piece); or

2) "drop" (re-enter) a previously captured piece on almost any vacant square.

Moves on the board

There are basically two types of pieces: those that can move only one step at a time in specified directions, and those that can range any number of unobstructed squares in specified directions.

The king, gold, silver, knight and pawn are step movers; the rook, bishop and lance are the ranging pieces.

Figure 2 shows the moves of all the step movers from the point of view of the person playing up the board (always

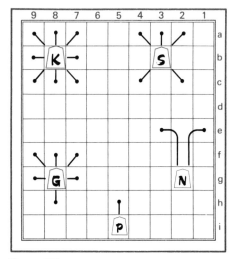

Figure 2 The step movers.

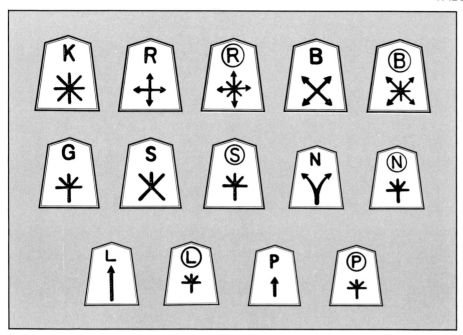

The Western equivalents of the shogi pieces opposite.

assumed to be Black, who moves first). For White all these moves would be reversed. The knight can go only forwards, but if need be it can jump over intervening pieces.

Figure 3 shows the moves of all the ranging pieces, again from Black's point of view. These pieces can move, on any one turn, in one of the specified directions and can go any number of unobstructed squares (i.e. they cannot jump). The lance, it should be noted, can go forwards only.

The restricted nature of these moves is more apparent than real, because of drops and because of promotions.

Each player has a promotion zone: the three rows (or ranks) furthest from him. Whenever a piece of his makes a move on the board (i.e. not a drop) into, within, or out of his promotion zone, it

may be promoted, so long as it is not a king or a gold, by being turned over on completion of its move. On subsequent turns that piece has to move in accordance with its promoted status until it is captured.

Silvers, knights, lances and pawns are all promoted to golds, but in power only, not in name. A promoted silver (a circled S on the western sets) has to be distinguishable from the real gold because when captured it reverts to a silver.

A rook, when promoted, adds the power to go one square diagonally (instead of ranging, not in addition to), and a promoted bishop can go one step orthogonally. Figure 4 shows all the promoted moves.

It may not always be desirable to promote a piece and so it is important to

note that, except in one common-sense case, promotion is always optional. If promotion is refused, it may be earned again by that piece whenever it subsequently makes a move wholly or partly within its promotion zone – and each time it can be refused.

Figure 5 shows some typical promotion-earning moves, all from Black's point of view. After all of these moves, except the pawn move, promotion is entirely optional. The case of the pawn is different not because it is a pawn, for there are cases where it is better not to

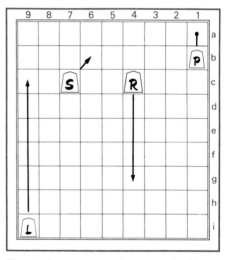

Figure 5 Typical promoting moves by Black.

promote a pawn, but simply because if the pawn was not promoted it would never be able to move again. That is the only time a promotion is compulsory, and so this rule applies to a pawn moving to the furthest rank, to a lance moving to the furthest rank, or to a knight moving to either of the two furthest ranks (these being the only pieces than can move only forwards).

Capture

If a piece, moving as described above, moves to a square occupied by an enemy piece, the enemy piece is captured. It is removed and placed at the right-hand side of the board near to the capturing player. It now belongs to him, and he is said to have it "in hand."

Promoted pieces, when captured, are automatically unpromoted.

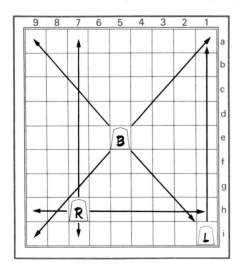

Figure 3 The ranging pieces.

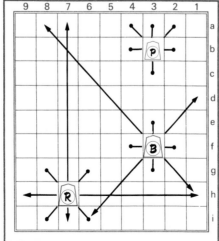

Figure 4 The promoted pieces.

Capturing the enemy king, however, ends the game, and as in western chess a king that is about to be captured next move, but is unable to make any move that will prevent this, is said to be checkmated. Figure 6 shows one of the most important checkmate positions in shogi: note that it is possible to checkmate with very few pieces (for this and

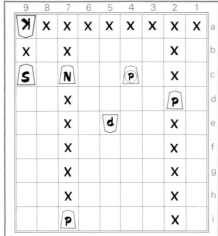

Figure 7 Prohibited drops (x) with a pawn in hand for Black.

other reasons draws are rare in shogi and stalemate is unknown).

Figure 6 Checkmate.

Drops

Instead of making a move on the board, a player can re-enter any one of his pieces in hand (if he has any) on almost any vacant square. He of course places the piece so that it is pointing away from him, showing it is his.

Pieces can be dropped only in the unpromoted state, but they can be dropped in the promotion zone and subsequently earn promotion in the normal way.

There are some restrictions on drops. These are:
1) pawns and lances cannot be dropped on the rank furthest away, and knights cannot be dropped on either of the two furthest ranks (or otherwise they would never be able to move);
2) no player can have two unpromoted pawns on the same file (column of squares) at the same time;

3) a pawn cannot be dropped immediately in front of the enemy king if in so doing it gives checkmate (but it is permissible to move a pawn on the board to give checkmate).

With a single pawn in hand, Black in Figure 7 can drop it on any of the unmarked squares; but he is not allowed to drop it on any of the squares marked x because of one of the restrictions above.

Notation

The official notation of The Shogi Association is introduced here. This system is western-oriented but has an underlying relationship to the Japanese system for the many players avid enough to move onto reading Japanese game scores.

The ranks are denoted by letters, a to i, and the files by numbers, 1 to 9. 1a is the top right (because that's where the Japanese start). A move is described by giving:
1) The initial letter of the piece moving, using N for knight. If it is a promoted piece, the initial is prefixed by "+".
2) The method of moving is then denoted by "–" for a simple move on the board, "x" for a capture or "★" for a drop.
3) Then the destination square is given.
4) Finally, if a piece is promoted "+" is added after the move, or if promotion was possible but was refused "=" is added.

Figure 8 Black to play and checkmate in two moves.

Occasionally, more than one piece of the same type can move to the same destination square. In that case, to show which piece actually moves, the starting square is inserted after the piece initial (e.g. G4i–5h instead of G–5h).

When diagrams are used, note that the pieces in hand are shown on each player's side of the board.

Simple problems

Some simple checkmate problems will illustrate some of the characteristic moves of shogi as well as providing some familiarity with the notation.

In Figure 8 Black has just one possible move which will force checkmate. There is only one rook move to check the white king: R–2i. But White simply captures it with Rx2i or Kx2i. So Black has to drop his bishop. B★2h looks good but after K–2i then B–3g (discovering an attack on the king), White's king can wander away with K–3h. Dropping the

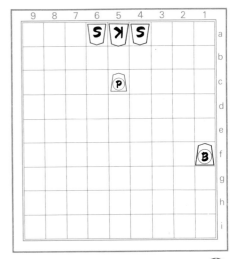

Figure 9 Black to play and force checkmate.

94

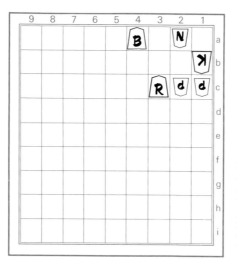

Figure 10 Black to play and force checkmate.

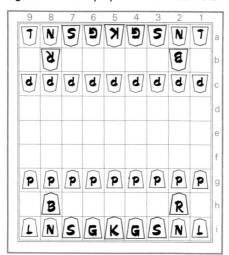

Figure 11 The initial set-up for an even game.

bishop further away is not straightforward. B★4f, say, fails after P★2h, Bx2h: the same position as above. But B★7c signals success, for then P★2h (forced) loses to Bx2h+. The promotion, earned by a move wholly or partly within the promotion zone, does the trick.

Figure 9: Black can checkmate, but not with +Bx6a, although that would work if he had a gold in hand (after Kx6a he could play G★6b). S★5b fails too: S6ax5b; +Bx5b, Sx5b gets nowhere.

The correct first move is +B–5b, a sacrifice, which is a very common tactic in shogi. If White plays S6ax5b, then S★6b is checkmate; S4ax5b allows S★4b, checkmate.

Figure 10 shows a typical problem as set in shogi magazines. Black has to force checkmate, but the conventional rules of such problems are that every move must be check (i.e. directly threatening to capture the king) and that White is assumed to have in hand all pieces not shown in the problem. These problems are not the artificial type of Mate-in-Two seen in chess; they represent situations seen in every game of shogi.

The correct first move here is Bx2c=. If Black promotes his bishop (Bx2c+) or his rook (Rx2c+), White plays K–1a and then Black is unable to continue checking White except by throwing away his pieces, e.g. with +R or +B–1b. P★1b is illegal: it is not permissible to drop a pawn to give checkmate on the move.

But if Black starts with Bx2c=, after K–1a he *can* play P★1b: check but not checkmate. For White can now play K–2b, only to succumb to R–3b+.

Starting a game

If an even game is played the game starts with the position as shown in Figure 11. Black plays first, but statistics over many, many years have shown this to give only a minute advantage.

But if the players are of disparate strength it is normal in shogi to play a handicap game. In this case the stronger player removes some of his pieces on a scale according to the difference in strength. Players are graded using a system of dan and kyu ranks, as in judo. Beginners start at about 15–kyu and progress to 1–kyu. The next grade up is 1–dan (which corresponds roughly to 1800 points on the chess Elo scale) and amateurs go up to 6–dan (2300 Elo). Professionals have their own dan/kyu system above this.

The handicap scale in commonest use is:

Grades difference	Stronger player removes
1	Left lance (lance on 1a)
2	Left lance in one game, bishop in the next game
3	Bishop only
4	Rook only
5	Rook and left lance
6	Rook and left lance in one game, rook and bishop in the next
7	Rook and bishop

Handicaps are used because they really work in shogi, and even bigger handicaps (four pieces: rook, bishop and both lances; or six pieces: rook, bishop, both lances, both knights) merit analysis in books and magazines. But in tournament play even games are the norm.

In a handicap game, Black is always the weaker player. Removal of White's pieces count as Black's first move, so that the first move actually made on the board is by White. The removed pieces are out of the game completely and cannot be dropped. All other rules are the same as in even games.

The opening

As in western chess there is a large corpus of opening knowledge, but in shogi this extends too to handicap play. But there is a huge difference: because, in shogi, the pieces are relatively slow moving and take some time to come into contact with the opposing forces, it is possible for players, to a considerable extent, to develop their own forces irrespective of what the opponent is doing. Even at professional level there are players who choose to play the same opening system year in, year out – as either Black or White.

But whichever of the many possible systems is chosen, the basic principles are the same: each player is trying to create a safe haven for his king, which he normally does by moving it to one side and surrounding it with two golds and a silver (this is called a castle, and there are about 40 standard castles); and to attack the enemy king he is trying to assemble an assault force normally based on his rook, bishop, one knight and the other silver, keeping lines open for these pieces to sweep forward.

Figure 12 illustrates a typical development. Black has played a Static Rook opening (that is, his rook stays on its original file). His king is in what is called the Boat castle, the king being in the stern of a boat created by the bishop on 8h, silver on 7i and golds on 6i and 5h. The rook, bishop, right knight and other silver are poised for attack in the centre and on the right.

White has played a Ranging Rook – a rook "ranged" across its original rank. In this case it is a Third-file Rook. Having second move, White is not so well developed as Black, but he is hoping to play G4a-5b which would create the Cape castle, which is the normal castle for a Ranging Rook player. This castle, formed by the silver

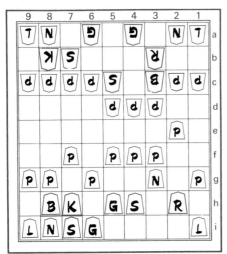

Figure 12 A typical opening: third-file rook.

on 7b and golds on 6a and 5b (the king having first sought the sanctuary of 8b), is so called because it resembles a straw rain-cape.

The next move in this position is P-4e by Black, initiating the middle game before White has time to castle properly.

Figure 13 is another type of Static Rook versus Ranging Rook game, this time a Fourth-file Rook by White but both players have chosen the ultra-defensive Bear-in-the-Hole castle. Black still follows the principle of attacking with rook, bishop, knight and silver, and White tries to, too, but is just that tiny step behind.

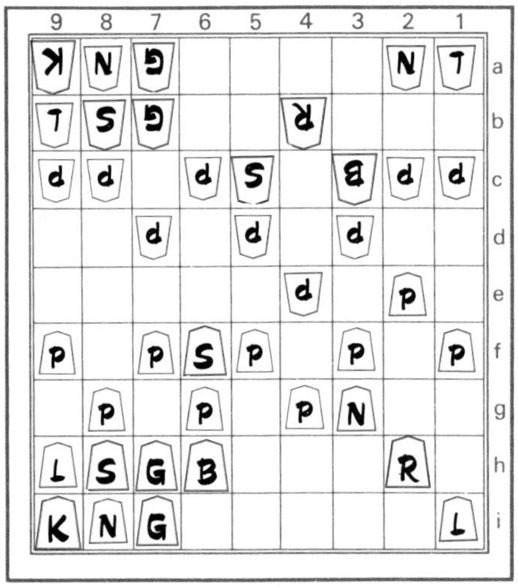

The middle game

Once the opposing forces come into contact the tempo of the game changes dramatically, for captured pieces can suddenly re-appear anywhere through drops, not least in the vicinity of the enemy king.

But the first sensible goal of the

Figure 13 A typical opening: fourth-file rook.

middle game is to create a bridgehead to support the incoming paratroops. This is done most often by breaching the opponent's defences to the promotion zone and promoting a pawn or a major piece (rook or bishop). The early part of the middle game is therefore concerned mainly with probing for weaknesses, or creating one, and once one is found a fight will generally ensue around it.

In the course of this fighting both players will get pieces in hand. A considerable amount of thought will go into getting the right combination in one's own hand for attack, while not allowing the opponent resources for a counter-attack.

The two factors uppermost in a good player's mind throughout all this will not be the gain or loss of his pieces, but the relative safety of the kings and the quality of the most active pieces, especially those in hand. Chess players introduced to shogi are always surprised to learn that there is no scale of the relative value of the pieces as there is in chess (queen = 9, rook = 5, etc.). In a general sense rooks and bishops are worth more than golds and silvers, which are worth more than knights and lances . . . but don't be surprised to see a rook sacrificed just to get a pawn in hand. At the back of all this is the fact that it is just too easy to get compensation for one's pieces (pieces in hand, safer king, more active pieces, the initiative, etc.).

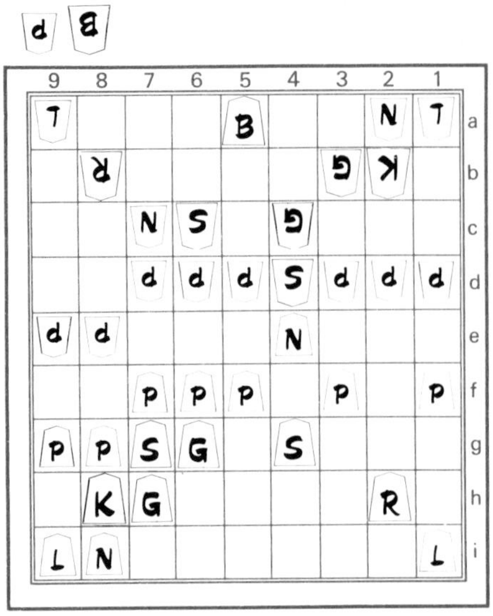

Figure 14 A typical early middle game.

Figure 14 shows a typical early middle-game position. Black has based his attack on the standard rook-bishop-knight-silver formula, there has been a flurry of exchanges, and the outcome has been that Black has disturbed White's castle by pulling the silver from 3c to 4d to escape the predatory knight, and has dropped his bishop at 5a, threatening to promote it at 2d or at 7c (capturing the knight). Black's king, meanwhile, is quite secure in a castle known as the Fortress.

The best moves from here are R-7b; Bx2d+, P★2c; +B−4f and Black has the advantage.

Figure 15, for contrast, shows a late middle-game position. Notice that White has five of the eight golds and silvers to Black's three, an extra lance on 8d and a promoted rook (he has both rooks and Black has both bishops). Yet Black, who has just played B★2f, has the better position.

The reason lies in the relative safety of the kings. Once the white gold on 4d has been displaced Black can play B★7a. The king has to go to 9b and then Black needs only a gold to checkmate with G★8b. It would be insufferable for White to have to continue the game in constant fear of exchanges of pieces that might result in a gold in hand for Black.

But, in addition, Black's promoted knight and pawn are keeping White's rook tied up and pose a threat to all his golds and silvers. In fact White has nothing better than G–5a to try to succour his king, and then play will proceed Bx4d, G–6a; +N–4c, P–3g+; +N–5c, P–4g+; G–5i, +P3g–4h; +Nx6c, Sx6c; S★6b and Black will win (the threat is B★7a, Gx7a; Sx7a=).

Figure 15 A typical late middle game.

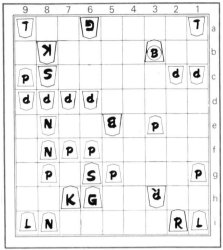

Figure 16 End game.

The endgame

The most characteristic feature of the endgame in shogi is that it is a race – a race to checkmate the opponent's king before he checkmates yours. Nothing is as important as speed and at this stage pieces can be sacrificed willy-nilly. Figure 16 is a representative case.

Black first carefully defends with N*5h and then, after B–2h+; Rx2h, Rx2h+, he has enough time to capture White's king through +B–5d, +R–3i; B*7c, Kx7c; G*6c, K–8b; +Bx6d, Kx9c; S*8b, K–9b; Lx9d, Sx9d; P*9c, K–8c; G–7c.

Yet had Black not played N*5h initially but attacked at once with +B–5d he would have lost the race: S*7g; Nx7g, Nx7g+; Kx7g, N*8e; K–7h, G*7g; K–8i, G–8h; Kx8h, Rx6h+; N*7h, +R–7g; K–7i, G*6h; K–8i, +Rx8g; P*8h, N–7g=.

An illustrative game

Just as chess has been the royal game in the West, so shogi has enjoyed imperial patronage for centuries in Japan. The following game, played in Tendo in 1983, was between Oyama Yasuharu, the foremost player of post-war years, and His Highness Mikasanomiya Tomohito, the nephew of Emperor Hirohito. The Prince, rated about 2–dan, is taking a handicap of rook and bishop and so removes these pieces from White's side as his first move. Oyama (White) plays the first move on the board.

1) . . .   S–6b
2) P–7f   P–5d
3) P–5f   S–5c
4) R–5h

This Central Rook is the Prince's favourite opening but it is rare in handicap games. White, having no rook, or bishop, has to use his silvers especially actively.

4) . . .   S3a–4b
5) S–6h   P–4d
6) S–5g   S–4c
7) K–4h   G–7b
8) K–3h   G–4b
9) S–4f   K–5b

Black has started to castle and already he has a bishop, rook and silver converging for an attack through the centre. White, in handicap games, has to try to combine castling with attack while avoiding weak points inside his own territory where, after exchanges, Black can drop pieces.

10) P–5e   Px5e
11) Sx5e   P*5d

It is a plus point for Black to have gained a pawn in hand.

12) S–4f   P–6d
13) G6i–5i   P–7d
14) G5i–4h

Completes the castle. Black is playing very strongly.

14) . . .   P–8d
15) P–9f   P–9d
16) P–1f   P–1d

Edge-pawn pushes and the decision whether to respond to them are among the most difficult strategical aspects of shogi. This combination of edge-pawn moves indicates a leisurely paced game.

17) B–6f   G–7c
18) N–7g   (Figure 17)

The last element in the attacking force. The focus is now switching from the centre, where Black's pressure has forced White to commit his forces, to the 8–file.

18) . . .   K–6c
19) P–8f   P–3d
20) P–8e   Px8e
21) Nx8e   G–7b

Figure 17 Illustrative game: position after 18) N–7g.

22) R–8h   P*8c
23) P*8d   Px8d
24) Bx8d   S–6b
25) P–7e   P*8c
26) Bx6b+

Sacrificing a major piece (rook or bishop) to force a permanent breach in the enemy camp is a basic theme of large-handicap games.

26) . . .   Kx6b
27) Px7d   G–5c
28) S*7c   Nx7c
29) Px7c+   Gx7c
30) Nx7c+   Kx7c
31) P*7d   Kx7d
32) P*7e

These repeated pawn drops form one of the commonest and most powerful tactics. Good players always strive to keep pawns in hand for such tactics.

32) . . .   K–7c
33) G*7d   K–6b
34) Rx8c+

The point of the bishop sacrifice on move 26. Once promotion has been achieved by a major piece Black should

expect to win easily. Note how untroubled Black's king has been.

34) . . .   S–5b
35) +R–8b   K–5a
36) G–7c   K–4b
37) +Rx9a   N–3c
38) L*6b   P–4e
39) S–5g   B★7g
40) L–6a+   Bx9i+
41) +L–6b   L*2d

Although his early play was faultless, Black has been a little heavy-handed in pushing home his attack. That has been enough to bring White back into the game and it is instructive to see how White conjures up an attack out of nothing by using pieces in hand, while simultaneously looking after his defence.

42) S–2h   N*3e
43) G4i–5h   +B–4d

This is the crucial point for Black. White's defences are threatening to become very solid and his attack is ready to go. Unless Black finds a way to win at once, he will lose – despite his superior numbers.

44) N*5f   +B–5e
45) +Lx5b   Gx5b
46) S*4d   +B–7g
47) P*5c   Gx5c
48) Sx5c+   Kx5c
49) +R–5a   (Figure 18)

And White resigned. Black made it just in time. He can guarantee winning the endgame race now because he has continuous checks up to checkmate (e.g. S*5b; G*6c, K–4c; +Rx5b).

Draws

For completeness draws should be mentioned. They can occur in two ways but never by agreement. First, repetition of the same position (all features: on-the-

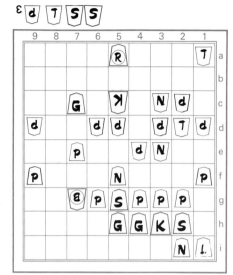

Figure 18 Illustrative game: position after 49) + R-5A and White's resignation.

board position, pieces in hand and turn to move, must be identical) four times renders a game void (that is, it has to be replayed, usually with colours reversed), unless one side is repeatedly checking the opposing king. In the latter case the checking side loses. This rule has been in force only since May 1983. Before that repetition of the same sequence of *moves three* times earned a draw. Draws by repetition occur about once in every 100 games.

About once in every 500 games a situation occurs where neither side can checkmate the other's king because it has advanced into the promotion zone and is too well protected (the poor backwards mobility of some of the pieces is a factor here). Figure 19 shows an example. In this case, called impasse, when the players agree to stop (or if they cannot agree, when one player has moved all his pieces into the promotion zone so that they cannot be captured) they count their pieces on the

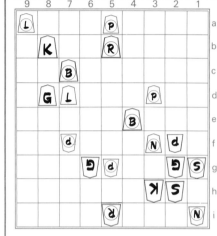

Figure 19 A game drawn by impasse (Black has 29 points, White 25).

basis that rooks and bishops count 5 and all other pieces count 1 (the kings and promotions being ignored). If both players have at least 24 points it is a draw (to be replayed), otherwise the player with fewer points loses. The position in Figure 19 was a draw. There is no agreed rule on impasse in handicap play.

Where to get more information

The presiding body for shogi in the West is The Shogi Association, PO Box 77, Bromley, Kent, UK. They supply books, magazines and equipment. Books and equipment are also available in all good games stores, and most Japanese shops can supply equipment. Japanese equipment naturally uses Japanese names on the pieces. These are shown on page 92.

The standard introductory work on the game is *Shogi for Beginners*, by John Fairbairn (Ishi Press, 1984).

REVERSI

Reversi was invented in England in the 19th century and gained a deserved popularity. It has continued to be played in moderation and is now enjoying a revival of interest.

SPECIAL BOARDS and men can be bought for Reversi, but the game can be played on the familiar board used for chess, draughts or checkers. Sixty-four men are required. These are identical counters, similar to draughtsmen, but with different colours on each side, usually black and white, red and white or red and black. For the purposes of this description we will assume they are black and white.

If a chess board is being used, colours of the squares on the board are of no significance. The board is shown in Figure 1. For ease of describing the game, each square has been given a number. The game is for two players.

Players toss to decide which colour each will play and each takes 32 men

squares on the board. The first two men played by each player must be placed in the four centre squares of the board, i.e. those numbered 54, 55, 44 and 45 in Figure 1. There are thus only two possible situations after four moves: the two men of the same colour are either diagonally opposite each other or are side by side in a rank or file (see Figure 2). As the orientation of the board is of no significance, all other positions are essentially the same. White's next move must be to place a man on a square adjacent to a Black man either diagonally or orthogonally (i.e. in a rank or file) so that the Black man is flanked by two White men. For example, in Figure 2(A), White may play on squares 63, 64, 65 and 66, while in Figure 2(B) he

flanked in more than one direction. All are captured. However men flanked when a captured man is reversed are not themselves captured. For example, imagine it is White's turn in the situation in Figure 3, and White plays at X on square 15. He captures the Black men at 45, 35, 25 in one direction, and at 24 in another. The new situation is at Figure 4. Notice that when the Black man originally at 35 was reversed (or for that matter, the Black man at 24) the Black man at 34 became flanked by White men, but is not captured.

A play is legal only if it captures one or more opposing men. If a player cannot make a legal move he misses his turn. Play continues either until each player has played all his 32 men (when the board is full), or until neither player can make a legal move.

The winner is the player with most men on the board at the end.

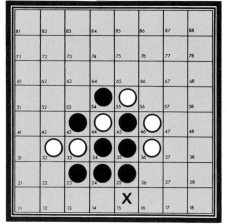

Figure 1

Figure 3

and places them before him with his own colour uppermost.

The Play

Each player in turn, beginning with White, plays a man to one of the

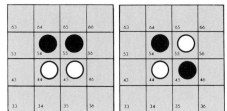

Figure 2

may play on squares 64, 53, 46 or 35. The man thus flanked is trapped and is reversed to show the colour of its captor. After White's third play there will always be four White and one Black man on the board.

Black, in his turn, must now play so that he captures and reverses a White man.

It is permissible to capture more than one man in a move. Should an unbroken line of two or more opposing men be flanked in a move, then all are captured and reversed. Similarly, a man may be placed so that opposing men are

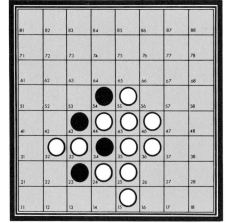

Figure 4

Strategy Reversi is a game of rapid changes, and it is difficult to foresee the results of plays more than a turn or two ahead. This makes it attractive for those who like a game where instinct and 'board sense' count more than study. Generally it is possible to identify the best squares to occupy. Men in the four corner squares are clearly safe from capture and these are good squares on which to get a man. Conversely, the three squares surrounding each corner are the most dangerous. The illustration at the top of the page grades the best (light) to the worst (dark).

CARD GAMES

PATIENCE GAMES

The amounts of skill and luck involved and the chances of success vary enormously between patiences. The eight games presented here are chosen to show the full range of this variation.

THERE ARE HUNDREDS of different patience games (called Solitaires in the U.S.A.), but several features are shared by nearly all of them. They are card games for one player, in which the cards are shuffled at the beginning, then laid out in some pattern, then the pattern is manipulated according to some set of rules with the object of getting the whole pack into order. If this is achieved then the patience is said to have "turned out", and the player has won. If the position becomes blocked, so that no more moves are possible, then the player has failed.

Specialised patience books use a lot of technical terms, which can be a bit off-putting at first. Here we introduce just two special terms, to distinguish between "building" which means putting cards in their final positions, and "packing" which means arranging cards in order in some intermediate working area, from which they will have to be moved on for the patience to turn out.

Of the games discussed here, Four Aces is the simplest and quickest. Klondike (also known as Canfield, Chinaman and Demon, though all those names are also used to refer to other games) is the best introduction to all the other games, and is probably the best one to start with if you are unfamiliar with patience games. Three Blind Mice is another relatively simple patience using one pack.

We then come to three representative two-pack patiences, Miss Milligan, Terrace and The Pyramids. These are all excellent games and are highly recommended to people who find Klondike a bit limited. The last two games here, Robin Post and Eight Kings, are relatively little known games involving some unusual features. They both require a lot of calculation and scheming to be turned out successfully.

Four Aces

This simple little patience is easy to play, and takes up very little space, which makes it ideal for children in bed with measles. It only turns out about one time in 25 games, but this makes it all the more exciting when you do succeed.

Use a single 52-card pack. Deal four cards face up, throw out the lower one of any two cards in the same suit (Ace counts high). Then deal another four cards face up on top of the previous ones (or into the spaces if the previous ones were thrown out). The top card of any pile may be thrown out whenever a higher card of the same suit shows at the top of one of the other piles. If a space is made (by the elimination of all the cards in one of the piles) then a single card may be moved into the space from the top of one of the other piles, and the card exposed by doing so may allow further eliminations.

When no more cards can be moved or thrown out, deal another four cards on to the tops of the piles and start again. Continue in this way until the pack is used up. If at the end you have reduced each of the four piles to just one Ace, then the patience has turned out (obviously you can't throw out the Aces since they are the highest in their suits).

Figure 1 shows a game just after the second set of four cards has been dealt. In the first set the ♣ 9 was eliminated by the ♣ 10.

From this position the ♣ A eliminates the ♣ J, then the ♣ A eliminates the ♣ 10 leaving a space. The ♥ 4 can then be moved into the space exposing the ♦ 2 which can be eliminated by the ♦ 5 leaving a space. The ♦ 5 can then be moved into that space exposing the ♥ 3 which can be eliminated by the ♥ 4. So we get down to just three cards: ♣ A, ♦ 5, ♥ 4. Then deal out another four cards . . .

Klondike

Also known as Canfield, Chinaman, Demon, or simply Patience, this is one of the best known of all patience games. The exact rules vary, and the variations alter the chances of success enormously.

Use a single pack of 52 cards. Shuffle thoroughly and deal out seven piles of cards face down, with one card in the first pile, two in the second, three in the third and so on to seven in the last pile.

Turn over the top card on each pile, but leave it on top of the pile, to give a position like that in Figure 2. Then start packing the exposed cards by forming them into sequences, alternating red and black cards, and descending (so that 8 goes on 9, 9 on 10 etc.).

During packing a whole sequence (or part of a sequence) may be moved together as a unit. Kings (with any cards packed onto them) may be moved into spaces. When a face down card is ex-

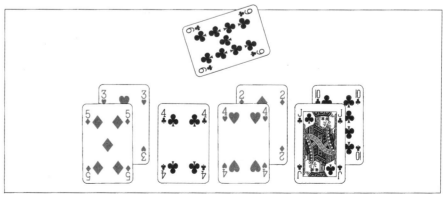

Figure 1 Four Aces soon after the start.

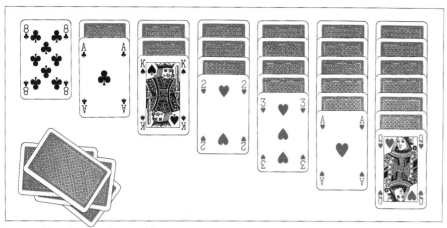

Figure 2 Klondike starting position.

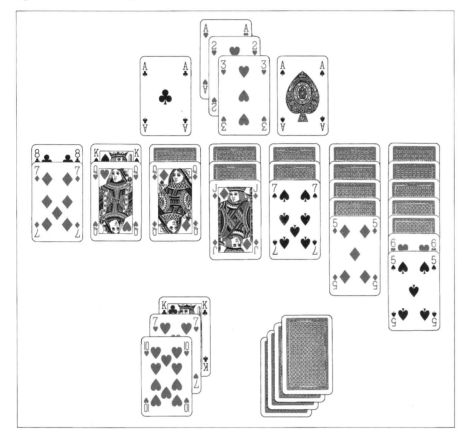

Figure 3 The same game after a few moves.

posed, turn it over.

As the Aces appear, move them to one side. The object of the game is to build all four suits onto the Aces in order up to the King. The top card of any pile (including the waste pile) may be used for building.

When no further building or packing can be done, turn over the first of the remaining cards. Build or pack it onto one of the exposed cards if possible, otherwise put it face up on the table to start the waste pile and continue turning cards from the pack. Only the top card of the waste pile is available for building or packing. No redeals of the pack are allowed. If you get to the end

of the pack without having built all the Aces up to their Kings then you have failed.

Figure 2 shows the starting position, and Figure 3 the way it might have developed a few moves later – the ♠ K has been moved into a space, and the ♥ Q packed onto it. The two Aces which were already exposed have been moved off to start the building, and the ♠ A has also appeared. The waste pile has three cards in it so far. Next, the ♥ 6 and ♠ 5 can be packed onto the ♠ 7, and another face down card turned over.

With these rules the patience comes out about three or four times in a hun-

dred. If you are forbidden from moving part of a sequence, it is even harder. In order to improve the chances of success variations may be tried:

1) Instead of insisting that sequences be built of alternating red and black cards, any card of a different suit may be allowed (though they must still be in descending sequence). This improves the chances of success to almost even. This variation is sometimes known as Thumb and Pouch.

2) Redealing the waste pile. This also improves the odds dramatically – the patience becomes easier the more redeals are allowed. With an indefinite number of redeals it should turn out about two-thirds of the time. Some people like to deal the pack onto the waste pile in threes. In this case at least two redeals are necessary to have any significant chance of success.

Three Blind Mice

A simple patience which more or less operates itself. This one does not turn out very often (about one time in ten) and has a way of getting stuck very near the end which you may find amusing or aggravating depending on temperament.

Use a single 52-card pack and deal out ten piles of five cards, overlapping so that you can see all the faces, as shown in Figure 4. All the cards in the seven piles on the left should be face up, but the bottom three cards in each of the three piles on the right should be face down. Keep the two odd cards on one side and play them wherever possible.

The object is to build each of the four suits in descending sequence (Queen on King, 8 on 9 etc.) from King down to Ace. This is done directly by building cards onto each other in suit. For this purpose the card being built onto must be on top of its pile, but the card doing the building can be anywhere except further down the same pile, so long as it is face up. If there are other cards on top of the one being built, they are carried with it.

When one of the "blind" cards is ex-

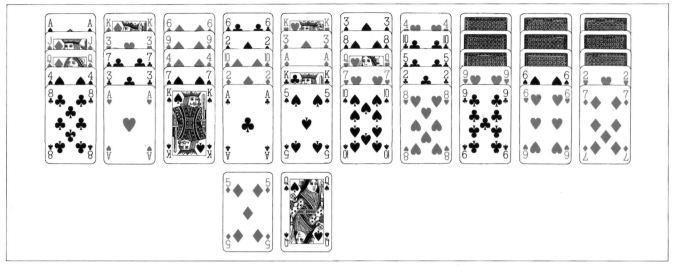

Figure 4 Three Blind Mice starting position.

posed it is turned over and can join in the play.

Kings may be played into the spaces which arise when one of the ten piles becomes empty.

Figure 4 shows the position at the start of a game. From here we can put the ♠ Q directly on to the ♠ K, but the ♦ 5 has to wait until the ♦ 6 is exposed.

The building might start with the ♣ 7 being played on the ♣ 8, keeping the ♣ 3 and ♥ A on top of it. This exposes the ♥ 3, so we can continue by putting the ♥ 2 (and ♦ 7) on the ♥ 3. Now one of the blind cards is exposed and can be turned over.

Miss Milligan

This is a classic patience, the enduring popularity of which must be due, in part, to its amazing ability to turn out from apparently hopeless positions.

Use two packs shuffled together, and deal out eight cards side by side, face up. Take out any Aces to start the building – the object of the game is to build all eight Aces in sequence and in suit up to their Kings. Having taken the Aces out, pack the remaining cards in descending sequence, red on black (or black on red) wherever they fit. You may also build any 2s which fit onto their Aces, and 3s on the 2s etc. Kings may be moved into spaces.

When no further building or packing can be done, deal out another eight cards on top of the piles (or into the spaces where piles have been emptied), then pause for another session of building and packing. Any card or properly packed sequence which fits may be moved from the top of one pile and packed onto the top of another pile. Aces are taken out as they appear, and building onto these Aces is allowed during the packing.

Figure 5 shows a position reached after three deals and some packing. From this position we can pack the sequence from ♦ J down to ♠ 6 onto the ♠ Q, then build the ♠ 2 onto the ♠ A, and the ♠ 3 onto the ♠ 2. No more packing can be done, so eight more cards are then dealt out.

Continue to alternate phases of packing and dealing until all the cards have been dealt out. You will probably have reached a pretty hopeless looking position, with all the cards you really need buried under something else, but at this point we introduce a new rule.

The rule is called "waiving" and the

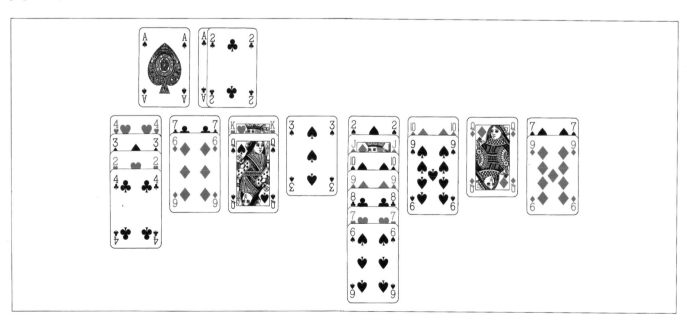

Figure 5 Miss Milligan in progress.

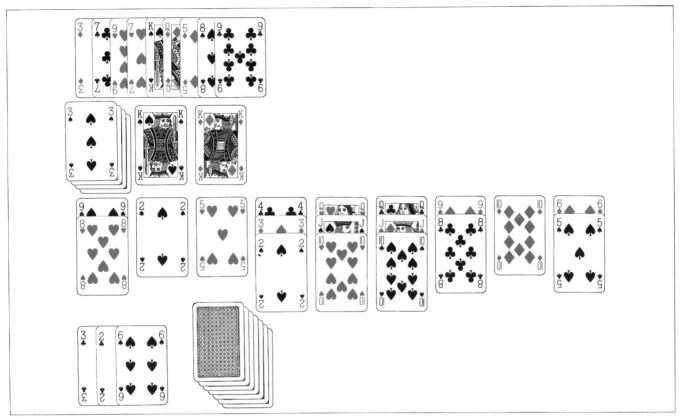

Figure 6 Terrace soon after the waste pile has been started.

process of waiving is simply to pick up the top card from one of the piles and hold it in your hand, continuing the play as if it didn't exist until you find somewhere to build or pack it. You may only waive one card at a time, but this is often enough to bring the patience out. Some people allow a whole sequence to be waived at once so long as it is properly packed.

A technique which is particularly useful in Miss Milligan is the transfer of parts of sequences. Suppose, for example, that you have an awkward sequence with a black Jack at the top of it blocking one of the piles, and that there is another black Jack exposed elsewhere. Then you can transfer the bottom part of the sequence, from the red 10 downward, to the other Jack, then waive the offending Jack and start work on the rest of the pile.

Terrace

Also known as Signora and Queen of Italy, this is an excellent patience which calls for considerable foresight. Its special feature if that all the blocking cards (the problems you will have to dodge round) are laid out in a line at the beginning.

Shuffle two packs together. Deal out 11 cards in an overlapping line, the "terrace", so that you can see what they all are. Leave space below them for the eight bases on which you will be building. Below that deal out four cards side by side, then stop and think.

At this stage you must choose one of the four cards. That card and the other seven of the same rank will form the bases for all the building, though you have to wait for the others to appear. The choice will depend on the cards in the Terrace.

Having chosen your base card, put it in the building area, fill the gap it occupied from the pack, and deal out another five cards to make a row of nine. These form the working area, where packing is allowed. Continue packing these cards, taking out base cards for building and filling in the gaps until you get stuck, then turn over cards from the pack to start forming a waste pile. When you get to the end of the pack, there is no redeal – if the cards are not all built onto the bases by then you have failed.

Cards are built up on the bases in sequence, alternating red and black cards and increasing, turning the corner from King to Ace to 2 when you reach it. The exposed cards in the working area, the top card of the wastepile and the top card of the Terrace are available for building.

Within the working area, packing is done in descending sequence, alternating red and black cards, turning the corner from 2 to Ace to King as necessary. Only one card at a time may be moved – sequences in the working area can only be moved by building – and gaps which appear may only be filled with the top card of the waste pile. Cards from the terrace may not be used for packing – they must be built directly. The only cards available for packing are single cards in the working area and the top card of the waste pile.

Figure 6 shows a game shortly after the wastepile has been started. Kings were chosen as base cards, and three of them have been found. One of these has been built up to a black 3, getting rid of the first two cards of the terrace in the process. In order to get rid of the next card, the ♣ 9, it will be necessary to find a red 4, a black 5, and so on up to a red 8 (the 5, the 6 and the 8 are already waiting in the working area, so this won't be too difficult). Note that it is illegal to pack the ♥ 8 and ♠ 9 onto the ♥ 10 in the working area, since only one card may be moved at a time.

The art of getting this patience to turn out is to work out in advance where the terrace cards are going, and not to do any building which does not contribute directly to this aim. For much of the time you will be turning

105

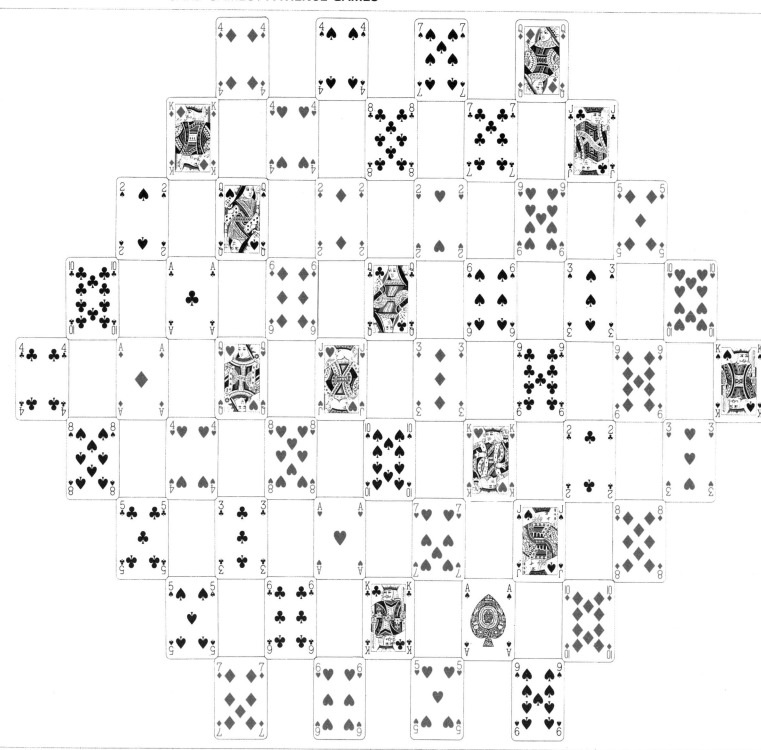

Figure 7 Robin Post starting position.

cards from the pack to the wastepile, waiting for some particular card to come up so that you can move the top card off the terrace. While doing this, though, you can prepare a "reception committee" for the next cards in line down the terrace. It hardly matters how big the waste pile becomes – it has an almost magical way of disappearing once the terrace has been got rid of. With care this patience can be turned out successfully about half the time.

Robin Post

This unusual patience involves a very pleasing layout (though it takes up rather a lot of space) and demands considerable care and analysis to be brought out successfully, though it comes out more often that not with accurate play.

Shuffle two packs together, then deal out 52 cards face up, in the hexagonal

pattern shown in Figure 7 – with nine rows of 4,5,6,7,8,7,6,5 and 4 cards in a "chequerboard" pattern with spaces the size of one card between each.

One Ace and one King of each suit are taken out as they become available, and the object is to build eight sequences in suit on these cards, running down from the Kings and up from the Aces.

Cards become available for play de-

to be able to unblock some part of the layout which is causing trouble.

When the position becomes blocked (or when you choose to stop moving cards) deal out the second 52 cards, in the same positions as before, so that some of them go on the tops of piles and some into spaces. Then continue playing as before until you are either blocked or successful.

Figure 7 shows the starting position. Considering the cards near the bottom, the ♥ 6 can be moved onto the ♠ 5, then the ♥ 5 goes on the ♣ 6 (possible now that the ♣ 6 has had one corner freed). Then the ♠ 9 goes on the ♦ 10, and these two cards together can be moved onto the ♦ 8 (with the ♦ 10 on top). Now the ♠ A and the ♣ K are free to be taken out to start the building – though it is important to remember that there are two of each of the cards in the pack, and whichever Aces and Kings are not used as bases are likely to become troublesome blocking cards.

The Pyramids

This game requires less space than most two-pack patiences, and more skill than many. It shows an extreme form of the irregular rhythm which a number of patiences share, with long periods when nothing seems to be happening, and occasional eruptions of activity. Much of the skill in the game lies in making the eruptions happen as often as possible.

Take two packs of cards, shuffle thoroughly and lay out a "pyramid" of nine cards face up, with one card in the top row, three in the middle and five along the bottom. The top four cards are reserves, and the bottom five are the working area where packing can be done.

As the Aces appear, one of each suit is arranged in a smaller pyramid to the left of the main one, with one Ace on top and three along the bottom row. As the Kings appear they are arranged similarly on the right. The Aces and Kings may be collected in any order, and building can start as soon as the first one appears. The object of the game is to build the Aces upward in

'Lawyers and Soldiers are the Devil's playfellows' is the caption to this old print, suggesting cards are sinful.

pending on how many other cards (or piles) they are touching at their corners. A card with two or more free corners may be taken for packing or building. A card with one free corner may not be moved, but it may be packed upon. Cards (or piles) with neighbours at all four corners may not be used at all.

Packing is done in sequence, ascending or descending, but not both on the same pile, red on black, or black on red.

A sequence or part of a sequence may be picked up together, and packed onto another card or sequence, reversing the order if necessary.

Cards may be reversed from the "King" pile to the "Ace" pile in one suit. This process is the key to getting the patience to turn out – each time the two ends of the building in one suit meet you have the opportunity to transfer cards from one pile to the other so as

Figure 8 The Pyramids starting position.

suit, in sequence, to Kings, and to build the Kings downward in suit, in sequence, to Aces.

Packing on the five bases is in suit, in sequence, upwards or downwards as you like but not both on the same base. Kings and Aces may not be packed on each other. In all packing, cards may only be moved one at a time.

When a space appears in the base of the pyramid, you are free to rearrange it. Only one card may be moved at a time, and cards from the top four (reserve) positions may only be moved if the spaces directly below them are empty. Notice that it is possible to

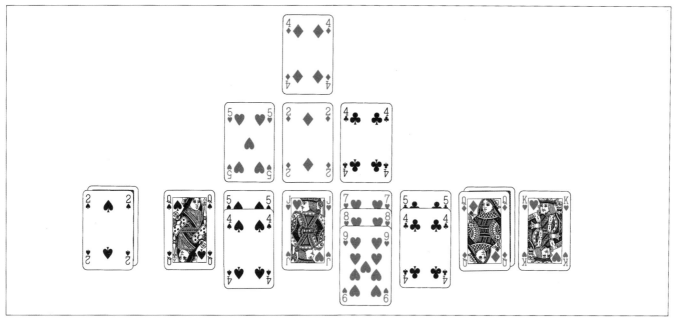

Figure 9 The Pyramids: the game in figure 8 after manipulation.

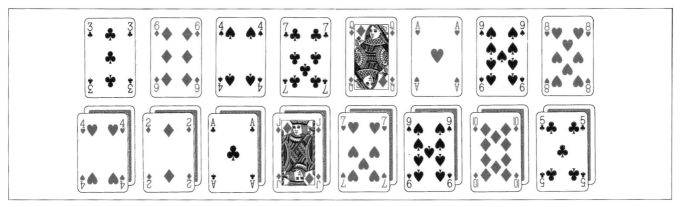

Figure 10 Eight Kings starting position. The bottom row is stacks of 12 cards.

Figure 11 Eight Kings: the same game after 20 moves. The numbers of cards in the bottom row vary.

move a long sequence from one base to another one card at a time – and that the sequence gets turned upside down when you do so. With a bit of practice the pyramid can be rearranged in almost any way you want, given just one gap at the bottom (though you may only have single cards in the reserve positions).

The remaining cards are dealt into three separate waste piles, three cards at a time to each pile. Deal cards to all three piles before doing any packing. Only the top card of each waste pile is available for use. When vacancies appear in the pyramid they must be filled from the waste piles before any further cards are dealt out.

When the cards are exhausted, collect the three wastepiles together, unshuffled, and redeal, this time to only two waste piles. For the second redeal there is only one waste pile, and after that no further redeals are allowed.

Figure 8 shows the starting position, and Figure 9 the same game after manipulation. This would start by taking the ♦ K out, then moving the ♠ 4 into the space where the King was, freeing the ♥ K, then moving the ♥ K out, moving the ♠ 2 into one of the spaces and building the ♦ Q on the ♦ K, and so on. The final position has been carefully arranged so that as many cards as possible will create a gap in the pyramid as the deal continues.

Most of the skill in this game lies in arranging the bottom row of the pyra-

mid carefully, since every time a gap appears there you can rearrange a lot of cards at once – especially at the beginning when there are three waste piles. The rule about having to fill gaps in the pyramid as soon as they appear is important – otherwise the patience comes out all the time. As it is the chances of success are about even.

Eight Kings

One of the problems with two-pack patiences is that it is difficult to shuffle the cards thoroughly enough. This patience is almost unique in that the winning position does not have most of the cards in sequence. Also, it makes little difference if the pack is badly shuffled at the start, so this patience can be used as a way of shuffling the pack. Speed and agility at mental arithmetic are a great help.

Deal out eight cards, side by side, face up as indicators. They should all be of different ranks, and none of them should be Kings. Below each of these put a stack of twelve cards, face up, as shown in Figure 10.

The object of the game is to assemble twelve cards in order above each indicator, finishing with a King. But the peculiar feature of this patience is that the sequences go in steps of different sizes; the indicator tells you what sized steps to take. If the indicator is 2 for example, the cards go up in twos: 4, 6, 8, 10, Queen (Jack = 11, Queen = 12, King = 13), then Ace, 3, 5, 7, 9, Jack, King.

When the number goes over 13, then subtract 13 to get back to a sensible number. This is quite easy for small indicators, but takes a little practice for the larger ones. If the indicator is 9, for example, the sequence is 5, Ace, 10, 6, 2, Jack, 7, 3, Queen, 8, 4, King. The first card above each indicator is found by doubling the value of the indicator, and thereafter you just add the indicator value to the top card of the pile subtracting 13 whenever the number reached is over 13.

The magic feature on which this patience relies is that the King always comes up 13th whatever indicator is used, and there is always just one of each of the other ranks in between.

The eight cards exposed at the tops of the stacks along the bottom are available for building. Build them on to the bases until you are stuck (or don't wish to continue), then take up the first stack and deal it out, one card at a time, on top of the others (including the gap you created by picking the stack up). Next time you are blocked deal out the second stack, and so on until the eighth stack, after which there are no more redeals.

Figure 10 shows the starting position – here the possible moves are to put the Ace above the 7, the Jack above the Queen, the 2 above the Ace or the 5 above the 9 – and Figure 11 shows the position 20 moves later when everything has become blocked and the first pile should be dealt out.

BRIDGE

Contract Bridge, to give it its full name, was invented by an American millionaire, Harold S. Vanderbilt, in 1926. It rapidly replaced Auction Bridge, which in turn had replaced earlier forms of a Russian card game, Biritch. Today, Contract Bridge reigns supreme, to the extent that it is now known everywhere simply as Bridge.

BRIDGE IS AT ONCE one of the world's most popular, widely played and skilful of all card games. For some, it is also a social advantage. It takes little effort to master the rules, a little more effort to become competent; but as in other good games, mastery belongs only to the hard-working and gifted.

Anyone taking up Bridge from scratch might be advised first to learn Whist, an easier game that has much in common with Bridge, but a knowledge of the rudiments of card play in trick-taking games is also useful background for the beginner.

The object of the game cannot be expressed in a sentence, though reduced to fundamentals it is to win tricks in play. After the deal players bid in an auction to establish the trump suit, if any, and the number of tricks that the highest bidder, who secures the contract, is committed to making. The hand is scored according to the outcome. Each time a game score is reached, a new game is started. The first side to win two games wins the 'rubber', which attracts a bonus score.

Every hand of Bridge therefore has two phases: the bidding and the play. Bidding is no formality. Not only is its purpose to find the right contract (or drive the opponents into a wrong one)

but bidding is also used to gather information – it allows players in effect to communicate with each other. Player interaction is a feature of the game.

Preliminaries

Bridge is a partnership game for four players. A standard pack of playing cards, excluding jokers, is used, though it is common practice to have two packs in contrasting back designs or colours for use in alternate hands, one partnership, termed for convenience North and South, dealing with one pack, and the second partnership (East/West) with the other. Each player should have a score pad, although in social Bridge it is not necessary for more than one player to keep the score.

The cards are ranked in the normal way from Ace (high) down to 2 (low). Suits are ranked also: spades (high), hearts, diamonds, clubs (low).

Players draw for or agree partnerships and a pack is then spread face

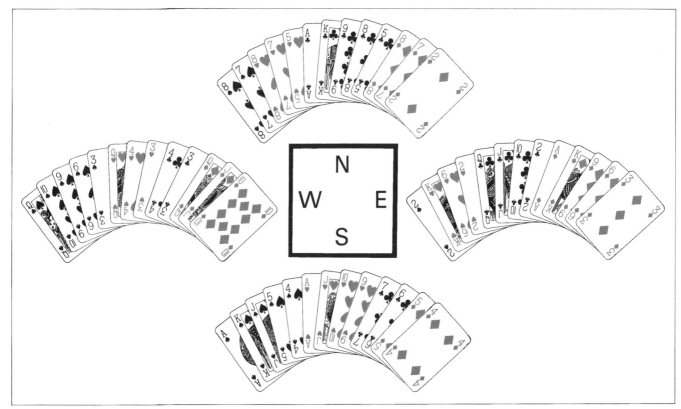

Figure 1 After the deal; hands sorted ready for play.

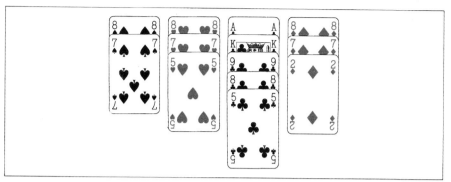

Figure 2 Dummy's hand displayed.

down on the table. Each player draws a card and exposes it. Highest card is dealer; if tied, higher suit takes precedence.

Dealer now selects one of the packs (which he and his partner will deal throughout the session). The opponent on his left shuffles and passes the pack to his partner to cut to dealer. Dealer deals out all the cards one at a time face down, starting with the player on his left and finishing with himself, when each player has 13 cards. During the deal, the dealer's partner shuffles the second pack and places it on his right ('If you're not demented quite, place the cards upon your right'). The deal passes to the left after each hand, and the same shuffle and cut procedure is followed – the player with the cards on his right passes them across to his partner to cut for the new dealer.

Players now pick up their cards and examine them. It is usual and useful to sort them into suits, colours alternating, and in descending order of rank. A deal, showing cards sorted, is illustrated in Figure 1.

Bidding

Bidding is the most difficult part of Bridge. During this phase, players bid individually, with partnerships competing for the right to nominate the trump suit or to elect for the hand to be played without trumps ('no trumps'). Bidders must at the same time declare the number of tricks they will attempt to make with their chosen suit as trumps (or without trumps). This is the contract. If it is accepted and subsequently fulfilled, the partnership is rewarded; but if it fails the partnership is penalised.

As is the practice in auctions everywhere, each bid, to be valid, must exceed the previous bid with the contract going to the highest bidder. Unlike in auction practice however, players cannot bid freely: the right to

bid passes from player to player in a clockwise direction and continues as many times round the table as is necessary to reach a contract. An important feature of the bidding is that although the players bid individually and without consultation, a player's bid is always binding on partner.

The dealer starts the auction. He may bid or pass ('No Bid') and he does this by making a statement to the effect. The lowest bid is One Club. It is a strange convention that the first six tricks ('the book') are not counted in the bidding, so 'One Club' means that the bidder is contracting on behalf of his partnership to make seven tricks with clubs as trumps.

Since each player has 13 cards and is obliged to contribute one card to every trick, there are 13 tricks, so a call of 'One Club' contracts to make only one more trick than the opposition.

The reason One Club is the lowest bid is because it is at the lowest permissible level (one) and clubs are ranked below the other suits. No trumps is the highest ranking, so the sequence at the one level in ascending order of bids is One Club, One Diamond, One Heart, One Spade, One No Trump. The next highest call after One No Trump is Two Clubs, and so on up to Seven No Trumps, the highest possible contract, which requires all 13 tricks to be made in no trumps.

So long as each bid exceeds the previous bid, bidding need not be (and very rarely is) sequential. For example, dealer might open 'Two No Trumps' when the next bidder would be free to call any bid at the three level or above.

A player on his turn may bid or pass. If the highest contract at that stage was with the opposition, then the player has another option: he can double the opponents' contract ('Double') instead of bidding or passing. This does not change the contract but increases the point values for the hand. Similarly, if

on a player's turn the contract is with his partnership but has been doubled by the opposition, the player may redouble ('Redouble'), again increasing the stakes but still in the same contract. Notice that a player cannot double his partnership's contract.

If a further bid is made after a contract has been doubled or redoubled, even if in the same suit as the contract, this automatically cancels the double or redouble, though the opposition is free to double the new contract. The contract is concluded when three players pass in turn.

Look back at Figure 1. North was dealer. A plausible, though not a model, bidding sequence in this hand might have gone:

North:	No Bid
East:	One Diamond
South:	One Spade
West:	Two Diamonds
North:	Three Clubs
East:	Three Diamonds
South:	Three Spades
West:	Double
North:	No Bid
East:	No Bid
South:	No Bid

The contract is Three Spades by North/South doubled by East/West. Bidding is discussed further under Strategy.

Play

Only three players participate in the card play subsequent to the bidding. The player who first bid the suit (or no trumps) which is nominated in the final contract plays the hand for his partnership. Partner becomes 'Dummy' for this hand and takes no further part in the game.

The player on the left of the declarer (contracting player) opens by leading face up on the table any card from his hand. Declarer now picks up his partner's hand and exposes it on the table, arranged in suits with the trump suit (if any) nearest the lead player. In the hand discussed above, South is declarer and would arrange Dummy's cards something like Figure 2 – there is no rigid

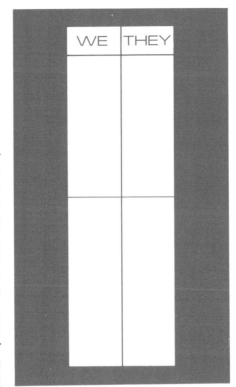

Figure 4 A score card.

procedure for displaying the hand.

Now declarer plays on behalf of Dummy, selecting a card in response to the opening lead. The usual trick-playing rules apply: it is obligatory to play a card of the suit led ('following suit') unless unable to do so, when any card may be dropped. Trumps (if any) are the controlling unit, any trump card beating any card of the other three suits. Otherwise, all suits rank the same during the play of the hand.

The partner of the player who led now contributes a card, and finally declarer does likewise. One player of the side that won the trick picks up the four cards, makes them into a packet and places them face down in front of him. The winner of the trick leads to the next trick.

Returning again to Figure 1, West leads to a contract of Three Spades Doubled, North becomes Dummy and South plays both hands. Figure 3 shows how the first trick may have been played. The winning card is the king of clubs, which came from Dummy. South claims the trick and leads to the second trick from Dummy. Notice that in dealing, bidding and playing of the hand, the movement is always clockwise, each player in turn.

Figure 3 The first trick.

Scoring

It is impossible to play Bridge well without understanding the principles of scoring, yet many people who indulge in casual Bridge are happy to leave the accounts to someone else.

They frequently ask 'How many

points do we need for game?' and only have a hazy idea of the penalties they are liable to incur when they double. Learn to score now!

A score card is printed in two columns headed 'We' and 'They' with a horizontal dividing line half way down (Figure 4). The column headed 'We' is used by the scorer to record the points earned by his side, and the 'They' column for the points scored by the opposition. Points that count towards game are entered below the break, progressively moving down the card, while bonus and penalty points, which do not count towards game, are entered above the line, progressively upwards. At the end of a rubber, each column is added up, the break then being ignored. The difference in points between the two columns determines the winner and the margin of the victory. In rubber Bridge, which is that usually played on casual and social occasions (tournament Bridge is the same game but is scored a little differently), the total is usually rounded to the nearest 100 and settled, if the game is being played for stakes, or carried forward to the next rubber.

If all the players are keeping the score, then of course partners should have identical score cards with opponents' cards also being the same but with columns transposed.

Game is 100 points. The only points

that count towards game are those for tricks bid and made – that is, for a successful contract. Thus only one side can score 'below the line' on a hand, and if the contract fails, then there is no score below the line.

For every trick of the contract, excluding always the first six, points are earned according to suit:

No trumps: 40 for first trick
30 for all subsequent tricks
Spades: 30
Hearts: 30
Diamonds: 20
Clubs: 20

Notice that game can be made in a single hand with three no trumps (9 tricks), that it requires four spades or hearts (10 tricks) – you don't have to score 100 exactly – and five diamonds or clubs (11 tricks).

However, games are often won by accumulating 'part scores'; that is, by winning two or more contracts, not necessarily in successive hands, that together sum to 100 or above. When one side wins a game, a horizontal line is drawn across the score card below the entry so that each game is started from scratch – there is no carrying forward of part scores.

When a side wins a game it becomes 'vulnerable'. A side that is vulnerable suffers stiffer penalties for failure, but also increased bonuses for success. If both sides win a game, then both are vulnerable pending the outcome of the final game to decide the rubber.

The table (Figure 5) give the points awarded for bonuses and penalties. Observe that except where overtricks are made – that is, tricks taken in excess of those contracted for – the suit in which a hand is played only affects the score below the line. Notice in particular the big bonus earned for winning a rubber, also for bidding and making a little slam (winning 12 out of 13 tricks) and a grand slam (all 13 tricks) – not an everyday occurrence!

Recall that all points for bonuses and penalties are entered above the line.

An example of a scored rubber should help explain the system. Sup-

BONUSES		
Overtricks – trick value (not vulnerable or vulnerable)		
if doubled:	100 per trick not vulnerable	
	200 per trick vulnerable	
if redoubled:	200 per trick not vulnerable	
	400 per trick vulnerable	
Rubber	700 if opponents not vulnerable	
	500 if opponents vulnerable	
	300 for game in unfinished rubber	
	50 for part score in unfinished rubber	
Little slam	500 if not vulnerable	
	750 if vulnerable	
Grand slam	1000 if not vulnerable	
	1500 if vulnerable	
Other bonuses		
For making doubled or redoubled contract – 50		
Bonus for honours:		
Four of trump suit:	100	
Five of trump suit:	150	
Four aces in no trumps:	150	

Note: Honours are the five top-ranking cards – A K Q J 10. To qualify for an honour bonus, which is awarded regardless of whether the contract is successful or not, the honours must be in one hand. The holder can be any player.

PENALTIES	
Undertricks – 50 for each trick.	
if doubled:	100 for the first trick and 200 for each subsequent trick (not vulnerable); 200 for the first trick and 300 for each subsequent trick (vulnerable)
if redoubled:	double the above

Note: Undertricks are the shortfall in a failed contract.

Figure 5 Bonus and penalty scoring.

pose North dealt, and a contract of Two Diamonds was reached by East-West. They got an overtick, and West held A Q J 10 of diamonds (four honours). The scoring of this hand is marked (1) in Figure 6. (The marking is to assist explanation: there is no numbering in practice.)

In the next hand, all players passed so the hand was abandoned and the deal passed to South. North-South tried for game with a call of Four Hearts, but were doubled and went two down (2).

East now dealt and East-West played the hand in Two No Trumps which were made. Since that concludes the game, a line is drawn below the score (3). East-West are now vulnerable.

In the next hand, North-South called and made a Small Slam in clubs (4).

Finally, North-South, now vulnerable also, went Two Spades which was doubled. They made the contract with one overtrick (5). Notice that the trick value of the contract below the line is doubled, and North-South also get bonuses for making the contract ('50 for the insult'), the overtrick and the rubber. North's score sheet (Figure 6) shows a gain for the rubber of 10(00) points.

Card Play

Card play is a science to which some people take easily, others do not. Fortunately, as far as Bridge is concerned there are a number of useful axioms which if followed flexibly promise the beginner that he will not be disgraced.

First, consider the sequence of play to a trick. The player who leads has the advantage of choosing the suit but it is the last player who is best placed because he does not have to declare his intentions until all others have played. The seating arrangements are significant. Unless you have the lead, you will always play after the player on your right, to your considerable advantage, and before the player on your left, an equal disadvantage. A simple example shows this: if you hold but K J in a suit (known, rather surprisingly, as a tenace!) and the opponent on your right holds the superior A Q tenace, then unless you have to lead the suit, you are bound to make a trick with the king, trumping possibilities aside. But if the A Q pair is with the player on your left, you will lose both tricks provided your opponent is not forced to lead the suit.

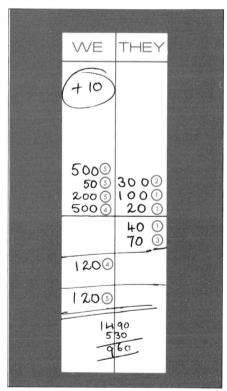

Figure 6 A scored rubber.

However, this situation is reversed for your partner, and this points up the first lesson of card play in Bridge: you and your partner are playing in effect a combined hand of 26 cards. Do not ask yourself 'How many tricks can I make?' but rather 'How many tricks can we make?' It does not matter which of you

Figure 7 A supporting hand.

makes the tricks! This is an obvious truism when you are declarer and are playing both hands, but it is easily overlooked when you only have your own hand to look at.

In every hand you are either attacking (attempting to make a contract) or defending. In either case you will have a target number of tricks to aim for, any made above that number being a bonus.

Many contracts are won or lost on the opening lead. A good opening lead is your highest card of a suit your partner has bid or a card of a suit bid by the opponent on your left which was not supported by his partner.

In defending against a No Trump contract, it is an honoured principle to lead the fourth highest of your longest suit. This gives valuable information to your partner since he can examine Dummy's hand and his own and so knows exactly how many cards in the suit higher in rank than the one led are held by declarer (who, incidentally, will equally be able to work out your partner's holding). Long suits are trick winners if there are no trumps!

The lead signals information. There are many other signals that can be used in card play. For example, if you have only two cards in a suit, by playing the higher one first, then the lower – reversing the natural order – you signal to your partner that you are void (no cards left in the suit in question). This is called a 'peter'. It is not a good idea if you have no trumps left with which to take advantage of a return lead in the suit!

A general principle to follow, unless there are obvious tactical reasons why you should not, is to play 'second hand low, third hand high'. That is, when a card is led and you are the next player, you should contribute your lowest ranking card, but if you are third player, the opposite is advisable – play your highest card.

Another sound principle is to 'cover an honour'; that is to say, if your right-hand opponent plays an honour and you hold a higher honour, you should play it, even though you strongly suspect that it will be beaten.

For example, partner leads a low club which draws the Queen; you follow with the King, 'covering the honour', which is beaten by the Ace. You will have lost the trick, but you will have drawn two honours for one – and you could well have promoted your partner's Jack or 10 to a trick-winner.

Three kinds of cards take tricks: high cards, trumps and low cards in a long suit. The first two groups need little explanation. In high cards, the Ace, King, and often the Queen, are likely winners. There are, after all, 13 cards in a suit, and given even distribution these should 'go round' three times when all but one player will be void.

But distribution is more likely than not to be uneven. A suit might break for example 5–3–3–2. Here the player with the long suit will have two more cards in it than anyone else and these are potential trick-winners.

Bidding

Before you can consider bidding you must evaluate your hand. You do this by estimating how many tricks you may hope to make. As we have seen, high cards, trump cards and low cards in long suits take tricks. These can be quantified to give a bidding value to the hand. The point-count system is now universally used for this purpose.

First, you give points to your high-card holding on the scale:

Ace: 4 points
King: 3 points
Queen: 2 points
Jack: 1 point

These values reflect, very roughly, the trick-taking chances of the individual cards.

On this count, the high-card value of the pack is 40 points, so if your hand totals 11 points or more you have a better-than-average holding of high cards.

Now for trumps. If you are short in a suit, you will be able to trump the opponents' high cards. So add points for distribution thus:

Void (no cards in suit):   3 points
Singleton (1 card in suit):   2 points
Doubleton (2 cards in suit):   1 point

You can also make allowances for long suits:

5–card suit: 1 point
6-card suit: 2 points
and so on.

With this system you make an opening assessment of your hand. During the bidding you may have to modify your estimate of its strength. If, for example, you have allowed 3 points for a void in what is clearly your partner's chosen suit, you have a bad 'fit' and you will have to scale down your ambitions accordingly.

Suppose though you pick up the hand in Figure 7 and your partner opens the bidding with One Spade. Your hand totals 10 high-trick points – an average holding; but with two good suits, a void and six of your partner's suit you are looking at almost certainly a game in spades (10 tricks, remember) with excellent chances of a slam.

The significance of distribution cannot be stressed enough; but remember that if you pick up an unbalanced hand then the chances are that other players will have unbalanced hands too. And that may mean that apparent trick-winning cards in your hand are worthless because there is no re-entry: your partner is void in the suit you control and you have no high card in your hand with which to take a trick and so gain the lead.

Bridge bidding systems proliferate but they share a common aim: to reach the best contract. Almost all systems combine natural with artifical bids. An artificial bid is used as a prompt or to signal information; a bid of Two Clubs for example may not necessarily mean that the caller has any clubs at all. However, it is forbidden to have a secret system. If you and your parnter wish to play a private system you are free to do so, but you must declare to your opponents the meaning of your calls. And it goes without saying that,

Figure 8

Figure 9

whatever system you employ, you should make your bid in an even voice and without undue hesitation – it is unethical to try and convey information to your partner improperly.

Most systems require that bidding starts low and advances in gradual steps. If you pick up a powerful suit and open the bidding with Four Hearts, then your partner has only a rough idea of the shape of your hand and because Four Hearts is a game call, he will be likely to pass. You may then find that you would have been better in another suit, or perhaps you missed a slam. By starting the bidding low and advancing slowly you can gather – and give – information to help both of you arrive at the right contract.

Forcing bids

One of the dangers of making exploratory bids at a low level when you have a strong hand is that your partner, who is not likely to have much anyway, will pass, leaving you in a bad or under-valued contract. The way round this is to make a forcing bid. A forcing bid is one which requires partner to respond regardless of his holding unless there is an intervening bid by the opposition, when partner may pass if he has nothing because you will get another opportunity to bid.

A Bidding System

No bidding system can cater for every eventuality, and the more artificial a system, the greater the possibility that you and your partner will find

yourselves in an absurd contract. Beginners are advised to bid as naturally as possible but this does not preclude the use of a sensible convention when occasion demands.

Always bid the full strength of your hand. The only exception is if you and partner are in a game contract when additional tricks will score the same whether bid or not.

Under-bidding is ill-rewarded. Overtricks are only entered 'above the line' remember, and they score very little. If you miss a game by bidding meekly then the opponents may take the game (or worse, the rubber) on the next hand, wiping off your part score.

Overbidding is sometimes justified as a sacrifice but only if the savings exceed the penalties. For example, if the opponents, who are vulnerable, call Four Hearts, an overcall of Four Spades would be sound if you forsee, say, eight tricks – if you are doubled but not vulnerable, then your loss would be only 300 points against 820 points saved. An advantage of an overbid in a situation like this is that it might tempt the opponents to overbid too because of the rewards at stake. If they reply Five Hearts, instead of doubling, then you have required them to make an extra trick – which they may not be able to make.

Below is an uncomplicated bidding system that will cater for most situations you are likely to meet. To be effective, your partner must of course play the same system. While the experts do not adhere rigidly to the systems

they play, it is not advisable for the beginner to induldge in what are called 'psychic bids'. Reflect that deviations from the agreed system are more likely to deceive your partner than anyone else!

It must be emphasized that bidding systems are a matter of taste (and more often of argument). There is nothing absolute about the system suggested here.

Opening Bid

With 12 points or less – pass

With 13 points or more – bid One of your best suit which must number at least four cards. Figure 8 shows an opening hand. Bid One Diamond. The hand in Figure 9 has a 13–point count but there is no good trump suit. This hand should be passed in the hope that partner will open the bidding.

When you hold a strong hand with uneven distribution that contains eight or more tricks (including the small cards of a long suit) bid Two of your best suit (other than clubs – see below) regardless, within reason, of the point count. This is forcing for one round. Figure 10 shows a hand which should be opened Two Hearts.

On those rare occasions when you pick up such a powerful hand that you can probably get game even if your partner has nothing, open Two Clubs. This is a convention which tells partner that he must not pass your bid until game is reached. Figure 11 shows one of these dream hands.

With 16-18 points – bid One No Trump with a well-distributed hand. This is the 'strong no trump'. (A 'weak no trump' with a point count of 13-15 can be used instead if preferred.) The hand in Figure 12 has a point count of 17 with a guard in every suit. This is a typical no-trump hand. The hand in Figure 13 also has 17 points but the distribution does not favour no trumps. Bid One Spade.

With 22–24 points – bid Two No Trumps. Remember not to credit short suits with points in no-trumps hands!

With a long suit (seven cards or more) and an Ace or equivalent in

Figure 10

Figure 11

another suit, you can open Three of your long suit regardless of point count. This is a 'pre-emptive' call and is basically weak. It challenges the opposition, who probably have the better high cards, to enter the auction at a dangerous level. A pre-emptive three call would be justified on the hand in Figure 14.

Responses

A response is a reply to partner's opening bid. Again, the point count strongly influences the call. Be careful not to count distribution points unless there seems a good possibility of a 'fit' with partner's hand.

Facing an opening bid of One in a suit, support with 6 points or more in high cards; otherwise pass. Three possibilities:

1) You have good support in partner's suit.

    6-9 points: raise bid to two
    10-12 points: raise bid to three

2) You have balanced hand.

    6-9 points: bid One No Trump
    10-12 points: bid Two No Trumps

3) You have a good suit.

6 points or better: bid your suit, if possible at One level. If you have at least 16 points yourself 'double jump' to indicate this. A double jump is to call at a one higher level than is necessary. For example, after One Heart, Two Spades would be a double jump.

Look at the hand in Figure 15. Partner opens One Diamond. Bid One Heart. Another example: partner opens One Spade and you hold the hand in Figure 16. Bid Three Clubs.

An opening bid of two in a suit (other than clubs) is forcing for one round:

1) With 7 points or less, bid Two No Trumps, which is a negative response.

2) With a fair hand, bid your best suit. If partner calls again you may pass unless he double jumps in a new suit when you must respond.

Remember an opening bid of Two Clubs is forcing to game so you cannot pass unless your right-hand opponent bids:

1) If you have no Ace or King, reply Two Diamonds (negative).

Figure 12

Figure 13

Figure 14

2) With some support and a balanced hand, bid Two No Trumps.

3) With some support and a long suit, bid the suit.

Facing an opening bid of One No Trump, pass if your cards are distributed evenly and you have seven high-card points or less; bid Two No Trumps with 8 or 9 points and Three No Trumps above that.

116

Figure 15

Figure 16

With uneven distribution and with seven high-card points or more, bid your long suit. With the hand in Figure 17, bid Three No Trumps in response to an opening One No Trump.

Facing an opening bid of Two No Trumps, bid Three No Trumps with four points or more, but if suit distribution is uneven, bid three of your longest suit.

Facing an opening bid of three in a suit, pass unless you have an exceptional hand which might yield game. High cards are essential: a long suit holding is likely to be worthless because it is liable to negate partner's long suit.

Blackwood Convention

The Blackwood convention is a useful vehicle for exploring slam opportunities. It works like this. Where a partnership believes that a slam may be

Figure 17

possible, one player, usually the stronger hand, calls Four No Trumps. This is an artificial forcing call which asks partner simply how many Aces he has. The reply is Five Clubs (no Aces or four

Aces), Five Diamonds (one Ace), Five Hearts (two Aces) etc. Now first caller can ask for Kings in the same way by calling Five No Trumps though this commits him to a small slam at least. Six Clubs means no King, Six Diamonds one King, and so on. Having established partner's holdings of Aces (and Kings also if desired) caller will sign off with his chosen contract.

Rebids

After the opening bid and response, the search is on for the right contract. Partner's call will indicate his point count, and if you add this to yours you will get an idea of the hand's potential.

With less than 20 points, the opponents will have the better high cards and the chances are that you will be defending. With a total of 21-25 points between you, anticipate no more than a

part score. With 26-32 points, a game call is on. A small slam usually needs 33-36 points and a grand slam 37-40.

If you make a part score towards game, then clearly you will need only

another part score to win the game. This puts pressure on the opponents who may resort to adventurous bidding to stop you getting the game and incur penalties as a result.

If you see no prospect of a game, then a safe call is to be preferred to a risky one. For example, if One No Trump looks solid but Three No Trumps impossible, it is better to stay at the one level than risk Two No Trumps.

Major and Minor suits

A feature of tournament Bridge is the emphasis placed on no trumps and the major suits (spades and hearts) at the expense of the minor suits (diamonds and clubs). This is largely on account of their scoring values. A call of one is quite easy to make as a rule, but a call of two is appreciably harder. Yet One No Trump earns as many points as Two Diamonds or Two Clubs. The most popular game contracts are Three No Trumps and Four Spades or Hearts. By contrast, a game call in a minor suit is rare – or at least it is rarely made – for to take all but two of the tricks in a hand is quite an achievement.

Suit ranking is also important. If your partnership is bidding for a contract in hearts and your opponents are similarly promoting diamonds, they will always have to bid at a higher level than you since hearts outrank diamonds.

Improving your Bridge

This article is no more than the briefest of introductions to a game that for some people is almost a way of life. It has been impossible to investigate in any depth the subtleties of bidding and card play that make Bridge such a fascinating game. Fortunately, there is a huge range of books on every aspect of the game, and most big towns have Bridge clubs where the beginner is welcome.

Meanwhile a big step forward can be made by memorising cards played. Start by counting trumps!

BLACK MARIA

Black Maria is probably the best English three-player card game. The rules are very variable, and so is the name. Some of the commoner alternative names are Hearts, Chase the Lady and Slippery Anne.

A STANDARD 52-CARD PACK is used for Black Maria, with the ♣ 2 removed so that the number of cards divides by three. Seventeen cards each are dealt out (all of them) and the game is of the 'trick-taking' type. The three players each play as individuals, the object being to avoid capturing tricks containing certain cards.

The dealer for the first hand is chosen at random, in later hands the deal passes round to the left. The deal is clockwise, one card at a time. After sorting their hands, each player selects three cards and passes them, face down, to the player on his right, then takes the three cards from the player on his left into his hand. The player on dealer's left then leads to the first trick.

The Play

Black Maria is a 'trick-taking' game without trumps. Play proceeds in a series of tricks in each of which one player leads a card, and the other two, in turn clockwise round the table, 'follow'. The player leading may choose any card he likes, but the others are obliged to follow with cards of the same suit if they can. The highest card of the suit led wins the trick, Aces being the highest cards, then King, Queen, Jack and so on down to 2. The player who wins each trick keeps the three cards it contains and leads to the next trick.

Penalty Cards

At the end of the hand, each player sorts through the tricks he has taken and adds up the penalty cards they contain (all scores are negative). The penalty cards are:

Each Heart	1 point
Ace of Spades	7 points
King of Spades	10 points
Queen of Spades	13 points
Total	43 points

As an exception, if one player takes all of the penalty cards (not necessarily all of the tricks) he is said to have "jumped over the moon" and scores plus 50 points.

Strategy

The top three spades are obviously the most important cards, since they have the biggest penalties attached to them. However the players holding these cards are not necessarily at a disadvantage. It is often easy to wait until one of the other players leads a suit of which you are void, and then play your high spades.

The danger of having the top spades is that one of the other players will start leading low spades. There are ten low spades, and so one of the three players is bound to have at least four of them. If you yourself have as many as four low spades, your high ones are almost completely safe. With only three, you are in some danger, though you can normally get away with it if you hold the Jack. The advantage of the Jack is that it enables you to win the trick, and change to another suit. It may be some time before the opponent leading spades gets the lead back.

If you do get caught with a high spade when one of your opponents is leading out the low ones, it may be necessary to take your punishment early – if you get reduced to just the ♠ K then the opponent can lead the ♠ Q (if he has been counting carefully) and give you both cards.

The hearts are penalty cards, but the penalty is not so big as long as both of your opponents are following suit – if you have any high hearts it is usually better to play them early.

The ♥ 2 is precious, and should normally be kept until last. As an example, suppose that the hand is down to the last three tricks, and that you hold the ♥ A, ♥ 2 and ♣ A, one of your opponents is out of hearts and the other opponent holds the ♥ 3, ♥ 4 and ♠ Q. You are on lead, and it is vital that you

lead the ♥ A first, then when you play the ♥ 2 your opponent is left leading the ♠ Q last. If you had panicked and played the ♥ 2 first, your opponent could give you the lead back, and you would be forced to lead the ♣ A, collecting the ♠ Q.

Clubs and diamonds may appear to be similar, but in practice the one card missing from the club suit seems to make it much commoner for players to be able to create voids in clubs than in diamonds.

These are the suits where the real damage is usually done. The typical sequence of events is for the first two or three tricks to be straightforward, and then for one of the players to run out of the suit and throw on the ♠ Q. The important thing is not to win the trick with the ♠ Q in it, and if you hold the lowest card of the suit you should keep it for that trick. It is not always possible to guess which trick that will be, so the player holding the bottom card will not normally want to lead the suit. It is a sure sign of an inexperienced player to lead the ♦ 2, say, to the first trick. It is often possible to guess how a suit is distributed by using information from the cards passed on at the beginning, and it is often good to play the cards which you were passed as early as possible, so as to take away the information your left-hand opponent has about your hand.

It is when playing clubs and diamonds that the advantages of holding the top spades become apparent. If you hold all the top spades yourself, then there is obviously no danger that your opponents will throw them on your club tricks, so it becomes possible to play quite recklessly in clubs and diamonds, and get rid of your embarrassing high cards in those suits cheaply early on.

When passing on at the beginning, the most usual thing to do is to try to create a void suit in clubs or diamonds. If you have few low spades it may be necessary to pass on the high ones – and if you have a lot of low spades, especially if they include the Jack, it is possible to pass on the high ones intending to lead spades whenever possible. Never

Some old French playing cards:
top, the eight of hearts; left, the
seven of clubs; right, the three
of hearts.

pass on low spades – not only will this
weaken your hand but it will also help
your right-hand opponent. Passing on
hearts is a bit risky since it may enable
your right-hand opponent to jump over
the moon. Normally it is bad to pass on
high hearts unless you keep either the
Ace of King as a protection. An

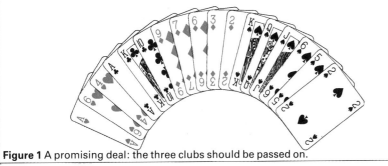

Figure 1 A promising deal: the three clubs should be passed on.

example hand is given in Figure 1.

Jumping over the moon is surprisingly easy – the problem is the heart
suit. It is necessary to have very few
hearts, or very high ones. The commonest way is to have an extremely long
suit in either clubs of diamonds, and to
get rid of all your other cards early on
while nobody is watching. An amusing
tactic for escaping from a very weak
position is to lead the ♥ A early on and
then follow with the ♥ J – one of your
opponents is very likely to beat this for
fear that you are going for the lot, and

you will have disposed of two embarrassing cards very cheaply.

Variations in the rules

The exact details of which cards incur
penalties, and what the penalties are,
whether "jumping over the moon"
counts as a good thing to do, and several
of the details of passing on the three
cards at the beginning, all vary from
one group of players to another. Some
of the main variations are discussed
here, with brief comments on their effect on the game.
1) The penalties for capturing hearts are
often much larger than the one point
each given here. In the extreme, each
heart is worth its pip value (i.e. 6 points
for the 6, 13 for the King etc.) This
makes the high spades relatively unimportant and also means that a player
holding a lot of the high hearts is

completely helpless. In this version it is
sometimes made illegal to lead hearts
until you have nothing else. The result
of these changes is a game with more
luck and less skill, which some people
prefer.
2) Some players forbid the passing on of
any of the top three spades, but this rule
seems to be based on the misunder-
standing that they are bad cards to hold
– it is usually unskilful to pass high
spades on, and this rule is not recommended.
3) A player holding the ♠ Q is sometimes forced to play it the first time he is
unable to follow suit. The reason for
this rule is to prevent deliberately vin-
dictive play (most often the player
hanging on to the Queen is doing so in
order to give it to his least favourite
opponent) and may be a good idea in
some company.
4) If the rule about "jumping over the
moon" is omitted, then some interesting features of the early part of the
game disappear – most of these features
depend on the player with a very good
hand being slightly worried that he
ought to try to take at least one penalty
card, while the player with a hopeless
hand tries to persuade the others that he
is trying to jump over the moon, so that
they make "sacrifices" to stop him
doing so.

CANASTA

Canasta was invented in South America during the early part of this century, and spread rapidly round the world soon after the Second World War. Recently it has declined somewhat in popularity, but it remains an entertaining game, and is easy to learn. It can be played by two, three or four players, though the three-player version is not very satisfactory.

TWO STANDARD PACKS are used, together with four Jokers, making 108 cards in all. Canasta is a "draw and discard" game, like Gin Rummy and Mah Jong – each player in turn draws a new card from the pack, and then discards one card, trying to form his hand into matching sets while doing so. It is sometimes possible, instead of drawing a new card from the pack, to capture the entire discard pile, and much of the skill in the game goes towards manoeuvring so as to be able to do this.

Combinations

In order to score, a combination of cards must be laid face up on the table. The only combinations allowed are sets of cards of the same rank – there are no sequences in Canasta. A combination must contain at least three cards. Jokers may be used to substitute for "plain" cards, and 2s may also be used like Jokers in this way. We refer to 2s and Jokers collectively as "wild cards". However a set may never contain more than three wild cards, and the plain cards must always outnumber the wild cards in one set.

A set of seven or more cards is called a canasta, and scores a large bonus. "Natural" canastas (containing no wild cards) score more than "mixed" ones. Examples of both forms are shown in Figure 1.

The 3s are covered by special rules. Black 3s may not normally be used for anything constructive – but are nevertheless good cards to hold – they are discussed later. Red 3s are bonus cards – a player holding one should immediately lay it face up in front of him and draw another card to replace it.

The score

When the game ends, each side adds up the value of their cards face up on the

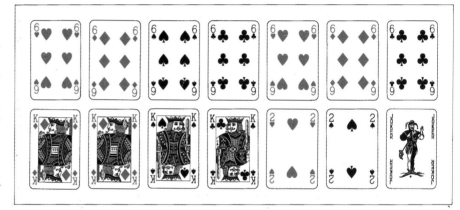

Figure 1 A natural canasta (this one worth 535 points) and a mixed canasta (worth 430).

table, then subtracts the value of any cards remaining in their hand. Scores are as follows:

Each 7, 6, 5, 4, or black 3	5 points
Each King, Queen, Jack, 10, 9, or 8	10 points
Each Ace	20 points
Each 2	20 points
Each Joker	50 points
Each red 3	100 points
All four red 3s	800 points
Each mixed canasta	300 points
Each natural canasta	500 points
Going out	100 points
Going out "concealed"	200 points

The object of the game is to be the first to 5000 points.

Capturing the discard pile

If a player is able to form a legal combination including the top card (that most recently discarded) of the discard pile, then he may do so instead of drawing a new card from the pack, and having done so he takes the remain-

der of the discard pile into his hand. The combination may involve the last discard, cards in the player's hand and combinations previously played on the table by him, but may not involve any of the previous discards. Having made his capture, and picked up the discard pile, the player may put down any further cards he wishes – these may include some of the cards he just picked up – and then discards to complete his turn. There is no restriction on discard-ing captured cards immediately.

It is illegal to make a capture using a wild card unless the player already has a wild card on the table before the start of his turn – otherwise the last discard must be matched with at least two plain cards of the same rank.

If a black 3 is discarded, it is always illegal for the next player to capture the pile – the main function of black 3s in the game is to act as safe discards.

If a wild card is discarded, then the pile is said to be "frozen". It is illegal for the next player to capture the pile, as with black 3s, but there are two additional restrictions which continue to apply until the pile is next captured: it becomes illegal to combine the top discard with cards already played on the table – the combination must be with cards from the hand; and it becomes illegal to capture the pile using a wild card, even if a wild card has already been used.

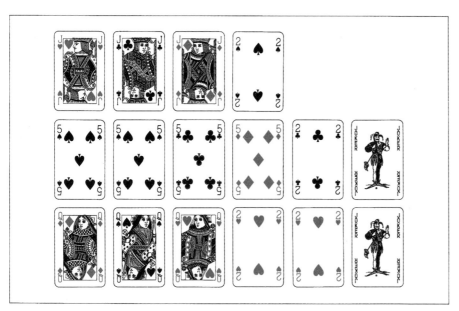

Figure 2 Sets satisfying the requirements of a first combination, worth 50, 90, and 120 points.

The first combination

The first time a player puts scoring cards on the table, they must add up to at least a minimum value, which depends on how close that player's side is to the target of 5000 points. This total may be achieved using several combinations, for example a total of 50 can be achieved with a set of three 5s (15) and a set of two Kings with a 2 (40). If (as usually happens) the first scoring cards are played while capturing the discard pile, this total must be achieved using only the last discard and cards in the player's hand.

The requirements depend on the side's score as follows:

Negative score	No restriction
0 – 1495	50 points required
1500 – 2995	90
3000 – 4995	120

This requirement is quite independent of any red 3s laid down. Examples of sets giving the points required are shown in Figure 2.

The deal

If there are four players, each receives 11 cards. With three players each gets 13 cards, and two players get 15 cards each. Cards are dealt one at a time, clockwise round the table starting on dealer's left. The top card of the remaining pack is then turned over to start the discard pile, and the player on dealer's left plays first. Before that, however, all the players holding red 3s put them down and draw replacement cards. The deal moves round to the left

in subsequent hands.

If the card turned over by the dealer is a Joker, a 2 or a red 3, then he turns another card to cover it, and the pack is frozen (so that wild cards and cards on the table may not be used to capture it).

Four players

With two or three players, each plays individually, but four players play as two pairs of partners. Partners sit opposite each other. In this case partners keep their scoring cards separately, and they must meet the requirements to score a certain number of points with their first combinations and to make one canasta before going out separately, but they can add cards to each other's combinations.

The end of the game comes when both partners on one side have gone out (or when the pack runs out). It is normally good play for the two partners to go out in immediate succession, and in order to be able to achieve this it is legal to say "Shall I go out partner?" before discarding. If your partner says "Yes" then you are obliged to go out.

Some special cases

It is normally illegal to put down a set of black 3s, but this may be done by a player on the turn in which he goes out. A set of black 3s may never contain any wild cards.

If the last card in the pack is a red 3, then the player drawing it does not discard on that turn.

Wild cards may be added to com-

pleted canastas, provided that they do not break the law that no more than three wild cards should appear in one combination. If wild cards are added to a natural canasta, though, it becomes a mixed canasta and only scores 300 points (it may be necessary to do this in order to go out).

The three of spades in an old French pack.

Strategy

In the early part of the game, the main objective is to be the first to capture the discard pile. Having done this, a player can often continue capturing the pile for the rest of the hand – each time he picks up he recycles the safe discards he has already used.

When a player has succeeded in making the first capture, and has the chance to go out, it is often good not to do so, but to keep going and make a really huge score. If, on the other hand, his opponent has made the first capture, he will often be stuck simply feeding him cards, and it is usually best to try to go out as soon as possible. Going out is a defensive tactic.

Black 3s should not be discarded too early. Capturing a pile of three of four cards is not very devastating, and it is usually better to hang on to black 3s until the pile gets bigger and a safe discard is really needed.

121

CASINO

Casino is an old Italian game, and probably derives its name from the word for a gambling house. It has often been mis-spelt as 'Cassino'.

CASINO IS FOR TWO PLAYERS, although it can be played by three or four (as described later). The full pack of 52 cards is used. Aces count as one, court cards (Kings, Queens, and Jacks) have no numerical value, and other cards have their pip value.

Cards are cut for dealer – lower card deals throughout the game. In the first deal, dealer gives two cards to his opponent, face down, two to the table, face up, then two to himself, face down. This is repeated, so that each player begins the play with a hand of four cards, and there are four cards in a layout in the centre of the table.

These hands are played, then dealer gives each player four more cards, two at a time, as before. When these hands are played, the process is repeated, and so on until the pack is exhausted. There are thus six deals in the game, and the dealer must announce the last one. If he fails to do so, non-dealer may cancel it or play it out at his discretion.

The object and the play

The object is to capture cards from the layout, and by doing so to score points.

Each player in turn, beginning with the non-dealer, plays a card until both players have exhausted their four cards.

A player has a choice of four plays:
1. *Pairing* A card from hand can be used to capture a card or cards of the same rank from the table, e.g. if player holds an 8, he may use it to take any 8s in the layout, placing the 8s from hand and table face down before him as a 'trick'. Court cards are captured in this way, e.g. a Jack can be paired with another Jack or Jacks. This is the only way court cards can be captured. Other cards can be captured in other ways.
2) *Combining* A card from hand can be used to capture two or more cards from the table if its pip total equals the added pip totals of the cards from the table. For example, an 8 can capture two 4s, a 5 and a 3, or a 6 and two Aces. As with

pairing, a player can take up more than one combination with the same card. For example, if the layout contains 3, 3, 4, 2, a player can take all four cards with a 6.

3) *Building* A player may play a card from hand to the layout to make up a total that he is in a position to capture with another card in his hand on the next round. For example, if there is a 3 in the layout, a player holding a 6 and a 9 may play the 6 to the layout, saying 'building 9s'. On his next turn he may take the 3 and 6 with his 9, if his opponent has not forestalled him.

A player cannot make a build unless he holds in his hand a card of the rank to capture it.

Nevertheless, he need not capture it on his next turn. He may prefer to capture another card with a pair first, or if his opponent makes a build which he can capture, he may prefer to take his opponent's build first, leaving his own for his next turn.

He can also create a multiple build. For example, a player adding a 6 to a 3 to build 9, as described above, may build another 9 on his next turn by adding, for example, an Ace from hand

to an 8 in the layout. On his following turn, he can play his 9 to capture both builds.

It is also possible to make a multiple build on 'single' cards. For example a player holding two 7s and finding a 7 in the layout, may add one 7 to that on the table, saying 'building 7s' and capture

both on his next turn with his second 7. Similarly, if there were a 4 and 3 in the layout, a player with two 7s can add his first 7 to the layout saying 'building 7s' and on his next turn capture his 7 and the 4 and 3 with the second 7.

Another alternative is to increase the builds.

To keep to the same example of a player building a 6 on a 3 to make a build of 9, if he also holds an Ace and a 10, he can play the Ace to the build saying 'building 10s' with the object of taking all three cards with his 10 on his next turn. Builds cannot be increased beyond a count of 10, of course, since the highest ranked card is 10 and a player making a build must have a card of the rank to capture it.

A player may increase a build of his own or his opponent. It is clearly a good play to increase an opponent's build, since he not only makes at least three cards available for capture by himself, but deprives opponent of capturing the build.

It is not allowed to increase a multiple build. For example, if a 5 is paired with a 2, and a 4 with a 3 by a player building 7s, it is not possible to add an Ace to one of these pairs to build 8s.

Note that if a 3 is added to another 3 by a player saying 'building 3s', this is a multiple build and cannot be increased, whereas if the player had said 'building

Figure 1 Hands for non-dealer (left) and dealer (right) with the layout centre.

6s', then any card lower than a 4 could be added to increase the build.

Note also that a build can only be increased by a card from hand, not from table. It follows that whenever a player makes a build or increases a build his opponent has one turn in which to capture or increase the build himself.

'A Game of Cards', painted by Judith Leyster in the 17th century (Musée des Beaux Arts, Rouen).

the layout varies during a game, and occasionally is nil, when a player on his turn has no choice but to trail.

General

The cards captured by a player together with the capturing card, are placed face down in front of the player. If on his turn a player takes all the cards on the table he registers a 'sweep'. He records this by turning one of his captured cards face up, so that at the end of the game he knows how many sweeps he made.

After the last card is played, any cards remaining on the table go to the player who last made a capture, but this is not regarded as a sweep.

Scoring

The object is to capture as many cards as possible, particularly those of scoring value. The scoring table is as follows:
Cards (for capturing the majority of the 52 cards): 3 points
Spades (for capturing the majority of the 13 spades): 1 point
Big casino (for capturing the ♦ 10): 2 points
Little casino (for capturing the ♠ 2): 1 point
Aces (for capturing an Ace): 1 point for each
There is no score for cards if each player captures 26.

This makes a total of 11 points, to which is added one point for each sweep.

Each deal can be regarded as a separate game, or players may prefer to add the points of two deals, so that each may deal once.

While most irregularities, such as a player attempting to capture cards illegally, can be corrected at the table by opponent pointing them out, it might happen that a player makes a build and is later found not to possess a card to capture it. In such a case the offender must forfeit that particular game.

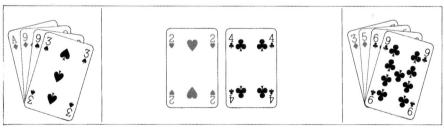

Figure 2

A player making or increasing a build that is not taken or increased by his opponent must have a card to capture the build, and he is not allowed to 'trail' while that build remains in the layout and the card remains unplayed.

4) *Trailing* A player who on his turn cannot pair, combine or build, as described above, must trail, that is he must play a card from his hand face up to the table layout. It is permissible to trail even if a player can pair, combine or build, unless he has a build in the layout, as mentioned earlier. Trailing is the way in which the cards in the layout are replenished. The number of cards in

123

Example hand

Figure 1 shows hands for non-dealer and dealer, and the table layout at the beginning of a game.

The game might proceed as follows:

1) Non-dealer pairs his ♦ K with ♥ K and places both cards face down before him.

2) Dealer captures both Queens from the layout with his ♦ Q, placing all three cards face down before him.

3) Non-dealer captures the ♥ 7 with his ♣ 7. As he has achieved a sweep, he puts one of these cards face up before him and adds the other face down to his pile.

4) Dealer trails his ♦ 6 to the table.

5) Non-dealer trails his ♥ 2 to the table.

6) Dealer can capture the ♥ 2 with his ♠ 2, but instead places his ♠ 2 on ♦ 6 and says 'building 8s'.

7) Non-dealer is forced to trail his ♣ 4 to the table.

8) Dealer plays his ♦ 8, capturing ♦ 6 and ♠ 2.

This leaves ♥ 2 and ♣ 4 on the layout, and dealer deals a second hand to both players. The new hands and layout are shown in Figure 2.

9) Non-dealer trails ♠ 3. He intends on his next turn to build 9s.

10) Alas for non-dealer, dealer has ♣ 9, which he plays to clear the table and score a sweep.

11) Non-dealer trails ♦ 9.

12) Dealer trails ♦ 3.

13) Non-dealer pairs ♠ 9 with ♦ 9, making the capture.

14) Dealer trails ♦ 5.

15) Non-dealer is forced to trail ♦ A.

16) Dealer plays ♣ 6, capturing ♦ A and ♦ 5.

This leaves only one card, the ♦ 3, on the table. Dealer deals a third hand to each player, and so on.

Dealer is doing well in this particular deal. He had captured 13 cards to non-dealer's six. He has three spades to non-dealer's one. He has already captured little casino and he has the only Ace to appear so far. Each player has one sweep.

Strategy

Playing casino well is a question of memorizing the cards played, so that the ranks of the cards still to come are known. It is necessary to be aware of the situation in the spade suit and to build and pair in combinations including spades. An Ace or casino held in the hand should be played carefully. Non-dealer in particular should keep it for the final trail if he cannot pair or build with it, giving dealer only one chance to capture it before he himself has a further four cards with which to capture it. When making a choice of cards to trail a player should attempt to trail a card giving him possibilities of building or capturing on a later turn.

Casino is an easy game to play and is sometimes regarded as a children's game, but it is less easy to play well and affords plenty of opportunities for judgement.

Three-handed Casino

As in two-handed Casino each player receives four cards per hand. There are four hands in each deal instead of six. The dealer remains the same throughout the game, and the player to the left of dealer (eldest) always plays first and dealer last. No points are won in the cards or spades categories if two players tie with the most cards. Eldest and dealer have an advantage over the other player, and for game it is best to total the points of three games with the deal rotating clockwise, so that each player occupies each position once.

Partnership Casino

In partnership casino for four players, partners sit opposite each other. Their captures are combined, so that each side scores as for the two-handed game. Each player must observe the rules of the two-handed game, however. For example, if one player is building 8s, his partner cannot build an 8 for him without holding an 8 himself in his hand.

Game could be decided by one deal, or by the higher total of points after four deals, with the deal rotating clockwise, thus allowing each of the four players to occupy each position at the table once.

Royal Casino

Royal Casino is a variant which is generally regarded as superior to the parent game. The only difference is that the court cards, rather than having no numerical value, are given the following values: Jack 11, Queen 12 and King 13. Additionally the Ace may be counted as one or 14 at the discretion of the player. Thus the court cards can be used in building as the others, for example a 6, 4 and 3 might be captured with a Queen.

Spade Casino

Spade Casino brings a variation to the scoring, applicable to all variants given above, by which instead of there being one point for capturing the majority of spades, each spade captured counts as one point, except Ace, Jack and 2 (little casino), which are worth two points each.

Draw Casino

Draw Casino is a variation in dealing applicable to all variants given above. After the first deal of four cards each, and four cards to the table, the remaining cards are placed face down in the centre of the table to form a stock. Thereafter, each time a player plays a card, he draws a replacement from the top of the stock pile, so that his hand remains constantly at four cards until the stock is exhausted, when each player plays his last four cards in the usual manner.

CRIBBAGE

Cribbage is at least 300 years old yet remains one of the best two-hand card games. It has long been a favourite of the English pub but was once fashionable in high society.

THERE ARE TWO popular versions, the classic five-card cribbage still widely played in Britain, and modern six-card cribbage favoured in the U.S.A. Seven-card cribbage is rarely played, and there are sundry other variants, including adaptations for three and four players.

There is little to choose between the five and six-card versions which are very similar anyway, but the five-card version is simpler if only because there is one less card to consider, and is therefore recommended to the beginner. Both versions, which are highly skilful if played intelligently, are given here.

Five-card cribbage

Cribbage is a game of scoring combinations with the object of being the first to reach the agreed game total. This is 61 for the two-player game, which will take on average half-a-dozen hands. Points are notched as they are earned, not at the end of each hand as in most games.

Play

Cut for deal, lower card winning; thereafter deal alternates. Dealer shuffles and then distributes the cards, one at a time face down, first to elder (or pone, his opponent) and then to himself and so on alternately until each player has five.

The players now examine their hands and select two cards which they contribute face down to form the 'crib' or 'cradle'. The crib belongs to the dealer and elder at once scores three points 'for last', but in the first hand of a game only, to compensate.

Now elder cuts and dealer turns over the top card of the lower packet. This is the 'starter'. If the card is a jack, the dealer at once scores two 'for his heels'. (Cribbage, as you will have noticed, is rich in jargon, a sure sign of a game's popularity.) The card remains face up;

the remainder of the pack is not used.

A hand is divided into two phases, the 'play' and the 'show'. In the play the two hands are integrated but they are valued, with the crib, independently in the show. Scoring is similar in both phases.

During the play there are two types of scoring combinations: two or more cards of the same rank, and three or more cards in sequence regardless of suit.

Aces are low and count one, court cards count 10 and other cards their pip value. Suits are not ranked. Here are the scoring combinations:
Pair (two cards of the same rank): 2 points
Pair royal (or triplet) (three cards of the same rank): 6 points
Double pair royal (four cards of the same rank): 12 points
Run (or sequence) (three or more cards in sequence, regardless of suit): 1 point for each card in run.

Notice that 'tenths' (court cards and 10s), although counting the same, are of different ranks: for example, QJ is not classed as a pair.

Elder starts the play by selecting one of his three cards and placing it face up in front of him on the table, at the same time announcing its value. For example, if a King is played elder would call 'Ten'. Dealer then plays a card similarly and announces the cumulative total of the two cards. If the dealer's card matches elder's card in rank, dealer scores two for a pair. Turns continue to alternate, each player announcing the cumulative value of the combined cards played to that stage and also announcing any score he makes with his play.

If either player makes the total 15 exactly he scores two points 'for fifteen'. The total may not exceed 31. If a player is unable to put down a card without exceeding 31, he calls 'Go' or knocks, and his opponent plays again if he can. The last player to put down a

card scores one point 'for go' or two points if his card brings the total to 31 exactly.

Runs do not have to be played in sequence to score: thus, 3,5,4 is a run and scores three points. The highest number of cards possible in a sequence is 7 to Ace – seven points.

Every time a card is played that completes a scoring combination, the player notches the appropriate number of points. This is true even if it extends a previous scoring combination. Thus in the run in the above example, the player who put down the 4 scores three points and if the second player has a 2 or a 6 he can now play it to score 4 points.

Similarly, the player who adds a third card of the same rank to a scored pair scores for a pair royal, and if his opponent comes out with the fourth card of the same rank, he notches 12 points for a double pair royal – a rare occurence, as you may imagine. Notice that it is possible for lower runs not to be scored: for example, if pip cards were played in the sequence 3,4,7,5,6 only a five-card run could be scored.

The play ends when all six cards have been played or neither player can put down a card without exceeding 31.

Show

Both players now pick up and display their hands for the show. Points are scored for combinations as in play (but not for 31) except that the starter is now considered as belonging to both hands so the players have in effect four cards each during the show.

Elder scores his hand first. If either player has the Jack of the starter suit he scores one point 'for his nob' (in some circles this is scored during the play if the card is exposed). Every combination of cards (two or more) that totals 15 scores two points 'for fifteen'.

There is an additional combination that only scores in the show: the flush. A flush is a hand in which the cards are all of one suit, regardless of rank. This scores three points, or four points if the starter is of the same suit. Notice that three cards of the same suit, of which

one is the starter, do not score.

Combinations are scored in every possible way, but only the highest combination can be scored. For example, a pair royal cannot also be scored as three pairs nor can a run of four be scored as two runs of three. The thing to remember here is that each scoring combination must contain at least one different card from those used in any other single scoring combination. Four show hands with their scoring values are illustrated in Figure 1.

When dealer has scored his hand, he picks up the crib and scores it similarly, including the starter to make a five-card hand. The only difference in scoring for the crib is that three and four-card flushes do not count. A five-card flush scores five points.

Scoring

The score is kept on a cribbage board, usually a flat oblong piece of wood with 60 small holes in two rows of 30, split into groups of 10 (5×2) for easy counting, on each side and an additional hole (the 'game hole') in the middle at either end. The centre of the board, which is not used, is often decorated. A cribbage board is illustrated in Figure 2.

Pegs or matchsticks are used as markers. Where pegs are used, these are usually in contrasting colours (red and white are common). Each hole counts one point. In a 61-point game the winner's peg travels the length of the outer row of holes, down the inner row and into the game hole at the end.

However, it is customary for each player to use not one but two pegs to guard against inaccuracies. This is how they are used:

1) On the first score, one peg is moved

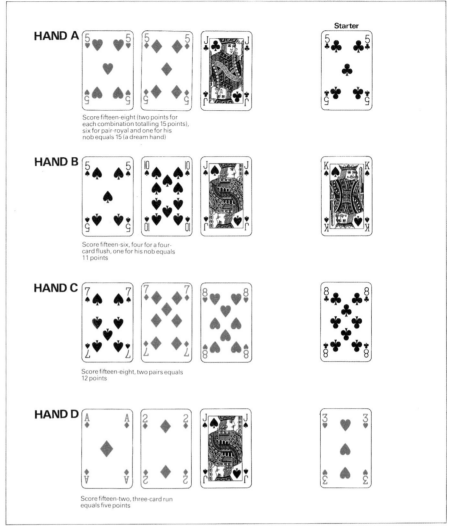

HAND A Score fifteen-eight (two points for each combination totalling 15 points), six for pair-royal and one for his nob equals 15 (a dream hand)

HAND B Score fifteen-six, four for a four-card flush, one for his nob equals 11 points

HAND C Score fifteen-eight, two pairs equals 12 points

HAND D Score fifteen-two, three-card run equals five points

Figure 1 Four show hands scored in five-card cribbage.

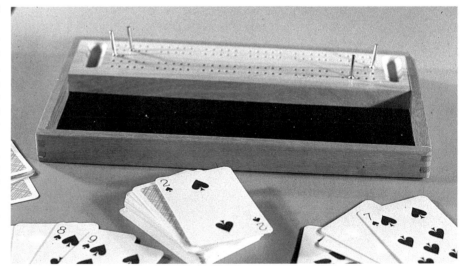

Figure 2 A cribbage board (right). Below left: scoring relating to Figure 3. Below right: scoring relating to Figure 5.

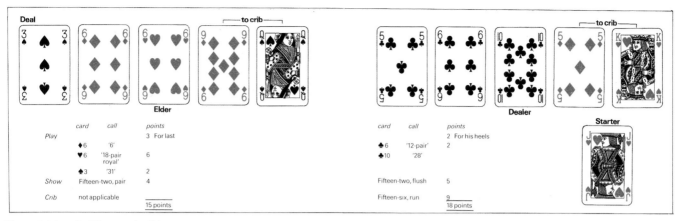

	card	call	points
Play			3 For last
	♦6	'6'	
	♥6	'18-pair royal'	6
	♠3	'31'	2
Show	Fifteen-two, pair		4
Crib	not applicable		
			15 points

card	call	points
		2 For his heels
♣6	'12-pair'	2
♣10	'28'	
Fifteen-two, flush		5
Fifteen-six, run		9
		18 points

Figure 3 A hand of five-card cribbage.

the appropriate number of holes along the outer line nearest the player and away from his game hole.

2) On the player's second score, the other peg is advanced the number of points earned beyond the first peg.

3) Thereafter, the peg behind is moved the appropriate number of holes beyond the lead peg. Thus it is the lead peg that records the score.

The idea is that the unmoved peg acts as back marker when the scoring peg is lifted. If only one peg were used it could often happen that the player, perhaps temporarily distracted, forgets which hole he lifted it from.

Of course, it is not essential to use a cribbage board. The score can be kept on a sheet of paper though this is rather tedious.

Example hand

A hand of five-card cribbage, duly scored, is given in Figure 3.

Six-card cribbage

This is played in much the same way as five-card cribbage, game normally being 121 up (i.e. twice round the board).

The deal is six cards each and again

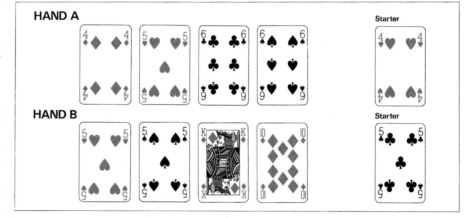

Figure 4 Two show hands scored in six-card cribbage.

both players contribute two cards to the crib, but elder does not score three for last. Elder cuts the pack and dealer turns up the starter, scoring two points for his heels if appropriate, as in five-card cribbage.

The only difference in the play concerns the 31 limit. As in the five-card game, one player scores a point for go or last, or two points for reaching 31 exactly. The cards played are then turned down and a new play up to 31 is started with the remainder, again one point being scored for go, and two

points for finishing on 31 exactly. A card must always be played if possible; thus if elder reaches 27 and dealer knocks, elder, holding a deuce, must play it and cannot knock in order to carry the card forward to the second play. Cards used in the first play cannot be used or included in scoring combinations in the second.

The show is scored in the same manner as the five-card game except that the lowest flush is four cards (complete hand) for four points, or with the starter for five points. Paralleling

Figure 5 A hand of six-card cribbage.

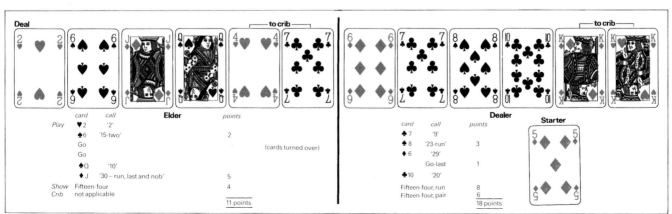

	card	call	Elder points
Play	♥2	'2'	
	♣6	'15-two'	2
	Go		
	Go		(cards turned over)
	♠Q	'10'	
	♦J	'30 – run, last and nob'	5
Show	Fifteen-four		4
Crib	not applicable		
			11 points

card	call	Dealer points
♣7	'9'	
♠8	'23-run'	3
♦6	'29'	
	Go-last	1
Fifteen-four, run		8
Fifteen-four, pair		6
		18 points

A 19th century painting by F.D. Hardy entitled 'A Mis-deal' (Wolverhampton Art Gallery).

the five-card game, a flush can only be scored in the crib if all five cards are of the same suit.

Two hands of six-card cribbage with their scoring values are shown in Figure 4.

Naturally, higher scores are to be expected in six-card cribbage. A complete hand with scoring is illustrated in Figure 5.

Muggins

This little refinement, which is optional and should therefore be agreed before play begins, adds to the fun of the game but is a bit harsh on the careless. If a player overlooks a score to which he is entitled his opponent may call 'Muggins' and peg the score for himself.

Lurching

The lurch is another option. In the six-card game, if one player is home before the other has gone half way round, the winner scores an extra game.

Strategy

Five-card cribbage

The first important decisions concern the discard to the crib. The players are in different positions. Elder's task is the easier; he will want to retain cards with

scoring potential both in the play and the show whereas poor cards he will gratefully contribute to the crib in order to minimise dealer's score with the hand. Dealer is differently placed, since both hands are ultimately his. Because the crib contains an extra card it holds more opportunities for scoring combinations. For this reason, dealer will be torn between retaining good cards in hand and allocating them to the crib.

What are good and bad cards in this context? The 5s are particularly useful since there are 16 'tenths' in the pack and the chances of putting together scoring combinations (fifteens) are excellent. For this reason, a 5 is the worst possible lead!

Low cards are useful in hand since they are of value in approaching 31. A discard by dealer to the crib of two cards in sequence – for example, 7 and 8 – is sound strategy, since if elder subscribes one of these, or a touching value (here a 6 or 9) dealer will score for a pair or run. Poor cards from elder's point of view and therefore natural choices to pass to the crib, are 9s and Kings, the latter because a run can only

be made one way – in descending order of rank, as Ace is low.

A sound lead for elder is a card below a 5 (since the addition of a tenth will not allow dealer to score for fifteen) or one of a pair, since if dealer then scores a pair, elder notches a pair royal.

Late in a game, it is important to remember that elder scores his show before dealer so that if scores are fairly level then elder has the better chance of reaching 61 first.

Six-card cribbage

Here the additional factor is the extra play. Experts value the bonus for last and are skilled at winning it. Plan your play accordingly.

Where you see the prospects for a run or pair royal, be careful to ensure that they fall in the same play: if you put down one of a pair and your opponent scores for a pair, you will not be able to score the pair royal if the cards are then turned over for the second play.

The laws of probability should be invoked, as in many card games, to get the odds working for you as far as possible. In six-card cribbage the average score per hand is about 12 points for elder and 17 points for dealer, the crib being worth about five points.

ECARTÉ

Ecarté is a trick-taking game, one of a widespread family of games in which each hand consists of five cards only. It was at one time the most popular card game in France, and it is the best of the 'short' trick-taking games for two players.

ECARTÉ IS PLAYED with the 32-card pack, i.e. the standard pack with the 6s, 5s, 4s, 3s, and 2s removed. The cards rank in each suit: King (high), Queen, Jack, Ace, 10, 9, 8, 7.

Each player draws a card from the pack to decide dealer – higher card deals. Dealer gives five cards to each player, beginning with his opponent, in two batches, of two and three or of three and two – whichever order he chooses remains the order for the rest of the game.

The 11th card is turned up on the table and fixes the trump suit. The remainder of the pack is put down beside it and forms the stock. If the card turned up is a King, dealer immediately scores one point.

The non-dealer begins by stating either 'I play' or 'I propose'. If he plays, the hands dealt are immediately played out. If he proposes, the dealer may then either refuse the proposal, by saying either 'I refuse' or 'I play', in which the hands are played out, or he may accept the proposal by saying 'I accept'. If the proposal is accepted each player may change any number of cards he wishes, non-dealer first. Non-dealer must change at least one by discarding face down to a 'dead' pile and drawing from the top of the stock. Dealer may change any number or none.

After the draws, non-dealer may play or propose again and dealer may again refuse or accept. This is repeated until either non-dealer says 'I play' or dealer says 'I refuse' or the stock is exhausted. If at the end not enough cards are left in the stock to satisfy either the non-dealer or dealer, he may take just those cards that remain. When the play commences each player must have five cards.

The Play

The non-dealer makes the opening lead, no matter who decides to play. If either player holds the King of trumps, he scores one point for it if he announces it before he plays to the first trick. It is not obligatory to announce the King of trumps, and a player may forfeit the extra point for the sake of withholding information from the opponent.

It is customary in Ecarté for the player leading to a trick to announce its suit.

Each player must follow suit upon each lead if able to, and *must win the trick if able to*, either by playing a higher card in the suit led, or by trumping if he is void.

The winner of each trick leads to the next.

The object and scoring

The object of the play is to make the majority of the tricks, i.e. three or more. This is called making the 'trick'. A secondary object is to make all five tricks, called making the 'vole'.

If the hands originally dealt are played out, the player who decides to play scores one point for making the trick, or two points for vole. If he fails to make at least three tricks, his opponent scores two points (no bonus for vole).

Once a proposal has been accepted (i.e. there has been a discard and draw from stock), then one point is scored for making the trick or two for making the vole, whichever player is successful.

Figure 1 Five *jeux de regle* hands, with varying numbers of hearts (trumps).

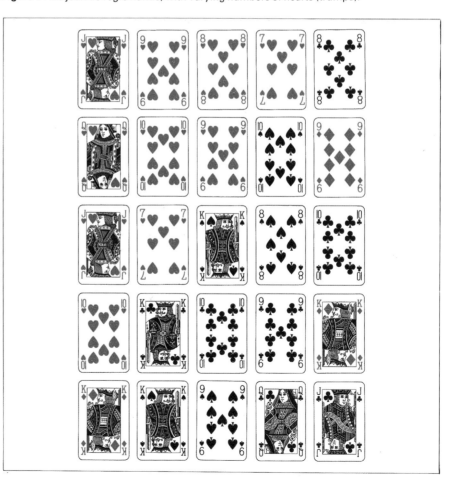

More dastardly cheating. A mirror being used to show the hand of a 17th century player in 'The Card Players' by Jan Steen.

The maximum points at stake on each deal are therefore three – two for vole and one for the King of trumps.

Game is to five points. A player with four points who is dealt the King of trumps may expose it immediately for a point, since he must win.

Strategy

There is not much opportunity for judgement at Ecarté, particularly in the play, since it is obligatory to win a trick if possible. The biggest decision to make is whether or not to propose or accept. A player who considers playing on the hands dealt should realise that he stands to score one point for making the trick, but to concede two if he fails. Therefore he should play only if his chances of taking the majority of tricks are 2 to 1 on or better. This is a question of probabilities, and the chances have been calculated for every hand.

The minimum hands which offer the required chances of success are known as the *jeux de regle*. For guidance, some of these are as follows:

1) *With four or five trumps:* any hand.
2) *With three trumps:* any two cards in the same outside suit.

Figure 2 Opposing ecarté hands (hearts trumps). Non-dealer should win whichever hand he holds because of leading first.

3) *With two trumps:* King, 7 in the same suit with 9 in another; Ace, 10 in the same suit with Ace in another; Jack, Jack, Jack or Queen, Queen, 7 in differing suits.
4) *With one trump:* four cards in an outside suit headed by King; three cards in an outside suit headed by King, Queen, or headed by King with a King in another suit; two cards in each of two outside suits, with the outside suits as strong as King, Ace and King, 7 or

Queen, Jack and Queen, Ace. If the cards in the outside suits are split 2,1,1, then the doubleton must be headed by King, or at worst be Queen, Jack, and one singleton must be King.
5) *With no trumps:* three outside suits all headed by King or Queen, Jack.

Examples of each category are given in Figure 1.

The strength of the trumps is comparatively unimportant.

The opening lead is of great value, however. The hands outlined above should always be played by non-dealer, because he has the opening lead. For the dealer, they represent the minimum requirement to play. Figure 2 shows two opposing hands, each of which should take three tricks if held by the player on lead.

When discarding it is best to retain only Kings and trumps. When three such cards are held it is better to play, unless there is a chance of improving the hand to make vole, and the hand is already strong enough to prevent opponent making vole. Thus, a player holding the King of trumps, or the Queen if the King is turned up, might try for vole, as he cannot concede it.

130

EUCHRE

Of the trick-taking games played with the short pack in which the hands consist of only five cards, Euchre has always been played more in the New World than the Old. It has been particularly popular in the United States.

EUCHRE IS PLAYED with the 32-card pack, i.e. the standard pack from which the 6s, 5s, 4s, 3s and 2s have been removed. It is best for four players, playing in two partnerships of two.

The cards rank from Ace (high) down to 7, except that in the trump suit the Jack is the highest trump (and is called the 'right bower'), while the Jack of the same colour as the right bower is the second highest trump (and is called the 'left bower'). Figure 1 shows the rank of cards in the trump suit (diamonds).

accepted or rejected by the players in turn. If the suit is accepted by any of them, the turn-up card becomes part of the dealer's hand. The dealer makes a discard, placing it face down crossways below the undealt cards. By custom, he does not pick up the turn-up but leaves it on top of the pack until he plays it.

Eldest hand has the first opportunity of accepting the proposed trump suit. To accept he says 'I order it up' (to signify that he orders the turn-up to be taken up into dealer's hand). To reject the proposed trump suit he says 'I

If a player makes trumps the same colour as the turn-up, he is said to be 'making it next', otherwise he is said to be 'crossing it'.

If all four players pass in this round, the cards are thrown in, and the deal passes to the next player.

Playing alone

The player who makes trumps (the maker) either by accepting the turn-up or by naming the suit himself, has the right to play alone. To do so, he must announce his intention before a card is led.

The partner of a player playing along lays down his cards face down on the table. He does not take part in the play, but the points won or lost are attributed to the partnership.

Figure 1 The rank of the cards in the trump suit (in this case diamonds).

It follows that the trump suit contains nine cards, the suit of the same colour as the trump suit (called the 'next suit') contains seven cards, and the two suits of the opposite colour (called the 'cross' suits) contain eight cards each.

Each player draws a card to determine partners, the two lowest playing against the two highest. The lowest denotes the first dealer. In the draw Ace counts low, below 7. Partners sit opposite each other, and the deal passes clockwise round the table.

Five cards are dealt to each player in packets of three and two, or two and three, as the dealer chooses, beginning with the hand on dealer's left (eldest).

On completing the deal, the dealer places the remainder of the pack face down on the table, turning the top card face up. The turn-up proposes the trump suit for the deal.

Making

The proposed trump suit can be

pass'. Dealer's partner may now accept the trump suit by saying 'I assist'. If he passes, the next player may 'order it up' or 'pass', and finally, if the three others have passed, dealer has the opportunity. If he accepts, he merely places his discard face down under the pack. If he rejects the trump suit, he puts the turn-up face up cross-ways below the pack.

If all reject the trump suit, eldest hand may now name any of the other three suits (not that of the rejected turn-up) as the trump suit, or he may pass. The other players then have the same opportunity in turn.

The play

The opening lead is made by the eldest hand, unless the maker plays alone, when the opening lead is made by the player to his left.

Players must follow suit to the card led. If unable to, a player may play any card. There is no obligation to trump or to win the trick if possible. The trick is won by the highest trump or the highest card in the suit led. The winner of a trick leads to the next.

Object and scoring

The object of the play is to win the majority of the tricks, i.e. at least three. If a side makes all five tricks it wins the 'march'. If a making side fails to win three tricks it is 'euchred'.

The side making trumps, unless the maker plays alone, scores one point for making three or four tricks, and two points for the march. The maker playing alone scores one point for three or

four tricks, and four points for the march. If the making side is euchred, whether in partnership or with maker playing alone, the opponents score two points.

Game is of five points, and it is customary for each side to keep its score by using two of the cards not wanted in the game, a 3 and a 4. The method is shown in Figure 2.

Strategy

The main decision lies in whether or not to make trumps. As the trump suit consists of nine cards, an average of just over five trumps will be dealt to the players, so the average trump holding of each hand will be 1¼ trumps.

Ordering up the trump is likely to give dealer a second trump in his hand, therefore, so eldest hand should bear this in mind and not order up the trump without three fairly sure tricks. The same applies to his partner.

Even with three likely tricks it might not be best for eldest hand to order up. If he is strong also in the suit of the same colour as the turn-up, particularly if he holds a bower, it might be better to wait until the second round to name trumps – he avoids thereby presenting dealer with a trump. If by chance dealer's side should take up the trump before eldest gets the opportunity to name trumps, then eldest has a hand likely to euchre them.

Dealer's partner should assist with two side Aces, or with one side Ace and two trumps, on the assumption that the turn-up will provide dealer with enough trumps to give his side the balance of power. If the turn-up is a high card, however, like a bower, he might pass to give dealer the chance to take it up and play alone.

All decisions will, however, be affected by the score. A side with four points is said to be 'at the bridge'. If the opponents have only two points or less, then the side at the bridge can risk being euchred, knowing it will not cost them the game. Eldest in this position will usually order up the trump to deprive the dealer's side the chance of

Figure 2 The method of scoring in Euchre, the arrangement of the cards representing one, two, three and four points respectively.

making it alone and scoring four. A side at the bridge with opponents on three points will be cautious, however, as being euchred will cost them the game.

Dealer will usually take up the trump when the opponents have four points, to prevent them naming trumps, particularly if his side have a low score. If the opponents have three points, though, he will beware of being euchred.

When dealer turns down the trump, the assumption is that he does not possess a bower, so eldest hand will usually make it next if he can – if not he usually passes. Dealer's partner, on the other hand, will prefer to cross rather than make it next. Of course, these niceties assume other things being equal – a player holding three sure tricks in any suit will name that suit.

Playing alone requires a hand like the two top trumps supported by two Aces or Ace and another trump, i.e. three fairly certain tricks and a prospect of five. Playing alone might be tried with a weaker hand if the opponents are at the bridge and a side has only one or two points.

There is little opportunity for judgement in the play. A player with top trumps will draw trumps at the earliest opportunity. With only five tricks it is usually best to take a trick whenever possible.

Two-handed Euchre

Two-handed Euchre is played exactly as four-handed euchre, except that the pack is reduced further to 24 cards, by removing the 8s and 7s, and there are no extra points for playing alone, since, obviously, each player plays alone throughout.

Three-handed Euchre

Three-handed Euchre is played as four-

handed euchre, except that during the play the player who makes trumps plays alone against the other two in temporary partnership. This requires a change in the scoring. A maker winning three or four tricks scores one point; if he wins the march he scores three points and if he is euchred his opponents score two points each. Scores are kept individually – the first player to reach five points wins.

Call-ace Euchre

Call-Ace Euchre can be played by four, five or six players. Each player plays for himself, although temporary partnerships may be formed.

The trump is made as in the basic game. The maker then has the option of playing alone or he may nominate a partner by saying 'I call on the Ace of . . .', naming a suit. The player holding this Ace then plays in partnership with the maker against the rest, but he does not reveal himself. Thus only the holder of the Ace knows who is playing with or against whom. The maker, in fact, does not know whether he has a partner or not, as the Ace named might not be in the deal, in which case the maker is playing alone. All is revealed during the play, of course, when the Ace is played.

A player playing alone scores one point for making three or four tricks. In a partnership hand the two players score one point each. For winning the march, a lone player scores one point for every player in the game, including himself. Players winning the march in partnership score two points each if there are four players in the game, three points each if there are five or six. If a lone player or a partnership is euchred, the other players score two points each.

GERMAN WHIST

German whist is a variation of whist for two players, which is a test of judgement and memory.

GERMAN WHIST USES a standard 52-card pack (no Jokers) with the cards ranking from Ace (high) down to 2 (low), as normal. Thirteen cards are dealt singly to each player. The dealer then places the remainder of the pack face down to form a stockpile. He then turns over the top card (i.e., the 27th) and leaves it on top of, or beside the pack – it doesn't matter which. This card indicates the trump suit for the hand; thus if the ♣ 7 was exposed, clubs would be trumps for the hand.

Elder (non-dealer) leads a card of his choice. A trick consists of two cards, one from each player, and the object is simply to capture the most tricks. The usual trick-taking rules apply.

The winner of the first trick, which he places beside him, then adds the exposed card (a trump, remember) to his hand and the loser then takes the top face-down card (i.e., the 28th) from the stockpile into his hand without showing it to his opponent. (A good variant, which makes for a different game strategically, requires the loser to show the card to his opponent.) The winner then turns up the top card of the pack.

Thus after the first trick, each player still holds 13 cards, the stockpile is reduced by two, and a new top card, which does not alter the trump suit, is exposed. Subsequent play follows the same pattern with the winner always taking the exposed card and the loser the unseen card, until the pack is exhausted.

Play then continues from hand until each player plays his last card to the 26th trick when the hand ends. The winner scores points equal to the number of tricks he has won in excess of his opponent. The loser does not score. For example, player A takes 19 tricks and player B takes seven tricks. Player A scores 12 points. Of course, if the tricks are shared neither player scores. Game is any agreed total – 50 points is usual.

Strategy The game is nicely balanced between two strategies: holding back a high card when the turn-up is a low card of a plain suit in order to be in a position to capture a trick when the turn-up is a high card or a useful trump – though without guarantee that the concealed card will be better than the turn-up – and taking the same trick cheaply with a relatively low card.

Memory can play an important part. When the stock is exhausted, each player in theory should know precisely his opponent's holding making the play hereon simply a matter of calculation. The common strategy of trick-taking games now prevails: establish a long suit by first clearing trumps (creation of a long suit, with adequate trump backing, should be an aim of the first phase).

Usually the 14th trick is an important one to win in order to impose one's strategy on the opponent after the hands have been stabilised.

Illustration from a German magazine of 1895. The game is a three-handed trick-taking game.

GIN RUMMY

The invention of Gin Rummy has been credited to E.T. Baker in a New York club in 1909. It is a variant of the parent game Rummy, which is frequently shortened to Rum, and acquired its name Gin by extension of the alcoholic drink theme. It became very popular due to the publicity it received when taken up by film stars in Hollywood in the 1940s.

GIN RUMMY IS A game for two players, using the full 52-card pack. The cards rank from King (high) to Ace (low).

Dealer is determined by the players each drawing a card from the pack: higher has choice of dealing first or not. If cards of equal rank are drawn, the suit determines precedence in the order: spades (high), hearts, diamonds, clubs. After the first deal, the winner of each hand deals the next.

The dealer deals ten cards to each player, one at a time, beginning with his opponent. The remainder of the pack is placed face down between the players to form the 'stock'. The top card of the stock is placed face up beside the stock and becomes the 'upcard', at the same time beginning a discard pile.

The play and objects

The non-dealer may take the first upcard into his hand or refuse it. If he refuses, the dealer has the option of taking it or refusing it. If dealer refuses it also, the non-dealer draws the top card from the stock and takes it into his hand, discarding a card (the new upcard) face up on the discard pile. The card discarded may, in fact, be the card picked up, and the player may merely look at it and discard it without physically adding it to his other cards. Thereafter each player in turn draws a card, either the upcard or the top card of the stock, and discards, so that the number of cards in each player's hand remains at ten.

The object of the play is to form the hand into sets of three or more cards. A set may be of two kinds: three or four cards of the same rank, or three or more cards in sequence in the same suit (Ace being in sequence with 2,3, not King, Queen).

Cards which are not included in a set are 'unmatched' cards. After drawing (and only then), a player may 'knock', i.e. terminate the hand, whenever the pip value of the unmatched cards in his hand total ten or less. For this purpose, court cards (King, Queen, Jack) count as ten points each, the Ace counts as one, and the other cards as their face value.

Knocking involves laying down the hand, arranged in sets, with the unmatched cards separate, and making the usual discard. The count of the unmatched cards represent points against the player. If all ten of the cards

Figure 1 Knocker (left) goes out with a count of three. His opponent lays off with ♥ J, 10, has a count of 11.

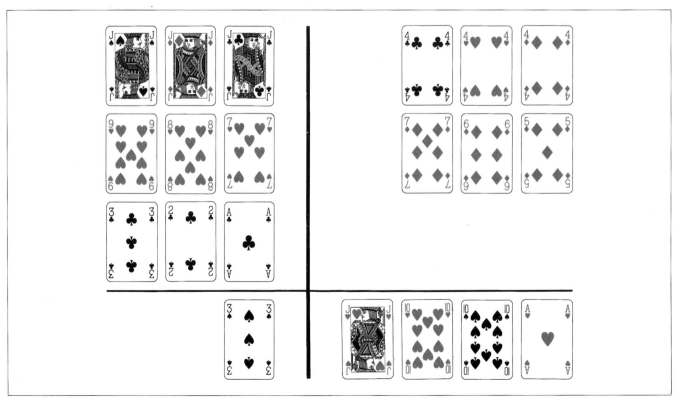

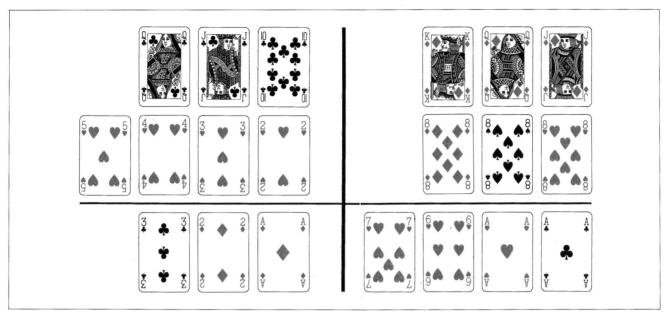

Figure 2 Knocker (left) is undercut when opponent lays off with ♥ A, ♥ 6 and ♥ 7 on his sequence.

are in sets, the player is said to 'go gin', and the count against him is nought.

If the player drawing the fiftieth card discards without knocking (i.e. there are only two cards left in the stock) the hand is abandoned and there is no score for that deal.

When a player knocks, there is one further stage before the calculation of the score, and that is the 'laying off'. The opponent of the knocker lays down his cards in sets, and, unless the knocker has gone gin, may lay off any of his unmatched cards on the sets of the knocker, thereby reducing the count against him.

Figure 2 shows a completed deal in which the opponent of the knocker can lay three unmatched cards on the knocker's sets.

Scoring

If the knocker has the lower of the two counts in unmatched cards, he scores the difference in the counts (in Figure 1 the knocker scores eight points). It is possible that the player who did not knock has the lower count. In this case he 'undercuts' the knocker and scores the difference in the count plus a bonus of 20 points. Should the count be equal, the opponent of the knocker still undercuts him, scoring the bonus 20 points, but nothing for difference in point count. Figure 2 shows a completed deal, in which the knocker is undercut.

It must be remembered that cards cannot be laid off on a knocker who goes gin. Going gin therefore guards against being undercut.

A player who goes gin scores a bonus of 25 on top of the point count.

The first player to score 100 points wins the game, but scoring does not end there. The winner of the game adds 100 points bonus to his score. Each player then adds 20 points to his score for each of his 'boxes' – each deal he won. The winner wins by the difference in the two scores. This difference is doubled if the lower did not score a point. This is called a 'shut-out' or 'schneider'. Figure 3 shows the score of a completed game.

There is a more complex scoring system, which was used in the days of popularity in Hollywood and which is

known as Hollywood scoring.

The scores are recorded on a sheet of paper ruled as in Figure 4. The first time a player wins a deal he enters the points in the first column only. The second time he enters the points in the second column and also adds them to the score in the first column. The third time he enters the points in the third column and adds them to the score in the first two columns. Thereafter points won are added to the scores in all three columns. Figure 4 represents a game in progress, showing some scores entered.

When the score of a player in a column reaches 100 or more, the column is closed. The player winning it scores a bonus of 100 points, and each player scores 20 points for each box won, as in the orthodox scoring. The winner wins by the difference in the scores, and if the loser fails to score in a column the difference is doubled. A player who is shut out in the first column must clearly make his first entry in the second column. A game ends when all three columns are won.

Strategy

Players must use judgement in deciding how long to hold high cards presenting a good chance of a set. For three or four draws it might pay to hold them, as high cards are likely to be discarded by the opponent. Many gin hands are won after only five or six draws, however, with six or seven cards in sets, and three or four unmatched. At this stage, therefore, a player should consider discarding these high cards in favour of lower ones.

Continued at foot of next page

Me	Thee
18	27
22	29
58	61
70	+ 60
75	121
92	
101	
+ 100	
+ 140	
341	

Figure 3 A completed score card.

KNAVES

Knaves is a trick-taking games for three, playing as individuals, combining both skill and chance.

A STANDARD 52-CARD pack is used, without the jokers. The cards rank in descending order from Ace (high) down to 2 (low). The suits are equal but the Jacks (Knaves) have a special significance, hence the name.

The cards are dealt out singly clockwise, starting with the player on the dealer's left, until each player has 17. The last card is exposed to determine the trump suit but is otherwise not used in the hand.

The object is to take as many tricks as possible, each trick scoring one point. However, there are penalties for picking up jacks in tricks as follows:

Knave of hearts: 4 points
Knave of diamonds: 3 points
Knave of clubs: 2 points
Knave of spades: 1 point

Thus a player who wins a trick containing the ♠ J scores nothing for that trick since the point earned for the trick is cancelled out by the penalty card. More than one Jack can be picked up in a single trick and minus scores are possible.

The usual rules for trick-taking card games are followed. The player to the left of dealer starts by playing any card to the table. The other two players contribute a card each to the trick clockwise in rotation. Players must follow suit (that is, play a card of the suit led) if possible, otherwise they may trump or discard. Highest trump wins the trick; if no trump is played, then the highest card of the suit led wins. Winner leads to next trick.

Game is 20 points up or any other agreed total. Each deal yields seven points (17 points for tricks less 10 for the Jacks although if a Jack is the turn-up trump then penalties in play are correspondingly reduced). A game is normally concluded in about six hands.

Strategy High cards are a mixed blessing, though mostly beneficial. They ensure tricks – but can also net unwanted knaves. Players holding Knaves naturally try to discard them or play them under high cards.

If one player is ahead on points, the other two players will combine to reduce his lead. If two players are together ahead, they will prefer to cede tricks to the back marker rather than their immediate rival; thus a pleasing feature of Knaves is its agreeable balance – runaway victories are comparatively rare.

The game is fun when played fast but can drag if play is over-cautious.

Gin Rummy : continued

Low cards, if drawn, ought to be retained, as clearly they reduce the loss if opponent wins, and they enable a player to knock as soon as he holds two or three sets.

A player in a position to knock will have to weigh the chances of being undercut. In the first four turns, a player might feel safe in knocking as soon as he can. From about the eighth turn, however, he might decide to knock only with a count of, say, five or lower. In deciding whether to knock he will consider the upcards which both players have taken and will try to calculate how many sets his opponent might have and what he might be able to lay off.

With an opportunity to knock with a low count it is usually a mistake to wait for gin. If opponent goes gin first it is a costly error.

Figure 4 Hollywood scoring, with a game in progress.

	Me	Three	Me	Three	Me	Three
Box 1	25	17	2	3	12	
Box 2	27	20	14		18	
Box 3	39		20			
Box 4	45					
Box 5						
Box 6						
Box 7						

PIQUET

Piquet is an ancient game of either French or Spanish origin, known in Elizabethan England as Cent, Sand or Saint. Combining elements of melding into sets with trick-taking, it is the most interesting and skilful of two-player games.

PIQUET IS PLAYED WITH the short 32-card pack, i.e. the standard pack from which the 6s, 5s, 4s, 3s and 2s have been removed. The cards rank from Ace (high) down to 7 (low).

The two players cut to decide the dealer. The higher card has the choice of dealing or not, and would be advised to deal, as there is an advantage in dealing first and being non-dealer on the final hand. The non-dealer is known as elder hand, the dealer as younger.

Each player is dealt twelve cards in packets of two or three. The remaining eight cards (the 'talon') are placed face down between the players. It is considered courteous by some players, but is not a rule, that the top five cards are separated from the bottom three.

If there are any cards left in the talon after both players have discarded and drawn, younger may turn them face up for both players to see, or leave them face down at his discretion.

Throughout the game each player is allowed to look at his own discards.

Carte Blanche

A hand without a court card (King, Queen, Jack) is 'carte blanche'. A player dealt a carte blanche scores ten points for it immediately. Elder must declare it on picking up his hand, younger as soon as elder has discarded and drawn. A player claiming carte blanche must show his hand to his opponent before he draws.

example game later). If younger has a longer suit, he announces 'Not good' and he will score the points in this category. If younger's longest suit is of the same length, he says 'Making?', asking elder to count the pip value of his suit. For this purpose, Ace counts 11 and court cards ten each. Elder announces his total, and if this is greater than younger's total younger says 'Good', and elder scores the points, otherwise he says 'Not good', and later scores them himself. If the totals are equal he says 'Same' and neither player scores.

2) *Sequences.* Elder announces the number of cards in his longest sequence (cards in sequence in the same suit). The sequence must be of at least three cards and the French terms tierce (three), quart (four), quinte (five), sixième (six), septième (seven) and huitième (eight) are used. Younger responds with 'Good', or 'Not good', or, if his longest sequence is of the same

Figure 1 Hands dealt in example game, elder on the left.

separated from the bottom three.

Elder (non-dealer) is now entitled to exchange from one to five of his cards by discarding cards face down and drawing an equal number from the top of the talon. He must exchange at least one card. If he exchanges less than five cards he may look at, and replace, those he was entitled to draw without showing them to younger (dealer).

Younger is now entitled to exchange cards up to the number that remain in the talon (which might be any number between three and seven). He, too, must exchange at least one (in America this obligation is usually waived).

Object and scoring

The score is made up in three ways: the count before the play, the count during the play, and the extraordinary scores, of which carte blanche, already mentioned is one.

Before the play, the hands are compared and score in three particulars as follows:

1) *Point.* Elder states the number of cards in his longest suit. If this is greater than the number of cards in younger's longest suit, younger says 'Good'. Before play begins, elder scores one point for each card in the suit (see

length, 'How high?' In this case elder announces the highest card in his sequence, and younger says 'Good', 'Not good' or 'Equal'. The player with the best sequence scores as follows: tierce three points, quart four points; quint and better ten points plus one for each card (e.g. septième, 17 points). The player who scores for best sequence may also score for any additional sequences he holds.

3) *Quatorzes and Trios.* Quatorze is four of a kind and trio three of a kind. Elder announces the rank of his highest quatorzes, or failing that of his highest trio (provided that it is of 10 or above). The

137

Figure 2 Hands in example game after the draw, elder on the left.

player holding the higher quatorze wins, or if neither hold a quatorze, the higher trio. Younger's response is 'Good', or 'Not good'. In this category there cannot be a tie, although it is possible that neither player holds a quatorze or trio, in which case neither scores. The player who scores in this category may also score for additional lower quatorzes or trios held. Points scored are 14 for a quatorze and three for a trio.

Scores for point, sequences, and quatorzes or trios are declared in the order given. A player can be asked to show the cards for which he is scoring in any category, but in practice this is seldom required, as each player can infer from his own hand most of the cards his opponent holds.

Sinking

It is not obligatory for a player to announce his best combination in any category. Sometimes it is good play to mislead an opponent by declaring less than is held. A player holding a quatorze of Aces, for example, might announce 'trio of Aces'. Should his opponent ask to see them he can be shown any three, or if, as is more common, the opponent asks which Ace is not being declared, the player can say which Ace he likes, as not declaring a card is not the same as stating that the card is not held. A player not declaring a combination does not score for it.

The play

Before plays begins, elder announces his scores for the three categories above. He then leads to the first trick, and since leading to a trick scores a point he immediately adds another point to his score. After elder has led to first trick, younger announces his scores for the three categories. Thereafter each player keeps count of his score out loud, announcing his score every time he plays a card.

Each player must follow suit to the card led. If unable to he may discard

any card he likes. The higher card of the suit led wins the trick. The player who wins a trick leads to the next.

A player scores a point for each lead he makes, whether he wins the trick or not. A player who wins a trick to which his opponent led wins a point. There is an extra point for winning the last trick (i.e. if the leader wins it he scores a point, non-leader scores two points).

The player who makes the majority of the tricks scores an extra ten points ('ten for the cards'). If the trick score is six each, neither player scores extra. A player who wins all 12 tricks scores a 'capot', and scores an extra 40 points rather than 10 points.

Pique and Repique

There are two extraordinary scores in addition to carte blanche and capot. If a player scores 30 points in hand combinations and in play before his opponent scores a point, he scores an extra 30 points for 'pique'. For example, if elder scores six for point, four for sequence and 14 for a quatorze, total 24, and then makes the first six leads to reach 30, his score immediately jumps to 60.

If a player scores 30 points in hand combinations alone before his opponent scores a point, he scores an extra 60 points for 'repique'. For example, if younger scores six for point, sixteen for sequence and fourteen for quatorze, total 36, his score immediately becomes 96.

Notice that because elder scores a point for first lead, younger cannot score for pique.

Example game

The example game is meant to show aspects of the play and scoring, and is not necessarily to be taken as an example of the best play.

Figure 1 shows two hands dealt at the beginning of a game.

Neither player can score for carte blanche. Elder has been dealt a poor hand. He decides that he must take five cards to give himself the greatest chance

of drawing an Ace, otherwise his opponent will probably score 14 for quatorze. He has little chance of winning the majority of tricks unless he keeps his clubs and draws Ace and another. As clubs also afford the best chance of scoring for point and sequences, he decides to keep his clubs and his three queens and to sacrifice his entire diamond suit and the ♥ 8 and ♥ 7. He discards these five cards, and draws ♦ Q, J and ♠ K, 10, 7. His bad luck continues – no additional clubs to improve his long suit, and no Ace. He has drawn a fourth Queen, but this quatorze will probably be beaten. He is almost sure to lose this deal, but realises that his opponent has not a long enough suit to score a repique.

Younger has been dealt a very promising hand. He can see chances of a quatorze with Aces and 10s. Also, with three Aces and a guarded King in the other suit, he knows that in the play he must be able to gain the lead on the second trick. With five sure trick winners and a probable sixth in the ♥ K, he is almost sure to win the majority of tricks. He wants to take all three cards left in the talon, but has no obvious discards. He would like to keep his spades in the hope of building a long suit for point, and a possible sequence, so he decides to discard his three 10s, giving up the chance of a quatorze in 10s. He drew ♥ A, 9 and ♦ 8. It was a lucky draw, because he drew the missing Ace. The missing 10 was not there, so he did not miss out on the 10s, but unfortunately he did not draw another spade.

The hands after the draw are shown in Figure 2.

The scoring for combinations takes place as follows:
Elder: 'Point of five'.
Younger: 'Good'.
Elder: 'Tierce'.
Younger: 'Good'.
Elder: 'Quatorze'.
Younger: 'Not good'.

Younger need not say 'How high?' to

Figure 3

Elder's 'Quatorze'. He knows that his is higher.

Elder now announces his score.

Elder: Point of five – five. Tierce – eight. I start with eight'. He then leads and announces: 'Nine'.

Younger now announces his score.

Younger: Quatorze – fourteen.

He then plays to the first trick, and since he wins it, says: 'Fifteen'.

The play might proceed as below. Elder has no prospects of more than a couple of tricks, and decides to lead his long suit. The winner of each trick is underlined and leads to the next. The players announce their score as they play to each trick.

Elder	*Younger*
♣ Q 'Nine'	♣ A 'Fifteen'
♥ Q 'Nine'	♥ A 'Sixteen'
♠ 7 'Nine'	♥ K 'Seventeen'
♠ 10 'Nine'	♥ J 'Eighteen'
♣ 7 'Nine	♥ 9 'Nineteen'
♠ K 'Nine'	♠ A 'Twenty'
♠ Q 'Ten'	♠ J 'Twenty-one'
♣ J 'Eleven'	♣ K 'Twenty-two'
♣ 8 'Eleven'	♠ 9 'Twenty-three'
♣ 9 'Eleven'	♠ 8 'Twenty-four'
♦ Q 'Twelve'	♦ 8 'Twenty-five'
♦ J 'Thirteen'	♦ A 'Twenty-seven, and ten for cards makes thirty-seven'.

With two cards each left, younger knows that elder has two diamonds, and can safely lead his ♦ 8 first, so that his ♦ A will win the extra point for last trick.

Partie

A game, called a 'partie', consists of six deals, in which each player deals alternately. At the end of the partie, the player with the higher score deducts from his score that of his opponent, and adds 100 to the difference to make his winning margin. If, however, one or both players fail to score 100, the winner adds both totals together before adding 100 to come to his winning margin.

Strategy

The major part of the strategy in Piquet lies in the discarding. The objects of discarding depend on whether one is elder or younger hand.

Because elder is safe from a pique against him, and because with first lead he has the advantage in the trick-taking play, and because he has the opportunity of exchanging five cards to his opponent's three, he can be on the offensive. He can try to achieve a big score, particularly by attempting to build a long suit.

Younger, on the other hand, must keep defence in mind. It is no good him building a long suit if he might never get in to lead, or might have to discard from his long suit before he gets the lead. He must keep stoppers in at least two suits, better still three, and without Aces must keep combinations like King and another, or Queen and two others.

Each player must try to work out the holding of his opponent. If a player is void in a suit, he must consider the possibility of his opponent holding a long suit, in which case it might be best not to try to score for point, but to attempt a score in other categories.

Players must also keep account of the score. If, on the last hand, only pique could win for elder he must clearly discard accordingly.

In Figure 3, the best discards for elder might be ♥ K, 8, ♣ Q, 10, 7. He needs only one diamond to be sure of making the majority of tricks, and has chances of scoring for point and sequence in this suit.

Younger, however, would do best to discard ♦ J, 9, 8, thus keeping a stopper in each suit. A discard of a heart and a club might allow his opponent to win several tricks in these suits.

In the play, the usual principles of trick taking games apply. A player should attempt to establish long suits, and should be aware of the chance to make an extra point by forcing his opponent to lead to the last trick in certain cases, in the way shown in the example game.

A lady playing cards with a gallant and being shown his cards by an accomplice with a mirror.

SKAT

Skat is a card game for three players. Originating in the south of what is now East Germany in the early part of the nineteenth century, it has become a popular pub game over most of German-speaking central Europe.

PLAYED AT THE HIGHEST LEVEL Skat is one of the most skilful of all card games, and it is particularly recommended for people who play Hearts (Black Maria, Chase the Lady, etc) but find that game too straightforward.

Outline

The pack is of 32 cards (as used for Piquet, Euchre etc), and consists of four suits: Clubs, Spades, Hearts and Diamonds, each suit containing Ace, King, Queen, Jack, 10, 9, 8, 7. Ten cards are dealt to each player, with the last two cards, "the skat", remaining face down on the table. There is an auction, and the winner of the auction plays alone against the other two players. Usually he takes the two cards of the skat into his hand, and discards two cards before play begins.

The play

Skat is a trick taking game, like Bridge, Solo Whist and Hearts. Play proceeds in a series of tricks, in each of which one player leads a card, and the other two, in turn clockwise round the table, follow with one card. The player leading can choose any card he likes, but the others are forced to play cards of the suit led, unless they have no such card when they are free to choose any card. The trick is won by the highest card of the suit led, except that one suit (called the trump suit) always beats the other suits and a trick to which trumps are played is won by the highest trump irrespective of the suit led.

The winner of each trick keeps the three cards it contains face down in front of him, and leads to the next trick. The player on Dealer's left ("Forehand") leads to the first trick.

The order of the cards

The four Jacks are always part of the trump suit in Skat, and they always rank in the order: Clubs, Spades, Hearts, Diamonds (Clubs are high). The 10s ranks between Ace and King.

The order of the trump suit is:
♣ J, ♠ J, ♥ J, ♦ J, A, 10, K, Q, 9, 8, 7 (11 cards)

And the order of the other three suits is:
A, 10, K, Q, 9, 8, 7 (7 cards)

There is also a contract, called "Grand", in which there are, effectively, five suits: the four Jacks, which are trumps, form a small suit by themselves, and the other four suits have seven cards each.

(Note that in all contracts the Jacks are treated exactly as ordinary members of the trump suit for the purposes of play, so that, for example, if hearts are trumps and the ♦ J is led, the other players are forced to follow with hearts [or Jacks] if they have any.)

The value of the cards and the object of the game

The cards have widely differing values as follows:
Ace = 11 points
10 = 10 points
King = 4 points
Queen = 3 points
Jack = 2 points
9, 8, 7 = 0 points.

This makes a total of 120 points in the pack. The object of the game is to capture half of these "card points" in tricks (Declarer needs 61 points to win, the defenders need 60 to beat him).

The skat counts as part of Declarer's tricks, so that if he discards two 10s for example, he already has 20 points – almost a third of his target.

Note that the Jacks, which are the most powerful cards for winning tricks, are not in themselves worth many points – this special feature of Skat is responsible for much of the interest and strategic richness of the game.

The score

Adding up the value of the cards captured and seeing whether Declarer has achieved 61 card points determines whether he has won or not. The amount of money he gets for doing so (or the score he gets if you're not playing for money) is determined in an unlikely sounding manner which takes a little getting used to. It is the product of two numbers which we shall call the "base value" and the "multiplier".

The base value depends only on the trump suit:
Diamonds = 9
Hearts = 10
Spades = 11
Clubs = 12
Grand = 20

The multiplier depends mostly on the number of top trumps the declarer holds, but various bonuses may be added:

1) If Declarer holds the ♣ J (the top trump), the multiplier is the number of trumps he holds in sequence from the ♣ J down.

2) If Declarer does not hold the ♣ J, the multiplier is the number of trumps he is missing, in sequence from the ♣ J down.

3) If Declarer plays "in Hand" i.e. he does not look at the skat, but just puts the two cards in his pile of tricks, he adds one to the multiplier.

4) If Declarer makes "Schneider" i.e. he takes 90 or more card points in his tricks, he adds one to the multiplier.

5) If Declarer announces that he is going to make Schneider at the beginning of the hand, then he adds another one to the multiplier in addition to the one for making Schneider. It is illegal to announce Schneider except when playing in Hand. If Declarer announces Schneider and takes fewer than 90 card points, then the multipliers for Schneider and Schneider announced still apply, but he loses.

6) If Declarer makes "Schwartz" (German for black – he takes all the tricks), then he gets another one added to the multiplier in addition to the one for Schneider.

7) If Declarer announces Schwartz then he gets yet another one added, but, as for Schneider, he may only announce Schwartz when playing in hand.

8) One is always added to the multiplier "for the Game".

9) If Declarer fails to make his contract he loses double the score he would have won, except when playing in hand.

Let us consider some examples:

1) Declarer plays in Hearts, holding ♣ J, ♠ J, ♦ J, and he takes 76 card points. He is "with two" Jacks (the ♥ J is missing) and claims:

"With two, Game three, times 10, makes 30."

2) Declarer plays a Grand holding ♥ J, ♦ J, and he makes 59 card points (not enough) and announces:

"Without two, Game three, off six, times 20, loses 120."

3) Declarer plays in Spades, in hand, holding ♣ J, ♠ J, ♥ J; and he announces Schneider. He makes 87 card points (not enough), therefore loses:

"With three, Game four, Hand five, Schneider six, Announced seven, times 11, loses 77."

4) Declarer plays in Clubs, in hand, holding ♣ J, ♥ J, ♦ J, and the Ace of Clubs. He makes 96 card points, and the ♠ J proves to have been in the skat (lucky). He claims:

"With five, Game six, Hand seven, Schneider eight, times 12, makes 96."

Null

In addition to the normal trump contracts, there is a contract called "Null", which is a contract to take no tricks at all. Card points do not count, and the hand stops immediately if the declarer takes a trick (he has lost).

The order of the cards is different in Null. There are no trumps, and the four suits each have eight cards: Ace, King, Queen, Jack, 10, 9, 8, 7 in that order (the 10s and Jacks are back where you would expect them to be).

In Null it is possible to play "Open" – Declarer exposes all his cards, and plays with them face up on the table. There are four contracts, depending on whether Declarer looks at the skat:

Null	23 points
Null Hand	35 points
Null Open	46 points
Null Hand Open	59 points

As with ordinary contracts, Declarer loses double the number of points if he has looked at the skat, but just loses what he would have won if he plays in hand.

Money

Skat scoring is designed for players who use piles of money on the table in front of them, and settle up after each hand – the rule is that Declarer is paid by (or pays if he has lost) each of the other players.

If you intend to play for honour (or if you, or the publican, do not like having money on the table) then the score can be kept on a piece of paper. After each hand add the score for that hand to the total under Declarer's initial. At the end each player pays each other the difference between their scores. (If you're not playing for money it's just the player with the biggest score who wins, which is simpler).

The deal

To determine the dealer for the first hand, cards are dealt out one at a time by whoever happens to hold them, face up, one to each player. The first person to get a Jack is dealer. Dealer shuffles, then someone else cuts, then dealer deals, clockwise starting with the player on his left, three cards to each player, then two to the skat, then four cards each, then another three each (the peculiar English habit of dealing cards one at a time is rare in central Europe). The deal moves round to the left on subsequent hands.

Bidding

The player on Dealer's left is called "Forehand", the other player is called "Middlehand". The bidding consists of an auction between the three players. The bids are numbers, and represent the number of points the player contracts to score if he became declarer. If someone else eventually becomes declarer then there is no obligation on the

bidder. If the declarer makes a higher score than he bid then that is fine – he scores the higher number. Note that these bids are scores, not numbers of card points – the contract is always to make 61 card points (unless Schneider is announced).

The process of bidding is for one player to call numbers in ascending order while a second player says "Yes" after each bid. Eventually one of them drops out of the auction by saying "Pass". The auction begins with Middlehand bidding and Forehand saying "Yes" (or "Pass"), then when one of these two has passed, Dealer starts bidding and the other of them says "Yes" (or passes).

One may only bid numbers which it is possible to score. The full bidding sequence starts with 18 (Diamonds with, or without, one Jack), then 20 (Hearts with one); 22 (Spades with one); 23 (Null); 24 (Clubs with one); 27 (Diamonds with two); 30 (Hearts with two); 33 (Spades with two); 35 (Null Hand); 36 (Clubs with two or Diamonds with three); 40 (Hearts with three or Grand with one); 44 (Spades with three); 45 (Diamonds with four); 46 (Null Open); 48 (Clubs with three); 50 (Hearts with four); 54 (Diamonds with five); 55 (Spades with four); 59 (Null Hand Open); 60 (Clubs with four, Hearts with five or Grand with two) . . . and so on up to 200 (Grand Hand with four with Schwartz announced) and, theoretically, 204 (Clubs Hand with eleven with Schwartz announced). In practice the auction never gets past 60 among skilful players.

A typical auction might go:

M: 18	F: Yes
M: 20	F: Yes
M: 22	F: Yes
M: 23	F: Yes
M: 24	F: Pass
D: 27	M: Yes
D: Pass	

(M is Middlehand, F is forehand, D is Dealer).

The result of this auction is that Middlehand has contracted to make at least 27 points.

If all three players pass, the hand is

thrown in and the deal passes on.

Overbidding

If Declarer overbids, either by accident or because he was hoping to play without several Jacks and finds one in the skat, then it is possible that he has absolutely no way to make his contract, even by making Schwartz. In this case he loses the next higher multiple of his base value above his bid. Suppose, for example, that a player holding:

♥ 10, K, Q, 9, 8, 7
♣ A, 10
♠ A, K

plays Hearts in Hand, after bidding up to 59 points. He makes 82 card points, but the ♠ J proves to be in the skat. Far from being "without five" as he had hoped, he is only "without one" and so scores only 30 (without one, Game two, Hand three). He loses 60 points for this, since that is the next multiple of 10 above his bid. It is always a bit dangerous trying to go without the Jacks because of the risk of finding one in the skat.

A few remarks on skilful play

Requirements to bid a suit contract The important cards are Jacks and Aces, and the average hand has 1⅓ of each of them. The advantages of getting the skat, discarding, and choosing trumps almost outweigh the disadvantage of being one player against two, and most hands with three cards which are Jacks or Aces can reasonably be bid up to the value of their lowest ranking long suit.

To bid Grand Here Jacks and Aces are especially important. Normally you need five of them (or perhaps four if you are Forehand, and have the lead). 10s to support your Aces are much better than 10s by themselves.

To bid Null You need 7s. Competent defenders will nearly always force you to take a trick if you have a three-card suit containing the Ace or King, or a four-card suit missing the 7, or a single card of a suit which is not 7,8 or 9.

Going in Hand If you have a rock-crushing collection of Aces and Jacks you might as well go in Hand to score for the extra multiplier, but there are

two common reasons for not doing so: (a) a holding which is almost sure to make game in Hand can be converted, using the skat, to one which is absolutely sure to make game and almost sure to make Schneider – the extra multiplier for Schneider is just as good as the one for Hand, and you are insured against dangers like a 5-0 trump split.

(b) many holdings which would make game in hand in a suit could be converted into a Grand given one more Ace or Jack from the skat. Since Grand is so much more valuable than the suit contracts it is often worth foregoing the multiplier for Hand in the hope of something bigger. If there are four particular cards any one of which would let you make Grand, the chance of finding one of them in the skat is about one in three.

Discarding the skat Declarer should try to create void suits where he holds one or two cards without the Ace. One odd low card can cost 21 card points. It is much better to have two low cards in one suit than one in each of two suits. Never discard an Ace.

Counting Counting is quite important in Skat. If you can only remember one number, then count trumps. If you can manage two, then count trumps and the number of card points the defenders have collected.

Choosing trumps If you have two suits of equal length, then choose the weaker one as trumps – this avoids devaluing your Aces.

Example deal

The following example hand (Figure 1) covers a number of other aspects of skilful play – you may find it easier to follow by laying the cards out on a table.

First, let's consider what the players should be prepared to bid:

Forehand: He has no chance in anything except Null. His Clubs and Hearts are safe, but he might be forced to take a trick either in Spades or Diamonds (the Diamonds are about as worrying as the Spades – any long suit missing the 7 is a liability in Null). He has a reasonable chance of improving one or both of these suits if he looks at the

skat, so he can bid up to 23.

Middlehand: He has a reasonable hand for playing in Clubs (he can even consider playing in Hand) but he would feel much happier if he could see the skat, and find another club, or a Jack, or an Ace. He can bid up to 24 (Clubs without one).

Dealer: He has quite a good hand. He can consider playing Hearts in Hand, but the ♠ 10 is a severe embarrassment – it is almost sure to be caught by the Ace. Ideally Dealer would like to look at the skat. If he finds an Ace, or possibly a Jack, he will be strong enough to play Grand, and if he can discard the embarrassing ♠ 10 into his trick pile, then Hearts are almost cast-iron. In a hand like this, with few losers, it is worth doing a calculation to see how many points the defenders can collect. In this case we would suppose that the defenders catch the ♠ 10 with the Ace and King, for 25 points, that they catch the ♦ Q with the Ace and 10, for a further 24 points making 49, and then we are left with the question of whether they can collect 11 points in trumps (assuming Hearts are trumps, of course). There are four trumps outside Dealer's hand, and he should be prepared for them to divide 3-1 between the opponents. In this case the defenders can arrange for at least one trick to happen when one of them is winning a trump, while the other is out of trumps and can throw on some valuable card like the ♣ 10. This will make up the required 11 points and Dealer will lose. Of course, in practice, the defenders will rarely manage to put the maximum possible number of points on his losing cards, but the calculation shows that Dealer is not quite safe playing Hearts in Hand.

The bidding goes as follows:

Middlehand : 18	Forehand: Yes
M : 20	F : Yes
M : 22	F : Yes
M : 23	F : Yes
M : 24	F : Pass
Dealer : Pass	

Dealer decides to pass since his Hearts Hand contract is not quite safe and he has very good chances of defeat-

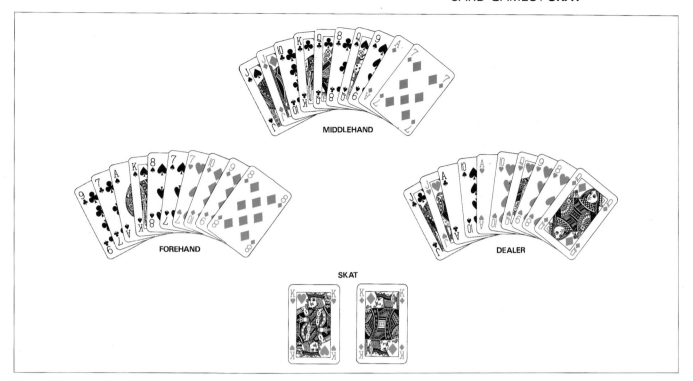

Figure 1 An example deal in Skat.

ing any contract Middlehand might try. This is rather cowardly – most players would bid up to 30 with Dealer's cards.

Middlehand looks at the skat, fails to find any of the key cards he was hoping for, and discards ♥ K and ♠ Q, getting 7 points home and creating a void in Hearts.

Middlehand then announces his contract: "clubs are trumps."

The play proceeds as follows (F = Forehand, M = Middlehand (the declarer), D = Dealer:

Trick 1: F Leads the ♠ A. Normal practice is for the player in front of the declarer to play long suits, while the other defender plays short suits – the reason soon becomes apparent. M follows the ♠ 9 and D plays the ♠ 10.
Score: M 7 points, Defenders 21
Trick 2: F leads the ♠ K. This is the position the defenders have been trying to create, with D, void of the suit led, playing after the declarer. This means that if M trumps the card led, D can overtrump, while if M throws away some odd card, D can put something valuable on (in this case, the ♥ A). M decides to trump with the ♣ Q, and D overtrumps with the ♣ A.
Score: M 7 points, Defenders 39
Trick 3: D leads the ♥ A. He expects M to trump this card, but it is far better to force M to trump than to allow him a free opportunity to get rid of an odd card. F plays the 7, and M trumps with the ♣ 10.
Score: M 28 points, Defenders 39

Trick 4: M leads the ♦ J. It is almost always best for the declarer to get rid of trumps as soon as possible. D wins with the ♥ J, and F plays the ♣ 7.
Score: M 28 points, Defenders 43
Trick 5: D leads the ♥ Q. He is saving the ♥ 10 for later, in case F is taking a Diamond trick which he (D) will want to put a valuable card on. F plays the ♣ 9. He is not expecting to win this trick, since M will probably want to trump anyway, but the ♣ 9 is worse than useless – if his partner wins another trump trick then F wants to be free to put the ♦ 10 on, and not to be forced to follow suit with the ♣ 9 which is worth no points. M wins with the ♣ K.
Score: M 35 points, Defenders 43
Trick 6: M leads the ♣ 8 – he makes sure that D's trump goes on a nice cheap card, and hopes that it is D, not F, who has the oustanding trump so that D will be embarrassed by having to lead Diamonds. D wins with the ♣ J, and F decides to play the ♠ 7, since he has been counting the points carefully. If he played the ♦ 10 the defenders would get to 55 points but would not have much chance of getting any more – he is hoping the ♦ 10 will take a trick.
Score: M 35 points, Defenders 45
Trick 7: D leads the ♦ Q. This brilliant play depends on his having worked out that F and M both have three diamonds (do you see how?). F plays the 9, and M, who rather enjoys having D on lead, plays the 7.

Score: M 35 points, Defenders 48
Trick 8: If D now plays a small Heart then M will throw away his ♦ K, and win the rest of the tricks. D therefore plays his ♥ 10, to force M to trump. F plays the ♠ 8, and M trumps with the ♠ J.
Score: M 47 points, Defenders 48
Trick 9: M plays the ♦ A, hoping that he has miscounted the points. D plays the ♥ 8, and F follows with the ♦ 8.
Score: Declarer 58 points, Defenders 48
Trick 10: M plays his last card, the ♦ K. D plays his heart, and F wins with the ♦ 10.
Final score: M 58 points, Defenders 62

So Forehand and Dealer win "without one, Game two, off four, times 12, loses 48".

Variations in the rules

The rules of Skat described above are among those most commonly used across central Europe, but Skat is the type of pub game in which local variations are common. Two of the more frequent variations are listed here:

Grand The base value for Grand is often taken as 24, not 20. This has little effect on the game except that Grand with one Jack outbids Null Open.

Contra As either defender plays to the first trick he may say "Contra", thus doubling the score for that hand. Declarer may, if he wishes, immediately say "recontra" or "re" which redoubles the score.

SOLO WHIST

Solo whist is a variation of the parent game of whist, in which each player plays for himself. It is usually called Solo, and is one of the better games for four players.

THE STANDARD 52-CARD pack is used. The cards are cut to determine the first dealer – thereafter the deal passes in rotation clockwise.

Dealer deals thirteen cards to each player in packets of three for four rounds, the last four cards being dealt singly. The last card of all, dealer's, is turned face up to show the trump suit for that deal.

There follows a session of bidding, in which a player may contract to make a certain number of tricks (or to lose them all).

The player on dealer's left (eldest) bids first. Each player must make a bid or pass. Once a bid has been made, a following player may make only a higher-ranking bid.

Bidding continues until a bid has been passed by the other three players. A player who passes may not subsequently re-enter the bidding, with one exception as noted below.

The player making the final bid plays against the other three, who are in temporary partnership.

The bids, from lowest to highest, are as follows:

1) *Proposal* The player making a proposal asks for another player to partner him in making eight tricks against the other two players. On his turn to bid, any of the other players may accept the proposal. The declaration of proposal and acceptance is usually called prop and cop, which are the words used when making or accepting the proposal.

This bid provides the only opportunity for a player to bid after passing, and it applies only to eldest hand. If eldest passes and another player makes a proposal which is passed all round, eldest, on his second turn, is allowed to accept if he wishes.

The players undertaking to make eight tricks in partnership remain at their seats – they do not sit opposite each other.

2) *Solo* This is a declaration to win five

tricks against the other three players.
3) *Misère* This is a declaration to lose all thirteen tricks. There is no trump suit.
4) *Abundance* This is a declaration to win nine tricks against the other three players; the declarer chooses his own trump suit, but does not need to name it until the bidding is completed.
5) *Royal Abundance* This is a declaration to win nine tricks with the turned-up suit remaining as trumps (note: it scores no more points than ordinary abundance but is a higher-ranking bid).
6) *Misère Ouverte* This is sometimes called 'Open Misère' or 'Spread'. It is a declaration to lose all thirteen tricks, with, after the first trick, the hand exposed on the table for the other players to see. There is no trump suit.
7) *Abundance Declared* This is a declaration to win all thirteen tricks; the declarer names his own trump suit in making the bid. A player making this bid is allowed to lead to the first trick.

The play

The normal rules of trick-taking games apply (see Whist). Players must follow to the suit led if able to, otherwise they may play any other card. The trick is won by the highest trump in the trick, or if there is no trump, by the highest card in the suit led.

Eldest hand leads to the first trick, except in the case of abundance declared, when declarer leads.

At the end of the hand the declarer has either fulfilled his contract or not, and scores accordingly.

If all players pass, the hands are thrown in and deal passes to the next player. The cards are shuffled before each deal.

Variations

Two variations are so common that new players might prefer to follow them.
1) Prop and cop is generally regarded as a boring and time-wasting bid and the majority of players dispense with it.
2) In abundance, the turn-up indicates trumps for the first trick, and declarer announces the new trumps only after the first trick is played. This can make a vital difference. If elder can guess declarer's suit correctly he can lead it on the first trick, with the likelihood that one of the declarer's trumps will itself be trumped.

A third variation is common and is a matter of taste.
3) At the end of a hand, when the tricks are collected up, or, if all players pass, when the hands are collected together for a re-deal, the cards are cut, but not shuffled. With the cards dealt in packets of three, this leads to freak hands with long suits, and more declarations of the higher values. Some players prefer the increased opportunities to make the big declarations; others find the hands artificial and unsatisfying.

Scoring

Scoring is usually with chips. Players making a contract receive chips to the following values from each player; players failing in the contracts pay the same amount to each player.

Prop and cop 2 units
Solo 2 units
Misère 3 units
Abundance 4 units
Royal abundance 4 units
Misère ouverte 6 units
Abundance declared 8 units

Note that prop and cop is not the same value as solo, since in the former two units are paid or received from two opposing players (i.e. profit or loss four units), while the latter involves paying or receiving from three opponents (i.e. profit or loss six units).

Scoring can be converted to a score sheet. It is suggested that all players start at 100 points, to avoid the necessity of minus totals.

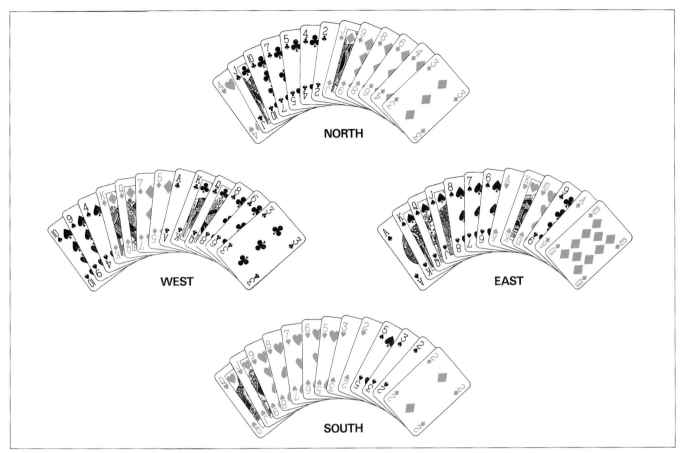

Figure 1 An example deal in Solo Whist (see text).

Strategy

Solo is not a difficult contract to gain. It is easy enough to see if a hand contains five tricks. It is dangerous to rely on an 'outside' hand, however, i.e. one with few trump winners. Aces often get trumped, and Kings are by no means easy to make. Many find the misère contracts the most interesting. The commonest cause of failure in a misère contract comes from regarding a long suit of low cards as safe when it does not include the 2. For instance, a player holding 8,7,6,5,4,3 in a suit will probably lose if any opponent who holds the 2 is the one with the next longest suit. Two or three rounds of the suit and the declarer could find himself holding three or four cards in his long suit and the only other card waiting to be led is the 2, which will put him down.

Example hand

Figure 1 shows four hands in which three players might reasonably bid in turn. Elder is West, and diamonds are trumps.

West has one sure trump trick, can probably win a heart lead with a trump and might make tricks from ♣ A, K, Q. There is no chance of making nine

tricks for abundance with clubs as trumps, but a bid of Solo is too risky.

North, if he can avoid being caught by the ♦ 2 is reasonably safe in the

An 11th century playing card.

other suits, and bids a hopeful misère.

East can bid abundance with confidence. With spades as trumps he should make seven spades, two hearts and a diamond. This gives him an extra trick for accidents.

South cannot see how he can be prevented from losing every trick, even if opponents can see his cards, and correctly bids misère ouverte, which he ultimately makes.

Looking at the hands all together it can be seen that only North's bid was beatable and that it would take such inspired defence that North might suspect the cards of being marked.

To defeat North's misère the play would have to proceed on the following lines. The underlined card wins the trick.

	West	North	East	South
1	♣ A	♣ J	♣ 9	♥ J
2	♣ K	♣ 10	♦ A	♥ 9
3	♣ Q	♣ 7	♦ 10	♥ 8
4	♠ 4	♦ J	♠ A	♠ 5
5	♦ K	♥ 4	♥ A	♥ 7
6	♦ Q	♦ 9	♥ K	♥ 6
7	♦ 7	♦ 8	♥ 10	♥ Q
8	♦ 5	♦ 6	♠ K	♥ 5
9				♦ 2

North is now beaten, as he holds the only remaining diamonds, the 3 and 4.

SPOIL FIVE

Spoil Five is a member of the Euchre family and is believed to be one of the oldest card games. It is related to Ombre, which has a somewhat similar ranking system and at one time was widely played in Europe. Spoil Five is reportedly the most popular card game in several parts of Ireland.

SPOIL FIVE IS A TRICK-TAKING card game for two players or more but is best for a good number – 5 or 6 is ideal.

A standard 52-card pack is used without jokers. The ranking of the cards is rather involved and owes more to tradition than common sense. It is likely to cause confusion at first.

There are two factors that affect ranking: the colour of the suit and whether or not the suit is trumps for the hand. There are three unusual features of the ranking:

1) The Ace of hearts is ALWAYS the third-ranking trump;
2) The first and second ranking trumps are respectively the five and jack of the relevant suit;
3) The plain (i.e. non-court) cards of the black suits are ranked in the reverse of the normal order (where Ace is low).

The ranking of the cards is shown in Figure 1.

Notice that the black suits have identical ranking, also that the Ace is the lowest ranking card in diamonds when a plain suit, but like the other Aces is ranked above the king when trumps. Notice also that there are fourteen trumps and only twelve hearts except when hearts are trumps.

Players complete as individuals and the objective is to win three tricks, or ideally all five but not four, with the alternative objective of stopping any other player doing so, hence the name Spoil Five.

Play

Each player starts with an agreed number of counters – 25 is about right. At the start of a game, every player contributes one counter a pool. Subsequently, dealer only contributes a counter to the pool at the start of each hand until the pool is won when again everyone chips in to form a new pool. The deal rotates clockwise in turn after each hand.

Fives cards are dealt to each player in batches of two followed by batches of three, starting with the player on the dealer's left. The next card is turned over to determine trumps. The remainder of the pack, which is not used, is put to one side and may not be examined.

If any player holds the Ace of the suit displayed (i.e., the Ace of trumps) he must declare it before playing a card to the first trick. This entitles him to the exposed card in exchange for any card in his hand which is discarded unseen. He may decline the trump if he so wishes, but if he fails to declare his Ace, the Ace is ranked as the lowest trump for that hand only.

If the exposed card is an Ace, then the dealer is entitled to it in exchange for any card in his hand. He can, if he wishes, decline it by saying 'I play with these'. It is usual etiquette for eldest (player on left of dealer) to invite dealer to exchange if he does not at once do so, before leading to the first trick.

Highest-ranking trump, or if no trump cards are played, the highest-ranking card of the suit led, takes the trick. The winner of a trick leads to the next.

The rules of card play do not follow the normal procedure for trick-taking games. After the lead, which may be any card of eldest's choice, other players must follow suit if a trump is led but no player is obliged to play any of the top three trumps (**5, J, ♥ A**) if a *lower* trump is led, whether or not a higher trump is later played to the trick. Instead, a player may discard from a plain suit. This action is called reneging. A player cannot renege if he holds any trump of lower rank but must then follow suit.

Example: Player A leads the **♥ A**.

Player B comes out with the 5 of trumps. Player C, holding only the Jack in trumps, may renege since it is one of the top three trumps and ranks above the card led.

Where a card of a plain suit is led, a player may either follow suit or trump, even if he holds cards in the suit led, but he may not discard unless he is void in the suit led.

The first player to win three tricks takes the pool. If a player takes the first three tricks however, he may take the

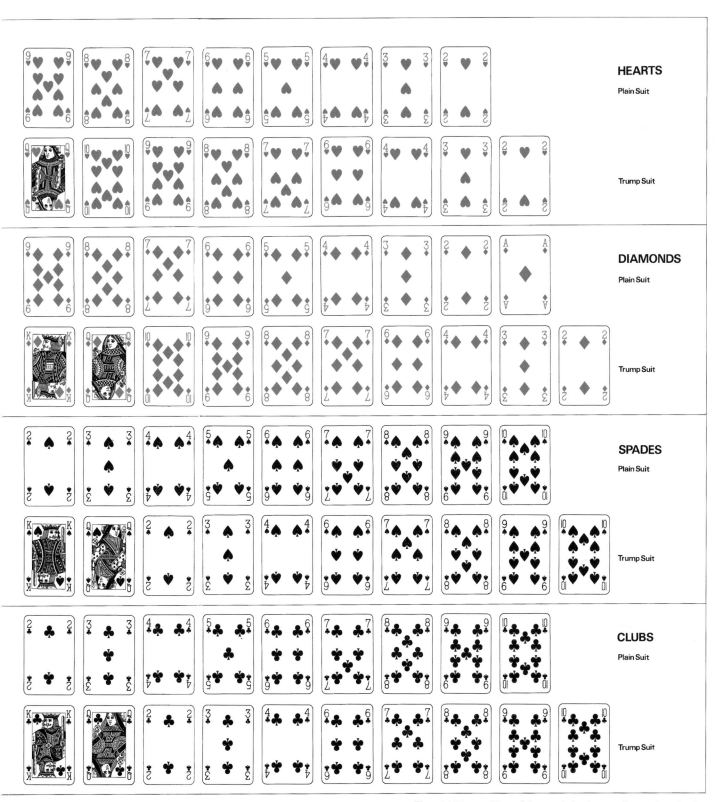

Figure 1 The ranking of the cards in descending order of value.

pool or elect to try for all five tricks. This is called jinxing. If he chooses the latter and fails to get all five tricks, he does not get the pool. If however he succeeds he collects the pool plus one counter from each of the other players.

A hand in which no player makes three tricks, or a player made the first three tricks, then elected to jinx and failed, is 'spoilt'. There are no payments, and the new dealer adds a counter to the pool as usual before the next hand.

Strategy The more players there are, the harder it is to win the pool. With five or six players most hands are spoilt – which does not mean that they are necessarily uninteresting.

At the start of the hand, each player must take the decision as to whether to go for three tricks or to attempt to spoil the chances of the other players. A decision on whether or not to jinx need not be taken until the first three tricks are won. When a player gets two tricks the other players will generally conspire against him.

It is not always wise to 'rob the trump' when eligible to do so since it discloses one of your cards to the opposition. Remember that even if you have the option on the Ace of trumps as dealer that the card is only the fourth-highest trump (third highest if hearts) and it may be wiser under some circumstances to reject it for the same reason.

TAROT

The name Tarot refers to a family of card games originating in Northern Italy around 1440. It is spelt variously (e.g. Tarokk, Tarocchi, Tarock) in the various countries where it is played, and versions of Tarot have been popular at some time across most of Europe.

THE PATTERN OF THE CARDS, the number of cards in the pack, and the rules of Tarot all vary from place to place, but the common feature is that the pack of cards has five suits, one of which is clearly different from the other four and is always trumps: the games are of the trick-taking type.

Fortune telling

Many English-speaking people will have heard of Tarot cards only in connection with fortune telling. However this is a relatively recent development, dating from an essay published in Paris in 1781. Tarot cards had been used widely for playing games for over 300 years before anyone thought of telling fortunes with them, and it is only in the last 100 years or so, and until very recently only in parts of Britain and France where the games are more or less unknown, that the cards have been commonly used for fortune telling. Suggestions of connections with the Hebrew Alphabet, with Gypsies, or with ancient Egypt have all been traced to specific fabricated documents. Tarot cards are a 15th century European invention.

The cards

Most Tarot cards for sale outside the Continent of Europe are designed for fortune telling, and are very difficult to play games with, especially for those not used to the Italian suits (Batons, Swords, Cups and Coins) which they use. Cards designed for playing with are readily available in France though, and can also be obtained elsewhere.

The pack of 78 cards (see Figure 1) contains:

(1) Four suits of 14 cards each: Spades, Hearts, Diamonds and Clubs. Each suit contains, in increasing order of rank: 1,2,3,4,5,6,7,8,9,10,V (= Valet, the Jack), C (= Chevalier, the Knight), D (= Dame, the Queen), R (= Roi, the King).

(2) A fifth suit, which is always trumps, and contains numbered cards 1 to 21.

(3) The Excuse, or Fool, which looks a bit like a Joker.

The game

French Tarot is a game for four players, each playing individually. Eighteen cards are dealt to each. The remaining six, known as the "Chien", are left face down on the table. There is an auction, the winner of which (usually) exposes

Figure 1 *(pages 150, 151)* The full pack of 78 tarot cards. The three oudlers (21 and 1 of trumps and the Fool) are marked with a dot.

A selection of Tarot cards from another pack.

Elaborate cards from an old pack.

the Chien, then takes those cards into his hand, discards six cards to start his pile of tricks, and plays alone against the other three players.

Rules of play

Tarot is a trick-taking game, like Bridge, Solo Whist, Skat etc, but the rules of play are slightly different. As in those games, the player who leads to each trick may play any card, while the following players must play a card of the suit led, if they hold one. However there are two additional restrictions: a player who has no card of the suit led must play trumps if he has any, and a player playing a trump must beat the highest trump so far played to the trick if he can, even if this means beating his partner's card. This second restriction only applies in trumps. The trick is won by the highest trump played to it, or by the highest card of the suit led if there is no trump played. The winner of each trick leads to the next one.

The Fool may be played at any time, but it never wins the trick. If it is led to a trick then the next card played determines the suit the other players must follow. It is normally impossible to lose the Fool – it is kept with his tricks by the person who played it. If that trick is not won by his side, though, he must give the opposition a card worth one point (see below) in place of the Fool. The Fool must not be played to the last trick – the penalty for doing so is that it is given up to the opposition in exchange for one of their one point cards. If the side with the Fool takes no tricks, then they still don't lose it, but get a total of four card points, while the opposition get 87.

Counting and the value of the cards

The values of the cards are as follows:
The three "Oudlers" (The 21 and 1 of trumps, and the Fool) 5 points each
The four Kings 5 points each
The four Queens 4 points each
The four Knights 3 points each
The four Jacks 2 points each
All the remaining cards 1 point each

The cards are counted in pairs – each pair is worth one less than the sum of the values of its two cards. The historical reasons for this perverse way of counting are too complex to discuss here, but if you get it right the two sides' scores should add up to 91 card points.

The Declarer's objective depends on how many of the three "Oudlers" he gets in his tricks:

With 3 Oudlers, he needs	36 points
With 2	41 points
With 1	51 points
With none	56 points

The deal

Players cut one card each: the player with the lowest deals (trumps are high). The player opposite Dealer shuffles, then the player on Dealer's left cuts, then Dealer deals, three cards to each player, starting on his right, and *anti-clockwise*. Whenever he likes during the deal, he deals one card to the Chien, until there are six cards there. The deal passes round to the right after each hand. Note that both the deal and the play are anti-clockwise in Tarot – this will feel a bit odd at first.

If a player has been dealt the trump 1, and no other trumps nor the fool, then he may (and usually should) annul the deal.

The auction

Each player in turn, starting on Dealer's right, must either bid or pass. The available bids are:
(1) *Prise:* Declarer gets to swap cards with the Chien.
(2) *Garde:* Exactly the same as Prise, but outbids it and is worth more.
(3) *Garde without the Chien:* The Chien goes into declarer's tricks, but he doesn't get to swap cards.
(4) *Garde against the Chien:* The Chien goes to the opposition.

Each player gets only one chance to bid and the highest bidder becomes declarer. If all four players pass (quite common), the hand is thrown in and the deal passes round.

The Chien

If the Declarer has bid Prise or Garde, the six cards of the Chien are exposed, then taken into his hand. He then discards six cards face down to start his pile of tricks. It is always illegal to discard Kings or Oudlers (the 5 point cards), and it is illegal to discard trumps unless the hand consists entirely of Kings and trumps. Any trumps must be discarded face up.

The score

If Declarer achieves his required number of card points, he scores 25 game points, plus one for each card point in excess of his target which he achieved. If he fails to achieve his requirement, he loses 25 points, plus one for each card point by which he failed. If his contract is Garde, the score is doubled, if it is Garde with the Chien, the score is multiplied by four, and in Garde against the Chien it is multiplied by six.

149

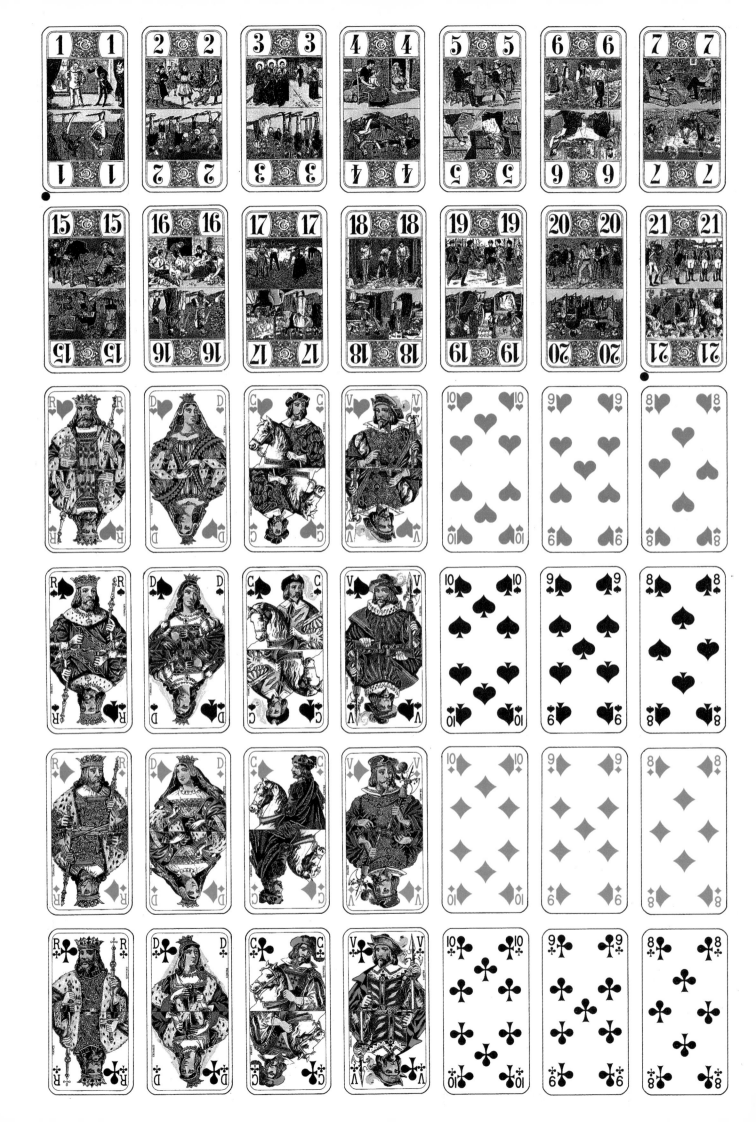

Payment

Declarer is paid his score by each of his Opponents. The recommended method is to score on a piece of paper, and to subtract Declarer's score from the total under each of the Opponents' initials, adding three times his score to Declarer's total. In this way the total of the four scores should always be zero.

Bonuses

In addition to the basic score for the game, each player may claim one of the following bonuses as he plays his first card. These claims are optional.

10 trumps (possibly including the Fool)	20 points
13 trumps (. . .)	30 points
15 trumps (. . .)	40 points

To make one of these claims, the appropriate number of trumps must be laid face up on the table for everyone to see. The Fool may be counted as a trump for this purpose, but it is illegal to expose the Fool as one of the trumps if there are any more trumps in the hand. It is legal to expose 10 trumps when actually holding, say 13. None of these bonuses gets multiplied (e.g. by four for Garde without the Chien). The bonus scores for whichever side wins the hand – it is paid to the Declarer by each of the defenders, or by him to each of them, depending only on whether he achieves his target of card points, and not on which side made the claim.

If the "Petit" (the Trump 1) is played to the last trick, then the side which wins that trick scores a bonus of 10 points. This bonus is multiplied (by two for Garde, by four for Garde without and by six for Garde against the Chien), and it is made independently of who wins the game, so that if declarer fails to reach his target, but wins the last trick with the Petit, then his losses are reduced by 10 (or 20, 40, 60 as appropriate).

Making all the tricks

If Declarer makes all the tricks, then he gets a bonus of 200 points (from each

An Italian 19th century tarot card (Victoria and Albert Museum, London).

player) in addition to his ordinary score and bonuses.

Declarer may also announce at the beginning of play that he is going to take all the tricks – in this case he gets to lead to the first trick (instead of the player on dealer's right). After this declaration Declarer scores 400 points if he is successful, and loses 200 if he fails to take all the tricks (though he still scores plus for making his ordinary target).

Declarer may announce that he will make all the tricks when he holds the Fool. In this case he can play the Fool to the last trick, when it wins the trick, and he can score the bonus of 10 for taking the 17th (penultimate) trick with the Petit. If he loses any of the first 17 tricks then the normal rules apply, and the Fool is lost if it is played to the last trick.

Some remarks on skilful play

What is needed to bid: Strong hands are ones with lots of trumps and kings. Possession of the Oudlers is, however, the overriding consideration in deciding

whether to bid, since they affect the target so much. Roughly speaking, to bid Garde:

with three Oudlers, three trumps and one king are needed

with two Oudlers, five trumps and two kings are needed

with one Oudler, seven trumps and three kings are needed

with no Oudlers, Garde cannot be bid.

It is unusual to want to bid Prise rather than Garde – a player expecting to lose should not bid.

To bid Garde against or without the Chien it is necessary to be much stronger than this – the only common suitable hands are those with all three Oudlers and a suit which is void or singleton (necessary to get the Petit home), so that it is possible to count which tricks are going to bring in 36 points. The average Chien contains seven points.

Hunting the Petit: Of the three Oudlers, the trump 21 is the highest card, so it can't be captured; the Fool can't be captured because of the rules, and so capturing the Petit is the only chance of reducing the target. Because of the rule that players are forced to overtake in trumps, it is sometimes possible to capture the Petit by leading small trumps – the player with the Petit is forced to play big ones – and then, when it is judged that he has only one or two trumps left, leading out the 21 and 20.

The last few tricks: Due to the requirement to play trumps when one cannot follow the suit led, it is common for the defenders to have a lot of Kings and Queens left at the end. This makes the last few tricks disproportionately valuable. Normally Declarer will try to keep some trumps for the end, but in any case he must get rid of his losing cards in the side suits early on.

Drawing Trumps: If Declarer has a long suit, especially if it includes the King and Queen, the most effective way to get rid of the opponents' trumps is usually to lead the suit out. Since the opponents are forced to trump, the long suit is as good as trumps once everyone else has run out of them.

WHIST

Like most trick-taking games, whist developed from the game of triumph. In the early 18th century it became fashionable among society, and gained popularity through the work of the famous writer on cards, Edmund Hoyle. For nearly 200 years it was the most widely played card game among the English-speaking, until it was overtaken in popularity by bridge.

WHIST IS A SIMPLER GAME than bridge and is still widely played by those who prefer a less taxing game. The full pack of 52 cards is used. In practice, it is usual to use two packs with contrasting backs, so that one pack is being shuffled while the other is being dealt. The cards rank from Ace (high) down to 2 (low).

Dealer deals one card at a time to each player, clockwise beginning with the player on his left (eldest) until the pack is exhausted and each player has 13 cards. The last card, however, he must turn face up in the centre of the table for all to see. The suit of this card becomes the trump suit for the deal, and when it has been noted it is taken up by the dealer to complete his hand.

Play

Eldest hand leads to the first trick. He may lead any card. Each player then plays a card in turn, if possible of the suit led. A player without a card in the suit led may play a card of any other suit. The four cards played form a trick, which is won by the player who played the highest card in the suit led, or, if the trick contains a trump, by the highest trump. The winner of a trick leads to the next trick.

One player from each side collects the tricks won by the partnership.

Scoring and object

The scoring differs in Britain and the U.S.A. In Britain there are complex systems involving game points, games and rubbers. The method given here is one of the simplest.

Scoring in Great Britain

A side scores one point for each trick that it makes in the deal in excess of six (e.g. a side making nine tricks scores three points). It follows, since there are only 13 tricks, that only one side can score for tricks in each deal.

After the hand has been played, a side may also score points for 'honours'. The honours are the Ace, King, Queen and Jack of the trump suit. A side that is dealt all four scores four points; a side dealt three scores two points. There is one restriction: a side with a score of four points at the beginning of a deal cannot score for honours.

A game is won by the first side to score five points. The points for tricks are scored before the points for honours. Thus a side reaching or passing five points with a score for tricks cannot be overtaken by the other side scoring for honours.

The object is to win a rubber, i.e. the best of three games.

Scoring in the United States

Scoring in the United States is simpler. There are no points for honours. Points for tricks are calculated in the same way, i.e. one point for each trick taken over six.

Game is the first side to seven points. The American system of scoring is more satisfactory than the traditional British system. It seems unfair to award a side holding the top four trumps, which gives a big advantage in the trick-taking, four-fifths of the points needed for a game just for being dealt good hands, as happens in Britain.

Strategy

Skill is a question of playing in collaboration with partner, working out where cards lay and leading cards which will help partner.

It is possible to give information to partner by the choice of card played. For instance there is a recognised order in which to lead cards from certain holdings in suits, and this is given in Table 1. If the game is to be played seriously, these leads should be learned by a player who does not wish to mislead his partner when leading, and who wishes to make the correct inferences from the leads of the other players at the table. Needless to say, passing information to partner in any other manner, such as by signals, tone of voice, gestures of disappointment or encouragement, are cheating and not to be practised.

It has been established by usage and practice that the second player to a trick usually plays low, and that the third player (partner of leader) usually plays as high a card as possible. It is also recognized that a player leading a low card is usually leading from a long suit or at least from a suit which he prefers to be led, and partner should respond, when getting the lead, by leading that suit back.

It is usually profitable for a player to lead a long suit, with the purpose of 'clearing' the suit, i.e. when the other players are out of the suit those cards still held are winners and can be beaten only by trumps. However, it should be noted that this is only profitable if the player has some outside winners which will enable him to get the lead. It is no use holding the last two clubs, say, if there is no prospect of gaining the lead and being able to 'cash' them. When leading from a 'broken' long suit (i.e. one which does not possess any of the combinations of top cards in Table 1) it is customary to lead the fourth highest card, which helps partner to calculate how many cards in the suit each partnership holds.

A player holding five or more trumps will usually do well to lead one, with the object of forcing out opposing trumps as quickly as possible, leaving himself with the only trumps left – but the composition of the rest of the hand will determine how far to follow this principle.

When a player plays an honour, it is usually profitable for the opponent following him to beat it with a higher honour.

Example game

The example game is meant to show some of the considerations which go through the players' minds. No doubt

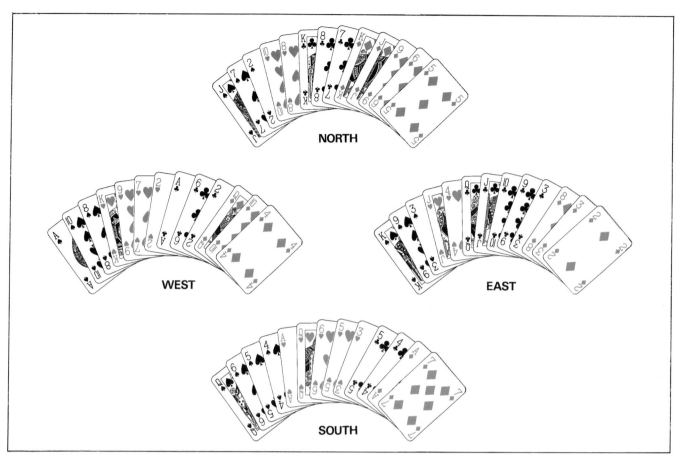

Figure 1 An example deal at Whist (see text).

TABLE 1

In plain suits

Holding	First lead	Second lead
A K Q J	K	J
A K Q	K	Q
A K x . . .	K	A
A K	A	K
K Q J x	K	J
K Q J x x	J	K
K Q J x x x . . .	J	Q
A x x x . . .	A	4th best of rest
K Q x . . .	K	4th best of rest
A Q J	A	Q
A Q J x	A	Q
A Q J x x . . .	A	J
K J 10 9	9	K (if A or Q falls)
Q J x	Q	
Q J x x . . .	4th best	

In the trump suit

A K Q J	J	Q
A K Q	Q	K
A K x x x x x . . .	K	A
A K x x x x	4th best	

x = small cards

. . . = or more small cards

the plays made are not always the best ones. The cards are dealt as in Figure 2. South dealt, and turned up the ♣ 4, making clubs trumps.

The play might proceed as follows, with the card winning the trick underlined. West leads to the first trick.

	West	North	East	South
1	♥ 2	♥ 8	♥ J	<u>♥ Q</u>

West decides to lead his fourth highest heart, hoping that partner might be able to win with the Ace and return the suit to West's King. East plays as high as he can.

	West	North	East	South
2	♦ 4	♦ 5	♦ 2	<u>♦ A</u>

South decides that, with only two small trumps, he might, by ridding himself of his two diamonds, be able to make one of his trumps by trumping a third diamond lead.

	West	North	East	South
3	♦ 10	<u>♦ K</u>	♦ 3	♦ 7
4	<u>♦ Q</u>	♦ 6	♦ 8	♣ 4

The plan works perfectly for South, as partner wins his second diamond lead and returns the suit, with the hoped for result. South is reluctant to lead hearts, as he knows that West probably began with four, which means that either North or East might be without one. He would prefer West, who does not have this information, to lead the suit, so that South would not waste his Ace. Therefore he leads his fourth spade.

	West	North	East	South
5	♠ 8	♠ J	<u>♠ K</u>	♠ 4

East realises he has three certain trump tricks, but decides not to lead them out. He returns spades in the reasonable hope that his partner holds the Ace.

	West	North	East	South
6	<u>♠ A</u>	♠ 2	♠ 3	♠ 5

West knows the ♥ A is against his side, and leads his final spade.

	West	North	East	South
7	♠ 10	♠ 7	♠ 9	<u>♠ Q</u>

South knows his remaining spade is the last, but leads it hoping that the trump it will draw from East will help his partner to make an extra trump trick.

	West	North	East	South
8	♥ 7	♥ 10	♣ 3	<u>♠ 6</u>

East decides now to test the trumps.

	West	North	East	South
9	<u>♣ A</u>	♣ 7	♣ Q	♣ 5
10	<u>♣ 2</u>	♣ 8	♣ 9	♥ 3

North considered winning with his king and leading a master diamond. This could have cost a trick, had East taken

Above The Christmas 'academicks' playing a rubber at whist.

Right An 18th century French engraving 'Le Partie de Wisch' (the game of whist).

the view that West held a final trump, as indeed he does. East could discard his ♥ **4** on the diamond lead, which would be won by West with his ♣ **6**, and East would have taken the two final tricks with ♣ **J, 10**.

East could do no better on trick 11 than leading another trump to drive out the King.

11	♣ 6	♣ K	♣ J	♥ 5
12	♥ 9	♦ J	♣ 10	♥ 6

East must finally lead the ♥ **4**, and South makes his Ace.

13	♥ K	♦ 9	♥ 4	♥ A

The North-South pair made the best of their cards in this game, winning seven tricks and scoring one point.

In Britain, the three honours held by East-West would score two points. The first game of the rubber is still to be won therefore, with West now dealing and his side leading by two points to one.

GAMBLING GAMES

BACCARAT

The game described here is sometimes called Baccarat à deux tableaux, and is the classical game popular in the great days of gambling in Europe between the wars. It is a casino banking game.

BACCARAT IS FROM the group of card games which includes Chemin de Fer and Punto Banco, and is the generic name of all such games.

The table layout is shown in Figure 1. It has spaces for 12 players and is in two halves, the half to the right of banker being tableau un, and that to the left tableau deux. The sections marked 1 and 2 at the centre of the table are betting spaces. A stake in the space marked 1, on whichever side of the table, is a bet that that side will beat the banker, and a stake in the space marked 2 that the other side will win. A stake on the line between the 1 and 2 is a bet à cheval on both sides of the table to beat the banker; it wins if both sides win, loses if both sides are beaten, and is a stand-off if one side wins and the other loses, or if there is a stand-off on the separate hands.

Six packs of cards are shuffled and cut and an indicator is placed above the bottom ten cards, which are not used. The cards are then placed in a shoe. All cards have their pip value, with Aces counting one and all court cards (King, Queen, Jack) ten.

A baccarat hand consists of two or three cards. The point count of the hand is the sum of the pip value, except that only the last digit counts, e.g. a hand of Queen, 4, 9, has a pip count of 23, and therefore a point of 3.

The object is to hold a hand with a higher point than the banker. A two-card hand with a point of 8 or 9 is a natural, and wins against all three-card hands, whatever the point.

After the players place their bets on the tables, the banker deals three hands of two cards each, one to each side of the table and one to himself. The players sitting next to the banker play the cards for their side of the table, and each continues to do so until he loses a coup, when the next player plays the cards for the side, and so on. A player may decline to play the cards.

The three hands are examined, and any hands with a point of 8 or 9 exposed. A point of 9 is called 'le grand', and 8 'le petit'. These hands win immediately, except that should there be two such, a point of 9 beats a point of 8.

If neither banker nor player has declared a natural, the banker first deals with tableau un. The player must stand or draw a third card. As he is playing for all the players on his side of the table, he is not allowed to do as he wishes, but must play according to the Table of Play, which gives his side best chance.

With a point of 0,1,2,3 or 4 he must ask for a third card. With 6 or 7 he must stand. Only with a point of 5 does the player have an option.

A player taking a third card receives it face up. The banker then deals similarly with tableau deux.

When both sides' hands are complete the dealer completes his own hand. There is a Table of Play for the banker, which is more complex than the players.

Because the banker is playing against both sides of the table simultaneously, his Table of Play can only be advisory, as he will be in different situations in relation to the two hands. Where there is a conflict, he might decide to make

TABLE ONE: **Banker's Table of Play at Baccarat**

Banker's point	Banker draws if player draws	Banker stands if player draws	Banker has option if player draws
3	0, 1, 2, 3, 4, 5, 6, 7	8	9
4	2, 3, 4, 5, 6, 7	0, 1, 8, 9	–
5	5, 6, 7	0, 1, 2, 3, 8, 9	4
6	6, 7	0, 1, 2, 3, 4, 5, 8, 9	–

Note: if the player does not draw, the banker stands on 6, and draws on 3, 4, 5

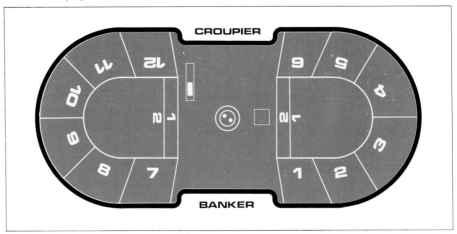

Figure 1 Table for Baccarat a deux tableaux.

the best play against the side with the higher stakes.

The banker is advised to draw on 0, 1 or 2, and to stand on 7. His best play for points 3 to 6 are shown in Table 1.

When all hands are complete, they are exposed and the bets settled. Equal hands are a stand-off and the bets are void.

There is no room for strategy in Baccarat, which is a game of chance.

BLACKJACK

Blackjack is the most popular card game in casinos in America, and rapidly becoming so in other parts of the world. It arose from the French game vingt-et-un, corrupted to van john in Britain and eventually to pontoon, which is a popular variation still played widely at home.

IN AMERICA THE game, known as twenty-one, acquired its casino name when, to encourage business, a casino began to offer double the winnings to players holding the Ace of Spades and either black Jack. Gradually the game took the name 'Blackjack'.

The rules, even in casinos, are not standardized, with British practice differing in general from American. In describing the basic game, the version common in American casinos is given first.

Four full packs of 52 cards are used, shuffled by the dealer and cut by a player by means of an indicator card. The dealer places a second indicator some 50 cards from the bottom of the joint pack to indicate the end of the deal. The cards are dealt from a dealing shoe.

The players (up to seven) sit at the spaces at the table (see Figure 1).

Cards have their pip value, with court cards (King, Queen, Jack) counting as ten, and Aces as one or eleven at the player's or dealer's discretion, although the dealer has no real choice, as will be seen.

The object of the game is to obtain a total card count, with two or more cards, higher than that of the dealer, but without exceeding 21. A player whose count exceeds 21 is said to have bust, and loses his stake.

Before the deal, each player puts a stake on the table before his space. The first card dealt is 'burnt', i.e. it is left face down on the table and takes no part in the game. The dealer then deals one card face up to each player, including himself, starting with the player on his left. He then deals each player a second face-up card, but his own second card is dealt face down.

If the dealer's face-up card is an Ace there is a possibility that his full hand is a blackjack or natural (Ace and a ten-count card, making 21). He asks the players if they wish to insure against this (explained later), and then looks at his other card. He also looks at his second card if his first card is a ten-count. In each case if his full hand is a natural, which cannot be beaten, he exposes it and settles immediately. If his full hand is not a natural he replaces the card face down and the deal proceeds as usual.

The dealer attends to each player in turn, beginning with the player on his left.

If the player has a natural, he wins and is paid immediately at odds of 3 to

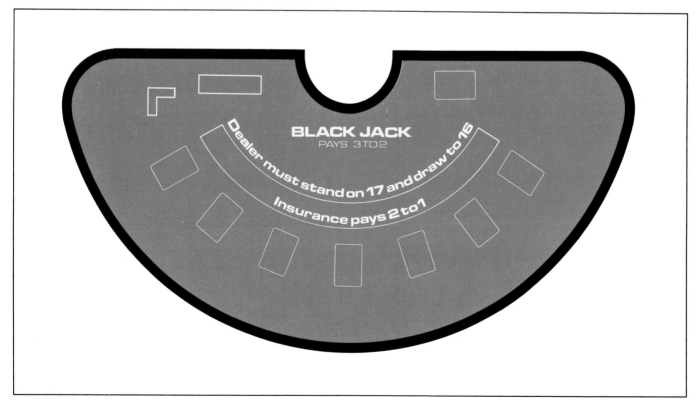

Figure 1 A Las Vegas Blackjack table.

2, as the table layout shows.

Otherwise he may stand on his total or he may ask the dealer for another card, which is usually done by beckoning or saying 'hit me'. He may continue to take cards until he is satisfied with his total. All cards are dealt face up. If a card takes his total past 21, he loses and dealer collects the stake and burns the cards.

A third option arises when the player's two cards are of the same rank (including any two cards with a ten count). He may split the pair. This involves treating each of the cards as the first card of two separate hands. The original stake stays on one card, and the player adds an equal stake to the other. The dealer then deals separate face-up cards to each hand, and the player plays each hand separately in turn, beginning with that on his right. Should the second card in either hand form another pair, he may split the hand further.

If a player splits a pair of Aces, he may not draw a third card to either hand. If a split hand results in a natural, the odds paid are 1 to 1, not 3 to 2.

A player's fourth option is to double down. This entitles him to double his stake and to receive a third card face down. This card must not be looked at by the player or dealer; it remains face down until the dealer has completed his own hand. The dealer then faces the card and pays or collects accordingly.

The final option open to the player is insurance, and occurs when the dealer's face-up card is an Ace, as mentioned earlier. He may insure against the dealer holding a natural by paying a premium of half his stake. The dealer asks, as soon as each player has two cards, which players want insurance. When all who wish to have insured, the dealer looks at his face-down card. If he does have a natural he pays all the insurers at odds of 2 to 1, and collects the losing stakes. Otherwise he collects the insurance stakes and proceeds as before. The insurance has the effect of the player saving his original stake if the dealer has a natural.

When the dealer has dealt with each player in turn, collecting and discarding the cards of all who bust, and removing their stakes, he plays his own cards, beginning by turning over his second card so that his hand is exposed.

The dealer has no options. If his count is 16 or less, he must deal himself an additional card. If his count is 17, 18, 19, 20 or 21, or if it reaches there in dealing extra cards, he must stand. If when dealing himself an extra card or cards he busts, he pays all players still in the game.

A vital difference between player and dealer occurs with the value of the Ace. Like the players, the dealer may count Ace as one or eleven, but if by counting it as 11 his count is one of the numbers 17 to 21, he must stand. For example, if his hand is Ace, 7, he must stand on 18 (known as a 'soft' 18), and cannot call his count 8 and draw another card.

When the dealer stands, he pays all remaining players with a higher point count, and collects the stakes from those with a lower count. All bets (except naturals, mentioned earlier) are paid at 1 to 1, or evens. When the dealer's and the player's hand are equal (including naturals), the bet is a stand-off, and the player retains his stake.

Variations

Common variations found in casinos in America are:

1) a dealer will draw on soft 17. This is a rule and will be displayed, probably on the table layout. The dealer still has no options.
2) insurance is not allowed in all casinos.
3) sometimes the player's cards are dealt face down. It does not affect the play, as the dealer, having no options, cannot profit from knowing the players' hands.
4) doubling down might be restricted to hands counting 11 only, or 10,11 or 9,10,11.

In Britain, restrictions were introduced to protect the poor player, not necessarily successfully, as follows:
1) the dealer does not deal a second card to himself until all the players in turn have completed their hands, and dealer is ready to play his own hand. Known as the 'London deal', this was designed to prevent casinos being cheated by collusion between a player and a dealer, who could signal his face-down card. It has the effect, however, of asking players to split hands and double down before they know if dealer has a natural, a situation which discourages the wise player from making these plays.
2) splitting is barred on pairs 4, 5 and 10.
3) doubling down is allowed only on 9,10 and 11.
4) insurance is allowed only when the player has a natural. It therefore has a different function. Since a player with a natural cannot lose, the function of insurance is not to save his stake, as in America, but to ensure a profit.

Strategy

Considerable judgement can be exercised at blackjack. It is a game where, from time to time, players have enjoyed an advantage over the bank. To acquire this advantage required great skill in counting cards, sometimes aided by electronic apparatus taped under the clothing. The advantage is considerably lessened by the current habit of using four packs, of which the last fifth or so are not used.

TABLE ONE: **The best plays in Blackjack**

Player		Dealer's face-up card									
	holds	2	3	4	5	6	7	8	9	10	A
	17	S	S	S	S	S	S	S	S	S	S
	16	S	S	S	S	S	H	H	H	S	S
	15	S	S	S	S	S	H	H	H	H	H
Hard	14	S	S	S	S	S	H	H	H	H	H
2-card	13	S	S	S	S	S	H	H	H	H	H
Total	12	H	H	S	S	S	H	H	H	H	H
	11	D	D	D	D	D	D	D	D	D	D
	10	D	D	D	D	D	D	D	D	H	H
	9	D	D	D	D	D	H	H	H	H	H
	19	S	S	S	S	S	S	S	S	S	S
	18	S	S	S	S	S	S	H	H	H	H
Soft	17	D	D	D	D	D	H	H	H	H	H
2-card	16	H	H	H	H	D	H	H	H	H	H
Total	15	H	H	H	H	D	H	H	H	H	H
	14	H	H	H	H	D	H	H	H	H	H
	13	H	H	H	H	D	H	H	H	H	H

Always stand on hard hands of 17 or more and soft hands of 19 and 20.
S = stand   H = hit   D = double down

Blackjack in an 1890 lithograph.

Counting involves keeping track of how many 10-count cards are played, and, if possible, Aces, medium cards (6-9) and low cards (2-5). As soon as the remaining pack is rich in one or another, the player can bet accordingly. For instance, if the pack is rich in 10-counts, and has few low cards, and dealer's face-up card is 6, he has an excellent chance of busting, and a player might double down on 8, or stand on 12, when otherwise he might not.

Assuming a normal distribution in the pack, the best plays, accepted by a majority of experts, are shown in Table 1 (for the American rules outlined above).

Experts are less in agreement over the question of splitting. Table 2 gives a reasonable consensus of opinion, again for the American rules.

Insurance is not recommended, unless a card-counter can work out the odds of success in a particular case. With normal distribution of cards, there are 16 chances in 51 that a dealer's face-down card will be a 10-count, and

as the odds of 2 to 1 offered would be fair if there were 17 chances in 51, the casino has an advantage of nearly 6 per cent. Insurance should not be regarded as insurance, but as a bet, at 2 to 1, that the dealer has a blackjack. In the long run, this bet will show a loss.

With the dealer having no options, and a tied hand being a stand-off, it might be wondered where the casino's profit comes from. It comes from the

TABLE TWO: **Advisability of splitting pairs in Blackjack**

Player's pair	Dealer's face-up card									
	2	3	4	5	6	7	8	9	10	A
A	S	S	S	S	S	S	S	S	S	S
10	X	X	X	X	X	X	X	X	X	X
9	S	S	S	S	S	X	X	X	X	X
8	S	S	S	S	S	S	S	X	X	S
7	S	S	S	S	S	S	X	X	X	X
6	S	S	S	S	S	X	X	X	X	X
5	X	X	X	X	X	X	X	X	X	X
4	X	X	X	X	X	X	X	X	X	X
3	S	S	S	S	S	S	X	X	X	X
2	S	S	S	S	S	S	X	X	X	X

S = split   X = do not split

Blackjack at the Four Queens Hotel, Las Vegas. Notice that this dealer draws on soft 17 (compare with Figure 1).

fact that the players play before the dealer. Thus the dealer wins from all players who bust, although he might later bust himself. In this one case, where player and dealer both bust, the tie is not therefore a stand-off.

It is difficult to estimate the casino's actual advantage overall, since the skill of the individual player must be taken into account. It has been estimated that a player who plays as if he were dealer, with the dealer's obligations, faces a disadvantage of over 5 per cent. A bad player who bets without much care or thought might face a disadvantage of about twice that, while a player who plays carefully and follows the guidance in the two tables herewith, might find he is in as even a game as can be found in a casino.

CRAPS AND OTHER DICE GAMES

Dice are the oldest of gambling implements, and the game of craps, which uses two dice, is the most popular gambling game in American casinos. It arose from an old English game called Hazard, which worked on very similar principles, and was nothing like the game Hazard which is still to be found in American casinos.

CRAPS IS NOT ONLY a casino game. The simple private game is described first. It requires only two identical dice.

Any number can play. They enclose the playing area, called the centre, which might be a carpet on the floor – preferably against a wall, so that the dice have something to bounce against.

The first player to throw the dice is the 'shooter'. He places the amount he wishes to bet in front of him. This is called his centre bet. He is betting that he will win, and inviting the other players to 'fade' his bet, i.e. to put up an equal amount to bet he will lose.

When his bet has been covered, the shooter rolls the two dice. The two faces uppermost when the dice come to rest determine the number thrown.

The bets are settled on the first roll should one of five numbers come up.

If the shooter rolls 7 or 11 (known as a 'natural') the shooter wins immediately.

If the shooter rolls 2, 3 or 12 (known as 'craps') the shooter loses immediately.

If the shooter rolls any other number i.e. 4, 5, 6, 8, 9 or 10, the number rolled becomes the shooter's 'point'. He continues to roll the dice until he rolls either his point, in which case he wins, or a 7, when he loses. The 7 is therefore a winning number on the shooter's first roll, but a losing number once he has established a point.

When the shooter wins he is said to 'pass', when he loses he is said to 'miss'.

While the shooter wins, he remains the shooter (unless he voluntarily passes the dice on) but when he loses he must give the dice to the man on his left, who becomes shooter.

Apart from the bets between the shooter and faders, the other players bet amongst themselves.

On the shooter's first roll, or on any other roll, a player may bet with another that the shooter 'comes' or 'don't come'. A come bet is one that the shooter will win, taking the next roll as if it were his first. A don't come bet is one that the shooter will lose. Come bettors are said to bet 'right', don't come bettors are said to bet 'wrong'.

Count d'Orsay calling a main at Crockford's, 1843. The game is Hazard, a forerunner of Craps.

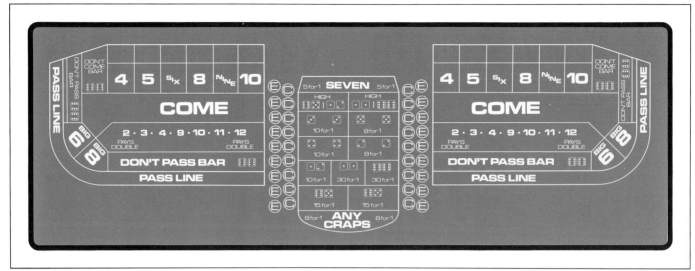

Figure 1 A typical layout of a Las Vegas Craps table.

The bet is always settled by the next 7 or earlier. These bets are made at even money.

Side bets are also made when a shooter has established a point. Players (including the shooter) may bet that he gets it or not. Since the odds are against the shooter making his point, these bets are not made at even money, but at the true odds. If the shooter's point is 6 or 8, the odds are 6 to 5 against the shooter making it. If the point is 5 or 9, the odds are 3 to 2 against. If the point is 4 or 10, the odds are 2 to 1 against. In some schools bets are made at even money on the shooter getting a point of 6 or 8 – this clearly favours the bettor who bets against the shooter.

Hard-way bets are popular side bets. When a player's point is 4, 6, 8 or 10, there is a possibility that he will make it by rolling the same number with each die, e.g. 2-2 for 4, 3-3 for 6, and so on. This is known as making it the hard way. The odds against making 4 or 10 the hard way are 8 to 1, against making 6 or 8 the hard way, 10 to 1.

That is the private game, as exemplified by the floating crap game in Damon Runyan's *Guys and Dolls*.

In a casino, all bets are made against the bank. The rolls are made on a table which is also the betting layout. Figure 1 shows a table typical of a Las Vegas casino.

Players still make the rolls, but the double-headed table is operated by four administrators: the boxman, the stickman and two dealers. The boxman is the overseer, the stickman handles the dice and looks after the bets at the centre of the table, and the two dealers settle the bets at their respective ends of the table. Betting is by means of the casino's chips, which are obtainable at

the tables, and are kept by each player in trays in the table railing.

As in the private game, a shooter wins, or passes, if he rolls 7 or 11 (natural) on his first roll, or if he establishes a point and rolls it again before he rolls a 7. He loses, or misses, if he rolls 2, 3 or 12 (craps) on his first roll, or if he establishes a point and rolls a 7 before he rolls his point.

The various bets to be made on the table are as follows (they are at odds of 1 to 1, or even money, unless stated):

1) *Pass:* a bet that the shooter will win. Also called a 'win', 'do' or 'front-line' bet. Chips are placed in the 'pass line' space on the layout. If the shooter throws a point, a point marker is placed in the appropriate numbered box near the top of the layout.

2) *Don't pass:* a bet that the shooter will lose. Chips are placed in the space on the layout marked 'don't pass bar 6-6'. This means that if the come-out roll is 6-6, which loses for the shooter, the bet on the don't pass line is a stand-off, and does not win. The bettor's stake is returned. This adjustment is necessary to give the casino its percentage advantage, because without it the odds would favour the gambler. Some casinos bar 1-1 instead of 6-6, others bar 1-2.

A player is allowed to remove his stake on the don't pass line if a shooter has established a point – the casino allows this because the advantage is with the bettor.

3) *Come:* a bet made after the shooter has established a point. The shooter's next roll is regarded as his 'come-out' roll, i.e. his first roll, for come bettors. They will win if he rolls a natural on this roll, and lose if he throws a crap. If he throws neither of these he will establish a point for the come bettor,

who will win if the new point appears before a 7.

Come bets are placed in the space on the layout marked 'come'. When the shooter establishes a point for the come bettor, the dealer moves the chips to the appropriate point box.

4) *Don't come:* the opposite of a come bet. The bet is placed in the space on the layout marked 'don't come bar 6-6'. The barring of 6-6 is also to adjust the odds in the casino's favour. The don't come bet wins if the shooter's next roll is crap 2 or 3 and loses if the next roll is a natural 7 or 11. If the shooter rolls 6-6 the bet is a stand-off and is returned.

If the shooter establishes a point for the don't come bettor, the chips are moved by the dealer into the blank space above the appropriate point number box. Thereafter the don't come bettor wins if the shooter rolls a 7 and loses if the shooter rolls the point number.

5) *Field bet:* a bet that any of the numbers 2, 3, 4, 9, 10, 11, 12 appear on the next roll. The bets are placed in the space on the layout above the don't pass line, which is sometimes marked 'the field'.

A roll of 2 or 12 pays double, as the layout indicates. In some layouts, 5 is included in the field in place of 4, but in this case, the casino will not pay double on 2 or 12.

6) *Big 6 and Big 8:* a bet that 6 or 8 will be rolled before 7. Bets are placed in the space marked 'Big 6' if the bettor wants to back 6 to appear before 7, or in 'Big 8' to bet that 8 appears before 7.

7) *Hard-way bets:* bets that the appropriate point, 4, 6, 8 or 10, is made the hard way (as explained earlier) before it is made the easy way, or before a 7 is rolled. Bets are placed in the box

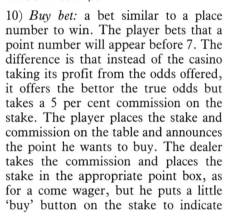

Figure 2 A free bet of five chips on an original stake of three chips.

on the layout marked with 3-3 for hard-way 6 and 4-4 for hard-way 8, for both of which odds of 10 *for* 1 (9 to 1) are offered, and in the boxes marked 5-5 and 2-2 for hard-way 10 and 4, at odds of 8 *for* 1 (7 to 1).

8) *Place number to win:* a bet that a particular point number will appear before 7. The odds paid are 9 to 5 on points 4 and 10; 7 to 5 on points and 9; and 7 to 6 on points 6 and 8. Because the odds are 7 to 6, bets on points 6 and 8 must must be made in multiples of six times the table minimum, and bets on the other place numbers to win must be in multiples of five times the minimum. The bets are placed on the line at the top or bottom of the appropriate point box. On points 6 and 8 some casinos offer odds of 11 to 10, and others 1 to 1 (evens).

9) *Place number to lose:* a bet that 7 will appear before a particular point number. The bettor must lay the odds of 11

10) *Buy bet:* a bet similar to a place number to win. The player bets that a point number will appear before 7. The difference is that instead of the casino taking its profit from the odds offered, it offers the bettor the true odds but takes a 5 per cent commission on the stake. The player places the stake and commission on the table and announces the point he wants to buy. The dealer takes the commission and places the stake in the appropriate point box, as for a come wager, but he puts a little 'buy' button on the stake to indicate

chip as commission, so to get the best value from a buy bet, the bettor must stake in multiples of 20 of the minimum. For example, if he places 21 chips on the table, the dealer will take one as commission, exactly 5 per cent of the stake of 20. But if he places 6 chips on the table, the dealer will still take one as commission, and the bettor is then paying a 20 per cent commission.

11) *Lay bet:* an opposite bet to a buy bet, i.e. a bet that 7 appears before a selected point number. The bettor is paid at the correct odds, and the bank exacts a percentage commission, but this time this is based on the hypothetical winnings rather than the stake. Points 4 and 10 pay odds of 1 to 2; 5 and 9 pay 2 to 3; and 6 and 8 pay 5 to 6. Thus to get the maximum value for his bet, a player must stake 40 chips on points 4 and 10; 30 chips on 5 and 9; and 24 chips on 6 and 8. All these bets win 20 chips, and the bettor must add

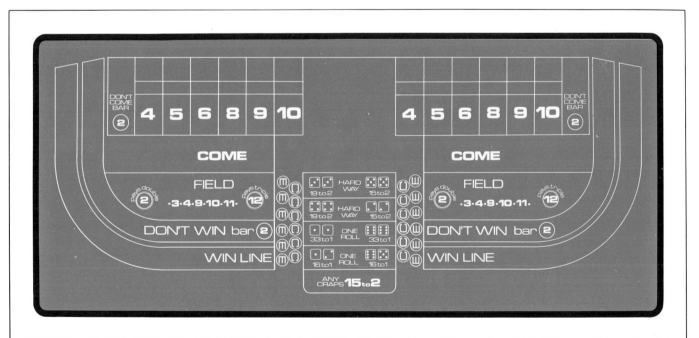

Figure 3 A typical layout of a British Craps table.

to 5 on points 4 and 10; 8 to 5 on points 5 and 9; and 5 to 4 on points 6 and 8. Stakes must be in multiples of 11, eight and five of the table minimum respectively.

that it is to be paid at the correct odds. These odds are 2 to 1 on points 4 and 10; 3 to 2 on points 5 and 9; and 6 to 5 on points 6 and 8.

A dealer cannot take less than one

one chip to the stake when making the bet. The dealer takes the one chip commission, and puts the stake in the blank box above the appropriate point number, with a buy button on it.

165

12) *Proposition bets:* bets made on any one roll of the dice. The player calls his bet, placing his stake on the table, and the stickman puts it in the appropriate position on the centre layout. At the top of the layout, the bet is 7 to appear on the next roll (odds 5 *for* 1, or 4 to 1). Next is the high bet, which requires five chips, one on the three numbers 2, 3 and 12, and two on 11. Should any of these numbers appear, the odds paid are 30 for 1, 10 for 1, 30 for 1 and 30 for 2 respectively, the chips on the three losing numbers being lost. The next four spaces are for the hard-way bets mentioned earlier. The spaces in the next two rows are for backing the numbers 1, 3, 11 and 12 individually, at the odds quoted. The bottom space, 'Any craps', is a bet that 2, 3 or 12 appear on the next roll – the odds are 8 *for* 1, or 7 to 1. The circles marked C and E are for bettors on craps and 11. The chips are placed to overlap both of the pair of circles pointing to where the player stands at the table. If 2, 3, 11 or 12 appears on the next roll the bettor wins and is paid odds of 4 to 1.

13) *Odds or free bets:* bets which the casino pays at true odds and without exacting a commission. They can be made only in conjunction with bets which do carry a house percentage. They are designed to encourage bets on the pass, come, don't pass and don't come lines, and work as follows.

If a player places a bet of one chip on the pass line, and the shooter establishes a point, the casino will allow him to add an odds bet of one chip to his stake. Should the shooter make his point, the casino will pay out on the original bet at the normal odds of 1 to 1 (in this connection it is called a flat bet), but will pay out on the odds bet at the true odds of the point number appearing before 7.

For example, a player makes a pass bet, and the shooter establishes a point of 4. The player can now make a free bet of one chip on the shooter passing, which is now in effect a bet that 4 will appear before 7. Should the shooter pass, the player will win one chip on the original pass bet, and two chips on the

Total possible combinations											Number of Ways	Odds Against
2											1	35-1
3											2	17-1
4											3	11-1
5											4	8-1
6											5	31-5
7											6	5-1
8											5	31-5
9											4	8-1
10											3	11-1
11											2	17-1
12											1	35-1

Figure 4 The 36 possible results from rolling two dice.

free bet, as 2 to 1 is the true odds of 4 appearing before 7.

The free bet is limited to the size of the original bet. This poses a problem, because the true odds on points 5 and 9 are 3 to 2, meaning that the free bet must be of two chips, or multiples of two. The true odds on points 6 and 8 are 6 to 5, requiring a free bet in multiples of five chips. In order to make his free bet at true odds, a player is required to add chips to his original bet, but this is a bad proposition, more than cancelling out the advantage of the free bet. Otherwise there will not be enough chips on the free bet to allow the casino to pay full odds, and the casino will pay at 1-1, in other words it will not be an odds bet at all. The casino will, however, allow a free bet of five chips on points 6 and 8 without the player increasing the original stake, if the original stake were three or four chips. The best stake on the pass line for a player wishing to take the maximum advantage of free bets is therefore three chips. It will allow a free bet of three chips on points 4 and 10, four on points 5 and 9 and five on points 6 and 8.

Don't pass, come and don't come bets have the same facility of free bets. On don't pass and don't come bets the odds for point numbers are 1 to 2 for 4 and 10; 2 to 3 for 5 and 9; and 5 to 6 for 6 and 8. The original bets should again be three chips for the maximum advantage of free bets, as stakes of six chips will be allowed on each free bet.

Free bets are placed on the original stake, but overlapping the edge (see Figure 2).

Craps in Great Britain

In the gambling boom following the legislation of the 1960s which allowed many forms of gambling preivously illegal, craps came to Great Britain. The Gaming Board was established to oversee fair play. The Board recommended the table layout shown in Figure 3. Some bets which are particularly disadvantageous to the player, such as Big 6 and Big 8, do not appear. Better odds than are available in Las Vegas are offered on other bets, particularly the one-roll proposition bets. The effect is to protect the uninitiated player rather than to make it easier to win.

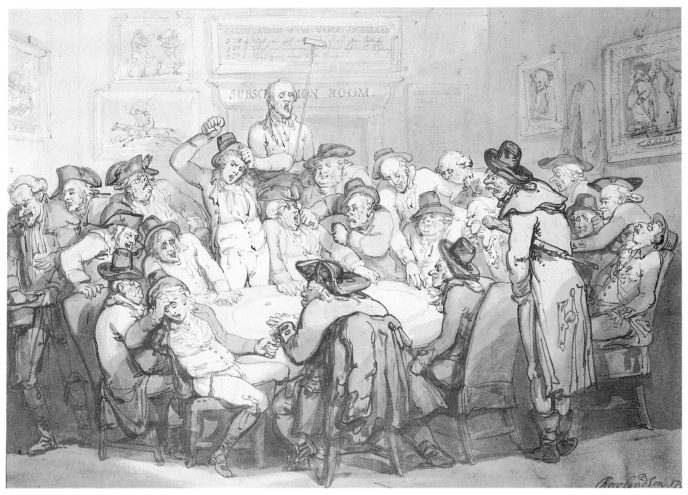

'The Hazard Room' painted by Thomas Rowlandson in 1792. The modern game Craps was based on Hazard.

Strategy

Craps is a game of chance. There is no room for skill. The difference between a 'good' player and a 'bad', is that the good player will bet where the casino has the smallest advantage. The newcomer should watch out for casinos which offer odds *for* one, instead of *to* one. The difference between 5 *for* 1 and 5 *to* 1 is a drop of 20 percent in the winnings, and this form of quoting odds is designed to mislead the uninitiated.

Figure 4 shows the number of results possible from two dice. There are 36 possibilities. The likeliest number is 7, the unlikeliest 2 and 12.

From this can be constructed Table 1, which works out the shooter's probability of passing.

It will be seen that, in the long run, the shooter will pass 976 times in 1,980 coups, just under half. This means that in private games, don't pass bettors enjoy an advantage over pass bettors of 1.41 per cent. This advantage would also be held by bettors in casinos, if the casino did not adjust the chances by barring 6-6. Thus the casino retains its

TABLE ONE: **The shooter's probability of passing**

Come-out roll	Number of times thrown	Number of winning coups	Number of losing coups
2 crap	55	–	55
3 crap	110	–	110
4 point	165	55	110
5 point	220	88	132
6 point	275	125	150
7 natural	330	330	–
8 point	275	125	150
9 point	220	88	132
10 point	165	55	110
11 natural	110	110	–
12 crap	55	–	55
Totals	1,980	976	1,004

advantage over pass bettors of 1.41 per cent and has an advantage over don't pass bettors of 1.40 per cent. The same advantages are held over come and don't come bettors. Casinos which bar crap 3 instead of 6-6 increase their advantage over don't pass and don't come bettors to 4.38 per cent.

An analysis of the odds offered on the other bets on the Las Vegas layout indicate the following:
1) On the field bet, the casino advantage is 5.56 per cent.
2) On Big 6 and Big 8 the casino advantage is 9.09 per cent, a silly bet as the casino offers better odds for the same bet on betting a place number to win.
3) On hard-way bets, the casino advantage is 11.11 per cent on hard-way 4 and 10; and 9.09 per cent on hard-way 6 and 8.
4) On place numbers to win, the casino advantage is 6.67 per cent on points 4 and 10; 4.00 per cent on points 5 and 9; and 1.52 per cent on 6 and 8 (much better odds than are offered on Big 6 and Big 8). See also buy bets.
5) On place numbers to lose, the casino advantage is 3.03 per cent on points 4 and 10; 2.50 per cent on points 5 and 9; and 1.82 per cent on points 6 and 8. Casinos which ask odds of 7 to 5 on points 6 or 8 increase their advantage to 6.49 per cent. See also lay bets.
6) On buy bets, the casino advantage is 4.76 per cent. A comparison with the advantage on place numbers to win shows that it is better to buy on points 4

167

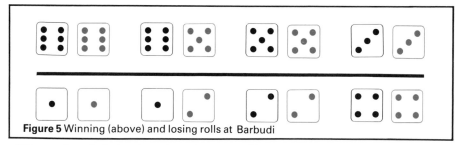

Figure 5 Winning (above) and losing rolls at Barbudi

and 10, but better to place points 5, 6, 8 and 9.

7) On lay bets, the casino advantage is 2.44 per cent on points 4 and 10; 3.23 per cent on points 5 and 9; and 4.00 per cent on points 6 and 8. A comparison with the advantage on place numbers to lose shows that it is better to lay on points 4 and 10, but better to place numbers to lose on points 5, 6, 8 and 9.

8) On proposition bets, the casino advantage on the various propositions are: 16.67 per cent on 7; 16.67 per cent on the high bet; 16.67 per cent on each of the bets on 2, 3, 11 or 12; 11.11 per cent on any craps; and 16.67 per cent on craps and 11.

9) On odds or free bets, a player who takes the free bets on every opportunity, and whose stakes on the free bets are exactly equal to his stakes on the pass or come lines, will reduce the casino advantage to 0.85 per cent. Bettors on the don't pass and don't come lines will reduce it to 0.83 per cent. A player who sets out to stake so that he can have a larger stake on his free bets than on his original bets, will reduce the casino advantage even more.

A player wishing to make the best use of his money, therefore, will back wrong and maximise his odds bets.

Barbudi

Barbudi, sometimes known as Barbooth, is a game requiring two dice. It is popular in Eastern Europe and Mexico, where, traditionally, miniature dice are used. Only two players are involved in the action, but, like craps, any number can play.

All players throw a die to determine first shooter. Highest is shooter, and the player to his right is fader. The fader puts up a stake as he wishes, and the players, beginning with the player on the right of the fader (the action goes anti-clockwise) cover the remainder. The fader withdraws any stake not covered. Players can decline their chance to be shooter or fader, when the opportunity passes to the right.

In placing his stakes, the fader must stipulate a one-shot or two-shot decision, the meaning of which will be seen.

When the fader's bet has been covered, the shooter and fader roll alternately, shooter first, to decide who wins the bets.

In a one-shot decision game, either player wins if he rolls 6–6, 6–5, 5–5 or 3–3. Either player loses if he rolls 1–1, 1–2, 2–2 or 4–4 (see Figure 5). Players roll until one rolls one of the winning or losing scores. Bets are settled immediately. If the shooter wins, he remains shooter. If the fader wins, he becomes shooter on the next round, and the player to his right becomes fader.

In a two-shot decision game, a roll of 6–5 wins only half the bet, and a roll of 1–2 loses only half. Then, if either player wishes, the game can end there, with the winning bettors taking half the opposing stakes while the losing bettors retain half. If this option is taken, a winning shooter remains shooter, a winning fader becomes shooter on the next round.

Alternatively, on a roll of 6–5 or 1–2 on a two-shot decision game, shooter and fader can agree to continue to shoot for the second half of the stakes. In this case all stakes are left on the table. If the shooter won the first half of the bet, he remains shooter for the second half, but if the fader won the first half, he becomes shooter for the second half. In effect, this means that whoever won the first half of the bet has the privilege of rolling first in the second half.

If the same side wins both halves of the bet, they collect the whole of the stakes. If each side wins one half of the bet, then both sides withdraw their stakes, and neither shows a profit on the round. When the second half of a two-decision game is played, both shooter and fader lose their roles, the player to the right of the fader becoming the new shooter, and the player to his right the fader.

Variation

Some players feel the two-shot game wastes time, and ban it. One-shot games last an average of three rolls. However, the 6–5 and 2–1 rolls retain some significance, because a shooter who loses by rolling 2–1, or by the fader

rolling 6–5, retains his position as shooter.

Strategy

The game is purely one of chance. When played at home it is an even game, with no advantage to either shooter or fader. It can be found in clubs and casinos, with the house taking a 5 per cent commission on all winnings (or, put another way, 2½ per cent on all money staked).

Strung Flowers

Strung Flowers is a Chinese banking game, suitable for any number of players. It requires three dice.

Each player throws the three dice to determine first banker. The player who rolls most 4s becomes banker; players who tie roll again.

Players put their stakes in front of them on the table. The banker covers each stake in turn. It is advisable to agree on a maximum beforehand. All stakes must be in multiples of three, the reason for which will become apparent.

The banker then rolls the dice, and continues to roll until he achieves one of the following significant rolls:

1. A roll which wins all bets immediately. These are (a) 4–5–6, known as 'strung flowers'; (b) any triplet; (c) any pair with 6.
2. A roll which loses all bets immediately. These are (a) 1–2–3, known as 'dancing dragon'; (b) any pair with 1 (known as 'Ace negative').
3. A roll which establishes a point for the banker. These are any pair with 2, 3, 4 or 5. The odd die represents the banker's point.

So the banker either wins all stakes, loses to all players, or establishes a point. In the last case, play must proceed until the bets are settled, and proceeds as follows.

The first player to the banker's left rolls the dice, and he too continues to roll until he throws a significant throw. If he throws a combination listed in (1) above, he beats the banker. If he throws a combination in (2) above, he loses. If he throws a point for himself, as listed

in (3) above, he wins if his point is higher than banker's, loses if it is lower, and ties, i.e. recovers his stake, if the point is the same. Herein lies the significance of the stake being in multiples of three. If the difference between the two points is three (i.e. the points are 2 and 5) the winner wins all the stake; if the difference is two, the winner wins two thirds of the stake; if the difference is one, the winner wins one third of the stake.

When the bets between the banker and the player to his left are settled, the next player rolls the three dice and so on.

The banker continues to hold the bank until he makes a point which loses to a player's point, when on the next round the bank passes to the player on the left. It can be agreed beforehand that a game will not end until all players have held the bank once.

Variation

A variation which dispenses with the terms strung flowers, dancing dragon and ace negative is a version of the game called four-five-six. Differences are as follows:

1) First banker is decided by the highest scorer in rolling three dice.
2) The banker puts up the stake and the other players cover it. If any remains uncovered, banker withdraws it.
3) Bets won or lost on point numbers are settled for the whole stake; the difference between the points is not significant.
4) The banker retains the bank until he loses his entire stake on a round (i.e. all players beat him) in which case it passes to the player on his left, or until a player rolling against his point rolls a triplet or 4-5-6, in which case the bank passes on the next round to that player.

Strategy

The game in both versions is purely of chance, players having no options. It should be appreciated, however, that there is an advantage to the banker of nearly 2½ per cent.

Qualify

Qualify is a banking game for any reasonable number of players, and requires five dice. Each player rolls one die to determine the first banker, highest becoming banker.

Each player puts up a stake (it is best to agree a maximum in advance), which is covered by a banker. The banker takes no part in the play.

The object of the play is to score 25 points or more.

The player to banker's left rolls the five dice, and puts aside the highest die as a contribution to his score. He then rolls the other four dice again, again putting the highest towards his score, and so on until he throws the last die singly. The total shown on the five dice represent the player's score.

If his score is 25 or more the player wins, and the banker pays; if it is 24 or less, the player loses, and the banker collects the stakes.

The dice then pass to the next player, and so on round the table, the banker settling with each in turn. At the end of the round, the bank passes to the player on the banker's left.

It is a simple game, but not without its interest. It might be thought that 25 is a high number to achieve (the maximum is only 30), but in three-quarters of cases a player will still be in with a chance up to his last roll, and should have at least an even chance on his last roll in half his turns. The banker does have a considerable advantage, however, so the bank should be held by all players an equal number of times.

Twenty-Six

Twenty-six is a banking game played by any number of players using ten dice. Players throw a single die to determine first banker – highest wins.

The player on banker's left puts up a stake (it is best to agree a maximum in advance) and nominates a point number from 1 to 6. He then rolls all ten dice from a cup 13 times, and a count is kept of the number of times the point appears. Banker should write down the

total after each roll to avoid disputes. The player's object is to roll the point 26 or more times, 13 times, or 10 or fewer times. Should he achieve this, he is paid by the banker according to his score, as set out in Table 2.

TABLE TWO: **Odds paid in Twenty-six**

Number of times point number appears	Odds paid
26	4 to 1
27	5 to 1
28	6 to 1
29	8 to 1
30 or more	10 to 1
13	5 to 1
10 or fewer	10 to 1

When all players have been dealt with in turn the bank passes to the player on dealer's left.

A point number can be 'expected' to appear 21.67 times on average, so a score of 26 or more is not easy to obtain.

The odds quoted in the table are thought to be fairest, and should enable the bank to show a small profit in the long run.

Variation

Fourteens is a similar game to Twenty-six, again using ten dice and a dice-cup. However, the turn comes quicker; each player throws the dice only five times.

The player does not nominate his point number until after his first roll, and must nominate whichever point appears most often on that roll, should it appear three or more times. He thus starts with a score of 3 or more. Should he not throw three of a kind on his first roll, he may nominate any point number he wishes, and is credited with a score of 3 for his first roll. The object is to score 14 or more on the five throws. If he achieves this the banker pays him at odds of 8 to 1. There are no bonuses for higher scores. The only consolation prize is paid if, after nominating a point number, he fails to throw it once on his last four throws, when the banker again pays him at odds of 8 to 1. Again the odds are calculated to give the bank a small profit.

Poker Dice

Poker Dice is played with the special set of five dive used also for Liar Dice. The six faces are shown in Figure 6. The

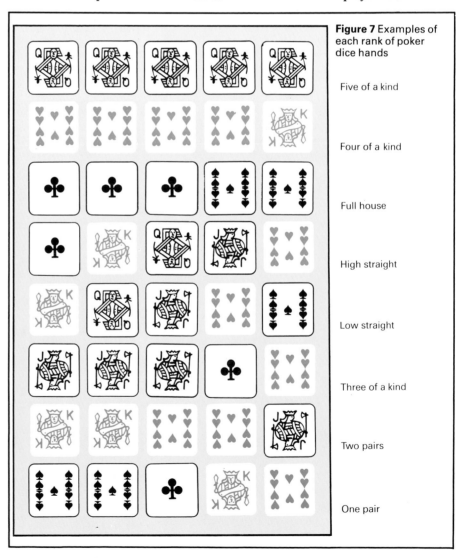

Figure 6 The six faces on each poker die.

player to play first on the first round is chosen by any agreeable method; thereafter the first player on succeeding rounds is the next in rotation clockwise.

Each player contributes an equal stake to a pool, to be taken by the winner.

On his turn, a player rolls the five dice, and can set aside any he wishes to keep, and roll the remainder a second time. The object is to get the highest ranking poker hand.

The poker hands are ranked as follows, highest first:
1) *Five of a kind:* all five dice showing the same rank.
2) *Four of a kind:* four dice showing the same rank.
3) *Full house:* three dice showing the same rank, and the other two dice showing a pair.
4) *High straight:* the five dice in sequence, Ace, King, Queen, Jack, 10.
5) *Low straight:* the five dice in sequence, King, Queen, Jack, 10, 9.
6) *Three of a kind:* three dice showing the same rank, with two odd dice.
7) *Two pairs:* two pairs of dice each showing the same rank, with one odd die.
8) *One pair:* two dice showing the same rank, with three odd dice.

Examples of each hand are shown in Figure 7.

The first player's throw is noted. As soon as it is beaten, if it is, the new best hand is noted, and so on. The player to have the highest hand at the end of the round takes the pool.

It is necessary to note the leading hand in detail, because hands of the same category are not equal. The faces of the dice are ranked from Ace (high) to 9 (low). Thus in five, four or three of a kind, the rank of the five, four or three decide precedence. In competing full houses, it is the rank of the three of a kind which decides – if they are equal, the rank of the pair. When two hands each of two pairs compete, the rank of the higher decides, if equal, the lower. With competing hands of one pair, it is the rank of the pair which decides. With four of a kind, three of a kind and two pairs the rank of the odd die or dice are not used to break ties.

Where two or more hands are exactly equal, the pool is shared, unless it is agreed beforehand that ties should be played off.

There is little opportunity for strategy. The last player in each round, however, knows exactly what hand he has to beat, and can retain and re-roll his dice accordingly. The later he rolls, the better chance a player has.

Figure 7 Examples of each rank of poker dice hands

Five of a kind

Four of a kind

Full house

High straight

Low straight

Three of a kind

Two pairs

One pair

POKER

Poker is an international card game, which in America is said to be the most widely played of all. It developed from other games using similar principles, probably acquiring its name from the German game Pochen (to bluff).

THERE ARE MANY variants to the game, not counting local amendments covered by 'house rules'. The original game called upon the players to bet upon the hands which they were dealt, with no opportunity to improve them, as in Brag (q.v.). This game, called 'Straight Poker', has been superseded by a game in which players may improve their hands by exchanging cards. This new game is often regarded now as the parent game, and is sometimes itself referred to as 'Straight Poker', but more correctly it is 'Draw Poker' or 'Straight Draw Poker'.

It is Draw Poker which is described first.

The game is for any reasonable number of players, five, six or seven being considered the best.

It is ideally played with chips for betting, with all players beginning with the same number of chips, and the following descriptions assume the use of chips, although, of course, currency might be used.

The standard 52-card pack is used, the cards ranking from Ace (high) to 2 (low). There is no rank of suits.

Object

The object of the game is to win the pot, i.e. the combined stakes of the players. This can be done in two ways: by building a better poker hand than the other players, so that at a showdown the hand will win, or by betting in such a manner that players holding better hands 'drop', or withdraw, before a showdown is reached.

Poker hands consist of five cards and they are ranked as follows, highest first:
1) *Straight flush*: a sequence of five cards of the same suit. An Ace may be high or low. Competing straight flushes are ranked by the highest card in the sequence, thus Ace, King, Queen, Jack, 10 (called a 'royal flush') is the highest and 5, 4, 3, 2, Ace is the lowest.
2) *Four of a kind*: four cards of the same rank, with an odd fifth card. Competing hands of four of a kind are ranked by the cards comprising the four, thus four Aces is highest and four 2s lowest.
3) *Full house*: three cards of the same rank with a pair of another rank. When competing it is the rank of the three cards which determines precedence, thus three Aces with any pair is the highest and three 2s with any pair the lowest.
4) *Flush*: five cards of the same suit not in sequence. Competing flushes are ranked by the highest card in the flush, if equal the second highest, and so on.

'The Gambler's Wife', a painting by Mrs Murray Cooksley from about 1904.

5) *Straight*: five cards in sequence but of two or more suits. An Ace may be high or low. Competing straights are ranked by the highest card in the straight.

6) *Three of a kind*: three cards of the same rank, with two other cards not a pair. Competing threes are ranked by the cards comprising the three, from three Aces to three 2s.

7) *Two pairs*: two cards of the same rank, two other cards of the same rank and an odd card. Where hands each of two pairs are in opposition, they are ranked by the higher of the two pairs, if equal by the lower, if still equal by the odd card. Thus two Kings and two 2s rank higher than two Queens and two Jacks.

8) *One pair*: two cards of the same rank, with three other cards of different ranks. With competing hands of one pair the rank of the pair decides precedence, if equal the rank of the highest odd card, if equal the next and so on.

9) *Highest card*: any hand which does not satisfy the requirements of the hands above, i.e. any five cards not including at least two of the same rank, and not in sequence or of the same suit. Competing hands of this kind are ranked by the highest card, if equal the second highest, and so on. Examples of each hand are illustrated in Figure 1.

The play

Before play begins it is best for players to agree when play will end, and also to agree on minimum and maximum bets and raises. For example, if the minimum bet is one chip, the maximum before the draw might be two chips and after the draw four chips. It might also be agreed to limit the number of raises any one player can make – a popular limit is three raises per betting interval.

The cards are shuffled and cut and any player deals them one at a time face up to his left, until a Jack appears. The Jack denotes first dealer.

The method of betting which follows is that most common in countries outside the United States. It is sometimes called the 'blind opening'. The method most popular in the United States is

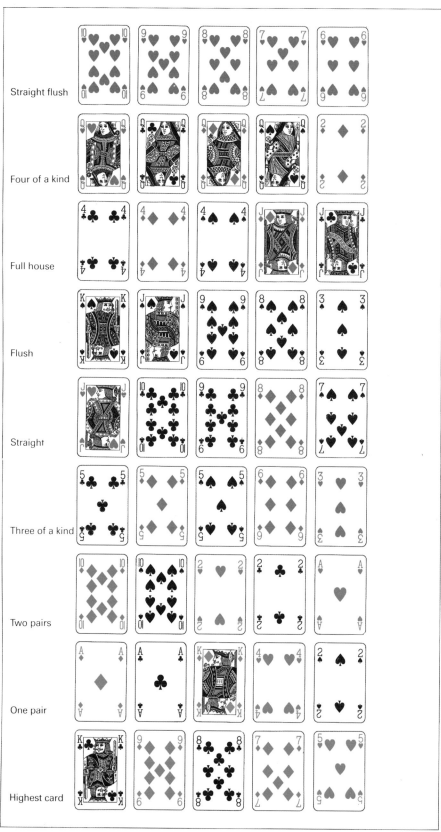

Figure 1 Examples of each rank of Poker hands.

described later under the variant 'Jackpots'.

Before the deal the player to the left of the dealer places one chip in the pot. This is known as the 'ante'. The player to his left puts two chips into the pot.

This is known as the 'straddle'. These players are betting blind. The dealer then deals five cards face down to each player, including himself, one at a time clockwise, and places the remaining cards face down in front of him.

The players examine their cards, and the first betting interval ensues. The first player able to make a voluntary bet is the player to the left of the straddle, and thereafter players bet in turn clockwise until the first betting interval ends.

A player on his turn to bet has three options, as follows:

1) *drop*, which means he discards his hand and takes no further part in that deal. Any chips he might have put into the pot are lost.

2) *call*, which means he places in the pot enough chips to bring his contribution during that betting interval up to the level of that of the previous players, but no higher.

3) *raise*, which means that he places in the pot enough chips to bring his contribution up to that of previous players, plus one or more additional chips (but no more additional chips than the maximum raise).

The players do not mix their chips in the pot, but place them towards the middle of the table and in front of them, so that the value can be seen.

The first player to bet voluntarily, i.e. the first player who decides not to drop, must put in four chips, known as a 'double'. Thereafter betting continues with each player choosing one of the three options. When the betting reaches the blind bettors the chips contributed to the ante and straddle count toward what they need to call.

When the stakes of all players who remain in are equal, the first betting interval ends.

The players now have a chance to improve their hands. The dealer picks up that part of the pack not dealt. Each player still in the game, beginning with the one nearest the dealer's left, may discard one or more cards face down, announcing the number discarded, and the dealer takes the equivalent number from the top of the pack and deals them face down to the player to bring his hand back to five cards. If the dealer himself is still in, he must announce how many cards he is discarding before dealing himself an equivalent number from the pack. With six or more

players, no player is permitted to discard and draw more than three cards. A player who does not discard any cards is said to 'stay pat'. The discards are collected by the next player to deal and placed in a pile face down, taking care that the faces are not seen by any players.

With seven or more players it might happen that the undealt pack will become exhausted before all players have discarded and drawn new cards. When the undealt pack is reduced to one card, the dealer must add this card to the previous discards (not including the discards of the player to be dealt with), shuffle them and ask the next player to be dealt with to cut the new pack thus formed. He then takes the pack into his hand and deals with the remaining players as before.

When all players still in have drawn, the second betting interval takes place.

The player who first bet, i,e. the first player to the left of the straddle, is the first to bet. He can drop or raise as before, but he also has a fourth option, to 'check', which means that he wishes to stay in, but does not wish to increase the stake. He announces his intention by merely saying 'check'. Each succeeding player may drop, raise or check, and if all players check, there is a showdown. As soon as somebody raises, however, the option to check disappears; the following players must call, i.e. equalize their stakes with the raiser, raise themselves, or drop. When all stakes are equal, the second betting interval ends, and the showdown takes place.

In the showdown, all players still in must expose their hands face up on the table, and the best poker hand wins the pot. If only one player remains in, however, as often happens, that player may take the pot without the obligation of showing his cards.

Each hand is separate, and the deal now passes clockwise.

Should a player run out of chips during the course of a hand, and have insufficient to call a raise, he may call for whatever chips he has. The other players continue the hand by creating a

side pot, into which go the stakes already bet which cannot be covered, and any additional raises. Thus the main pot is equalized and frozen.

Should the same thing happen during the betting in the side pot, a second side pot may be opened. At the showdown, all players who have not dropped compete for the main pot, but only those who contributed to a side pot or pots are eligible to win those. A player who drops in a side pot (except for running out of chips) loses his right to be in the showdown for any pots.

Example hand

Six players, A, B, C, D, E and F, are dealt the hands in Figure 2. A is the dealer, with B on his left and so on round to F on his right. Before the deal B puts one chip into the pot as ante, and C puts two chips into the pot as straddle. D is the first to bet, and as he holds a good hand, with three Aces, he had no hesitation in putting in the four chips required (the double). E has little prospect of improving to a good hand and will not risk four chips on his collection of cards, so he drops.

F decides to risk four chips. Were he to draw the ♠ 5 or ♠ 10, he would be almost certain to win the pot, while any spade would give him an excellent chance, and any 5 or 10 a good chance.

A decides his pair of 3s are not worth much and drops. B, who already has a chip in the pot, and is an adventurous player, decides to stay in by putting in another three chips, hoping that he might complete a flush by drawing another diamond. C, who has two chips in the pot, adds another two, hoping he might draw an 8 or a 5 to complete a full house.

The first betting ends there with four players still in, each having contributed four chips.

In the draw, D is dealt with first. He discards ♦ 8, ♦ 5, and dealer gives him ♥ 5, ♦ 2.

F discards ♥ 2 and is given ♥ 3.

B discards ♣ 10 and is given ♥ 10.

C discards ♦ 6 and is given ♥ 9.

The first chance to bet now falls to D, who raises by two chips. F, whose hand

is now worthless, drops. B, who failed to complete his flush, also drops. C does not think he has much chance of winning, guessing by D's discard of two cards and his subsequent raise that he probably holds three of a kind at least. If he drops, he will lose his four chips. He can call, which will cost him two more chips, and give him the chance of taking the pool of 20 chips (winning 14), or he can raise – with the object of convincing D that the card he drew completed a good hand, and hoping that D will drop.

In the event, C drops, limiting his loss to four chips, and D wins the pot without the need to show his cards.

As it happens, therefore, a bold player at D could have won the pot with a hand of no value whatever, had he bet in the way D actually did.

Jackpots

The most popular version of Poker in the United States is Jackpots. This version evolved to encourage betting and at the same time to prevent very weak hands from winning pots by default. With its increasing popularity, the convention of the blind ante and straddle bets from the two players to dealer's left has disappeared.

In Jackpots, each player puts in an ante of one chip before the deal, or, if all agree, the dealer may put in one chip for each player, which, if all players deal the same number of times, amounts to the same thing.

Each player receives five cards, as in the previous game.

The player to the left of dealer has the first opportunity to bet. In Jackpots, however, no player may open the betting without a pair of Jacks or a higher-ranking poker hand. The options of the first player, therefore, are:

1) open, which means that he has a hand of the required strength and wishes to bet. He adds to the pot his stake. Minimum and maximum stakes should be agreed beforehand.

2) check, which means that he is not making a bet but is staying in the game with the right to bet in the second round. A player without the require-

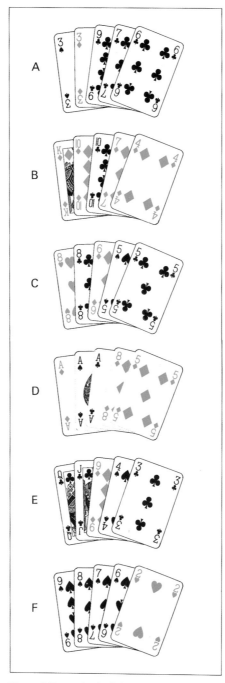

Figure 2 Example deal described in the text.

ment to open must check, of course, and a player who has the requirement may also check if he wishes.

After a player has made a bet, subsequent players must drop, call or raise.

If every player, including dealer, checks, the deal is passed. Each player puts another chip into the pot (or all the chips are put in by the next dealer, if that is the system being followed).

When all bets are equalized, the first betting interval ends and the draw takes place. When the opener discards, his discards are left face down before him and are not collected up. This is because on demand he must be able to

prove afterwards that he held a hand high enough to open.

The second betting interval and the showdown follow the procedure already described.

Progressive Jackpots

When a hand of Jackpots is passed, and all players have put in a second ante, the requirement to open becomes a pair of Queens or better, known as a Queenpot. Succeeding passed hands increase the requirements to open to Kingpots and Acepots, which is where the progression usually ends. The requirement remains at a pair of Aces or better until a hand is not passed. As soon as a bet is made, the next hand reverts to Jackpots.

Wild cards and Freakpots

By agreement beforehand, any card or cards in Draw Poker may be used as 'wild'. A wild card is a card which its holder can use for any other card he wishes.

Sometimes a Joker is added to the standard 52-card pack, and is used as a wild card. It might be used as an ordinary wild card, but is sometimes used as a limited wild card, when it is known as the 'bug'. This restricts its use: it may be counted only as an Ace, or as any card necessary to make a flush or a straight.

It is customary to use 2s as wild cards. A game in which all four 2s are wild is known as Deuces Wild or sometimes a Freakpot. In some schools a wild card may not be used to count as a card which is already held. This rules out the possibility of a hand of 'five of a kind', since to have five of a kind it would be necessary to hold a duplicate card, i.e. two cards of the same rank and suit.

In other schools a wild card may duplicate another, and it is allowed to hold five of a kind, which thus becomes the highest ranked hand, above a straight flush, unless the straight flush is a royal flush, i.e. it is headed by an Ace.

In these schools, a flush might be headed by two or more Aces, and beats a flush containing only one.

Late stages in the World Poker Championships at Killiney Castle, Dublin, in 1983.

Stud Poker

Stud Poker is a variation of Poker in which there is no draw, and in which all but one card in each hand is exposed. More people can conveniently play than can play Draw Poker, and also the game is a more interesting one for a small number of players. There are four betting intervals, and maximum stakes should be agreed before the start. It is usual to have one maximum for the first three rounds and to double the maximum for the fourth round, or for earlier rounds in which any player has a pair showing.

The procedure for deciding dealer is as described for Draw Poker.

The dealer gives one card to each player face down, and then deals a second face up. The face-down card is the 'hole card'. He then sets the pack aside while there is the first betting interval.

The players look at their own hole cards but then replace them face down on the table. They are not exposed until the showdown.

At the first betting interval the player with the highest card showing must open the betting, and it is the dealer's function to indicate which player that is. If two or more players have equal cards showing, the player nearer dealer's left must open the betting. Subsequent players must drop, call or raise until all bets are equalized. Players who drop at any stage must turn their cards face down.

The dealer then deals a second face-up card to all players still in, and indicates who has the first opportunity to bet. This is the player with the highest ranking poker hand, which at this stage might be the highest pair, or it might still be a high card (as in complete hands, Ace, 2, takes precedence over King, Queen).

At this and subsequent betting intervals, the player nearest dealer's left has the opportunity to bet first if two or more hands are equal. After the first betting interval, however, the player whose turn it is need not bet, he may check. If all players still in check, then the betting interval ends, as all bets are

still equal, but as soon as a player raises, other players must call or raise themselves to remain in.

The dealing of the third and fourth face-up cards and the following betting intervals proceed in the same manner, except that when dealer gives each player his face up card he must point out possible straights or flushes.

Thus if a player has ♥ K, ♥ 3 showing, and he receives ♥ 9, dealer says 'possible flush' as he deals the card. However possible flushes and straights are not significant in deciding who bets first: a hand showing ♥ 5, ♣ 2, ♠ 2 (a pair) takes precedence over ♠ 10, ♥ 9, ♦ 8 (a possible straight, but as yet only 10 high).

When all players have five cards, and the final betting interval has ended with all bets equalized, those remaining in expose their hole cards in a showdown, and the best poker hand takes the pot. Should all players except one drop during the game, the final player does not have to show his hole card in order to take the pot.

Poker variations

There are enough variations of Poker to fill a book by themselves. These include Whisky Poker, in which a widow hand is used, High-low Poker, in which the pot is divided at the showdown by the highest and lowest hands, Spit in the Ocean, in which each player receives four cards only, and a card is dealt face up to the table to represent the fifth card in each players' hand (it is a wild card, as are the other three of its rank),

Seven-card Stud, in which players pick their best hand from seven cards dealt, and so on.

Other variations arise through the recognition of special hands, such as a 'skip straight', a sequence of 'odd' or 'even' cards, e.g. Jack, 9, 7, 5, 3, ranking above three of a kind but below a straight, or a 'round-the-corner straight', e.g. 3, 2, Ace King, Queen, ranking below a skip straight. Another popular special hand is a 'blaze', a hand containing five court cards. It ranks between two pairs and three of a kind (it could, of course, qualify for these two categories as well – the holder naturally chooses the higher category).

Some special hands are outlandish, such as 'big tiger', a hand with cards ranking from King to 8, and not containing a pair, and 'little tiger', with cards ranking from 8 to 3 similarly.

Regular schools might invent their own special hands, of course.

Strategy

Poker is a game of skill. Its advocates claim that it is more skilful than Bridge, in that it is more certain in Poker that the best player will win.

The skill arises from mathematics and psychology; more precisely the ability to calculate probabilities quickly, to bluff opponents and to draw the correct inferences from the opponents' play.

In Draw Poker, it is necessary to know the comparative values of each hand by having an idea of the probability of being dealt it. Table 1 sets out these probabilities. Before the draw, it

TABLE ONE: **The incidence of Poker hands**

Hand	Number in pack	Approximate probability of being dealt
Straight flush	40	65,000 to 1
Four of a kind	624	4,166 to 1
Full house	3,744	693 to 1
Flush	5,108	508 to 1
Straight	10,200	254 to 1
Three of a kind	54,912	46 to 1
Two pairs	123,552	20 to 1
One pair	1,098,240	4 to 3
High card	1,302,540	evens

TABLE TWO: **Probabilities of hand improvement**

Holding before draw	Number of cards drawn	Improvement to	Odds against drawing	Odds against any improvement
One pair	3	Two pairs	5 to 1	5 to 2
		Three of a kind	8 to 1	
		Full house	97 to 1	
		Four of a kind	359 to 1	
One pair and a kicker	2	Two pairs	5 to 1	
		Three of a kind	12 to 1	
		Full house	119 to 1	
		Four of a kind	1,080 to 1	
Two pairs	1	Full house	11 to 1	11 to 1
Three of a kind	2	Full house	15½ to 1	8½ to 1
		Four of a kind	22½ to 1	
Three of a kind and a kicker	1	Full house	15 to 1	11 to 1
		Four of a kind	46 to 1	
Open-ended four straight	1	Straight	5 to 1	5 to 1*
One-sided or inside straight	1	Straight	11 to 1	11 to 1*
Open-ended straight flush	1	Straight flush	22½ to 1	22½ to 1*
One-sided or inside straight flush	1	Straight flush	46 to 1	46 to 1
Four flush	1	Flush	4¼ to 1	4¼ to 1*
Three flush	2	Flush	23 to 1	23 to 1*

* The odds against improving to a pair, or in the case of a three flush to threes or two pairs are not considered.

is necessary to know the odds against improving any hand with the draw. Table 2 gives this information.

In the first betting interval, Table 2 might be used as a rough guide on whether to enter the betting. For example, if the pot contains 15 chips and it requires four chips to come in, the table is offering odds of just under 4 to 1 for a win. A player attempting to fill a straight will probably regard these odds as not good enough, since the odds are greater against him improving. Of course, the strength of the hand both before and after drawing, and the possibility of future raises must also be considered. Therefore, although in the situa-tion mentioned, the odds of improving a four flush are just over 4 to 1, a player might think it worth entering the bet-ting on the grounds that if he does im-prove, his hand is very likely to win. Also, although the odds against impro-ving three of a kind are 8½ to 1, three of a kind might be good enough to win the pot in itself.

The table shows that it is not general-ly profitable to keep a 'kicker' (i.e. an odd card, usually a high card, such as Ace). However, a good player will vary his play to confuse opponents.

The betting interval after the draw is where bluffing plays its part, and where knowledge of the betting habits of the opponents can be used. If opponents are known, for example, never to bet against a player drawing one card only, it might be possible for a player drawing one card and failing to fill a flush to bet heavily and bluff the opponents into dropping.

Good players will bear in mind the following precepts:
1) Do not be impatient. Keep dropping when the hands are poor. The worst hand after the deal is rarely the best hand after the draw. It is useless to gamble on a miraculous draw.
2) Do not keep betting when for once you have a good hand if you think another player has it beaten. It is the good hands which are second best that cost the most money.
3) Do not throw good money after bad. Players are often reluctant to drop when they have made a substantial contribu-tion to the pot. Each bet must be valued on its merits separately. It is better to let the pot go than lose even more at-tempting to win it. Similarly, treat each hand on its merits. If you are losing, do not increase the stakes or bet on poorer hands in an effort to recoup.
4) Do not show excitement when the good hand eventually comes along. Play it like the others.
5) Do not overvalue bluffing. Betting heavily on a poor hand will not necessa-rily scare off the other players. It is better to rely on the table of probabili-ties, and to bet with confidence when you know you have a good hand.
6) In Stud Poker do not bet if, with your hole card, you cannot beat the cards your opponents are showing. For instance if your hole card is an 8, and you have a 7 as second card, do not stay in if there are already an Ace and a King showing. Similarly, when one player has a pair showing, do not stay in if you do not have a pair even with the hole card.
7) In Stud Poker do not continue bet-ting hoping to complete a flush or straight. As Table 2 shows, even with four cards of the same suit it is still over 4 to 1 against completing the flush. An opponent showing a pair of Aces is bet-ter than 4 to 1 to beat you.

BOULE

Boule is a game not unlike roulette. It is found in French and Swiss casinos. It has less glamorous equipment, a noisier atmosphere, smaller stakes and might be thought of as 'poor man's roulette'.

THE EQUIPMENT for boule consists of a sunken dish containing 36 cups (Figure 1). Each cup is numbered, four cups for each of the numbers 1 to 9. The cups numbered 1, 3, 6, 8 are coloured black, those numbered 2, 4, 7, 9 are red, and those numbered 5 are yellow. The number 5 fulfils a similar function to the zero in roulette.

Each dish has two or three tables containing betting layouts (Figure 2). When the players have placed their stakes on the layouts, the croupier sends a rubber ball travelling around the rim of the dish, and the winning number is decided by the pocket into which the ball drops.

The bets are of two kinds. *En plein* is a bet on any single number, including 5. The stake is placed on the appropriate number of the layout. The odds offered are 7 to 1.

All other bets are on a combination of four numbers and are offered at odds of 1 to 1, or even money. Stakes placed on the space marked Noir are on a black number winning, on Rouge on a red number. Stakes on Manque are on the numbers 1, 2, 3, 4; those on Passe on the numbers 6, 7, 8, 9. Bets can be made on the odd numbers (known as impair at roulette) by placing a stake in the space on the layout containing 1, 3, 5, 7 in a diamond shape, on the even numbers (pair) in the space containing 2, 4, 6, 8.

All even-money bets are lost when the number 5 wins. There is no 'in prison' or le partage rule as in roulette.

The advantage to the casino on every bet is therefore 11.11 per cent, making boule a very unfavourable game for the gambler, who is almost certain to lose over a relatively short period. Nevertheless, the tables in French casinos are usually well patronised.

Vingt-trois

Vingt-trois is a new game in French casinos, and is an improved form of boule, using space-age equipment. This consists of a wheel with 27 pockets enclosed in a plastic dome. When a croupier operates apparatus from outside, the wheel spins and a ball bounces around inside. The ball eventually drops into a pocket to denote the winning number and colour.

The pockets contain the numbers 1 to 14 but not equally.
Numbers 1, 2, 3, 4 have one pocket each
Numbers 5, 6, 7, 8, 9, 10, 11 have two pockets each
Numbers 12, 13, 14 have three pockets each

The pockets are coloured alternately red and black, except the three containing number 13. These are white. Number 13 performs the function of zero in roulette and 5 in boule.

The only even-money bets are on Noir and Rouge (black and red). They lose when number 13 appears.

Successful bets on a one-pocket number are paid at odds of 23 to 1; on a two-pocket number at odds of 11 to 1; and on a three-pocket number at odds 7 to 1. The number 13 can be backed.

The effect of these odds is to give the casino an advantage of 11.11 per cent on all bets, as in boule. Players seeking a fair gamble will prefer French roulette to either of these alternative games.

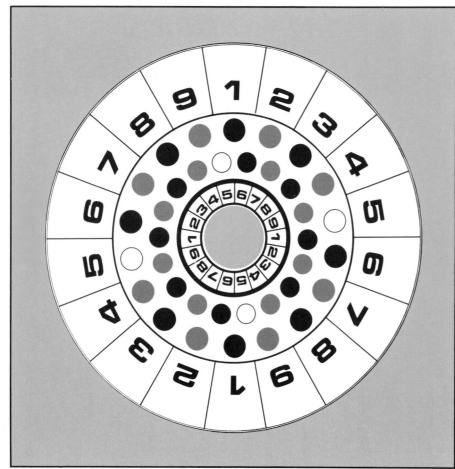

Figure 1 A Boule dish.

Above A Boule dish and table at a Boulogne casino in 1963.

Right An Oscar Wilson print dated 1897 called 'Petits Chevaux'. This game was a fore-runner of Boule, run on the same principles.

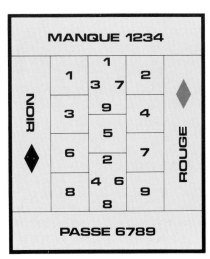

Figure 2 A Boule staking table.

179

BRAG

Brag developed from a Spanish card game called Primero, which was popular in England in the time of the Tudors.

BRAG IN ITS TURN is an ancestor of Poker, and Poker has itself influenced a modern version of Brag.

Traditional game

Brag is a game for from five to eight players, using the full 52-card pack. The first dealer is decided by any agreed means, and thereafter the deal passes in rotation clockwise after each hand.

The dealer puts a stake up to an agreed limit into the centre of the table and deals three cards face down to each player.

In turn, each player, beginning with the player on the left of the dealer, after examining his cards, must either put into the centre a stake at least as high as the dealer's or drop out for that particular deal. A third alternative is to raise the stake. If a player raises the stake, subsequent players in their turn must put into the centre at least the amount of the new stake or drop out. When a stake is raised, all players who have already staked must on the next turn add to their stake to bring it up to the new level, raise it themselves, or drop out and forfeit the stake already made.

The betting stops when all except one player has dropped out, in which case that player may take the entire stakes without showing his hand, or until those players still in the game have all staked an equal amount. Once that stage is reached nobody can raise any more. The hands are then compared and the player with the best hand collects the stakes. If two hands are equal highest, the stakes are shared.

Evaluation of hands

There are three wild cards in Brag: the ♦ A, ♣ J and ♦ 9. They are called braggers and can count as any rank the holder wishes.

In the traditional game flushes and sequences are of no value. The highest hand is a pair royal, consisting of three cards of the same rank. A pair royal without a bragger beats a pair royal with bragger. Where hands are of the same kind, the rank of the cards decides precedence.

The cards rank from Ace (high) to 2 (low). Braggers are of equal rank, e.g. if two pair royals of equal rank each include a bragger the hands are equal.

The next highest hand is a pair, with again a natural pair taking precedence over one with a bragger. Where pairs are of the same rank, the rank of the odd cards decides precedence.

Hands without a pair are given precedence by the rank of the highest card, if equal by the second highest, and if still equal by the third.

A bragger is regarded as a natural card if used to represent its own rank, e.g. ♦ A, ♠ A and ♥ A is a natural pair royal.

Figure 1 shows the possible hands.

Three-stake Brag

Three-stake brag is a variation. Each player puts up three stakes of equal amount before the deal. The dealer deals the first two cards to each player face down and the third face up. The first stake is won by the player dealt the highest face upwards card. For this round the braggers take their natural position in the pack. Should two or more players have the same equal highest card, the player nearest the dealer's left wins the stakes. The second stake is won in the usual way by the players examining their hands and betting, raising and dropping out in the way described above. If nobody bets the best hand wins the stakes.

The third stake is won at the end of the deal by the player whose hand has a pip value nearest to 31 (over or under). Aces count 11 and court cards 10. All players show their hands so that each knows the total to beat, because, beginning on dealer's left, a player whose total is lower than 31 may draw one or more card from the top of the pack until he is satisfied. If a player who draws reaches a total over 31, however, he busts and cannot win. Should two or more totals be equal, the player nearest the dealer's left wins the stakes.

Modern Brag

Modern Brag is played in the same way as traditional Brag, but there are no braggers and a wider variety of hands are recognised.

The hands rank in order:
Prial Three cards of the same rank. Aces are high and 2s low, except that a prial of 3s beats everything.
Running flush Three cards of the same suit in sequence. The highest ranking is Ace, 2, 3, then Ace, King, Queen down to 4, 3, 2.

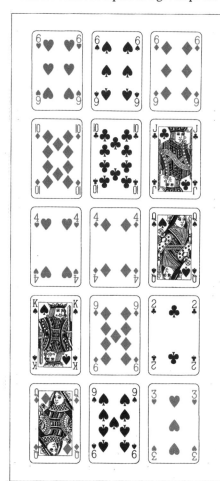

Figure 1 Rank of hands in traditional Brag. From the top: pair royal, pair royal with bragger, pair, pair with bragger, high card.

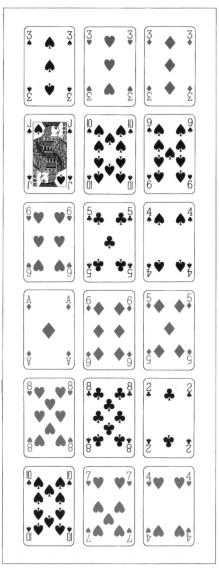

Run Three cards in sequence, but not of the same suit. Again Ace, 2, 3 is the highest ranked, with 4, 3, 2 the lowest.
Flush Three cards of the same suit. Competing flushes are ranked by the highest card, if equal the second, if still equal the third.
Pair Two cards of the same rank. A pair of higher rank beats one of lower. If two pairs are equal, the odd card determines precedence.
High card Hands lacking any of the above combinations are ranked by the highest card, if equal the second, if still equal, the third.

Examples of these categories are shown in Figure 2.

There are many variations in modern Brag, and players should agree on the precedence of runs and prials etc. before the game starts. Similarly, some schools allow wild cards, popularly the black 2s, and this should be determined beforehand.

Strategy

Psychology and mathematics play parts in Brag. It is necessary to know first how good a hand is. This can be shown by Table 1, which gives the probability of being dealt hands of each type in modern Brag.

TABLE ONE: **Probability of being dealt each hand in modern Brag**

Hand	Total in pack (no wild cards)	Probability (per cent)
Prial	52	0.2+
Running flush	48	0.2+
Run	720	3.2
Flush	1096	5.0
Pair	3744	17.0
High card	16440	74.4
	22100	100.0

Having determined the value of a hand in mathematical terms, it is necessary to learn the betting habits and mannerisms of the other players in order to form an idea of the strengths of their hands. At the same time, of course, it is necessary to confuse them by not betting to a pattern and by not betraying by behaviour the strength of one's own hand.

Figure 2 Rank of hands in modern Brag. From the top: prial, running flush, run, flush, pair, high card.

A John Lomax drawing entitled 'The Bitterness of Dawn'.

CHEMIN DE FER

Chemin de fer is a version of Baccarat, sometimes called Baccarat à un tableau or Baccarat-Chemin de fer. However, the game known in America as Baccarat-Chemin de fer is the game known elsewhere as Punto Banco (q.v.).

THE MAIN DIFFERENCE with Baccarat is that the players hold the bank in rotation. Hence the name of the game: the sabot, or dealing shoe, moves round the table (Figure 1) like a train on rails.

The first banker is decided by ballot or auction, the player agreeing to put up the biggest bank being given it. He may withdraw it when he wishes, but may not add or subtract from it, unless it exceeds the casino maximum or is not covered by the players, when he must withdraw the excess.

When the bank passes, it is offered to the next player in an anti-clockwise position, and if he refuses it to the next, and so on.

Because the casino does not hold the bank, it takes a commission. In France and Nevada it is likely to be 5 per cent of the banker's winnings per coup, in Great Britain a charge per shoe.

There are only two hands in Chemin de fer – the banker's and the players'. The players put up their stakes, beginning with the player on the banker's right, until the amount in the bank is covered. One player can cover the whole bank by calling 'banco'.

A player who calls banco and loses is entitled on the next coup to call 'banco suivi', which takes precedence over other calls, and entitles the player to stake the whole amount of the bank on the next coup.

A third preferential call is 'avec la table', ranking lower than the other two calls, by which a player announces his intention to cover half the amount of the bank. Should two or more players call 'avec la table' or 'banco', preference is given to him nearest banker's right.

Six packs of cards are shuffled and cut and placed in the dealing shoe with an indicator between the seventh and eighth cards from the bottom, to mark the end of the shoe.

The banker deals two cards face down to the active player and two to himself, one at a time. The active player is the player with the highest stake.

As in Baccarat, a hand consists of two or three cards. The object is to obtain a point nearer to 9 than the opponent.

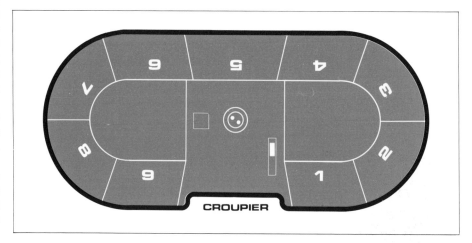

Figure 1 A Chemin de Fer table.

The point is calculated by adding together the pip values of the cards in the hand (Ace counts as one, King, Queen, Jack as 10) and taking the last digit as the point (see also Baccarat). A two-card hand with a point of 8 or 9 is a natural and wins against all three-card hands, irrespective of the point. A natural 9 beats a natural 8.

The banker and player examine their hands, and if either has a natural the cards are exposed and the bets settled.

Otherwise, the player first, and then the banker, must decide whether to stand on his hand as it is, or draw a third card.

The player must draw with a point of 0, 1, 2, 3 or 4, and stand with a point of 6 or 7, whether he is playing only for himself or for several players. His only option is when his point is 5. This is the same rule as in Baccarat. The banker, too, must follow the same banker's Table of Play as in Baccarat. This is set out again in Table One. Unlike Baccarat, however, the banker *must* follow the rules in the Table of Play. As he is playing against only one hand, there is no conflict for him as in Baccarat. He has the choice of whether to draw or stand, therefore, in only two situations.

Some casinos in Britain allow faux tirages, or false draws, whereby banker and player may draw or stand as they see fit, but only in those coups where a player is playing for himself only.

TABLE ONE: **Banker's Table of Play at Chemin de Fer**

Banker's point	Banker draws if player draws	Banker stands if player draws	Banker has option if player draws
3	0, 1, 2, 3, 4, 5, 6, 7	8	9
4	2, 3, 4, 5, 6, 7	0, 1, 8, 9	–
5	5, 6, 7	0, 1, 2, 3, 8, 9	4
6	6, 7	0, 1, 2, 3, 4, 5, 8, 9	–

Note: if the player does not draw, the banker stands on 6, and draws on 3, 4, 5

FARO

Faro is a card game which was the most popular gambling game in America in the late nineteenth century, but is now likely to be found in only a few places in Nevada.

A STANDARD 52-CARD pack is used. In the old casinos the cards were dealt from a dealing box, there would be a staking table marked with one entire suit of cards, usually spades (Figure 1), and a casekeeper would use a counting device, an abacus-like piece of equipment, with which he kept track of the cards played (Figure 2). There were also copper tokens used to distinguish between types of bet.

Players can bet on any rank of card, either to win or to lose. In each case the stake is placed upon the appropriate card on the table layout, but if it is a bet that the rank will lose a copper token is placed on the chips.

When all bets are placed, a dealer plays a card from the box. This card is called 'soda' and has no effect on the game. The next card is dealt from the box and is a loser, while the card exposed in the box is a winner. The bets on these two ranks are settled at odds of 1 to 1 (or evens). Stakes not affected are left on the layout, and there is now an opportunity for players to make additional bets if they wish.

The winning card is then taken from the box and begins a win pile. Now the next loser is played from the box onto the losing pile, exposing the next winner; bets are settled, and so on.

Behind the 24th winning card in the box, there will only be three cards left. Their ranks are known (from the casekeeper) and players now bet on their order. If the three ranks are different, odds of 4 to 1 are offered against naming the order (the correct odds are 5 to 1, the casino edge 16⅔ per cent). If there is a pair in the last three cards, the odds offered are 1 to 1 or evens (the correct odds are 2 to 1, the casino edge 33⅓ per cent). The standard bets on winning and losing cards are not settled on the last three cards.

On the standard bets, the casino claims its profits when the losing and winning cards in a pair are of the same rank. The casino takes half the stakes on that rank, giving it an advantage of about 1½ per cent.

It is possible to play the game privately without the equipment found in a casino. Players should hold the bank for one deal each, and the banker should keep track of the cards played.

Figure 1 The staking table for Faro.

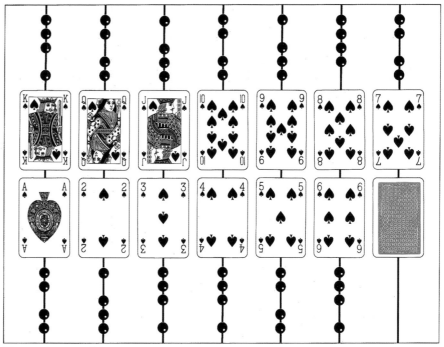

Figure 2 A counting frame.

HOGGENHEIMER

Hoggenheimer is a card game which is sometimes called English roulette, because the stakes are placed upon the 'tableau' in a similar manner.

IT IS PLAYED WITH a standard pack of cards from which the 6s, 5s, 4s, 3s and 2s have been removed. It also requires a Joker, but it is necessary that the back of this card is indistinguishable from the others. Therefore a 'clean' Joker should not be used – one of the discarded 2s would be better.

Each player should be banker in turn. The cards are shuffled and cut, and the banker lays out all but the last one face down in four rows of eight cards. These rows represent, from the top, spades, hearts, diamonds and clubs respectively, and from the left Ace down to 7 in each row. The last card is placed face down on one side.

Players place their bets by putting a stake on a card or a combination of cards. They are betting that the card or combination will be turned face up before the game ends.

When all bets are placed, the banker turns over the odd card, and places it in its place in the layout, taking up the card which is already there and exposing it. He then places this card in its appointed place, exposing the card already there, and so on. The game ends when the Joker is exposed, and the banker settles the bets. It is possible, of course, for the Joker to be the card set aside, in which case the banker wins all stakes.

Figure 1 shows a completed game.

The bets possible and the odds, are as follows:

1) On a single card, stakes 1 and 2 on the layout. Stake 2 is successful. The odds are 1 to 1, or evens.

2) On any two adjacent cards, stakes 3 and 4 (successful) on the layout. The odds are 2 to 1.

3) On four cards in a street or column, stakes 5 (successful) and 6 on the layout. The odds are 4 to 1.

4) On four cards in a square, stakes 7 (successful) and 8 on the layout. The odds are 4 to 1.

5) On eight cards in a suit or row, stakes 9 (successful) and 10 on the layout. The odds are 8 to 1.

The odds quoted are the true ones and give no advantage to either banker or player.

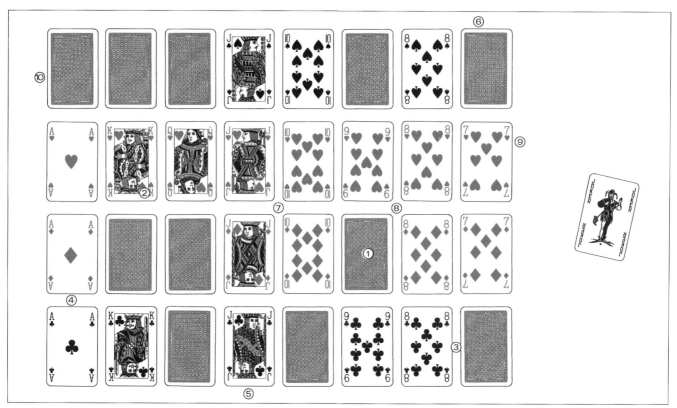

Figure 1 A completed game of Hoggenheimer, with some winners and losers.

MONTE BANK

Monte Bank and Lansquenet are two very simple games of chance which involve no more than betting upon whether a card of one rank or suit will turn up before another.

Monte Bank

Monte Bank is a game for any number of players. The full pack is used with the 8s, 9s and 10s removed. The first banker is chosen by any method agreeable. Thereafter the bank passes to the left, each player holding it for five hands.

After the shuffle, and another player cutting the cards, the banker draws two cards from the bottom of the pack and places them in a row face upwards on the table. This is known as the bottom layout.

The banker then places two cards from the top of the pack face up in a row to form the top layout.

Players place their bets on whichever layout they choose. It is best to have an agreed maximum stake before the game begins. The banker then turns the pack upwards. The exposed bottom card is known as the 'gate'. If either layout includes a card of the same suit as the gate, backers on that layout win. If a layout does not include a card of the same suit as the gate, the banker collects the stakes on that layout.

Should a layout contain two cards of the same suit backers of that layout are paid treble if they win. Figure 1 shows top and bottom layout and gate. Top layout wins, bottom layout loses. Had the gate been a heart, both layouts would have won; a spade and both would have lost.

Unless there is one card of each suit in the two layouts, there is a slight advantage to the banker.

Lansquenet

Lansquenet is a German game. Any number may play, and the full pack is used. The first banker is chosen by any method agreeable to all, thereafter the bank passes to the left after each deal.

After a shuffle, the cards are cut by another player. Banker then deals the

Figure 1 Top layout (♥ J, ♣ 7), bottom layout (♦ 8, ♥ 5) and gate (♣ 2).

top two cards of the pack face up in a row to the table. These are known as the hand cards. He then deals a card face up to himself and one face up to the players. If either card is of the rank of a hand card it is put with them and another card dealt in its place. A maximum stake should be agreed beforehand. The players place their stakes on the players' card, each announcing the amount of his stake. A player may not subsequently bet on another card in the same deal except at the same stake. Players are betting that a card of the rank of the banker's card

will appear before a card of the rank of the players' card.

The banker then draws cards one at a time from the top of the pack and turns them face up.

Should he turn up a card of the rank of the players' card, the banker takes the stakes on that card and the two cards of that rank are added to the hand cards.

Should he turn up a card of a rank not shown on the table, that card becomes another players' card, and players may put stakes upon it.

Should he turn up a card of the rank of the banker's card, he pays out at level stakes to all the players with stakes on the cards on the table, and his deal ends.

Figure 2 shows the row of two hand cards, a banker's card and several players' cards, with various stakes.

The game is an even one, with no advantage to bank or player, since every time a bet is struck, there will be three

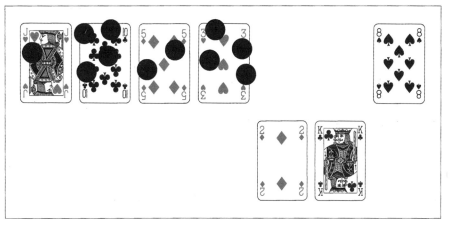

Figure 2 The hand cards (♣ K, ♦ 2), banker's card (♠ 8) and four players' cards with stakes.

cards of the rank of the banker's card and three cards of the rank of the players' card remaining in the pack.

The reason a player is barred from varying his stake during a deal is to prevent players from doubling up on a new players' card each time he loses. This would not bring him a mathematical advantage, as every bet still has an equal chance of winning or losing, but would tend to spoil the game for the remaining players.

NAPOLEON

Napoleon, commonly called Nap, is a simple card game for any number up to six, four being ideal.

THE FULL PACK of 52 cards is used. The cards rank from Ace (high) to 2 (low).

Players draw for first dealer, lowest dealing first. Ace counts low for this purpose. Five cards are dealt to each player, one at a time, in a clockwise direction.

Bidding

After the deal, there is one round of bidding, beginning with the player on dealer's left (eldest). Each player in turn must make a bid higher than the previous bid or pass.

A bid of Two is a contract to make two tricks, with the bidder naming a trump suit, a bid of Three a contract to make three tricks, and so on. A bid of Five (i.e. a contract to make all the tricks) is called Napoleon, or more commonly 'Nap'. A bid of Two is the lowest permitted, except that if all other players pass, dealer must bid, and he is allowed to make a bid of One.

The play

The highest bidder (declarer) leads to the first trick, and the first card led indicates the trump suit. The usual procedure of trick-taking games applies. Players must follow suit if they can, if not they may play any card they wish. A trick is won by the highest trump, or if it contains no trumps, by the highest card in the suit led.

The other players form temporary partnerships against the declarer, the object of the game being to make the contract on the one hand and to defeat it on the other. Tricks made in excess of the contract are of no value.

Scoring

Settlement is made at the end of every deal. Declarer receives from, or pays to, each player according to the following scale:

One	1 unit
Two	2 units
Three	3 units
Four	4 units
Napoleon	Declarer receives 10 units if successful.
	Declarer pays 5 units if beaten.

After each hand the deal passes to the next player in a clockwise direction.

Strategy

It is difficult to evaluate a hand as, unless there are more than six players, there will be more cards sleeping than in the deal. Each hand must include at least two cards of the same suit. A good hand will include at least three trumps, with preferably Ace and another in a second suit. Declarer must expect at least one hand against him to contain two trumps.

In the play there is little room for judgement. With only five tricks to play for, it is usually best to take them whenever possible.

Variants

To add variety to a simple game players allow some extra bids, as follows:

Wellington A bid of Nap can be overcalled by a bid of Wellington, which is also a contract to make five tricks but doubles the stake (in some schools it doubles the stake only when the declarer loses). It cannot be bid unless Nap is bid first.

Blucher Where Wellington is allowed, Blucher is also allowed as a bid to win five tricks but at triple stakes (again in some schools only when declarer loses). It can only be bid over Wellington.

Misère A bid of Misère, or Misery, is an undertaking to lose all tricks, without a trump suit (although some schools make the declarer's opening lead the trump suit as usual). The bid ranks between Three and Four and is paid as Three.

Peep Each player at his turn to bid may look at the top card of the stock by paying a chip to a pool. The eventual declarer, if he has paid to look at the card, may take it up into his hand, discarding another. The pool is taken by declarer if he is successful, or otherwise by the first player to make a successful bid thereafter.

Nonchalance and annoyance at the card table – the game is Bridge but it looks as if there might be stakes involved.

NEWMARKET

Newmarket is a modern version of an old card game called Pope Joan. There are many versions which differ slightly from each other, and the game goes under many names, most commonly Boodle and Stops in Britain, Michigan, Chicago or Saratoga in the United States.

ANY NUMBER FROM three to eight may play. The full pack of 52 cards is used, plus any Ace, King, Queen and Jack of differing suits from another pack. These four cards are placed face upwards in a row in the centre of the table and are known as the boodle cards.

The cards rank from Ace (high) to 2 (low).

The first dealer is decided by any method agreeable to the players; subsequently the deal passes clockwise. The dealer has an advantage, so all players must deal an equal number of times.

Before the deal each player places a chip on each of the boodle cards and another in a pool or kitty (see Figure 1).

The cards are dealt one at a time clockwise, beginning with an extra hand (the widow) between the dealer and the player on his left. The whole pack is dealt.

The dealer, after looking at his hand, may exchange it for the widow. Having picked up the widow, he cannot change back. The hand not taken remains face down on the table throughout the game.

The player on dealer's left (eldest) leads a card of any suit, but it must be the lowest card he holds in that suit. He plays the card to the table in front of him, rather than to the centre. He announces the rank and suit of the card played.

The holder of the next higher card in the suit then plays it, followed by the holder of the next higher and so on, until the suit is stopped, either by the Ace being reached or by the next higher card in the suit being in the widow, in which case it will become apparent that no player can go. A player with a sequence can play it on the same turn. After the first card in a suit, players playing subsequent cards need announce only the rank.

The player who played the last card before a stop begins a new suit by leading his lowest card in any other suit he chooses, announcing both rank and suit. If the only cards he has are of the suit which has been stopped, he must pass, and the player on his left starts the new suit.

When a player plays a card he plays it into a pile before him, and may not spread the pile to remind himself of cards previously played.

The object is twofold. The first object is to play a card that duplicates a boodle card. A player so doing wins the chips on that card. The second object is

won on boodle cards or from the pool on that deal, and if another player was unable to play the boodle card in the suit withheld he must pay him the number of chips on that card.

Strategy

Dealer must use judgement in deciding whether or not to exchange his hand for the widow. The boodle cards in the hand, and the number of chips on each boodle card, will influence the decision. If in doubt he should change, taking care to remember the cards of his original hand, since they become the stoppers. During the play, a player will prefer to lead cards in suits in which he holds boodle cards, otherwise he will lead long suits in the hope of gaining the pool.

A player should remember the cards

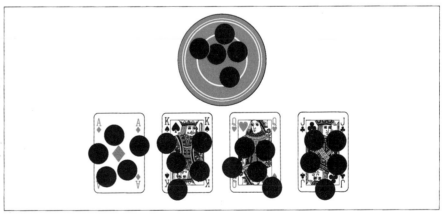

Figure 1 The four boodle cards and the pool in Newmarket.

to be first to get rid of all the cards in the hand. The player who does so wins the pool. Play ends when one player has played all his cards. Any chips on boodle cards not won at the end of the deal remain on the cards to be won on a subsequent deal.

A player who is found to have played a card other than his lowest in a suit must replace any chips he won on any boodle cards in that deal, and must pay each of the other players one chip each as a penalty. A player found not to have played a card when able, thus causing a false stop, must replace any chips he

played. Often a card held will become a stopper by another player leading the next higher. Such a card should be led at the first opportunity.

PUNTO BANCO

Punto Banco is a casino banking game of the Baccarat family growing in popularity in America and Europe, and likely to oust Baccarat and Chemin de Fer from many casinos, except, perhaps, in France, where the old traditions of Baccarat are valued.

PUNTO BANCO IS THE GAME which is kown in Nevada casinos as Baccarat-Chemin de Fer. The table layout is shown in Figure 1.

The game is a simplified version of Chemin de Fer played on a double-ended table like that of Baccarat à deux tableaux. It lacks the small degree of skill which other Baccarat games have in that all decisions are covered by a Table of Play, and no options exist for a player with a point of 5. Its popularity among players depends on this automatic quality, and among casinos on the guaranteed house edge.

Six packs are shuffled and cut and placed in a shoe, with a marker above the seventh card from the bottom to indicate the end of the shoe.

There are two hands, the players' and the banks, but these do not have the same significance as in Chemin de Fer, for instance. The players in rotation may play the bank hand, while a casino croupier plays the players' hand. All players may bet on either hand to win, and all bets are against the casino.

A player wishing to bet that the players' hand wins, places his stakes in the area marked 'punto' (or on some tables 'players'), just in front of his position at the table. A player wishing to bet that the bank's hand wins, places his stake in the little box marked 'banco' (sometimes 'bank'), numbered to correspond with his place at the table.

Each hand consists of two or three cards. The pip value of the cards is added together (with Ace counting as one and King, Queen, Jack as 10 each) to determine the point of the hand. Should the total pip count be a number with two digits, the second is the point of the hand. The hand with the higher point wins, except that a two-card hand with a point of 9 or 8 is a natural, and beats any three-card hand irrespective of its point. The evaluation of the hands is thus the same as in Baccarat and Chemin de Fer (q.v.).

Two cards are dealt by the 'banker' to each hand. If either is a natural it is exposed and bets are settled. Otherwise player and bank in turn complete their hands by either standing or drawing a third card. Both player and bank are performing mechanical functions, because neither has any options as to their play. They both must follow the respective Table of Play as set out in Table One.

Of the two hands it is calculated that the hand representing the bank has a slight advantage over the hand representing the players. Therefore the casino pays successful backers of the players' hand at odds of 1 to 1, or even money, whereas successful backers of the bank's hand are paid at odds of 19 to 20, in other words a 5 per cent deduction on what would be paid at odds of 1 to 1. The difference represents the casino profit, which amounts to around 1.25 per cent, about average for the best casino games.

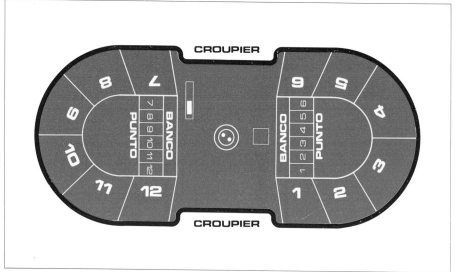

Figure 1 A Punto Banco table.

TABLE ONE: **Tables of Play for Players and Banker at Punto Banco**

Player's point		
0, 1, 2, 3, 4, 5	draws	
6, 7	stands	

Banker's point	draws if player draws	stands if player draws
0, 1, 2	0, 1, 2, 3, 4, 5, 6, 7, 8, 9	–
3	0, 1, 2, 3, 4, 5, 6, 7, 9	8
4	2, 3, 4, 5, 6, 7	0, 1, 8, 9
5	4, 5, 6, 7	0, 1, 2, 3, 8, 9
6	6, 7	0, 1, 2, 3, 4, 5, 8, 9
7	–	0, 1, 2, 3, 4, 5, 6, 7, 8, 9

RED DOG

Red dog, also called high-card pool, is a simple gambling game for up to ten players, using the conventional 52-card pack of playing cards.

THE CARDS RANK from Ace (high) to 2 (low). The suits are not ranked. To determine first dealer, each player is dealt a card face up – highest deals. Thereafter the deal passes in rotation clockwise. Each player, including dealer, puts an agreed amount into a pool.

Dealer gives each player five cards, one at a time face down, beginning with the player on his left (with nine or ten players, each player is dealt four cards only). The remainder of the pack he places face down to form the stock.

Beginning with the player on dealer's left, each player on his turn bets that he has a card in his hand to beat the card on the top of the stock at his turn.

The player examines his hand, and stakes an amount between one chip and the total amount in the pool. He announces his stake and places it alongside the pile in the centre of the table.

The dealer then turns up the top card of the stock. If the player's hand contains a card to beat it, that is a card of a higher rank in the same suit, he shows that card, and dealer pays him the amount of the stake from the pool. The rest of the player's hand is discarded face down.

If the player cannot beat the turned up card, he displays his hand face up for the other players to see before it is discarded face down. Dealer adds the chips staked to the pool.

Each player is dealt with separately and in turn.

On his turn, a player may pay one chip to the pool as a forfeit in preference to betting. By doing so, he avoids the need to show his hand.

If a winning bet removes all the chips from the pool, each player contributes the same number of chips as before to form a new pool.

At the end of a deal, the cards are collected and shuffled and the next player deals. If at the start of a new deal the pool has dropped below the original amount, each player contributes an equal number of chips sufficient to bring it back to at least the same amount.

Strategy

It is easy to evaluate the hand before betting. At the beginning of the deal a player has five cards in his hand. Of the other 47 he can work out how many he can beat and how many beat him. During the play, as cards become exposed, both totals might be reduced. When it is his turn to bet, if there are more cards that he can beat than will beat him, he has an advantage.

Throughout the game the pool belongs to all the players jointly. The object of forfeiting a bet when almost certain to lose is to prevent other players having the advantage of knowing which small cards have already been dealt.

Slippery Sam

Also called Shoot, Slippery Sam is a banking variation of Red Dog. The dealer puts in the entire pool (it is best to agree a minimum beforehand), and deals three cards to each player except himself. The betting and settling is as for Red Dog. The dealer keeps the bank for three rounds unless the entire pool is won, when it passes to the next player. At the end of three rounds, the dealer withdraws the pool, or he can choose to deal one further round. He would be advised not to, as this is rare among banking games in that the advantage is heavily with the players.

Farmer's Joy

Farmer's Joy is a variation of Red Dog and Slippery Sam which Lord Stockton enjoyed when he was Harold Macmillan, the British Prime Minister. It is a more interesting game than the others.

Each player contributes equally to a pool, which is replenished when necessary in the manner described in Red Dog. The dealer deals three cards to each player one at a time face down.

Figure 1 Hands which offer almost equal chances of winning and losing in (from top) Red Dog, Slippery Sam and Farmer's Joy.

The players leave their hands face down on the table. The dealer then turns cards face up one at a time from the top of the stock until a 7 or lower appears. This card becomes the turn-up.

Each player in turn then bets an amount, varying from one chip to the entire pool, that he holds a card in his unseen hand to beat the turn-up. He then turns over his cards and adds or subtracts from the pool accordingly.

The deal passes clockwise after each round.

The first player's chances depend on the ranks and suits of the cards exposed before the turn-up, and the rank of the turn-up. The chances of subsequent players alter as each hand is exposed. The chance of winning can always be calculated precisely. In the majority of cases it will fall somewhere between 6 to 4 on and 6 to 4 against.

Figure 1 shows hands in Red Dog, Slippery Sam and Farmer's Joy, all of which have almost equal chances of winning or losing. The optimum staking strategy in all these games is to bet the maximum when the odds are favourable and the minimum when they are not, which makes the games boring as the means for serious gambling. They are much better played for small stakes and social enjoyment.

ROULETTE

Gambling games in which a ball fell into marked pockets on the rim of a bowl were popular in Europe in the early 18th century. E.O. (for even-odd) was fashionable in English spas, while hoca was played in casinos in Europe.

THE INVENTION OF the roulette wheel made other games of the type redundant. With its bright green cloth, lettered in gold, the polished wood table, the glittering wheel with its red and black numbers and chrome fittings, the ivory ball clicking round, the multi-coloured chips scattered on the layout, roulette is the epitome of the glamour of gambling. While it became the centre of activity in the palatial casinos of Monte Carlo, France and Germany, it has never been popular in the United States. This is less because Americans prefer the brasher vulgarity of craps than because roulette players in America have never been given a fair deal by the proprietors.

Roulette is essentially a casino game. It is possible to buy wheels and table layouts in games shops for use at home, but it is difficult to capture the aura and sense of social occasion which accompanies a busy roulette wheel in a casino.

The game described first is as it is played in casinos. There are differences in European and American practice which are noted as they arise.

The French roulette wheel, used in most countries of the world except the U.S.A., contains 37 pockets. One, marked zero, is green, the remainder are alternate red and black, and are numbered 1-36 in a manner designed to alternate as far as possible odd numbers and even numbers, high numbers and low numbers. The wheel is illustrated in Figure 1.

The American roulette wheel, which is also found in some other countries, particularly where gambling is illegal,

contains 38 pockets, including two zeros, a single zero and a double zero. The order of the numbers around the perimeter is different to the French, but the red numbers on the French wheel remain red on the American. The American wheel is shown in Figure 2.

The layout of the table, on which bets are made, also varies in France and America. The French layout, or 'tableau', is shown in Figure 3. The layout is repeated on each side of the wheel, with the lower numbers being closer to the wheeel on each side.

The American layout is shown in Figure 4. This is rarely double-headed. The wheel is set at the end showing the zeros. In Britain, where the French wheel is used, the American single-ended layout is preferred, without the double-zero, of course.

All betting is based upon the pocket in which the ball settles when the wheel is spun. Stakes are placed upon the table layout. One of the croupiers (le tourneur in France, the wheeel roller in America) spins the wheel and sets the

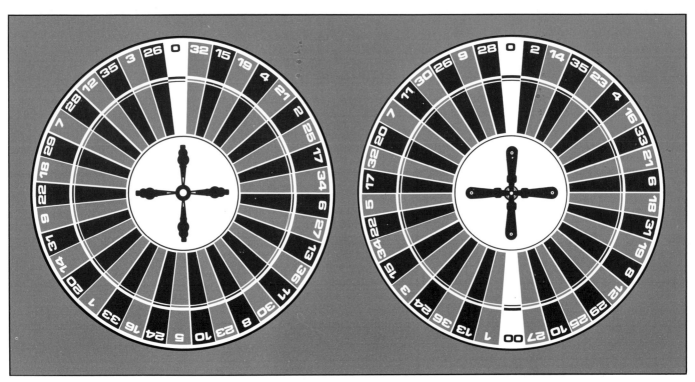

Figure 1 The French roulette wheel.

Figure 2 The American roulette wheel.

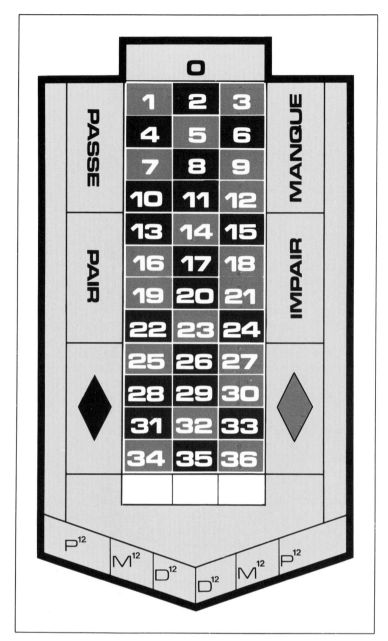

Figure 3 The French roulette table.

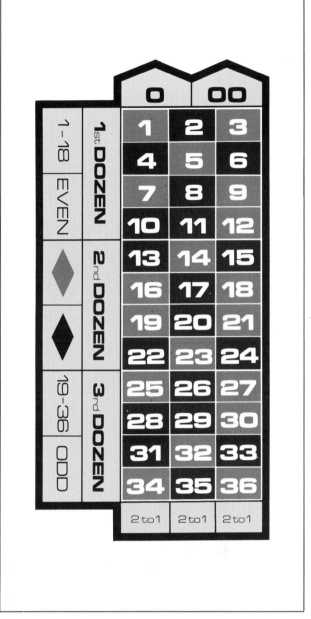

Figure 4 The American roulette table.

ball rolling around the rim in the opposite direction. Bets can be made while the wheel is spinning, up to the time the croupier calls 'rien ne va plus'. In English-speaking countries this is more likely to be 'no more bets'.

Settlement is made after each spin, with one exception, to be explained later. Bets are made using the casino's chips. In Europe, each player will use the same chips, which vary only with denomination. In America, and generally where the American-style table layout is used, chips will be issued at the table, and each player's will be of a different colour.

The bets fall into two categories, those offering even money and those offering odds. The even money bets are

as follows:

Rouge: a bet that a red number will win. Stakes are placed in the rectangle which on both tables is marked by a red diamond.

Noir: a bet that a black number will win. On both tables the black diamond indicates the staking area.

Pair: a bet that an even number will win. The spaces are marked 'pair' or 'even'.

Impair: a bet that an odd number will win. The spaces are marked 'impair' or 'odd'.

Manque: a bet that a low number (1-18) will win. The spaces are marked 'manque' or '1-18'.

Passe: a bet that a high number (19-36) will win. The spaces are marked 'passe'

or '19-36'.

The even money bets differ from the others in the procedure when zero wins, as will be explained later. The other bets are as follows:

En plein: a bet on a single number. This is also called a straight bet. The stake is placed on the appropriate number on the layout. Zero (and double-zero in America) can be backed. The odds paid are 35 to 1.

A cheval: a bet that one of two adjacent numbers on the table layout will win, such as 17 and 20. This is also called a split. The stake is placed on the line between the two numbers. Zero can be combined with an adjacent number. The odds paid are 17 to 1.

Transversale plein: a bet on any three

191

Roulette in Monte Carlo in 1890. 'Rien ne va plus' by J. Berand.

numbers in a row on the table layout, such as 16, 17, 18. This is also called a street. The stake is placed on the line at the edge of the row. Zero can be combined with any two of 1,2,3 by placing the stake on the corner common to the three numbers. The odds paid are 11 to 1.

En Carrè: a bet on any four numbers forming a square on the table layout, such as 31,32,34,35. This is also called a square. The stake is placed on the intersecting lines at the centre of the square. Zero can be backed with 1,2 and 3 by placing the stake on the outside corner common to the zero and the row. The odds paid are 8 to 1.

Transversale simple or sixain: a bet on six numbers forming two adjacent rows or

streets, such as 7,8,9,10,11,12. This is also called a line. The stake is placed on the outside corner common to the two rows. Zero cannot be backed in a sixain. The odds paid are 5 to 1.

Colonne: a bet that a number in one of the three columns on the table layout will win, for example 1,4,7,10,13,16,19,22,25,28,31,34. This is also called a column bet. The stake is placed, on the French table layout, in the blank rectangle at the foot of the column. On the American table layout, the rectangle is marked 2 to 1, which represents the odds paid.

Colonne à cheval: a bet that a number in one of two adjacent columns will win. This is also called a split column. The stake is placed on the line between the

two rectangles representing the column bet. The odds paid are 1 to 2, or 2 to 1 on.

Douzaine: a bet on twelve numbers, the lowest (1-12) the middle (13-24) or the highest (25-36). This bet is also called a dozen. The stake is placed, on the French layout, in the parallelograms marked P^{12}, M^{12} and D^{12}, P (première) for 1-12, M (moyenne) for 13-24, D (Dernière) for 25-36. (On the American table, there are large rectangles marked '1st dozen,' '2nd dozen' and '3rd dozen'. The odds paid are 2 to 1.

Douzaine à cheval: a bet on the 24 numbers represented in two adjacent dozens. This is sometimes called a split dozen. The stake is placed on the line between the spaces used for betting on

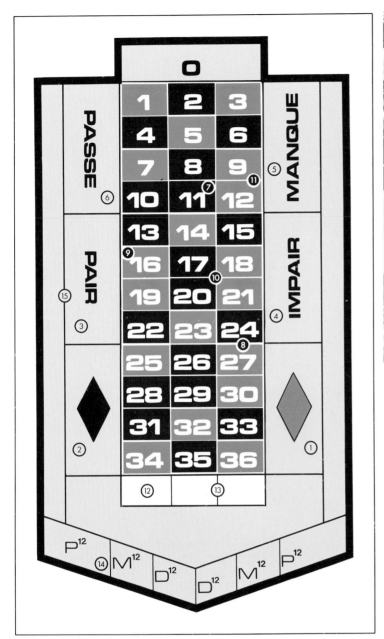

Figure 5 Examples of placing stakes on the French roulette table.

Above Roulette (with a double zero!) at Ostend – a painting by C.H. Kuechler.

Top A painting by Reginald Cleaver showing an evening in the Roulette room at Monte Carlo, 1902.

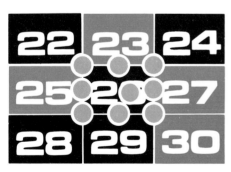

Figure 6 Completing a number (26)

the individual dozens. The odds paid are 1 to 2, or 2 to 1 on.

It can be seen that there is a logical principle behind placing the stake on the table layout. The bets allowed are all those where it is possible to place the stake so that its meaning is unambiguous. Figure 5 shows a layout on which each of these bets have been made.

Figure 6 shows a popular bet, in which a number is backed singly and in combination with all its neighbours, i.e. in four splits and four squares. This is called 'completing the number'. It takes nine chips, and if the number itself wins, it shows a profit of 135 chips. If one of the four numbers in the corners win, the stake is merely saved, with no profit. If one of the other four numbers win, the profit is 27 chips.

When the wheel is spun, the croupier will announce the winning number and its colour. In most casinos a marker will be placed on the winning number on

the table layout until the settlement is made. The croupiers are equipped with long rakes with which they will rake in all losing chips. It is the custom in the payout for the chips won on the even money bets to be placed alongside the chips of the original wager, so that the winner can pick them up together. On the straight bets on a single number the chips won will be placed in front of the winner, who must retrieve his original chip himself, or, as many players do, leave it on the number for a further spin.

When zero wins, the conventions differ. In American casinos, and those playing to the American practice, all bets that do not actually include zero, lose. In France, Britain, and casinos following the French practice, all those bets on numbers and combinations of numbers that do not include zero lose, but stakes on the even money bets are not entirely lost. Half the stake is lost, and the other half retained by the player, a system known in France as 'le partage'.

French casinos offer an alternative to le partage, which involves putting the stake 'in prison'. This involves the croupier moving the stake onto the line drawn at the edge of the staking rectangle, where it remains for the next spin. If the bet wins on the next spin, the player retains the whole stake, but if the bet loses, the whole stake is lost. The 'in prison' and le partage conventions amount to the same thing in effect: a loss of half the stake when zero appears.

Top Left A roulette table well stacked with chips.

Left Roulette in progress at the Grand Hotel casino, Rhode Island.

Right Another view of Roulette at the Grand Hotel casino, which uses a single-ended French table.

It is sometimes thought that the zeros represent the casino's advantage in roulette, but this is only half true, as bets can be made on zero singly or in combination just like any other number, and it pays the same odds. It is truer to say that the casino's advantage comes from the odds offered being based on there being 36 pockets on the wheel, whereas there are, of course, 37 or, on American wheels, 38.

This means that, on the French table, on bets other than the even money bets, the player will expect to lose on average one chip in 37, a casino advantage of approximately 2.70 per cent. On the even money bets, the advantage is halved, to approximately 1.35 per cent.

In American casinos, the casino's advantage is doubled, and is not reduced on the even-money bets. It remains at 5.26 per cent approximately on all bets. This is why roulette has never been as popular in America as elsewhere, particularly since craps offer the wise gambler a much smaller house advantage to overcome.

One of the attractions of playing roulette, particularly in casinos, is the opportunity it affords for players to invent and follow staking systems.

The serious player might have a 'tableau des voisons' to help. This is a chart which shows for each number on the roulette wheel the numbers which are its neighbours (see Figure 7). He might also keep his own chart recording the results of all the spins at the table – the casino might even supply results of previous day's spins.

The best-known system is the 'martingale', or doubling up system. On an even-money chance, a player stakes one unit. Should he lose, he stakes two units on the next spin, subsequently four units, then eight, and so on. As soon as he wins he stops the progressive doubling and starts again at one unit. Calculation will show that whenever he wins, his winnings will equal all his previous losses in the run plus one unit. Therefore this system cannot lose. This would be true, but for one thing. Casinos stipulate a minimum and maximum stake on each bet. The maximum

12	35	3	26	0	32	15	19	4
5	24	16	33	1	20	14	31	9
15	19	4	21	2	25	17	34	6
7	28	12	35	3	26	0	32	15
0	32	15	19	4	21	2	25	17
30	8	23	10	5	24	16	33	1
2	25	17	34	6	27	13	36	11
9	22	18	29	7	28	12	35	3
13	36	11	30	8	23	10	5	24
1	20	14	31	9	22	18	29	7
11	30	8	23	10	5	24	16	33
6	27	13	36	11	30	8	23	10
18	29	7	28	12	35	3	26	0
17	34	6	27	13	36	11	30	8
16	33	1	20	14	31	9	22	18
3	26	0	32	15	19	4	21	2
23	10	5	24	16	33	1	20	14
4	21	2	25	17	34	6	27	13
14	31	9	22	18	29	7	28	12
26	0	32	15	19	4	21	2	25
24	16	33	1	20	14	31	9	22
32	15	19	4	21	2	25	17	34
20	14	31	9	22	18	29	7	28
36	11	30	8	23	10	5	24	16
8	23	10	5	24	16	33	1	20
19	4	21	2	25	17	34	6	27
28	12	35	3	26	0	32	15	19
25	17	34	6	27	13	36	11	30
22	18	29	7	28	12	35	3	26
31	9	22	18	29	7	28	12	35
27	13	36	11	30	8	23	10	5
33	1	20	14	31	9	22	18	29
35	3	26	0	32	15	19	4	21
10	5	24	16	33	1	20	14	31
21	2	25	17	34	6	27	13	36
29	7	28	12	35	3	26	0	32
34	6	27	13	36	11	30	8	23

Figure 7 The tableau des voisons.

is likely to be no more than 1,000 times greater than the minimum. This allows the gambler to double up only nine times – on the tenth he is over the limit. In practice, after ten losers (by no means impossible) a backer seeking to win £1 or $1 will already have lost 1,023 and will be a brave man if he is still doubling up, and wishing to bet £1,024 or $1,024 in order to win one.

The martingale can be modified so that instead of doubling the stake is raised in a slower progressive manner, such as 1, 2, 3, 4 or 1, 1, 2, 2, 3, 3 etc. It limits the stake, but, after a run of losers the eventual winner does not cancel out all the previous losses.

The d'Alembert system is a variation on the martingale, designed to produce the effect of the larger stakes being on the winners, and at the same time to keep the stakes within bounds. The gambler starts with a stake of one unit, increases it by one after each losss, and decreases it by one after each win, stopping the progression as soon as it is in profit and starting again. For example, if he lost his first four bets, his losses would amount to 1 + 2 + 3 + 4 = 10 units. His next stake would be five units. If it won, his stake would reduce to four units, and after another win to three units. If this won, his three winning bets would have gained 12 units, putting him two units up on the progression.

This system has the advantage, as the example shows, of being capable of showing a profit even if the winners are fewer in number than the losers.

The ultimate system in this respect is the Labouchère, which provides a win when the number of winners is little more than half the number of losers.

A row of numbers is written down, for example 1, 2, 3, 4. The stake is the sum of the two numbers at opposite ends of the row, in this case 1 + 4 = 5 units. Should the bet win, the 1 and 4 are crossed out, and the next stake becomes the two numbers at each end of the row again, which would be 2 + 3 = 5 units. Should this bet win, the whole sequence is crossed out, and the profit is 10 units.

Whenever a bet loses, the amont of the losing stake is added to the row of the numbers. Therefore every winning bet crosses out two numbers from the row, while every losing bet adds only one. It follows that the row of numbers is certain eventually to be crossed out. And every time the row is crossed out, the profit is the sum of the numbers in the row – in the example given 10 units. Table 1 shows a possible progression, based on the row of numbers 1, 2, 2, 3. It shows that eight wins and 12 losses eventually wipes out the row of numbers with the promised profit of the sum of the row, i.e. eight units.

Notice, however, that the stakes in

Croupiers laying out chips prior to a Roulette session at the Baden Baden casino.

TABLE ONE: **The Labouchère system in operation**

Row	Stake	Result	Running Profit/Loss
1 2 2 3	4	L	−4
1 2 2 3 4	5	L	−9
1 2 2 3 4 5	6	W	−3
2 2 3 4	6	W	+3
2 3	5	L	−2
2 3 5	7	L	−9
2 3 5 7	9	W	level
3 5	8	L	−8
3 5 8	11	L	−19
3 5 8 11	14	W	−5
5 8	13	L	−18
5 8 13	18	L	−36
5 8 13 18	23	L	−59
5 8 13 18 23	28	W	−31
8 13 18	26	L	−57
8 13 18 26	34	W	−23
13 18	31	L	−54
13 18 31	44	L	−98
13 18 31 44	57	W	−41
18 31	49	W	+8

this unremarkable sequence got quite high – at one time 98 units were lost with another 57 staked.

It is the drawback of all staking systems, that, in relation to the expected win, a large capital is needed to start with, because an adverse series of spins soon leads to large stakes and a test of the gambler's nerve.

All these systems can be played in reverse, whereby the player can increase the stake after a win and decrease it after a loss. This limits losses while providing a prospect of a big win. The gambler should set a target for his win, otherwise he will just keep going until the inevitable loss.

For instance, if a player wrote down a row of figures 1, 2, 2, 3 as above and played the Labouchère in reverse, with a target of winning 100 units, he might achieve this as shown in Table 2. Of course, if he had lost the first two spins, as in Table 1, he would have lost his eight units immediately. Notice that to win 112 units he has needed 15 wins to only seven losses, but has never risked more than his original eight units.

Systems which rely on predicting the winning numbers are usually based on mistaken understandings of the law of large numbers, or, as it is popularly called, the law of averages. Thus, on the strength of any particular number being expected to win on average once in 37 trials, system backers will back a number which has not appeared for this

TABLE TWO: **The Labouchère system played in reverse**

Row	Stake	Result	Running Profit/Loss
1 2 2 3	4	W	+4
1 2 2 3 4	5	W	+9
1 2 2 3 4 5	6	L	+3
2 2 3 4	6	W	+9
2 2 3 4 6	8	L	+1
2 3 4	6	W	+7
2 3 4 6	8	L	−1
3 4	7	W	+6
3 4 7	10	L	−4
4	4	W	level
4 4	8	W	+8
4 4 8	12	W	+20
4 4 8 12	16	L	+4
4 8	12	W	+16
4 8 12	16	L	level
8	8	W	+8
8 8	16	W	+24
8 8 16	24	W	+48
8 8 16 24	32	W	+80
8 8 16 24 32	40	L	+40
8 16 24	32	W	+72
8 16 24 32	40	W	+112

number of spins, or more cautiously, twice or three times this number, 74 or 111 spins. Usually this system is coupled with a progressive staking plan.

A number which has not appeared for a long time is called a 'sleeper'. Sometimes the law of averages idea is extended to the last digits of the numbers on the wheel. These are called 'finals'. The finals of 2 are 2, 12, 22 and 32. Thus all digits up to 6 have four finals; 7, 8, and 9 have three. The lower finals can be expected on average once in nine spins. Some gamblers bet on sleeping finals.

A pecularity of the table layout is that the middle column contains eight black numbers and only four red, while the third column contains eight red and only four black. Some players like to use this imbalance by betting on the centre column, say, and also on red. The idea is that if they lost their column bet, they have a better than even chance of saving their stake, as the other two columns contain 14 red numbers to only 10 black.

This is true, but does not lead to a profit. The column bet will continue to lose at the rate of 2.70 chips in every 100, while the bet on red will continue to lose at the rate of 1.35 chips in every 100 (bearing in mind the 'in prison' or 'le partage' rules), and two losers cannot be combined to make a winner.

It is sadly true that whatever system is used at roulette, whether it is a progressive staking system or a system based on the law of averages, over a long run the casino advantage is certain to tell. Whatever has happened on previous spins does not affect what happens in the next spin. Thus the sequence of numbers which has won the previous 10 or 10,000 spins is immaterial, as is the amount of chips won or lost by any particular player on those spins. Each spin is a separate entity, and on each spin the player is at a disadvantage on every bet.

High society Roulette and a big winner on a curious table layout.

Roulette at home

If roulette is played at home, the host, or whoever provides the equipment, might wish to become the bank, paying out the winners and taking the losing stakes. Over a long period he is sure to make a profit. Players might want to share however.

If no more than ten want to share in the bank, the easiest way is to fix the bank at 1,000 units, made up of ten shares of 100 units each. Players then buy a share each. Should any shares be over, all players may buy a second share, then a third, and so on, until all shares are exhausted. Should there by more players wishing a second share than there are shares, lots must be drawn. The units paid for the shares form the bank's working capital. At the end of the game, the capital remaining in the bank is shared among the shareholders. Thus, if the 1,000 units had become 1,850, each player receives 185 units back per share. Occasionally, the bank may lose, of course. If the bank's capital becomes exhausted, then a new bank must be formed with new capital.

It is suggested that one player operates the bank and does not take part in the play. A banker who plays will not be able to operate the bank quickly enough for the other players. In regular schools, the banker can be chosen on a rota basis. To give the banker an interest, perhaps a tenth share in a 1,000-unit bank could be sold to nine players for 110 units each, the banker having the tenth share free. It is essential for minimum and maximum stakes to be fixed for a game at home. It is suggested that the maximum stake on each betting position be arranged so that the maximum win is roughly the same on each bet, as shown in Table 3. Notice that if chips were used, denominations of 1, 5 10 and 50 would be quite sufficient. The capital in the bank to start should not be less than about 50 times the maximum stake for even money bets.

It is as well to decide the length of the game in advance, particularly if the bank is shared. This avoids acrimony when some want to stop and others do not. If a session of about four hours is required, it could be agreed to play 100 spins, divided into two halves with an interval after 50 spins. The banker should begin with two charts, each ruled up with spaces to record the results of 50 spins, and should note the results so that everybody is satisfied that the correct number of spins takes place.

TABLE THREE: Suggested minimum and maximum stakes for private games

	Minimum Stake	Maximum Stake	Odds	Maximum Win
En plein (single number)	1	5	35-1	175
A cheval (two numbers)	1	10	17-1	170
Transversale plein (three numbers)	1	15	11-1	165
En carré (four numbers)	1	20	8-1	160
Transversale simple (six numbers)	1	30	5-1	150
Colonne and douzaine (twelve numbers)	5	80	2-1	160
Colonne and douzaine à cheval (24 numbers)	10	300	1-2	150
All even-money bets	5	200	1-1	200

Raking in the chips at the Grand Hotel, Rhode Island casino.

200

TRENTE ET QUARANTE

Trent et Quarante is a casino game mostly confined to France and not played in America. It is sometimes called Rouge et Noir.

THE BETTING LAYOUT is shown in Figure 1. Four bets are possible, and stakes are placed on the appropriate places in the layout.

Six packs of cards shuffled together are used. A dealer, called a tailleur, deals two rows of cards. He does not use a dealing shoe, but deals from a batch of cards held in the hand.

The dealer first deals a row representing noir. He continues to add cards the row until the pip count of the row equals or passes 31. Aces count as one and court cards (King, Queen, Jack) as ten. When the row equals or passes 31 the dealer announces the point. The point is the number by which the pip count exceeds 30, and thus can range from one to ten.

The dealer then deals a row repre-

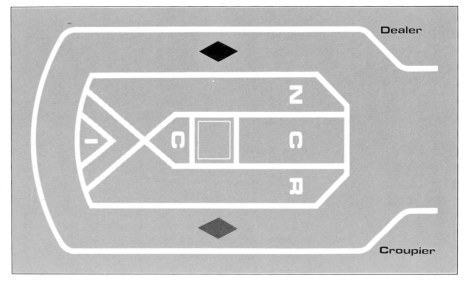

Figure 1 A Trente et Quarante table.

An engraving by Sydney Hall of the last days of Trente et Quarante at the Baden Baden casino, 1872.

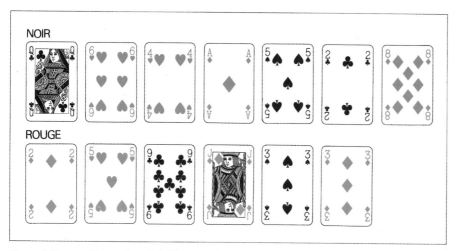

Figure 2 The two lines of cards in Trente et Quarante.

senting rouge in similar manner. The row with the lower point is the winning row. Figure 2 shows rows representing noir and rouge, noir having a point of six and rouge of two.

The four bets possible are all even money bets. They are as follows:

Noir: a bet that this will be the winning row. Stakes are placed in the section on the layout marked N and containing a black diamond.

Rouge: a bet that this will be the winning row. Stakes are placed in the section on the layout marked R and containing a red diamond.

Couleur: a bet that the first card dealt is of the colour of the winning row. Stakes are placed in the section marked C.

Inverse: a bet that the first card dealt is of the opposite colour of the winning row. Stakes are placed in the section marked I.

Should the points of the two rows be equal, bets are void and the stakes returned. However, should both rows total 31, known as a refait, only half of the stake is returned and the other half lost. Alternatively a player may prefer his stake to remain on the table 'in prison'. If it wins on the next spin he reclaims all of it; if it loses he loses all of it. The effect is the same whichever option is chosen.

It has been calculated that a refait occurs fractionally more than once in 40 deals, giving the casino an advantage of 1.28 per cent.

However it is possible for a player to buy insurance against a refait at a cost of one per cent of the stake. A casino operating this system will only allow it on stakes above a certain minimum. A special small chip called a jeton is placed beside an insured stake, and such a stake is returned entire to the player on a refait. Insurance lasts for one hand only. A player who insures on every hand faces a casino advantage of one per cent.

Apart from accepting the opportunity to insure, which slightly reduces the house advantage, there is no opportunity for judgement in Trente et Quarante – it is a game of chance only.

Trente et Quarante being played at Monte Carlo around 1895.

The Green Table.

PHYSICAL GAMES

SNOOKER

Snooker is believed to have been invented by British Army officers in India in the late 19th century. It developed from two games played on a billiard table. One, called Pyramids, used 15 red balls and a cue ball – stakes were paid to each player for each red potted. Another, called Life Pool, used coloured balls – each player paid up each time his colour was pocketed.

A VARIATION, BLACK POOL, used a black ball as a 'rover'. When a player potted an opponent's ball, he could earn a bonus by pocketing the black.

It is said that officers in the Devonshire Regiment joined the games together in a way resembling modern snooker. A snooker at that time was Army slang for a new cadet at the Royal Military Academy at Woolwich (from the French 'neux'). When a subaltern missed an easy pot at the as yet unnamed game, one of the officers, Sir Neville Chamberlain, dismissed him as a 'regular snooker' of a player. The

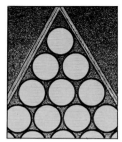

name stuck, the game spread (Lord Kitchener probably played), it was brought back to England, and eventually snooker supplanted billiards as the most popular game played on a billiard table.

A Resumé of the Rules

Snooker is played on a standard snooker or billiard table. It is played by two players (or two pairs, playing alternately), using cues, and requires 22 balls, arranged at the start of the game as shown in Figure 1.

Points are awarded for scoring strokes, and from opponent's fouls.

Scoring strokes consist of the legal potting of the 21 object balls. The 15 reds are worth one point each, and the six 'colours' are valued as follows: yellow two points; green three; brown four; blue five; pink six and black seven.

Scoring strokes are made by potting reds and colours alternately until all the reds are off the table, and then the colours are potted in ascending order of value, yellow to black.

Players determine order of play by tossing a coin. The first player begins the 'frame' by playing from in hand, that is he places the white cue ball anywhere within the D and strikes it with the tip of the cue.

In the first stroke of any turn the cue ball must hit a red, while reds remain on the table. The ball to be struck is known as the ball 'on', and at the beginning of the game red is on.

If the striker succeeds in pocketing a red, he scores one point, and continues his break by nominating any colour he wishes. The cue ball must hit that colour ball, and if it is pocketed the striker scores the points appropriate to that colour.

Red balls pocketed remain off the table, but colours potted are immediately re-spotted, i.e. returned to the spots on which they started the game.

Having potted a colour, the striker continues his break by playing reds and colours alternately until he fails to score on a stroke, when the break ends and it

becomes his opponent's turn.

The opponent plays from wherever the cue ball has come to rest.

It is a foul for a player to cause the cue ball to be pocketed. The break ends, and the next player plays from in hand (i.e. from the D).

When the last red is pocketed, the striker may nominate any colour in the usual way. If he pockets that colour, the ball is re-spotted. The next ball on is then the yellow. The six colours are potted in ascending order, and at this stage remain off the table.

The player with the highest score when all the balls are cleared from the table wins the frame.

When only the black is left, the first score or foul ends the frame, unless it brings the scores level, in which case the black is spotted, the players draw lots for choice of playing, the first player plays from in hand, and the next score or foul ends the frame.

If one player is more than seven points ahead when only the black is left, it is customary for the black not to be played, as it is impossible for his opponent to win.

Re-spotting balls

Red balls are never re-spotted, even if pocketed illegally. Colours pocketed illegally are immediately re-spotted. If a colour has to be re-spotted and its spot is occupied, it is placed on the highest value spot available. If all spots are occupied, it is placed as near as possible to its own spot on an imaginary line between that spot and the centre of the top cushion. In the case of the pink and black, all of that space might be occupied, in which case the ball is re-spotted as near as possible to its own spot on an imaginary line between the spot and the centre of the bottom cushion.

Touching balls

If the cue ball comes to rest touching a ball which is not on, the striker must play away from that ball without moving it.

If the cue ball comes to rest touching a ball which is, or can be, on, the referee shall state 'touching ball'. The

striker must play away from it, as before, otherwise his stroke will be called a 'push stroke' (see under fouls and penalties). The striker may nominate that ball, in which case he is deemed, in playing away, to have struck it (i.e. no penalty is incurred), or he may nominate another ball, in which case he is deemed, in playing away, not to have struck the touching ball.

Snookers and free balls

If the cue ball comes to rest in a position such that it is impossible to hit directly the ball or balls on, because other balls are obstructing the path, the striker is said to be 'snookered'. The laying of snookers is an important part of the game.

However, if a player is snookered by means of a foul shot, the referee shall call 'free ball'. A snooker, in this case, is considered to occur if the striker cannot hit freely either side of the ball on, i.e. he must be able to make a fine contact with the ball on both sides. If the non-offending player decides to take the next stroke (he may ask the offender to play again – see under fouls and penalties), he may nominate any ball as on. For this stroke, the nominated ball shall be regarded as the ball on, and shall acquire its value. For example, should the ball on be red, and the ball nominated as the free ball is the blue, and the blue is potted, one point shall be scored. The blue is re-spotted and the striker is next on a colour.

If in the course of the stroke the free ball is hit first, and the ball on is pocketed, whether the free ball is also pocketed or not, the ball on is scored.

A player awarded a free ball is himself committing a foul if he fails to first hit the free ball or (except when only pink and black remain on the table) if he snookers his opponent behind the free ball.

Fouls and penalties

When a foul is committed the break ends. The offending player does not score any points for the offending

Figure 1 The layout at the start of the game. Key: 1 reds; 2 yellow; 3 brown; 4 green; 5 blue; 6 pink; 7 black; 8 white cue ball; 9 baulk line; 10 the D.

stroke, but keeps the points made in the break previously. The opponent scores the points appropriate to the foul. Should more than one foul be committed in a stroke, the highest value penalty shall be incurred.

Any colours pocketed during a foul stroke are re-spotted. The next stroke is made from where the cue ball comes to rest (if the cue ball is pocketed, it is played from in hand).

The non-offending player may request the offending player to play again, but cannot change his mind having made the request.

The minimum penalty for a foul is four points. The following are fouls and incur a penalty of four points or the higher one prescribed.

a) Fouls with penalties of the value of the ball on:
1) Striking when the balls are not at rest.
2) Striking the cue ball more than once.
3) Striking with both feet off the floor.
4) Striking out of turn.
5) Striking improperly from in hand.
6) Causing the cue ball to miss all object balls.
7) Causing the cue ball to enter a pocket.
8) Causing a snooker with a free ball

(see under snookers and free balls).
9) Causing a jump shot, i.e. a shot in which the cue ball jumps over another ball, except where it first strikes an object ball and then jumps over another.
b) Fouls with penalties of the value of the ball on or the ball concerned, whichever is the higher:
10) Causing a ball not on to enter a pocket.
11) Causing the cue ball to hit first a ball not on.
12) Causing a push stroke i.e. a stroke in which the tip of the cue remains in contact with the cue ball when the cue ball hits the object ball or after the cue ball has begun its forward motion.
13) Striking a ball incorrectly spotted.
14) Touching a ball with other than the tip of the cue.
15) Forcing a ball off the table.
16) Causing the cue ball to hit simultaneously two balls other than two reds or a free ball and the ball on.
c) Fouls with penalties of seven points:
17) Committing a foul after potting a red and before nominating a colour.
18) Using a ball off the table for any purpose.
19) Playing at reds in successive strokes.
20) Using as the cue ball any ball other than the white.

Replayed shots

At all times the striker must try, to the best of his ability, to hit the ball on. If the referee considers this rule to be infringed he shall:
1) Call foul.
2) Award the non-offender the relevant penalty.

3) Ask the non-striker if he wishes to have the balls replaced and the striker play again.

Techniques

Snooker is one of those games where physical co-ordination is of paramount importance, but because it is a game, like golf, in which strokes are made while the ball is still, it also requires a good temperament. There is no room for anxiety, loss of nerves, excitement or anything else which will throw the stroke a little off groove. A player must at all times be able to make a shot with confidence, and that confidence can only come with constant practice.

An aspiring player should possess his own cue. The rules merely state that a cue should be not less than 3 feet (910 mm) in length and show no substantial departure from the traditional shape and form.

Most experts agree that an ideal length for a cue is such that when it is stood upright with the butt on the floor, the tip should be about one inch (25mm) below the shoulder.

The cue should be thick at the butt end, but not too thick to make it unwieldy to hold loosely in the hand, and taper towards the tip, which should be between 10 and 11 mm in diameter.

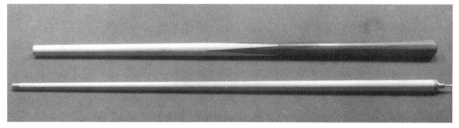

A modern two-piece cue.

The tip should not be hard, so that it hits the ball solidly. It should be soft and holding, allowing a springy feeling as the tip comes into contact with the cue ball.

The snooker professionals prefer quite heavy cues, weighing 16½ to 17½ ounces (470 to 500g approximately). Generally, the heavier the cue the easier it becomes to impart screw and stun.

209

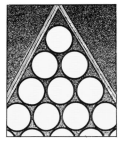

The stance. Note the position of the feet, giving steadiness.

Beginners and amateurs often prefer lighter cues, however.

The balancing point of the cue should be near where the points of the butt meet the shaft. The cue should be fairly rigid.

Since the 1970s it has been possible to buy two-piece cues. The two halves screw together to make a perfectly aligned cue. An alternative long shaft is sometimes available, giving an extenson to the cue which enables it to be used where the half-butt would normally be required. The half-butt is a special long cue with a long rest which is usually part of the equipment of the table. The top players much prefer to use an extension of their own cues rather than the half-butt. Further refinements to the extended cue theme include extensions which fit to the butt end of cues, and even three-piece cues, by which a normal two-piece cue is extended by a third piece which fits between the two halves.

One of the attractions of a two-piece cue, in addition to those which arise from actually using it, is the comparative ease with which it can be carried around. Obviously it will fit into a case

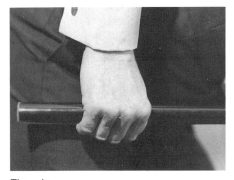

The grip

2ft (0.61m) long rather than, say, 4ft (1.22m).

A player buying a cue should try several, practising shots in the shop if possible.

The way to hold the cue when playing is the next thing to get right. The grip should be firm, but not tight. A floppy grip will mean that the cue is not under control. An over-firm grip

will lead to rigidity and a loss of feel. The strength of the grip might be discovered by laying the cue on the table and picking it up with one hand, with the butt resting on the middle joints of all four fingers. The strength needed to lift the cue is about the same strength with which the cue should be held when making a stroke. The cue, when the stroke is made, will be resting on the middle points of the four fingers, and actually gripped by the thumb and first two fingers.

Having gripped the cue correctly, the next item to get right is the stance. The legs should be apart, with one forward of the other. The front foot should be pointing forward in the direction of the shot, with the back foot pointing outwards, nearly at right angles. Assuming the player is right-handed, the back leg will be the right, and it should be rigid. The left leg, the forward leg, should be bent, with the weight of the body on it as the player leans forward. The feet should be flat on the floor, so that the whole stance should be firm.

The legs do not move during the stroke. Only the cue arm moves, and the body must not rock. When beginning to practise, it is worth practising the stance, a part of the game often overlooked. The right space between the feet should lead to the stance being comfortable and firm, so that the temptation to bend the back leg or lift the back heel of the ground will not arise.

As the player leans over the table to

make his shot, the left hand is placed on the table to form the third leg of a tripod on which the stance is based. Where there is room, most players lay their elbow on the table or cushion as another point of contact. Many players make their strokes with the elbow slightly bent. Others prefer to keep the left arm rigid, which they find helps to keep it still. All players have to keep their arm straight on occasion, as the positions of the balls will require it.

The hand on the table is called the

The normal bridge.

bridge hand. The fingers are straight and press downwards, gripping the cloth. Ideally, the distance between the bridging hand and the cue ball is at least 6 in (15cm). Some players like a longer distance, up to 15 in (40cm).

The cue is guided with the help of the thumb. This is cocked, with the base of the thumb pushing hard into the cloth. The inside of the raised thumb, the

Left Steve Davis playing down the left-hand cushion using the rail to support his bridging hand.

Below Alex Higgins shows his cueing action in tournament play.

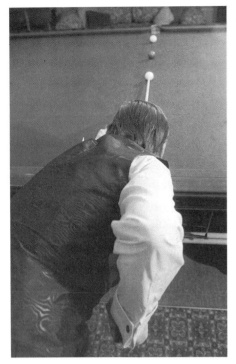

Far left The stance from the back showing the elbow and wrist in the same line as the cue. *Left* the stance from the front, showing the chin over the cue. *Below* Keeping the cue as horizontal as possible while striking through the ball.

space between the thumb and first finger, provides the groove through which the cue is pushed.

The chin should be directly over the cue – in fact the cue should almost wear a groove in the chin. Most players sight with both eyes equally, in which case the path of the cue will be directly below the nose. Some players sight predominantly with one eye, in which case that eye will be directly over the cue. The late Joe Davis, the most successful of all snooker players, sighted with his left eye, and therefore turned his face slighlty outwards.

The shot will be lined up by looking at the cue ball and object ball, assessing the angle at which the object ball must travel when hit, and deciding where the cue ball must hit the object ball to achieve this angle. Having settled into the stance, a player's eyes will switch from the point at which the cue ball will be struck and the point on the object ball at which he is aiming. During this time the cue will possibly be drawn back and moved forwards in rehearsal of the stroke. This is known as 'feathering'.

As the cue is drawn back to make the stroke, the eyes take their last look at the cue ball and as the cue is pushed forward the eyes transfer to the point on the object ball which is the target.

Before the cue is drawn back to make the stroke, the cue should be as horizontal as possible. It cannot be exactly horizontal, as the cue ball will require striking at a point lower than the

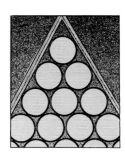

cushion rail, so the cue must always be slightly higher at the butt than the tip. But, except in exceptional circumstances, such as the addition of swerve, the cue should be regarded as horizontal.

The elbow will be directly above the cue, and the forearm will be perpendicular, i.e. at right angles to the cue. With a perfect cue action, the tip and butt of the cue, the chin, the hand, forearm, elbow, upper arm and shoulder should all be in the same vertical plane.

To visualise the perfect stroke, it is easiest to regard the right elbow as a hinge. The drawing back of the cue represents the opening of the hinge. The backswing varies from player to player and from shot to shot, and might be anything between 5 and 12 inches (130 to 300 mm).

The cue is then pushed forward in a straight line, representing the closing of the hinge at the elbow. The cue drives through the ball and follows through. For the smooth and accurate working of this 'hinge', it is necessary that all other parts of the 'machinery' remain absolutely still. Any movement of the bridging hand, feet, legs or shoulders will throw the cue off line. This is the importance of the follow through. If the head looks up to see the effect of the shot, the cue will be jerked and the shot go awry.

Having got the basic mechanics right, it is necessary to practise so that all the actions become automatic. Since everything stems from correct striking of the ball, a good practice is to set the cue ball on the brown spot and play it up the table over the blue, pink and black spots so that it hits the top cushion and returns over the same spots (see Figure 2). If the ball returns to either side of the spots it might mean that the cue ball is being struck slightly off centre, or that the stance is too open or closed.

Potting is the next practice exercise. The dead straight pot is not necessarily the easiest, but it provides the first practice. One method is to place the blue ball on its spot and to practise potting it into the top pockets. Take the

Figure 2

Figure 2 Playing over the centre spots.

Below Playing the cue ball when it is tight against the cushion.

Bottom: The looped bridge, in which the forefinger loops over the cue.

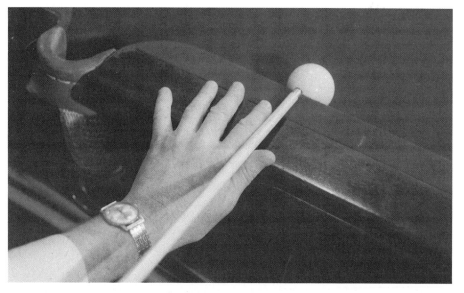

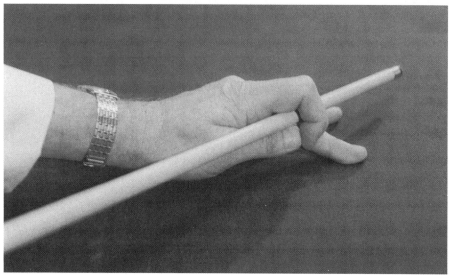

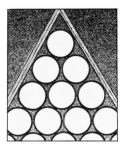

cue ball farther back from the object ball until the blue can be potted regularly from a position on or behind the baulk line.

Potting at an angle is best practised by concentration on one angle at a time. For instance, one can place the green on its spot and practise potting it from a position, say, 2 in (50mm) up table from the yellow spot. Or one can place the pink on its spot, and practise potting it from a position say, half-way between the blue spot and a centre pocket. The black ball is an important one in break building and practising potting it from its spot is always useful. It should be practised from a position where the cue ball is the same distance from the top cushion as the black, and from positions where the cue ball is further from the top cushion and nearer (a cut).

When straightforward pots (i.e. those with no hindrance to the stance of bridging hand) are mastered, then it is time to practise shots with improvised bridges.

Practise strokes with the cue ball tight against the cushion. The bridge must now be made with the fingers flat and gripping the cushion rail, while the palm of the hand presses against the side of the table. The cue is still kept as horizontal as possible, although it is possible to hit only the top of the cue ball. It is a tendency to try to dig down into the ball which involves raising the cue butt and the bridge and usually results in an instability which causes the shot to go wrong.

Sometimes the orthodox groove for the cue has to be amended. If the cue ball is about 6 in (150mm) from the cushion it might be best to advance the hand so that the tips of the fingers are pressing into the cushion itself, which supports the cue. The cue is still thrust forward between thumb and forefinger, but the forefinger can now loop over the cue for extra control.

This grip, with the hand on the cushion and the forefinger curled round the cue, can also be used to play the cue ball up the table from the right-hand cushion, i.e. nearly parallel to the

Using the rest. Mark Wildman follows the usual practice of taking two fingers over the cue.

cushion rather than directly away from it. When the cue ball is close to the left-hand cushion and is to be played up the table the bridge is different. This time the first finger or two might press into the table itself, with the third and fourth finger flat on the cushion. The cocked thumb can provide a fairly normal channel for the cue.

The cushion is not the only obstruction to easy bridging. There may be intervening balls, and the bridge must be raised. With the tips of the four fingers pressed into the table, almost

perpendicularly, the palm of the hand is horizontal and parallel to the table. The cocked thumb provides a high channel enabling the cue to pass above the intervening ball or balls and strike the cue ball. It is important to remember the other aspects of striking correctly, particularly keeping everything still while only the tips of the fingers are pressed into the cloth, and keeping the cue as near horizontal as possible rather than digging downwards into the ball or 'scooping' it.

All of these awkward bridges should

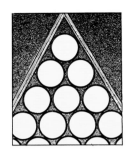

(300mm) behind the butt, and the shot is sighted along the whole length of the cue. The action of the stroke is now a push with the force coming mainly from the wrist and forearm. The right albow juts out, and there is much less control than with the normal shot. It is easy to play across the cue ball and it is necessary to follow through in order to keep the ball straight. Effort should still be made to keep the cue as horizontal as possible. Because, by the nature of the shot, the cue tends to point downwards, there is a tendency to drop the right hand as the shot is made, which produces a scooping action. If the cue is almost horizontal it is easier to push it through the ball, thus making a more accurate shot.

Strokes should be practised using all the rests, including the spider rest, a rest with a particularly high bridge used for playing strokes over intervening balls. It is impossible to avoid using the rest in matches, and it is essential that players feel at home with it.

After the ability to pot the balls, the next most important skill at snooker is that of controlling the cue ball. Breaks are kept going by ensuring that when one ball is potted the cue ball ends in a position which enables the next to be potted. The behaviour of the cue ball is governed by the way in which it is struck. It can be made to stop, follow-through, screw back, or move to either side.

To impart spin to the cue ball, it is necessary to have a good tip to the cue. It should be domed, not flat, and should be slightly soft and springy. It should not be so hard that the cue ball skids away on contact, nor so soft that the power is absorbed in a spongy way. It should be soft enough to bite on the ball and transmit a feeling of touch and control. Chalking the cue helps to give this holding effect, but if too much chalk is applied some will transfer to the cue ball and cause 'kicks' whcn cue ball and object ball meet. Little and often is the method with chalk.

If the cue ball is struck dead centre, it will behave in what might be called a normal way.

Kirk Stevens bridging on both table and cushion to play along the right-hand cushion.

be practised at length, so that no situation which can arise at the table will cause dismay.

Of course, there will be occasions when it is impossible to make a bridge at all, because the cue ball is out of reach. The rest is required. The action with the rest is quite different.

The head of the rest should be brought to within about 12 in (30 cm) of the cue ball. The handle of the rest is held lightly in the left hand. Where possible, the left elbow rests upon the table or cushion rail.

The cue is gripped right at the end of the butt. It is supported by the thumb underneath and gripped by as many fingers coming over the top of the cue as the player finds comfortable. The majority of top players appear to bring the forefinger and second finger around the cue, with the third and little fingers bent back, the middle joint of the bent third finger resting against the cue, with the little finger clear. Other players bring three fingers round the cue.

The cue does not run under the chin, as the head is held back about 12 in

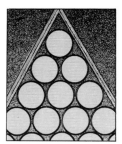

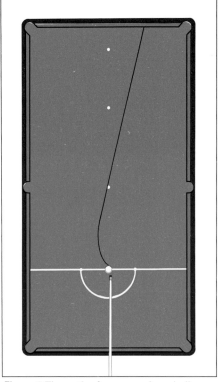

Figure 3 The path of a swerved cue ball.

Below Imparting, from the top, screw, stun and spin.

Below Imparting, from the top, screw, stun and spin.

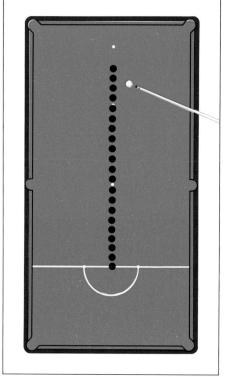

Figure 4 A practice set-up.

Imagine the cue ball as a clock face. If it is struck at 12 o'clock, top spin will be imparted, and when it strikes the object ball, the effect of the spin will be to keep the cue ball rolling. The effect might be seen by setting up a straight pot into a corner pocket. By imparting top spin it is possible to make the cue ball follow the object ball into the pocket.

Striking the cue ball below centre, midway on a line drawn between 8 o'clock and 4 o'clock, will impart some back spin – about enough to stop the cue ball dead on impact with the object

ball. To stop the cue ball dead, or bring it to rest anywhere close to the point of impact with the object ball, is known as 'stun'.

Striking the cue ball lower will impart enough back spin to bring it back after impact with the object ball. Striking it at 6 o'clock will bring it back dramatically. This is known as 'screw'. A good practice is to place the blue on its spot, and the cue ball half way between the blue and a middle pocket, and to pot the blue into the far middle pocket while imparting enough screw to bring the cue ball back into the near middle pocket.

The distance between the cue ball and object ball affects the amount of spin required to make the cue ball behave as required. If the two balls are close together, less spin will be needed than if the two balls are far apart.

The important thing when playing the stun and screw shots is to keep the cue horizontal as before. There is a tendency when imparting screw to raise the butt and dig down on the ball. The effect is not the same as striking the ball firmly forwards with a near horizontal cue. It follows that the bridging hand must be tilted when imparting screw, so that the thumb is flat on the table and not cocked, and the fingers raised and pressing down at the tips. The bridging hand is raised when imparting follow-through.

If the object ball is struck at an angle, rather than full ball, the spin will work in a similar manner, but less dramatically. For instance, if stun is imparted the cue ball will not stop dead, but it will not travel as far from the point of impact as otherwise.

As well as stopping the cue ball and making it run forward or back, it is possible to make it move to one side by imparting 'side'.

The effect of side is complex. First of all it affects the path of the cue ball towards the object ball. Imagine a cue ball struck at 3 o'clock, i.e. with right-hand side applied. The cue ball will begin by veering to the left, then as the spin takes effect it will swerve gradually to the right. When it makes contact with the object ball, reverse spin will be imparted to the object ball. It is so little that in most cases it can be ignored, but in theory the object ball will serve from right to left.

Side is often imparted to a cue ball to affect the angle at which it will rebound from a cushion; for example, a ball

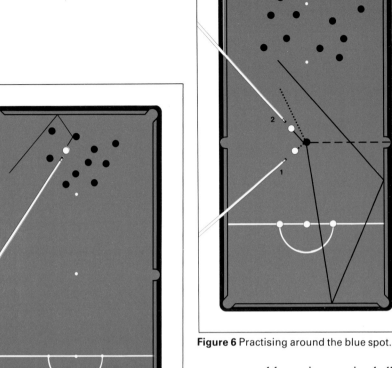

Figure 6 Practising around the blue spot.

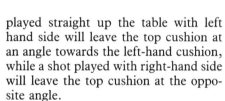

Figure 5 Practising around the black spot.

played straight up the table with left hand side will leave the top cushion at an angle towards the left-hand cushion, while a shot played with right-hand side will leave the top cushion at the opposite angle.

Side can be used to swerve the ball around another, and is useful for getting out of snookers. The stroke is made with a lot of spin. The ball is struck with side and also below centre. The bridge is raised so that only the tips of the fingers are pressed into the cloth. The butt is raised and the cue punched into the ball with hardly any follow-through. The cue ball follows an arc, but it is not an even arc. The ball is thrown off line sharply on impact and comes back in a more gentle curve (Figure 3).

The most exaggerated use of side comes with the massé shot. This shot is very difficult to play, but can swerve the cue ball almost in a semi-circle. It can be played only over a short distance, and is most useful to negotiate snookers where cue ball and object ball

are separated by an intervening ball, all three balls being close together on a cushion. The bridge and the cue are almost vertical. The back of the hand faces the cue ball, or the hand might be turned so that it is at right angles to the cue ball. The second, third and little fingers are pushed into the table, or usually the cushion, since these shots are played when the ball is close to the cushion. The first finger is bent backwards and the cue comes down guided between first finger and thumb. The cue strikes the side of the cue ball, forcing it into the table and spinning it round in a tight semi-circle.

An important aspect of the imparting of spin is the nap of the cloth. The nap of a snooker table runs up the table, from baulk to top cushion. The strength and effect of spin will alter according to whether the cue ball is travelling with the nap, against the nap or across the nap.

Playing side is not an exact science. Even the best players cannot be certain how the cue ball will behave. Thus they are reluctant to use side if there is more than about 2 feet (60 cm) between cue ball and object ball.

Practice routines can be set up to make the practice of all the above shots more interesting. One useful practice is to line up all the 21 object balls between the black and brown spots (see Figure 4) and, starting from anywhere, pot

each of them in any order into any of the pockets.

The most useful practices so far as game situations are concerned centre around the black and blue spots. Big breaks are often built around a sequence of successive blacks, and is true to say that a player who cannot pot the black from its spot confidently will never make a top player.

Figure 5 shows the black on its spot and an assortment of reds just below it. The practice is to pot alternate reds and blacks. It will be found necessary to bring the cue ball back off the top cushion at various angles in order to be on the next shot, and simulates a position frequently found in matches. A possible first shot is shown.

Figure 6 shows a similar practice involving the blue. It often happens in a break around the black and reds that a player gets out of position and has to go down for the blue. Therefore with the reds scattered around the pink and black spot, the practice involves potting reds alternately with blues from the spot. The aim should be to bring the cue ball back slightly past the blue, so that when the blue is potted into the middle pocket the cue ball can return directly for a red (shot 1). If the cue ball finishes the wrong side of the blue, the practice will involve playing it into baulk and back up the table (shot 2).

The main thing to remember about practice is that it must be enjoyed. A practice session which becomes a chore does more harm than good – a lackadaisical attitude creeps in and it is no good practising and perfecting that.

When all the shots have been mastered, the rest is a question of tactics and choice of shots, and that will come with experience.

217

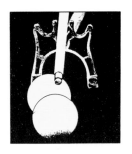

BILLIARDS

Unlike its big brother, snooker, which was conceived in recent times, billiards has been played as an organised sport for nearly two hundred years.

THE FIRST ATTRIBUTED professional appeared in the early 19th century, and Jonathan Kentfield became the precurser of a long line of professional billiards players who, throughout the last century and into the present, found fame and modest fortunes, played before royalty and travelled the world on their "green baize tickets", spreading the three-ball game.

Australians, New Zealanders, South Africans and Indians challenged for the premier event in the world of amateur billiards, the British Empire Championship, whilst at the same time, professional players of even higher standards were performing in the match arenas at Burroughs and Watts Hall and Leicester Square Hall in London's West End.

In the mid-1930s the warning light flashed on professional billiards. The rules had not been revised to take account of the fast increasing standards of some of the top players. In particular, Walter Lindrum from Australia and Britain's Joe Davis had begun to master the art of scoring from long runs of nursery cannons and had become so proficient that huge breaks were being made from this stroke alone. This delicate little shot, to make the cue ball strike the opponent's white and the red in the same movement, necessitates the deftest of touches and the three balls hardly move. One can understand how a run of 500 or so of these delicate little cannons, involving the same repetitive stroke, artistic to the connoisseur, did nothing for the average paying spectators, and they began to stay away. "What shall we do?" mused Walter and Joe as their pay packets got smaller. Too late! A change of rules was made that severely restricted cannon play, but the crowds did not return.

As interest in billiards began to wane, snooker, a curious 22-ball game with unclear origins and based on potting,

was beginning to appear and, although it was to take another 40 years, it had gained a foothold at the expense of billiards, which was to take it to the very pinnacle of popularity as an indoor sport in Great Britain.

Meanwhile the decline of billiards continued, although there were still plenty of amateur exponents and a handful of professionals fighting it out between themselves. In the last few years both of the governing bodies, amateur and professional, have made efforts to regenerate interest. In 1985 a tournament was televised nationally in

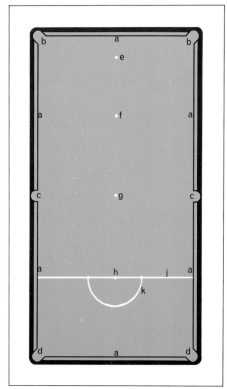

Figure 1 The billiard table. a) cushions; b) top pockets; c) centre pockets; d) bottom pockets; e) the spot; f) the pyramid spot; g) the centre spot; h) the baulk line spot; j) the baulk line; k) the D. The area below the baulk line is 'in baulk'.

Opposite Mark Wildman, 1984 World Billiards Champion, practising top of the table.

Great Britain, and the World Professional championships also received a substantial cash boost. These factors alone will generate grass roots interest and the popularity of this lovely old game, the father of modern snooker, looks set to grow.

A Resumé of the Rules

Billiards is for two people, or four playing as two sides. It is played with cues on a standard billiards or snooker table (see Figure 1). Three balls are required, a 'plain' white, a 'spot' white (i.e. a white ball with a black spot) and a red. Each player has his own white as his cue ball. The object is to score more points than the opponent, or opposing side, in an agreed period, or to be the first to reach an agreed number of points.

A traditional way to choose who plays which ball and who goes first is by 'stringing', i.e. each player together plays his ball up the table from the D, and the player whose ball stops nearer the bottom cushion has choice. Alternatively, players may merely toss a coin.

Play starts with the red ball placed on the spot, and first player playing his ball from 'in hand', i.e. from any point within the D.

A player playing from in hand must play the ball out of baulk (although it may be played against a cushion in baulk to hit a ball out of baulk). A ball in baulk cannot be hit when playing from in hand, unless the cue-ball hits a ball or cushion out of baulk first.

A player continues to play until he fails to score with a stroke, when the turn passes to his opponent. A complete turn is called a break.

Points are scored for the following strokes:

1) *Cannons*, when the cue ball strikes both other balls (impossible, of course, in the first stroke, or when the opponent's ball is not on the table). Two points are scored for each cannon, and only 75 cannons may be scored consecutively.

2) *Hazards*, of which there are four kinds as follows:

(a) a *pot* of the red (i.e. knocking the red

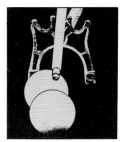

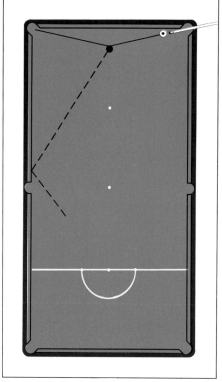

Figure 2 The 'half-ball' angle.

into a pocket), scoring three points.

(b) a *pot* of the white (i.e. opponent's ball), scoring two points.

(c) *in-off* the red (i.e. the cue ball going into a pocket after hitting the red), scoring three points.

(d) *in-off* the white, scoring two points.

Pots are sometimes called winning hazards and in-offs losing hazards. Only 15 consecutive hazards may be scored.

If more than one hazard, or a combination of hazards and cannon are made in the same stroke, all are scored. When an in-off occurs with a cannon, it scores two or three points according to whether the white or red was hit first.

In a break, if the red ball is potted, it is immediately replaced on the spot (if occupied, on the pyramid spot, if that is occupied, the centre spot). However, if it is potted from the spot or pyramid spot twice in succession in one break, without another score in conjunction, it is placed on the centre spot (if occupied, the pyramid spot; if occupied, its own spot). If the opponent's cue ball is potted, it remains off the table until the end of the break, when the opponent brings it back into play from in hand. When the cue ball is pocketed, the striker brings it back into play immediately by playing it from in hand.

Should the striker's ball come to rest touching another ball, the red is replaced on the spot, the non-striker's ball, if in play, is placed on the centre spot, and the striker plays from in hand.

Should a player not hit another ball in making a stroke, he is penalised two points, awarded to his opponent. Two points are also lost should a player commit a foul. A foul is committed by striking:

1) when the balls are not at rest.

2) the cue ball more than once.

3) with both feet off the floor.

4) out of turn.

5) improperly from in hand.

6) with a ball incorrectly spotted.

7) a ball other than the cue ball.

A foul is also committed by making:

8) a jump shot (when the cue ball jumps over another ball – except when it jumps a ball as the result of striking

another ball).

9) a push stroke (when the tip of the cue remains in contact with the cue ball (a) when the cue ball makes contact with the object ball, or (b) after the cue ball has commenced its forward motion).

10) more than 15 hazards.

11) more than 75 cannons.

12) by touching a ball with other than the tip of the cue.

13) by forcing a ball off the table.

14) by using a ball off the table for any purpose.

Following a foul, the next player may play from where the balls are at rest, or, if he prefers, from in hand, the red and white being spotted on the spot and centre spot respectively. In this connection a miss is a foul, except when the striker is playing from in hand and there is no ball out of baulk.

The Structure of the Game

Everything about the billiards or snooker table – they are the same thing – was devised for billiards originally, and snooker quite simply geared itself to it.

The spots used for spotting the colours at snooker all serve more ancient purposes.

The black spot is the billiards spot or red spot, where the red is replaced after being potted. If that spot is occupied, say by the cue ball, it would be placed on the pink spot or pyramid spot, and,

if that spot is covered, by say the other white, it would go onto the blue spot or centre spot.

The baulk line serves a most important purpose at billiards as opposed to snooker, where its only function is to support the 'D' or semi-circle, to which area one is confined when playing from hand. This is the "in-between shot" time, after a successful in-off has been played. The cue ball is returned to striker who may play from any position in the D. Whilst deciding on which shot to select, the ball may be held in the hand. When playing from hand, the ball must be struck forward and cross the baulk line, whereas of course at snooker, striker may play back into baulk.

The billiards ball was originally made from ivory, but the few sets remaining are now collectors' items. Today composite plastic compounds are used to produce the same sized and weighted articles, as for snooker. Notwithstanding the change-over from ivory, the special relationship between the precise location of the billiards spot and the middle and top corner pockets remains unchanged, and the in-off red into the corner pocket, to score three points, is one of the most important and often played strokes in the game.

Figure 2 shows the natural angle for in-off red into the corner pocket when red is on its spot. When the ball is on the line between the pockets and the spot it requires "middle of the ball" striking of the cue ball and even, or "half ball", contact on the red ball.

The manifest difference between scoring at billiards and snooker, is that when the white enters the pocket at snooker it is a foul shot and terminates the visit to the table, whereas at billiards this shot, the in-off or losing-hazard, together with the pot red or winning hazard and the cannon, form the backbone of the scoring. With each in-off, the cue ball is returned to striker in hand, who selects the best shot for the construction of his break, which is the total number of points scored in continuous play in the visit to the table without "breaking" down. When this

Mark Wildman, playing from hand with both object balls in baulk, scores a cannon off three cushions.

eventually happens, it is the turn of the opposition to play from the position that has been left, but this time, he will play the other white ball. For ease of identification one white ball has a black spot running through its central core.

The game starts with one player "breaking" off by striking the cue ball, which must contact the red ball occupying the billiards spot. Since the opponent's ball is not yet on the table, the safety shot – knocking one ball, usually red, into baulk – will be the objective. Remember, one may not strike backwards into baulk when in hand so, if at the start of the game striker can play both balls behind the line, he has laid the billiards equivalent of a snooker.

These days, games in local leagues are usually played on the "two hundred up" basis; first player to pass that mark wins, but competition can be played on a time basis also; the winner at one or two hours for instance.

In the early days of professional billiards, games were often of a week's duration and, aided by unlimited nursery cannons and the now banned push stroke, some quite astronomical breaks were made. The most famous of these was by Tom Reece who, just after the turn of this century, made a break of 499,135 with the use of the anchor cannon, the break taking just over five weeks to complete.

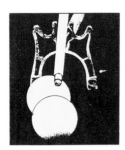

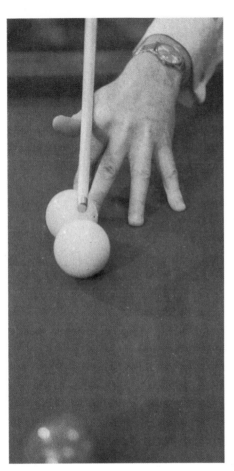

Bridging over an intervening ball; . . . using the rest; . . . and using the spider rest.

Today, with the use of nursery cannons, anchor cannons and all other cannons severely limited, and restrictions placed on consecutive pots off the spot – two only are allowed before the red ball has a one pot excursion to the middle spot – the breaks are very much smaller. A break of 1000 has not been achieved at professional championship level since the 1930s and it is fairly safe to say that within the immediate years of the game's rebirth, there is little prospect of seeing one. Administrators within the game believe that, in this frenetic age, the shorter the game, the more exciting it becomes. A match comprising the best of five short games is more attractive to the media because it offers the chance of five crises rather than one, as in a long game. So, for the immediate future, the professional

championships look as though they will be firmly geared to that principal and games of 300 points up are going to make the scoring of a 400 break mighty difficult. The days of artistic perfection in the setting of top hats and tails have gone. The game is now one of short sprints, hopefully for increasing millions of television viewers.

Professional status is the goal of today's aspiring amateur snooker player. Until very recently, the two games were indivisible as far as professionalism was concerned. The World Professional Billiards and Snooker Association controls both professional games and status at snooker also included billiards status. As the two games evolved, it was decided to separate the two and now players may become "billiards only" professionals.

This is rather a curious position as, should a billiards professional give an exhibition and wind up the evening with a frame or two at snooker he plays the frames as an amateur!

Technique

Why is it though that billiards players seem to improve with maturity? Fifty years appears to be the normal peaking age, whereas snooker players have usually started to decline in performance by the age of forty. By the same token, is it just coincidence that of a handful of senior snooker playing professionals, three of them are well-known billiards players – Rex Williams, Fred Davis and Eddie Charlton? Could it be that incessant practice years ago at long in-off reds from the middle spot into the corner pocket, necessitating

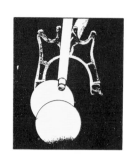

Norman Dagley, long-time World Amateur Champion, playing a cannon.

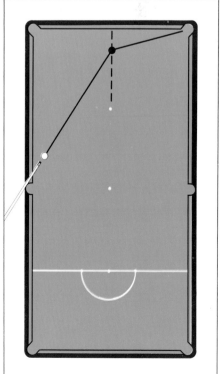

Figure 3 Various contacts: from top, quarter-ball, half-ball and full-ball.

perfect striking of both cue and object balls and an almost exaggerated follow-through of the cue, has stood the test of time better than the staccato-type action of snooker, in executing stun and screw-back shots so frequently?

The basic details of stance, grip and cue action are discussed in the section on snooker.

The billiards stroke is by necessity a smooth plain ball follow through shot, except of course where side, top, or bottom spin is called for. Bottom spin is only occasionally required for screw in-off shots and screw cannons, and for potting the red, but top spin, or run-through, is regularly used.

The in-off shot is the basic stroke of all players and its practice will soon familiarise the student with the half ball angle or throw-off. This is the natural angle of departure of the cue ball after striking half of the showing face of the object ball, assuming the cue ball has been struck accurately at middle. Contact against less than half-ball is called fine contact and more than half-ball is called full-ball. There are varying degrees of contacts divided like the quarters of the moon (see Figure 3).

A fool-proof way of establishing whether or not half-ball contact has been made is by playing the stroke described in Figure 4.

The red ball is on the billiards spot and cue ball twelve inches (305mm) from the middle pocket, in direct line from centre of middle pocket to the billiards spot. Strike the cue-ball fractionally above centre and plain ball – no side. Play with just enough weight to carry the white off the red into the

Figure 4 A half-ball in-off red practice stroke.

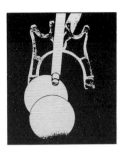

Practising the long in-off red from the centre spot.

right-hand corner pocket, for an in-off red. If half ball contact has been made, the red ball will bounce off the top cushion and run back down the table over the pink spot. It is that accuracy of striking half-ball shots that needs to be strived for in order to form the foundations of a skilful game. After successfully executing this practice shot, it should be tried at heavier weight of shot. Always the objective is the successful combination of both in-off and the propelling of the red ball on a straight path over the centre spots.

There are a great number of recurring half-ball losing-hazards but one in particular is a must for practice. This is the long in-off red from the centre or blue spot when played from hand. Once again the cue ball should be struck fractionally above centre and with sufficient force to take red round off side, top and then side cushion again, back into the open for another in-off into either a middle pocket or again into a corner, depending upon the speed at which it has been played.

The art of compiling large breaks depends upon how well the three balls are controlled; at snooker only two are normally required to be in harness.

When a cannon is played all three balls will be moved. If a pot or in-off is played, normally only two are moved. There are exceptions: when these shots are played in conjunction with nudges on the third ball for positional reasons. The six-shot pot red and in-off in one shot is often played, especially when the object white is in good drop cannon position.

The most points possible in one shot is a 'ten shot': pot red, cannon, pot white and follow through with the cue ball, which is deemed in-off red, the first ball of contact. The shot is purely an exhibition shot since the object white stays down when potted, which would almost certainly mean end of break.

Generally the top players have a pattern of play, or blueprint, upon which their game is based. The large breaks are made by way of the pot-red cannon sequence at the top end of the

Ideal position at the top (red is on its spot) for making a break.

table, by the billiards spot. This is universally known as "top of table play". If position gets obscure it is simple to play an in-off red to knock it over the middle pocket. A quick return to the top can then be made by potting red into the middle pocket and running on with the white to the billiards spot, if the position of the white ball requires it.

It is getting to the top of the table that is the problem to the less proficient.

There are two basic approaches.

The more foolproof way to the "top" is to use the basic in-off game to lay the path.

The object is to try and position the object white between the billiards spot and the top cushion and then to pot the red and run through to a position from where top of the table play is possible. The position of object white and red in Figure 5 would probably have been the result of some four or five in-off shots.

With cue ball to hand play a slow thin in-off white (Figure 5, shot 1), to take the white as indicated to stop between red spot and cushion. White is returned to hand; now play a pot red into the opposite middle pocket (Figure 5, shot 2) to take white cue ball, to position X in Figure 5. The balls are now in the perfect position (Figure 6). Now take a gentle cannon, knock the red towards the pocket, hardly moving the other white, pot the red, then start again. Sounds easy doesn't it!

The other approach to the "top" is with the aid of the "drop-cannon", as in

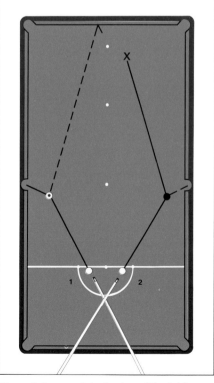

Figure 5 Approach to the top of the table.

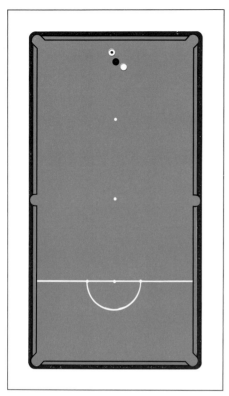

Figure 6 The position after Figure 5.

Figure 7. Once again the position of white ball 18 inches (457mm) out from the side cushion and just above the middle pocket, could well have been the result of previous planning, but, with the red on the spot and the white cue-ball to hand, the opportunity of gathering all three balls together

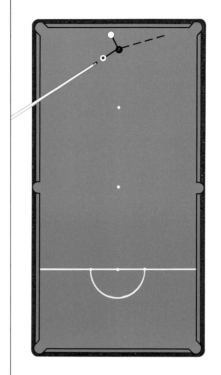

Figure 8 Top of the table play (1).

between the spot and cushion should be taken. Play half ball contact on to object white at sufficient strength to knock the red off its spot on to the top cushion and off again, to leave a pot into the corner pocket. Meanwhile the object white will have arrived in the vicinity behind the spot. Once again the pot red cannon sequence can begin.

Figures 8, 9, 10 and 11 show a typical top-of-the-table scoring sequence and it is important to note that the pot in Figure 9 has been made to leave the cue ball in such a position to enable the cannon in Figure 10 to be taken off the top cushion. It will be noted that in Figure 11 the three balls are almost in their original positions as at the commencement of the sequence shown in Figure 8.

The secret of billiards is to develop a sound in-off game first, with constant practice at the long in-off from the middle spot. This will enable the student to acquire instinctive recognition of half-ball angles in any situation on the table.

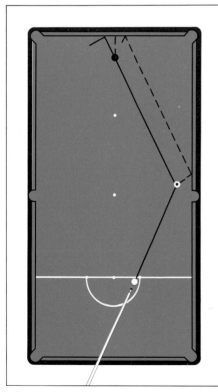

Figure 7 A 'drop-cannon'.

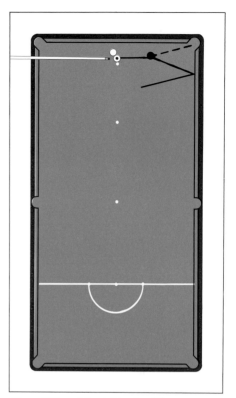

Figure 9 Top of the table play (2).

Top of the table development would follow, based on strong foundation of half-ball contact knowledge and this "mysterious" department of the game will be found to be absorbing. There are so many variations involving intricate little cannons, cushion first pots, not to mention pitfalls, that the learning, even

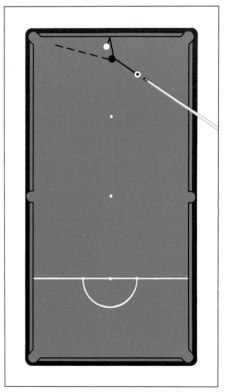

Figure 10 Top of the table play (3).

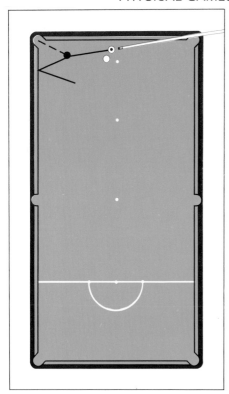

with the very best of players, is never finished.

The biggest danger at the "top" is the cover, or line up: all three balls landing, almost touching each other in a straight line, on the top cushion, with cue ball on the outside (Figure 12).

The situation is hopeless to the layman but, with all seemingly lost, the grand master raises his cue butt above his head and, in a subtle dropping of the cue down on to the cue ball, propels it out into the "green field" and, as if on a string, back again in a perfect arc to make the cannon.

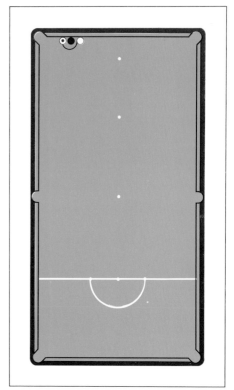

Figure 11 Top of the table play (4).

Figure 12 A cannon from a massé shot.

Above Good position at the top.

Below The position after the cannon.

Right Mark Wildman playing a massé shot.

POOL

Like all table ball games played on the green beize, pool can be traced back to billiards, caromball, and right back to the 15th century when the French played table croquet with two wooden or ivory balls being propelled through two hoops when pushed by a mace, later called a cue.

WHAT IS STILL not clear is where pool originated. There was a game played many years ago in England played on a snooker table whereby players each had their own coloured ball and three lives. The object was to pot your opponent's ball and take away your opponent's three lives before he could take yours. Groups of players could play this in one game with each attempting to clear all the balls on the table at the least expense to himself. This was a gambling game with stakes being put into the 'pool'. It did not gain much popularity and bears no comparison to the game of pool known today.

The most common theory is that pool started in the United States, but here history is difficult to trace because all references are to pocket billiards and to this day the governing body of pool games in the States is the Billiard Congress of America, where most games are variations of pool and are called such. There have also been claims that pool was invented in Australia where it has been popular for years.

By comparison, pool in the United Kingdom is still an infant, though many had seen the game played on the cinema or television screens. In the early 1970s an enterprising company brought coin-operated pool tables over from Italy and installed them in public houses in the north of England and Scotland. Other operators soon saw the potential and in

Eddie Charlton, Australian snooker champion, playing pool with red and yellow balls.

a short space of time the game had started its run of popularity and soon spread to most areas of Britain.

Rules used were decided by each operator and varied from area to area but all were based on the American 8-ball game. This was the game most acceptable to a coin-operated table.

Tables varied, some having conventional pockets, whilst others had round holes in the slate. There was no standard size: they ranged from 5 x 2½ ft (1.52 x 0.76 m) to 7½ x 4 ft (2.29 x 1.22 m). Cue balls were either larger or smaller than the object balls to enable them to return to the table outlet via trays or runners within the table interior. The object balls always stayed inside the table, once potted, until released by a coin or coins.

In 1975 a number of the coin machine operators involved in pool joined together and formed the British Association of Pool Table Operators, thus starting attempts at standardisation.

They agreed to, and printed, a standard set of playing rules for 8-ball. British manufacturers were now constructing their own pool tables to certain specifications.

With the increase in the skills of many players and the prospects of individual sponsorships, at the request of the players, the Professional Pool Players Organisation was formed.

In 1983 England joined the European Pocket Billiard Federation and competed in the European Pool Championships held in Holland. The following year the Championships were held in London.

By this time B.A.P.T.O. and the National Associations had come to terms with each other. In 1983 they met and agreed on a set of rules which meant, for the first time, the rules were standard throughout the country.

The two pool games played in the European Championships have been 8-ball and 14-1, with 9-ball added to the list in Austria in 1985. Playing rules adapted are basically the same as used in the U.S.A.

Pool on the European mainland is played in clubs and restaurants and is mainly for individual players. There are more players playing pool in Britain, possibly three million, more than the whole of Europe put together; but nowhere near the estimated thirty million playing in the States.

There is more in common in the game between mainland Europe and the U.S.A. regarding rules and equipment, with many of the Swedes and Germans competing in American Tournaments.

Equipment

In Britain there are over 80,000 coin-operated pool tables in daily use in pubs and clubs throughout the country. These tables (see Figure 1) are mostly 7 x 3½ ft (2.13 x 1.07 m) or 6 x 3 ft (1.83 x 0.91 m) which are ideal sizes for many of the confined areas of British pubs. There are a few 8 x 4 ft (2.45 x 1.22 m) available but these are in the minority. All these sizes of pool table are operated by placing coins in the slot at the side of the table to release the balls. All balls potted, except the white, remain in the tray until the completion of play and the next amount of coins used. The white ball will return to the outlet because of its different size which allows it to slip the running rails inside the table.

The diameter of the object balls is 2 in (51 mm) and all are the same weight. The cue ball is 1⅞ in (48 mm) diameter and lighter. Object balls can be either numbered spots or stripes, or non-numbered balls (7 reds and 7 yellows), plus black. In Britain balls are not nominated when potting, hence no need for numbers, whilst the reds and yellows are more convenient for television and for the uninitiated.

Pocket sizes are standard on all tables, no matter the size, with the standard width being 3½ in (89 mm). When cue ball is in hand players shoot from the D which has a circumference of 11 in (279 mm) on a 6 ft (1.83 m) table and 12 in (305 mm) on a 7 ft (2.13 m) table.

Cues need to be shorter, especially in confined spaces, and are much lighter than their American counterparts. Tips vary from 8mm to 10 mm with some even smaller depending on a players whim.

The majority of American tables (see Figure 2) are either 9 x 4½ ft (2.74 x 1.37 m) or 10 x 5 ft (3.05 x 1.52 m). These are not coin-operated but are booked by players at a central control desk or operated by a time switch on the light. The pockets are large, an average of 5 in (127 mm) width for the four corner pockets and nearly 6 in (152 mm) for the centre pockets. The balls return to the outlet once potted and can be replaced on the table when rules allow. All pool balls are 2¼ in (57 mm) in diameter and weigh from 5½ to 6 oz (156 to 170 g).

This automatically leads to larger and heavier cues, usually over 20 oz (567 g), and tips of 13 mm.

The cost of conversion to American-size tables in Britain is prohibitive and it is hardly likely that the breweries would look too kindly at losing possibly three-quarters of their sites. The attitude of the players would have to be taken into consideration too. In Britain the accent is on tactical play, allied to potting ability. Only one game is played throughout the country: 8-ball (except at tournaments, where a variation of 14-1 is played, and occasionally speed pool). The 9-ball game is to be introduced but only on a limited scale. There is no nomination at any time.

In America, many variations of pool are played with 8-ball, 9-ball and 14-1 being the most popular. Potting is paramount and nomination essential in most games.

Rules – General

Despite the fact that there are many different games of pool there are some rules which are general for all games and in all countries. These are:

1) Legal shots require that the cue ball be struck only with the cue tip.

2) A ball is considered as a pocketed ball if as a result of an otherwise legal shot, it drops off the bed of the table into the pocket and remains there. A ball that rebounds from a pocket back onto the table bed is not a pocketed ball.

3) It is a foul if a player shoots when at

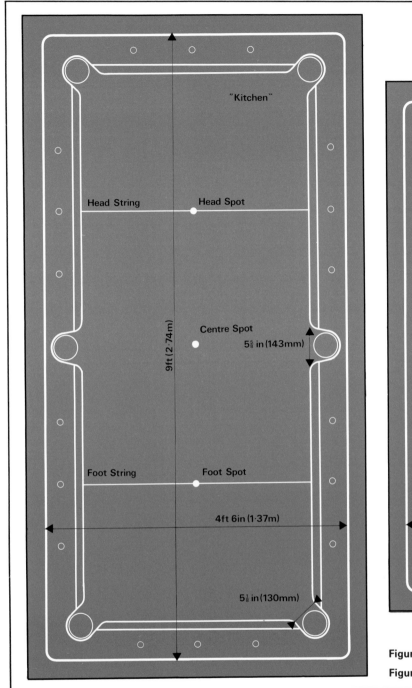

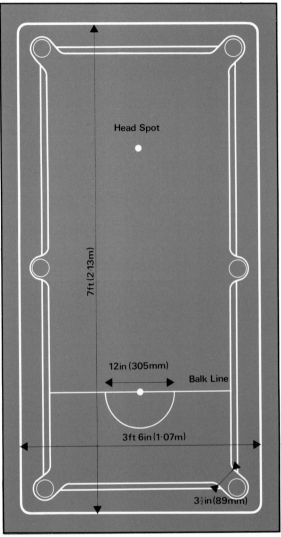

Figure 1 *Above* The British table.

Figure 2 *Left* The American table.

least one foot is not in contact with the floor.

4) It is a foul if a player shoots while the cue ball or any object ball is in motion.

5) A stroke is not complete until all balls on the table have become motionless after the stroke.

6) It is a foul to strike, touch, or in any way make contact with the cue ball in play or any object balls in play with anything (the body, clothing, chalk, bridge, cue shaft, etc.), except the cue tip, which may contact the cue ball in the execution of a legal shot.

7) It is a foul if the cue ball is struck more than once on a shot by the cue tip.

8) When the stroke results in the cue ball being a jumped ball, the stroke is a foul.

Though the penalties for fouls differ from game to game the following apply to all games:

(1) The offending player's turn (visit) ends.

(2) If the foul is made on a stroke, the stroke is invalidated and any pocketed balls not counted.

If the balls are moved by a non-player during a match (or a player bumped such that play is directly affected), the balls shall be replaced as near as possible to their original position.

Unless individual game rules apply, players alternate visits at the table, with a player's visit ending when he either fails to legally pocket a ball, or fouls.

8-ball Pool

The most common pool game played is 8-ball. In this game players must legally pocket seven balls of one group and then legally pocket the black. All balls are used, racked as in Figure 3. The following are the rules followed in Britain.

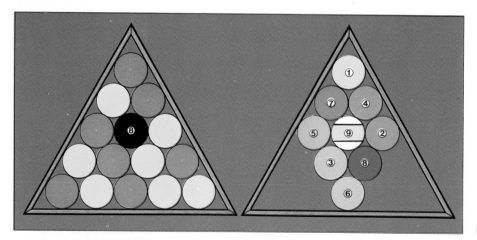

Figure 3 *Far Left* Racking for 8-ball pool.
Figure 4 *Left* Racking for 9-ball pool.

Les McMackin posing during a tournament.

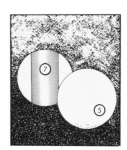

Left Dave Dolman in action.

Below: Jim Rempe, World Champion, using the red and yellow balls while playing in Britain.

231

Starting player must make an open break, with at least two object balls striking a cushion or a ball being pocketed. If he fails to do so the opposing player may accept the balls as they lay or demand a re-rack.

The table remains 'open' until, after an open break, a player legally pockets a ball from a group. If a ball is potted from both groups simultaneously, the player must choose which group he wishes to play, and continue.

Combination shots are allowed provided that the player hits a ball of his own group first.

Apart from fouls already defined, it is also a foul to: go in off (i.e. to pocket the cue ball), hit oppenent's ball before one's own, fail to hit any ball, hit the black ball before one's own (unless one's own balls are all potted), pot an opponent's ball, knock a ball off the table, and play out of turn.

Following any foul, the offending player loses his next turn at the table, and his opponent is entitled to two consecutive visits to the table. This means the oncoming player may go to the table on his first visit and pocket as many of his own balls as he wishes, and after failing to pocket a ball, he still has another visit. The oncoming player may also play any of his opponent's balls or the 8-ball black for his first shot only, in other words, he may play the cue ball onto any ball without any penalty. If he pots any ball or balls directly or by combination, he is deemed to have potted a legal ball or balls and continues with his break, with the exception that he may not pot the 8-ball black which would mean loss of game (unless he is on black).

It is loss of game if a player intentionally and unmistakenly seeks to gain advantage by playing directly at a ball not of his own group. A player not making any attempt to play his own group will lose the game.

If a player pockets the black before he pockets all the balls in his group he loses the game.

A player potting the black and any other ball on the same stroke will lose the game.

In general, push strokes are allowed. When a player has the cue ball in hand he plays from any position on or within the D and in any direction.

Those basically are the British rules for 8-ball. They differ in the United States and Europe as follows:

1) If a player does not make an open break his opponent can accept the balls as they lay, or, have the balls re-racked and shoot the opening break shot himself.

2) When shooting, a player must make the cue ball contact a ball and then either pocket an object ball or cause the cue ball or any object ball to contact a cushion. Failure is a foul.

3) When a player has the cue ball in hand behind the head string, and all his object balls are also behind the head string, the object ball of his own group nearest the head string may be spotted on the foot spot at his request. In America when cue ball is in hand a player can only shoot forwards.

4) The 8-ball may not be pocketed legally unless, prior to the shot, the shooting player designates to his opponent or the referee which pocket he is shooting for.

5) Push shots are not allowed.

6) Penalty for fouls: Incoming player has choice of either accepting table in position and shooting, or, shooting with the cue ball in hand behind the head string.

Those are the basic differences between British and American 8-ball pool.

14–1 Pool

The only other game played in England which can be compared with American Pool is 14–1.

Played in England, usually as a sideline at tournaments, it is played as a game for one with as many players as wish to enter trying to make the highest score on the day.

Balls are racked at random on the head spot and the oncoming player shoots to break the pack. If he pockets a ball on his first shot he continues until he fails to pocket a ball. If no balls are pocketed on the break shot he is

allowed one more visit to continue his sequence. If he pockets all 15 balls on his visit (they have remained inside the table), the cue ball remains at the place where it came to rest, and the object balls re-racked and the player continues his break until such time as he fails to pot.

The balls are then re-racked for the next player to make his attempt at the highest score for the day. The record so far is 122 balls potted.

In America, 14–1 is more a competition game with players opposing each other. The object of the game is to score a pre-determined point total prior to the opponent (usually 150 in major tournaments).

Any ball legally pocketed counts one point for the shooter.

Every shot the shooter takes must be designated. At the break he must designate a ball and a pocket into which that ball will be pocketed and accomplish the shot, or, cause the cue ball to contact a ball and then a cushion, plus cause two object balls to contact a cushion. A breaking violation is a loss of two points.

All other violations are a penalty of one point. If three fouls are committed in successive visits there is an additional penalty of 15 points deducted.

A player continues shooting until such time as he either fails to pot a designated object ball, or commits a foul. A player can call a safety shot if the considers he cannot pot an object ball but cue ball or object ball must contact a cushion. When safety is called any object ball potted is re-spotted.

When the 14th ball has been potted, the remaining object ball and the cue ball remain where they lay, and the rest of the balls are re-racked. If either object ball or cue ball, or both, finish in the area where the triangle should be placed, then, if it is the object ball it is placed on head spot, if it is the cue ball it is placed behind the head string.

7) All illegally pocketed balls are re-spotted with no penalty.

232

Jelly Baby Holt among the spots and stripes.

9–ball Pool

The game of 9–ball pool has not yet been played in Britain but there are moves to introduce it at tournaments. It was included in the European Pool Championships for the first time in 1985. Very popular in America, the rules are relatively simple.

The object of the game is to pot the 9–ball before your opponent. The only balls used are object balls numbered 1 to 9 plus the cue ball.

The balls are racked in a 'diamond' (1–2–3–2–1) with the 1–ball on the foot spot and the 9–ball in the diamond's centre; other balls may be placed at random (see Figure 4).

A legal shot requires that the cue ball's first contact be with the lowest numbered ball on the table. A player must then pocket a ball, or, cause the cue ball or any object ball to contact a cushion. Failure to meet this requirement is a foul. A legally potted ball entitles the shooter to remain at the table until he fails to pocket a ball on a legal shot.

It is loss of game if a player commits three successive fouls.

If a player legally pockets a ball, then cannons into another object ball that ball counts as a legal shot. For example if a player strikes the 1 ball legally, then cannons into the 9 ball and causes it to be pocketed, that player wins the game.

Penalty for fouls: the incoming player awarded cue ball in hand.

Other games

Those are the most popular tournament games of pool played throughout the world. Most other games are variations on a theme such as '6–ball', '7–ball', '10–ball' are all variations of '9–ball'. This also applies to 'Rotation' where all 15 balls are used.

'Bank–Pool' demands that every shot be a double off the cushion before a ball is pocketed. Straight in is illegal.

'One-Pocket' is a game in which only two pockets are used for legal scoring. Each player has his own legal pocket and the object is to score eight object balls in his own target pocket first.

Other popular games are: Bottle Pool, Bowlliards, Bumper Pool, Cowboy, Cribbage, Cut–throat, Forty–one, Golf, Line-up, Mr & Mrs, Odd Ball, One-Ball, Pea Pool, and Sides.

Tactics

Americans play the more positive pool. Tables are larger, giving more space, and with pockets being larger there are few opportunities for players to cover or impede a pocket. Potting, coupled with cue-ball control, are the orders of the day. Little or no advantage can be obtained from foul shots.

The opposite applies in Britain, where it is a positive advantage to try and induce opponent to commit a foal. The advantages are enormous with two visits to the table and on the first shot of the first visit to be able to hit or pocket any ball or balls on the table.

With the smaller tables, giving less space to move, and the smaller, tighter, pockets, there are ample opportunites to snooker an opponent or to cover a pocket with a ball, thus making it inaccessible to your opponent unless a foul is committed.

This makes for dull, dour, play to the average spectator but, for the lovers of the game, it is enthralling and interesting and often likened to a game of chess. It can be a battle of wits but comes to life once a player goes for home.

DARTS

Forms of darts were no doubt played by archers in medieval days, and it is known that Anne Boleyn gave Henry VIII a richly ornamented set of 'dartes', but the modern game dates back only to the end of the 19th century.

AROUND THE TURN OF the century the folded paper flight was invented, an all-metal barrel was invented, and the arrangement of numbers round a modern standard dartboard was devised.

In 1908 a publican called 'Foot' Anakin was prosecuted in Leeds for allowing darts, 'a game of chance', to be played on his premises. He demonstrated in court that darts was a game of skill (according to legend he threw three double-20s) and the case was dismissed. From that time darts grew in popularity in England and eventually spread to many other parts of the world. In 1977 a biennial World Cup was begun, and in the first four tournaments 25 countries took part.

There are several games of darts, and

there are a number of dartboards in existence. Figure 1 shows the standard international dartboard, also known as the London, trebles or clock board.

It is divided into 20 sectors, each given a value of from 1 to 20. A narrow band around the perimeter of the scoring area forms a doubles ring, in which a dart scores double the value of the sector. Closer to the centre is a narrow trebles ring, in which a dart scores treble the score of the sector. In the centre is an inner bull, of value 50, and around it an outer bull, value 25.

The standard dimensions of the board are as follows:

Overall board diameter, including the non-scoring area around the edge, 18 in (457 mm)

Diameter of scoring area, 13.38 in (340 mm)

Outside edge of treble wire to centre of bull, 4.21 in (107 mm)

Outside edge of double wire to centre of bull, 6.69 in (170 mm)

Inside diameter of outer bull, 1.25 in (31.8 mm)

Inside diameter of bull, 0.5 in (12.7 mm)

Inside width of double and treble rings, 5/16 in (8 mm)

There are numerous other traditional and regional boards, some almost extinct, others still to be found fairly frequently. A selection is shown in Figure 2. The most interesting of these is the Manchester, or log-end, board. The scoring area is only 10 in (254 mm) wide, and there is no outer bull or trebles ring. The doubles ring is only ⅛ in (3.175 mm) wide. The numbers are arranged differently to all other 20-sector boards, and it must be admitted the arrangement is more logical than on the standard board. Never are more than two odd or even numbers adjacent, while on the standard board there is a run of four consecutive odd numbers. Also the sums of adjacent pairs of numbers range from 17 to 25, while on the standard board the range is 16 to 26.

The darts are thrown at the board from an agreed throwing distance, which might be marked by a line on the floor or by a raised oche, a strip of wood

Figure 1 The standard international board.

behind which the players stand. The British Darts Organization have specified a height and length of an oche: 1.5 in (38 mm) and 24 in (610 mm)

The B.D.O. have specified dimensions for all aspects of the setting up of the board, and these are shown in Figure 3.

The minimum throwing distance of 7ft 9¼ in (2.37 m) is the approved distance of the World Darts Federation, a body set up in 1976 to regulate the sport on an international basis. It is the distance used in the World Professional championship.

However, other throwing distances are used, principally 8 ft (2.44 m), which the *News of the World* used when it began its championship in 1927. For many years this was the principal championship in darts, and the throwing distance has not changed. Other throwing distances commonly found are: 7ft 6in (2.29 m), 8ft 6in (2.59 m) and 9ft (2.74 m).

Whatever the throwing distance, and however it is marked, the B.D.O. rules regarding the throw are clear:

'During matchplay no player shall tread on any part of the raised oche, nor shall the player deliver any dart with his feet in any position other than behind the toe edge of the raised oche.

A player wishing to throw a dart, or darts, from a point either side of the raised oche must keep his feet behind an imaginary straight line extending on either side of the raished oche'.

In other words, the oche, or line, should be regarded as continuous, extending indefinitely on either side, and both feet must be completely behind the back of the line.

The equipment which an aspiring player will own himself is a set of three darts. A dart consists of a needle point fixed to a barrel. At the rear of the barrel is attached a flighted stem, which may consist of up to three separate pieces, i.e. a flight, a flight securing device and a stem. The B.D.O. fix an overall maximum length of 12 in (30.5 cm) and a maximum weight of 50 grams.

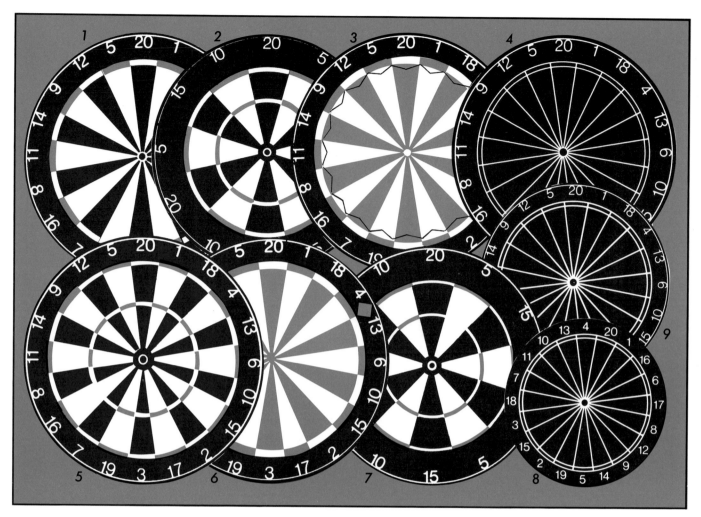

Most of the leading players today use darts with tungsten barrels. As tungsten has a high density, darts made from it can be of a good weight while still being very slim. This is useful to a player who expects at times to squeeze more than one dart into the treble-20 bed. Some players prefer brass-barrelled darts, which usually have thicker barrels.

Stems for tungsten darts are usually of fibre glass and screw into the barrel, while the flights, which fit into slits in the stem, are usually of plastic or paper. Flights fold up and the set can be carried in a flat leather wallet.

Players find the weight and the barrel shape most important when buying a set of darts. Few darts are lighter than

Figure 2 Traditional and regional boards. 1 The Yorkshire or Kent doubles board, with no trebles. 2 The wide fives board. 3 The Tonbridge board – the outer ring counts treble, the triangles double. 4 The black Irish board. 5 Champion's Choice boards with narrow doubles and trebles. 6 The Staffordshire or Burton board – the diamonds count 25. 7 The narrow fives board, with narrow doubles and trebles. 8 The Manchester or log-end board, with its own arrangement of numbers. 9 The Lincoln or Medway board, like the black Irish but only 15 in (381 mm) in diameter.

12 grams or heavier than 40 grams, and most fall into a 16 to 30 gram range.

Barrels come in many shapes and designs. Four of the more common are shown in Figure 4. The straight barrel is of even weight and thickness; the centre-weight barrel has its width and weight where the thrower grips it; the torpedo barrel has its weight and maximum thickness where it meets the point; and the bomb shape tapers both to the point and more gently back to the flight.

Most barrels have some sort of ridges or knurls cut into them to give the thrower a good grip. Some players

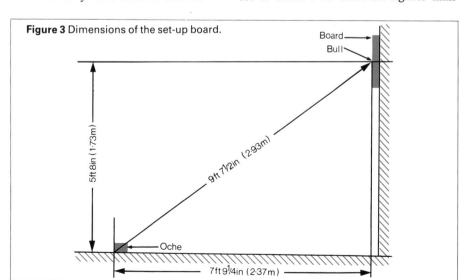

Figure 3 Dimensions of the set-up board.

Board
Bull

5ft 8in (1·73m)

9ft 7½in (2·93m)

Oche

7ft 9¼in (2·37m)

237

prefer a smooth barrel. Some like to improve their grip by chalking the barrels.

The weight and shape of the darts a player uses are purely a question of personal choice, and each player has his own preferences. The best darts equipment shops will have a practice board on which players can try various sets of darts before making a purchase. It is a good idea to make a careful choice and buy the best that can be afforded – with care darts should last many years.

The Games

The basic game of darts, as played in the World Professional championships, is a race between two players each trying to be first to reduce a score of 501 to zero exactly, ending with a double. In this connection the bull counts as a double (i.e. double-25).

A turn, or throw, consists of three darts, and players throw alternately. The 'bust' rule applies, i.e. if a player scores more than he needs, reducing his score to below zero (or to zero or 1, which cannot be scored with a double), then he scores nothing for that turn, and he reverts back to the score he required before the opponent's last throw.

A match is concluded by the dart scoring the required double, and any darts thrown in error afterwards are not counted.

For a dart to score, it must have the point remaining in or touching the face of the scoring area of the dartboard until after it has been called by the referee or scorer and retrieved by the thrower. In other words a dart dropping out of the board before the thrower can retrieve it after the throw does not count.

The player to throw first is decided by lot or by tossing a coin. Should a match consist of several games, the right to throw first alternates. If a match is of several 'sets', each set to consist of a number of games (in this case called 'legs'), the right to throw first alternates with each set, as well as with each leg within a set.

The total score of a throw (i.e. the three darts) is deducted from the starting total of 501 after each throw.

Variation
The standard game is the one most often played in public houses in Great Britain, but a number of variations are common.

The game is more frequently of 301 up, and it is customary to start, as well as finish, on a double, i.e. no darts count until a double is scored.

First throw is often decided by each player throwing one dart at the bull, the nearer to throw first. In some games, by arrangement beforehand, a player throwing all three darts in the same doubles or trebles bed automatically wins the game.

Most pub games are scored with chalk on a blackboard situated by the board. It is customary for continuous action to be maintained by players desiring a game to 'take the chalks', i.e. to score for the current game and to play the winner. In busy pubs there might be a string of initials on the blackboard of players awaiting a turn to take the chalks.

A number of other games are popular, and a selection follows:

Round the Clock
Round the Clock is a simple race game for any number in which each player, beginning with 1, has to score each number before passing on to the next, ending with the outer and inner bull after scoring the 20. A number scored out of sequence does not count.

There are numerous variations. One is to count doubles or trebles at face value. Thus a player on 4 and scoring treble-4 will count it as 12 and go straight to 13 as his next number.

That makes a shorter game. To make a longer game it might be required to score each number three times before moving on to the next, in which case doubles and trebles count as scoring the number two or three times.

Good players might like to play the game going round the board on doubles only.

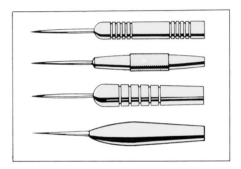

Figure 4 Common shapes of barrel.

Shanghai
Shanghai is another round-the-board game for any number of players, although it is not a race game. In the first round, each player throws at 1, and registers his score, all doubles and trebles counting as two and three respectively.

In the second round, all players, whether they scored on 1 or not, throw at 2, scoring as before, and so on round the board, or as far round as one wishes – a popular version goes as far as 9. In this version, the numbers 3, 5 and 7 are penalty numbers, and a player who fails to score on these is eliminated.

A player who scores a single, double and treble of a number on one throw is said to have gone 'Shanghai' and wins the game, although the round is completed in case another player can score Shanghai, in which case the player with the higher score of the two wins.

Cricket
A popular dartboard game in countries which play cricket is a game in which two players score against each other, each having an innings, and scoring 'runs' and taking 'wickets'.

The players toss for innings, and the player representing the bowling side throws first. He aims at the bull and the outer bull. The bull scores two wickets and the outer one. His object is to take 10 wickets as quickly as possible.

Meanwhile the player 'batting' scores his total for each throw, except that if he hits a bull or outer bull that counts as wickets against him. By the same token a player bowling who throws a dart

Jocky Wilson jams the outside of his foot against the oche in his stance.

outside the treble ring gives whatever the dart scores away to his opponent as 'extras'.

An innings ends when the 'bowling' player takes his tenth wicket. However, the 'batting' player is allowed the same number of darts to complete his innings, so throws one, two or three more darts according to the dart with which the 'bowler' took his tenth wicket.

A match can, of course, be of one or two innings each.

Mickey Mouse
In the United States, Mickey Mouse is very popular, but for some reason compatriots of the famous cartoon char-acter call this game Cricket, a sport which has failed to capture their popular imagination, despite missionaries bringing it from England in 1859.

It is a game of tactics for two players in which, in the United States, the

	A	B	C
	100	100	100
ANY 15	160	50	115
TREBLE 16	208	98	57
SINGLE 20	248	118	97
DOUBLE 4	124	126	48
25			
SINGLE 19			
TREBLE 12			
DOUBLE 14			
ANY 18			
BULL			

Figure 5 Scoreboard for 'Halve-it'.

numbers 15 to 20, plus the bull and outer bull, are used. In England, the numbers 10 to 20 are used, making for a longer game.

Each number remains in play until both players have hit it three times. A treble counts as three hits, a double as two. The bull and outer are regarded as one number, 25, the outer counting as a single and the bull as a double.

A player can score on any number while it remains in play, but must hit a number three times before he can score on it. The game ends when each number has been hit three times by each player. Two scoring charts have to be kept, one registering each player's score, the other how many times each player has hit a number.

The game sounds complicated, but an example will make it clear. Suppose Player A begins by throwing at 20, and scores a treble and two singles. This immediately gives him the three 20s he needs to score on this number, and two extra 20s which give him 40 points. From now on every 20 he throws will score, until Player B also scores three 20s to eliminate the number.

Suppose Player B concentrates on 19 for his first throw, and scores three singles. From now on every 19 he throws will score.

It will be noticed after these throws that Player A cannot score on 19, because as soon as he throws three 19s the number is eliminated, but at the same time he has to throw three 19s to stop Player B scoring. Player B is in the same position regarding Player A's 20s.

On every throw each player has to choose, therefore, between building up his own score on a number established for himself, of establishing a new number, or off knocking out his opponent's number.

The player throwing first has a considerable advantage, and therefore the game should be played over two legs with each player having the advantage in turn.

Scram

Scram is a simplified version of Mickey Mouse. The players do not score simul-taneously, but one is the scorer and the other the stopper. All the numbers are used, except the bull and outer. The scorer throws first and scores everything he throws. The stopper then throws. Every sector he hits is put out of the game, and the scorer is forced to score on other sectors.

The stopper will clearly attempt to eliminate the higher numbers first, and will begin throwing at 20, then 19 and so on. The scorer will throw at the highest sectors left in the game. The score is kept in two columns. In the first the numbers 1 to 20 are written, and each is wiped out as it is hit by the stopper. The other column keeps the scorer's running total. When all numbers are eliminated, the scorer's total is noted and the players change roles. The higher scorer wins.

Fox and Hounds

Fox and hounds is a good game to play if practice on the doubles is required. It is a race game for two players, one representing the fox and the other the hounds. The fox goes first. Beginning on double-20 he must go round the board in an anti-clockwise direction, scoring a double, then a single, on each number in turn. His object is to get completely round the board, scoring double-1, before being caught. The player representing hounds throws second, and starts on double–18, two beds behind the fox. He needs to score only the double before going on to the next number. The tendency therefore will be for the hounds to begin catching the fox. The fox is considered caught if the hounds throw any double before him. If the fox scores double-1 first he has safely reached home.

Halve-it

Halve-it is a game in which a number of specific categories are written down the side of the scoreboard. To score each category is the object in each round. Figure 5 shows a scoreboard for a game in which three players are taking part. It is partly completed.

Each player starts with 100 points.

Each total that a player scores in any category is added to his score, but if he fails to score in any category his score is halved.

In the illustration, the first category is 'Any 15'. This means that all darts in the 15 sector score. Player A has scored four 15s (a treble and a single) and Player C has scored one. Player B, on his turn, failed to score a 15 and his score was halved.

The second category is treble-16, and only trebles count. The third category is single–20, and only singles count. A treble–20 on this throw is bad luck.

Play continues with each player in turn throwing at each category, with the player with the highest total at the end the winner.

The categories written down the side can be, of course, whatever the players like, and can vary from game to game.

Technique

Watching the world's top players will reveal that all have different methods. There is clearly more than one way to play darts. But there are also a number of similarities among the top players, and it is by identifying these that the aspiring player will reach the top.

Clothing might not seem of importance to a darts player, but in fact a player wishing to appear in a B.D.O. tournament should note that 'players are not permitted to wear jeans, or trousers or skirts made in a "jeans style" with denim or corduroy material'.

Comfort is the main object in choosing clothes. The most important item is the shoes. A darts player spends a lot of time on his feet. He will not be able to do himself justice if his feet are aching because of corns, or a badly fitting shoe. A player might reserve one pair of shoes for darts playing. His height will then always be the same in relation to the board – alternating plimsolls with heels will require adjustments to the throw.

Socks are important, too, in keeping the feet comfortable. Working upwards, comfortably fitting slacks (or, if they prefer, skirts for the ladies) are best, topped off with a loose fitting shirt (or blouse) which enables free movement of the arms. Most professional players prefer a short-sleeved shirt, worn outside the trousers, with a breast pocket for their darts. The B.D.O., by the way, bans headgear, unless permission to wear it is granted (a Sikh would receive such permission).

Fitness is not usually associated with the top darts players, many of whom are overweight and clearly drink and smoke. However, many of them do take steps to maintain a level of fitness. The claims that the drinking settles the nerves or that the smoking helps concentration might be regarded with scepticism, but it is also true that some of the 'offenders' also diet and exercise.

Being on one's feet most of the day, playing or giving exhibitions in the evening and practising during the day, as most professionals do, is, in fact, extremely tiring, and a player who is fit must have a considerable advantage over one who isn't.

Stance is a question of comfort. Most right-handed players stand with the front foot (the right) pointing straight at the board or slightly to the left of it. The back foot is about 12 in (30 cm) behind the front foot and at an angle of about 45° to it. The weight is on the front foot with the body leaning slightly forward, which usually raises the back heel a little from the floor.

Some players, notably the world number 1, Eric Bristow, throw with the outside of their front foot jammed against the oche. This stance enables Bristow to lean forward more than most players when throwing. Other players prefer a squarer stance, with the back foot brought round to be nearly level with the front foot.

Balance is the aim of the stance. A player should be able to reproduce his throw time after time without toppling or leaning to one side.

Grip is not as natural as the beginner might think. Most new players grip the dart as they would a pencil, but most of the top players grip it differently. Many support the point in some way.

The thumb grips the dart on one side and the index finger on the other. The index finger usually comes over the top of the dart. Some players grip the dart with the point almost sticking into the middle finger. Others hold the middle finger alongside the barrel and the point. Bristow, who holds the dart well back, has the point against his third finger.

A beginner, therefore, should not pick up the dart as he would a pencil and throw it. He should study the grips of the successful professionals and experiment with similar grips. Perhaps he will be surprised, and find one to improve his accuracy.

Throw The important thing about the throwing action is that it should be smooth and free, and that the player should be able to repeat it as if his arm were a piece of well-oiled machinery. The elbow should be regarded as a hinge, a fixed pivot. The backswing should bring the dart up level with the eye. Most players bring the dart back to a position in front of their right ear, but a few players who sight with a dominant left eye bring the dart back across their face to a position in front of the left eye.

The eyes are focused on the bed at which the dart is aimed. The lining up of the dart with the target becomes a natural action.

Finally, with the elbow and shoulder remaining in position, the forearm is brought forward at an even pace and the dart released. The wrist is loose, the action smooth and there is a full follow-throw as the dart is released and the arm straightens. If the follow-through is omitted, the dart will drop. The follow-through also helps to keep the whole action free from jerks or snatches.

Practice is the only way to become proficient at darts. Practice must be of a good quality, however, with the player enjoying it. Enthusiasm leads to improvement. Boredom leads to faults.

Variety is necessary. One way to introduce variety is to draw up a programme for, say, 30 minutes' practice.

Ten minutes might be spent on practising going out from a large number, say 125. Try it four ways: treble-18, treble-13, double-16; treble-18, treble-17, double-10; treble-20, treble-19, double-4; treble-20, treble-15, double-10. Try each way five times each, keeping a note of how many times you go out – this becomes the record to beat in succeeding practices.

Ten minutes might be spent going out from 1,001, finishing on a double. Again, a note should be kept of how many darts it takes.

Ten minutes might be spent going round the board on doubles, throwing three darts at each double. Keep a record of how many doubles are scored, with a view to beating it next time.

By setting targets and keeping records like this, practice can be made interesting and, better still for enthusiasm, progress can be charted.

When a player can score doubles and trebles regularly in practice he will not be over-awed when it comes to matches, and will be able to reproduce his practice form regularly.

TABLE TENNIS

First known as ping-pong, the sport of table tennis originated as a Victorian parlour game popular in genteel households. The name described the noise made by the small hollow ball as it struck the players' racket and then the surface of the table.

AS PING PONG INCREASED in popularity a need was recognised to standardize the rules of play in order that players could enjoy friendly competition on equal terms.

The International Table Tennis Federation, established in 1926, now governs the sport worldwide and what was originally a simple pastime has developed into a very complex and interesting sport played extensively throughout the modern world by people of all ages.

Rules of play

Choice of Ends and Service

A coin is tossed. If the winner chooses whether to serve or receive first then the loser may choose at which end of the table he wishes to play, or vice versa.

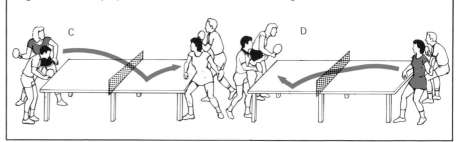

Figure 1 Order of play in doubles. The striker is shown in green.

The winner also has the right to ask the loser to make the first choice.

In a game of doubles the team who have the right to serve must then decide which one of them will serve first; similarly the opposing team must decide which of them is to receive first. In the remaining games the first receiver is determined by the identity of the server; once the server has been chosen this becomes clear, as he must serve to the player who served to him in the preceding game.

Change of Ends
Throughout the match players change ends after each game with only one exception. In the final game ends are changed when the first player or team scores 10 points. If players or the umpire forget to change ends until a later point in the game the change should take place immediately the mistake is realised but all points scored up to that point are counted.

Definitions
A 'rally' is the period during which the ball is in play. If a 'let' is called during the course of the rally no score is recorded. A 'point' is a rally, of which the result is scored.

The ball is introduced into play by the 'server' and returned by the 'receiver'. The 'racket hand' is the hand in which the racket is held, the other hand is the 'free hand'. A player is deemed to strike the ball if he contacts it with either the racket or the racket hand below the wrist.

If the ball passes under the projection of the net and its supports outside the table it is said to have passed 'over or around' the net.

Order of Play
In singles the server shall first make a good service, the receiver shall then make a good return, each player shall then make a good return alternately. In a game of doubles the order shall be:
1) The server shall make a good service
2) The receiver shall make a good return

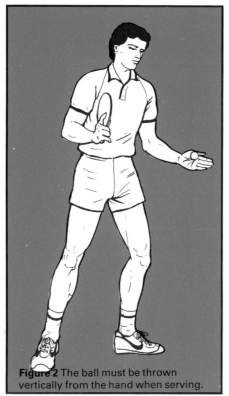

Figure 2 The ball must be thrown vertically from the hand when serving.

3) The partner of the server shall then make a good return
4) The partner of the receiver shall then make a good return

This sequence continues throughout the rally.

A Good Service
Service begins with the ball resting in the palm of the free hand which shall be stationary, open and flat. From this point until the ball is struck both the ball and racket must be held above table height.

The server must throw the ball so that it rises within 45° of the vertical, he must not impart spin. The ball is considered to be 'in play' from the moment that it ceases to be stationary.

The ball shall be struck on its descent so that it strikes the server's court once before crossing over or around the net to strike the receiver's court.

At the moment the ball is struck it must be behind the end line of the table or an imaginery extension thereof.

In doubles, the ball shall touch the

Figure 3 A good service.

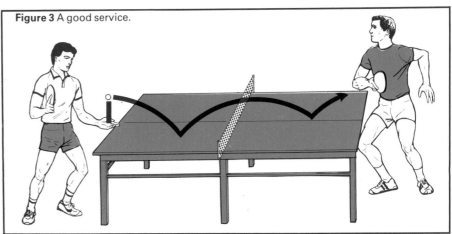

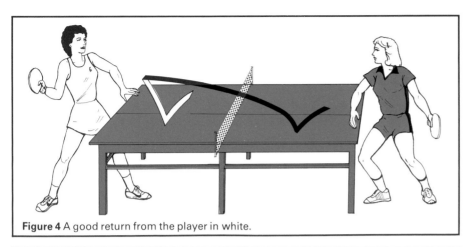

Figure 4 A good return from the player in white.

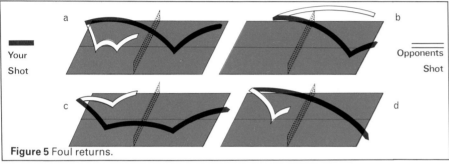

a b

c d

Your
Shot

Opponents
Shot

Figure 5 Foul returns.

Figure 6 Order of service in doubles.

2) Player B then serves to the partner of player A, player C.

3) Player C then serves to player D.

The complete sequence is repeated until the end of the game.

When the score reaches 20-all or the expedite system comes into operation the same service order is maintained but each player serves only a single point.

The player or team which served first in the opening game shall receive first in the second game.

In subsequent games of a doubles match the player nominated to serve first must do so to the player from whom he received in the previous game.

In the final game of a doubles match the order of receipt changes once more when the players change ends, one team having scored 10 points.

If an error in the order of service or receipt is noticed it must be corrected immediately but the total points scored are still counted.

Scoring
A 'match' may consist of either 3 or 5 games. Play is continuous throughout except that any player is entitled to claim an interval of not more than five minutes between the third and fourth games of a match and not more than one minute between any other successive games of a match.

A Game A player or team reaching a total score of 21 points shall be declared the winner of a game unless both players or teams reach a total of 20 points. In this case the game is won by the player or team first scoring subsequently 2 points more than the opposing player or team.

A Point is scored by a player if his opponent:
1) fails to make a good service.
2) fails to make a good return.
3) strikes the ball twice successively.
4) allows the ball to strike his court twice successively.
5) touches the playing surface with anything other than his racket or racket hand below the wrist.
6) moves the playing surface.

server's right-hand court and then the receiver's right-hand court.

A Good Return
The ball must normally be struck so that it passes over the net, either directly or having been deflected by the net or net posts, to land on the opponent's court.

A return is not good if:
A) the ball is allowed to bounce more than once before the return is made.
B) the ball is volleyed.
C) the ball is struck in such a way that it hits the striker's court before passing over the net.
D) the ball is hit so that it crosses over or around the net but does not contact the opponent's court.
E) the ball is hit directly into the net.

The ball is automatically considered to be out of play if it contacts anything

other than the net, net posts, table top, racket or racket hand below the wrist or when the rally is ended by any of the points (A) to (E) above.

If the racket is dropped, a return by racket hand alone is not considered good; similarly if the ball is struck by a racket blade surface (most likely to apply to a player using the penholder grip) which does not comply with the regulations regarding racket coverings then the stroke is a foul.

Change of Service
In both singles and doubles the service passes from one player to the next after every five points which have been scored.

In doubles the sequence is:
1) The serving team must decide which player is to serve. The server A then serves to the player nominated B.

7) touches the net or net posts with racket, body or clothing.

8) stamps his foot during service.

9) strikes the ball out of sequence during a game of doubles irrespective of whether he does so by mistake.

Techniques

Becoming a good player involves buying the right equipment, learning the basic strokes, and practice. Practice soon involves having a coach or other players to play against, and this section assumes that the aspiring player will join a club.

The Racket

There is no restriction to the size of a table tennis bat but the laws state that the blade must be of wood, flat, rigid and continuous throughout and that the covering of each side shall be a maximum thickness of 4mm. A quite incredible amount of technological development has taken place over recent years into table tennis rubber. Long gone are the days of the world famous Barna bat which was simply a wooden blade covered on both sides by a sheet of rubber with the pimples facing outwards.

The bat coverings favoured by the majority of players today feature a layer of sponge covered by a sheet of reversed pimpled rubber (see figure 7). These two layers are produced as a single sheet and commonly referred to as 'rubber'. As players are now permitted to use a different type of rubber on opposite sides of the racket the number of combinations available is startling.

Anyone intending to enter recognised competitions should check that any complete racket or new sheets of rubber which are purchased have the ITTF stamp of approval (Figure 8) and that the rubbers on each side of the racket are of an obviously different colour, e.g. red and black, otherwise disqualification is possible.

This must be bewildering if you are a novice, but do not despair. If you are purchasing a bat for the first time then you should look for something which will give a good balance between the

Figure 7 Section of racket.

three important factors of speed, spin and control; once you have mastered the basic strokes you will be in a position to decide what style of game suits you best. Then is the time to consider more specialist equipment.

A medium/soft wood blade will provide control and is to be recommended in preference to a fast hard wood blade which offers speed at the expense of

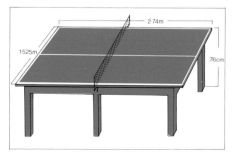

Figure 8 The ITTF stamp of approval.

control. When choosing a blade the most important factor is that it should have a comfortable handle. A variety of weird and wonderful shapes are to be found on the sports shop shelves but if they do not feel comfortable in your hand that is the best place for them. Try a range before making your decision.

The thickness of the rubber on your bat will determine its speed. Rubber is manufactured in four thicknesses, from

0.5 to 2.00 mm. Either 1.00 or 1.5 mm is recommended for beginners. Touch the rubber by sliding your forefinger over it. The tackier this feels the more 'grip' the rubber will have on the ball and the greater the amount of spin it will be able to impart. The price of the bat will, to a great extent, be determined by the quality of the rubber.

The cheaper rubbers will give less spin and speed but are ideal for beginners as they have a high control factor. As with everything in life it is better to walk before you can run and therefore a bat which may well fall at the lower end of the price scale will be best suited to your initial needs.

The Ball

The most popular type of balls are made from celluloid, although others made from a similar plastic are available. There are three recognised grades of ball: 1★, 2★ and 3★. The higher the star the better will be the ball's qualities of roundness and thickness. The more expensive 3★ ball will give the most even bounce and reliable angle of trajectory and is in turn the more expensive. This is the quality used in all major competitions but for practice purposes a 2★ ball is quite adequate.

The Table

The measurements given for the table tennis table in Figure 9 are those of a competition-size table. The playing surface should be dark matt green in colour with a 2cm wide white line running along each of the four sides, known as the base and side lines. The thin white line which runs along the centre of the table parallel to the side lines divides

Figure 9 Measurements of table.

Desmond Douglas as English junior champion in 1973.

each court into a left and right side for the purposes of doubles play; it bears no relevance during singles competition.

The quality of a table is determined by the thickness of its playing surface. Leading manufacturers normally produce a range from 15-25 mm in thickness. Although the 15 mm surfaces are adequate for recreational play, the more expensive 25-mm surfaces will provide a more predictable bounce and are used exclusively in major competitions. If you intend to purchase a table it is well worth considering the advantages offered by the new space-saving rollaway models which can be easily moved for storage by one person; some rollaways offer a playback facility which will allow you to practice even when your partner is unavailable (see Figure 10).

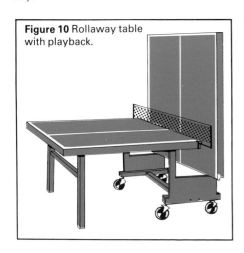

Figure 10 Rollaway table with playback.

The Chinese, indisputably the world's leading nation of table tennis players, have been known to practise on sheets of hardboard supported by stacks of bricks, which clearly shows that the best equipment is not an absolute necessity. What really counts is the amount of time which you are prepared to devote to practice.

The Net
The net which divides the table into two equal courts is held in position by a pair of posts. The posts are fixed to the table by means of a simple screw fitting and should be positioned to straddle the table joint. The bottom of the net should be as close as possible to the table top, thus minimising any possible confusion which might arise as to whether in the course of a rally the ball passed under or over it.

The Venue
Table tennis is truly an indoor sport, ideally suited to a room where there is a total absence of natural light and where the walls are of a uniform dark matt colour. For recreational purposes a space 5m x 10m is adequate for a single table. While it is possible to play in a smaller area players have a tendency to compensate for the lack of space by developing completely unorthodox strokes. You will be wise to bear in mind the maxim, 'old habits die hard.' Your ability to learn the more conventional strokes at a later date might be affected by learning in too cramped a space.

In many circumstances you will have no control over the type of lighting used, but if you are equipping your own table tennis room it is well worth considering the installation of tungsten halogen lamps. Unless correctly phased, fluorescent lighting will cause an undesirable stroboscopic effect on the ball.

Clothing
Competitive table tennis is played in clothing specially designed for the purpose. Both men and women now play in short-sleeved shirts and elasticated shorts. This specialist clothing is comfortable to wear and allows the player to move with ease into the many positions which he must adopt during the course of a game. If you are merely interested in table tennis at a recreational level an expensive outfit is not an absolute necessity, but whatever you choose to wear it should be loose fitting and feel comfortable. Tight jeans are certainly not to be recommended as they will

What the well-dressed player wears.

Figure 11 The penhold grip.

Figure 12 The Western or shakehands grip: forehand and backhand.

greatly hinder your ability to make any fast and controlled movements.

A tracksuit of some description will prove to be a valuable investment as it is important to keep warm during rest periods. Think of your muscles as sticks of toffee – if they are warm they will stretch easily but if they are cold they become brittle and you will be more prone to injury.

Ideally, dark coloured clothing should be selected but the only colour which is actually forbidden within the laws of the game is white; as you can imagine the human eye has great difficulty in tracking a small white ball moving at speed against a white background.

Shoes

Light footwear will enable you to develop the nimble footwork which is a very vital part of this game. A range of special table tennis shoes are available from leading sports shops and in relation to many varieties of training shoes they are moderately priced, but you must consider the value of spending your money on a pair of sturdy all-purpose training shoes which give adequate support for a variety of sports activities compared to table tennis shoes which are of a lightweight material and have only a thin rubber sole giving little support to either the arches of your feet or your ankles.

Specialist table tennis shoes have the advantage of being much more pliable than most other sports shoes allowing the wearer to balance his weight on the balls of his feet and insteps in preparation for the quick movements and frequent changes of direction which the game requires.

If you do buy table tennis shoes you will find that a pair of well-cushioned sports socks will help to protect against painful blisters.

Grips

The two completely different styles of grip of which there are many variations are the 'Western' or 'shakehands' grip and the 'penhold' grip. The penhold grip (Figure 11) is favoured by Asian players. The Chinese and Japanese styles are slightly different but both penhold styles make use of only one side of the racket. Upon examination, you will see that there is a great similarity between these grips and the manner in which a pair of chopsticks are held.

Applying backspin on the forehand.

Applying backspin on the backhand.

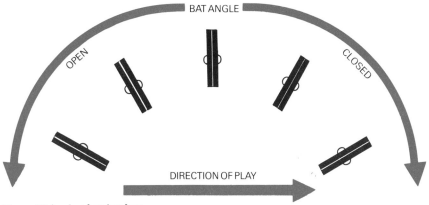

Figure 13 Angle of racket face.

The Western or shakehands grip (Figure 12) which is popular throughout Europe, the Soviet Union and the United States, utilises both surfaces of the racket as shown.

The angle of the blade is controlled by the pressure exerted by your thumb and forefinger, the other fingers merely giving balance to the racket. While it is sensible to place the forefinger along the edge of the racket in order to minimise the possibility of it obstructing a backhand shot this is very much a matter of personal choice.

Whichever grip you choose to adopt it is important that you find it comfortable for both forehand and backhand play. As a novice you may find it possible to change your grip during a rally but as you improve and become involved in longer and faster rallies the need to change grips will hinder your progress.

Spin

Your enjoyment of the game will be greatly enhanced if you are able to recognise the types of spin which different shots impart. Understanding spin will not only help you to decide which shot to play but what type of bounce to expect when an opponent's return lands in your court.

The type and amount of spin produced is related to the angle of the racket face and the direction and speed of the racket arm which are used (see Figure 13). The two major types of spin are 'backspin' and 'topspin'.

The more open the racket face then the greater the amount of backspin which is imparted to the ball upon contact (Figure 14). When a backspin return lands it will 'kick' off at a higher angle.

To play a topspin shot a closed bat face is used (Figure 15). The more closed the face the greater the amount of topspin which is imparted. When the shot lands it will dive down.

A third type of spin, 'sidespin', is rarely see in its pure form; it is normally used in conjunction with either topspin or backspin. As its name suggests this spin will cause the ball to swerve in

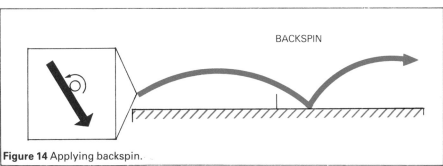

Figure 14 Applying backspin.

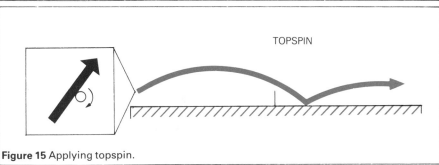

Figure 15 Applying topspin.

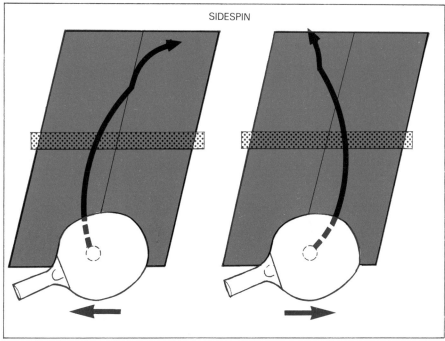

Figure 16 Applying sidespin.

249

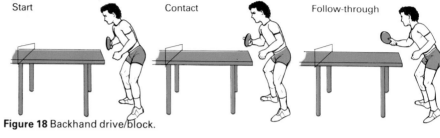

Start   Contact   Follow-through

Figure 17 Backhand push.

Start   Contact   Follow-through

Figure 18 Backhand drive/block.

Start   Contact   Follow-through

Figure 19 Forehand drive.

Start   Contact   Follow-through

Figure 20 Forehand push.

flight and to veer off either to left or right when the return contacts the table. By pushing the racket head from left to right across the back of the ball the return will swerve to the left on contact with the playing surface (Figure 16). By pulling the racket head from right to left across the back of the ball the return will swerve to the right on contact with the playing surface.

Combined with either of topspin or backspin this can add another dimension to your basic strokes.

The Foundations

When we see the game's leading exponents demonstrate a vast array of dynamic strokes either on TV or live in the arena, there is a tendency to devote hours of practice to the immitation of those glamorous shots. What must be remembered is that each of the top players has, as the basis of his game, a complete mastery of the basic strokes. He is a winner because his game is built on firm foundations. As with any other active sport there is no substitute for practice and this should begin with basic strokes.

Appying topspin on the backhand.

A backhand block.

Backhand Push

This is the stroke (Figure 17) which is perhaps the easiest of all to learn.

Stance Take up a position close to the table. Your weight should be slightly forward on the balls of the feet, the shoulders and feet both facing the direction of play and the feet slightly more than shoulder width apart.

Stroke The push is a short stroke created by pivoting the elbow. Little wrist or shoulder movement is required. As its name suggests the ball is pushed back over the net by using a slow, smooth downward stroke. The point of contact should always be in front of the stomach; remember to move your feet in order to place your body in line with the ball. If you are lazy and stretch to play a return you are likely to loose control of the stroke.

Backhand Drive and Backhand Block

Stance This is the same as for the backhand push.

Stroke (a) *Backhand Drive:* like its forehand counterpart this is a short stroke. If we liken it to a clock the movement of the racket starts at 9 o'clock and finishes at 12 o'clock (see Figure 18).

(b) *Backhand Block:* derived from the backhand drive, this stroke is a particularly useful means of counteracting a heavy topspin return. It is an even shorter stroke than the drive. As the ball is contacted earlier it will be necessary to move slightly nearer to the table in order to maintain control and avoid the need to stretch.

Forehand Drive

Stance Stand close to the table and square to it with the left foot slightly further forward than the right. At the end of the stroke the shoulders should be square to the direction in which the ball has been hit.

Once again the weight should be slightly forward on the balls of the feet. A slight crouch is important as it increases the space between elbow and trunk and allows free movement of the racket arm.

Stroke The forehand drive is a short stroke created by a pivoting action of the racket arm at the elbow together with a quarter turn of the upper body about the hips (see Figure 19). As the stroke is played the shoulders rotate to finish square to the direction in which the ball has been played, causing the body weight to transfer naturally from the right to left foot. Ideally a table tennis player should recover his balance directly the stroke is executed. If body-weight is evenly distributed you will be equally well prepared to move to the left or right to play your next stroke. For this reason more advanced players favour a completely square stance when playing the forehand drive.

Forehand push

Of the basic strokes this is, for most players, the most difficult one to master, but it is an invaluable stroke for players of all levels; the forehand push is frequently seen in use at the very highest level of competition. In the game situation, if the ball is placed short to the forehand and low over the net it is impractical to think of using a topspin shot but a controlled forehand push can be very effective. Placed either wide or deep to the base line it can put an opponent under pressure and force him to make an error.

Stance This is the same as for the forehand drive.

Applying topspin on the forehand.

A forehand block.

Figure 21 A short service.

Stroke Created by pivoting the elbow, the forehand push is a short stroke where the racket is moved slightly downwards and forward to push the ball over the net. As with the forehand drive the shoulders should rotate smoothly to finish square to the direction of the shot (see Figure 20).

There is no hard and fast rule which dictates that these strokes must be learned in the order which has been outlined. The most important factor is that equal practice time should be devoted to each of them. By adhering to this principal you will develop an all-round game. Remember that a player who has areas of his game which are obviously weak will taste very limited success as his opponent may quickly discover and exploit them.

Footwork
You may often think that your failure to make a good return is caused by a poor stroke but often the real cause lies elsewhere. Even the leading table tennis players can only execute their shots to best advantage if through nimble footwork they are able to project their body into the correct position from which to make each stroke.

Footwork is a vital part of the game of table tennis which is often overlooked during practice. Man is by nature a lazy creature, and this tendency often results in a player stretching to reach a shot when in fact he ought to move his entire body towards the ball. By straightening the racket arm it is easy to lose the vital element of control which will reduce the effectiveness of the shot being played and cause a loss of balance which in turn will make it more difficult to recover in time to play the next shot.

Static practices are useful as they enable you to concentrate on stroke technique, but once a reasonable degree of proficiency is achieved practices incorporating footwork are more valuable. It is useful at this point to practise with a player of a higher standard who can act as a controller by placing the ball accurately to different points on the table, in sequence. In this way footwork can be learned to such a degree that it becomes virtually automatic; in a game situation this will allow you to devote more of your attention to other vital aspects of play.

There are two recognised types of footwork, *'stepping'* and *'running'*.

Stepping When close to the table, the feet are moved in short steps. At this distance balance is a vital factor and care must be taken to avoid crossing the feet as this will increase the time needed to recover. Vertical trunk movements should be kept to a minimum as energy used in bobbing up and down between strokes is energy wasted.

Running A defensive player positioned well back from the table must cover a much greater distance than his attacking counterpart; running footwork is far more functional at this distance. In this type of footwork the feet may be crossed; as the ball must cover a far greater distance the defender has a longer period in which to effect his recovery.

A forehand service.

A backhand service (after the ball has been struck).

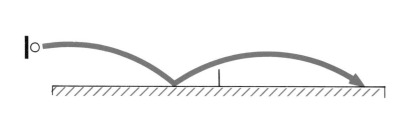

Figure 22 A long service.

The Next Step

Once a player has mastered a variety of footwork sequences the next step is for the controller to simulate match conditions by changing the placement of shots at random, gradually building the practice to include each of the shots learned.

Service

The service is not merely a way of introducing the ball into play but the first opportunity which you have to place your opponent under pressure. Unlike other strokes of a rally you have complete control over the stroke which you wish to play and the area of the table in which you wish to place it. By using your service points wisely, varying the speed, spin and placement of each serve, you can quickly uncover an opponent's weaknesses and by exploiting them force poor returns which will enable you to use your own attacking shots at an early stage in the rally.

If you are able to reproduce only one or two different serves an opponent will soon learn to return them and the advantage of service will be lost. Therefore, it is sensible to spend time building a repertoire of different serves.

Short service Over recent years a short service has been considered to be rather negative as it could easily be pushed back by an opponent. The latest style of short service (Figure 21) is a little more awkward to deal with; by playing a low ball which will bounce midway between the net and the baseline of your opponents court he will be forced to decide whether to strike the ball early with topspin (when really it is too low) or to move hastily back in order to play a push stroke.

When practising this service aim to make the ball bounce twice, the second bounce being as near as possible to the baseline. You will achieve this with little difficulty by striking the ball at net height and aiming its first bounce midway between your own baseline and the net. If you find that your service is bouncing high on your opponent's court, allowing him to attack the ball, the cause is probably that you are striking the ball above net height.

Long service To be effective a long service must bounce very near to your opponent's base line (Figure 22). If it lands in the middle of his court it will bounce too high and is likely to be returned with interest!

Practise long and short services with both your backhand and forehand, and once you can achieve regular success playing along the diagonals practise serving down the line.

Finally it is well worth developing a service down the centre of the table to your opponent's crossover point. In right-handed players this falls midway between the breastbone and the right shoulder. It is a 'no man's land' where neither a forehand nor backhand stroke will feel comfortable. If you use that tactic repeatedly it will loose its value as your opponent will anticipate and move accordingly, but it can certainly be worth the odd point.

If you can conceal the type of service which you intend to play, almost until

A high toss service.

Stance to receive service.

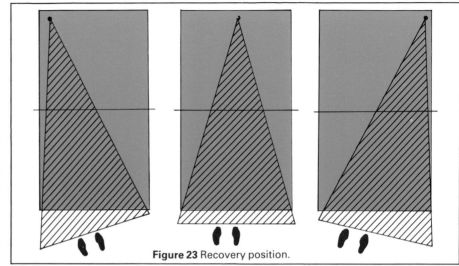

Figure 23 Recovery position.

the point of contact, you will confuse your opponent and prevent him from anticipating the stroke. Therefore it is worthwhile practising a similar backswing for a number of different serves.

Receiving

Having looked at the variety of service ploys which can be adopted, and considering the difficulties involved in dealing with the elements of spin, speed and length, you must now be wondering how on earth as the receiver you will be able to cope with the task of playing an effective return.

The art of return depends upon your degree of readiness and your ability to read the clues displayed by the server. By adopting a slightly crouched stance with your weight evenly distributed on the balls of your feet you will be best prepared to move in any direction. The position which you assume should be square to the direction from which the service is to be played.

Anticipation

Some players are naturally gifted and are able to anticipate their opponent's service or return almost before he plays the stroke. Although it is generally thought that anticipation is a quality which everyone has to differing degrees and which cannot be greatly improved upon through practice, you will find that as you become more familiar with the different table tennis strokes, it becomes easier to see what sort of shot your opponent is going to play. As with any fast ball game it is important to watch the ball but at certain points, especially when receiving service, pay attention to his general body position and the angle of his bat as this may give you vital clues of what is to follow.

In a game situation a player cannot afford the luxury of admiring each stroke – he must immediately recover to a position which will give him the best opportunity of playing his next shot successfully. The position to which he recovers is not related to the table but to the placement of the shot which he has just played for it is this which governs the boundaries of the playing surface within which the opponent can place the return stroke.

The areas to be covered are shown in Figure 23. If you are right-handed, by standing slightly to the left your bat will be central to the area which you must cover and therefore you will be best prepared to face either a backhand or a forehand return.

Receiving service on the backhand.

Receiving service on the forehand.

Index/Glossary

255

March (Euchre): the making of all five tricks by one player or side 131
Martingale (Roulette): a staking system 196
Massé (Snooker, Billiards, Pool): a shot which swerves the cue ball sharply 217
Matador (Domino Game) 38
Meld (Card Games): a set of matched cards, either by rank or sequence
Merelles (alternative name for Nine Men's Morris) 60
Michigan (alternative name for Newmarket) 187
Mickey Mouse (Darts Game) 239
Middle Game (Chess) 26, 30; (Chinese Chess) 47; (Shogi) 96: the development of a game after the opening
Middlehand (Skat): the player between Forehand and Dealer 141
Mill (alternative name for Nine Men's Morris) 60
Misère (Solo Whist) 144; (Napoleon) 186: a declaration to lose all the tricks
Misère Ouverte (Solo Whist): a declaration to lose all thirteen tricks, with the hand exposed on the table 144
Miss (Craps): to lose (i,e, the shooter) 163
Miss Milligan (Patience Game) 104
Monte Bank 185
Moultezim: a Turkish version of Backgammon 17
Muggins (Cribbage): an announcement by which a player scores for himself points that his opponent has overlooked
Muggins (Domino Game) 37

Napoleon 186
Natural (Baccarat) 158; (Chemin de Fer) 182; (Punto Banco) 188: a point of 8 or 9 with two cards 158
Natural (Blackjack): an Ace with a ten-count card 159
Natural (Craps): a roll of 7 or 11 on the come-out roll 163
Newmarket 187
Next Suit (Euchre): the suit of the same colour as the trump suit 131
Nine Men's Morris 60
Noir (Boule) 178; (Roulette) 191: a bet on black numbers
Noir (Trente et Quarante): a bet that this will be the winning row 202
Notation (Chess) 23, 30; (Chinese Chess) 46; (Shogi) 94
Null (Skat): a contract to make no tricks at all 141

Object Ball (Snooker, Billiards, Pool): the ball to be struck by the cue ball
Oche (Darts): a raised strip to indicate the throwing distance 236
Odds bet (Craps): a bet paid at correct odds, allowed in certain circumstances by a casino 166
On (Snooker): the ball to be played next is the ball on 208
Open (Poker): to begin the betting in games of the Jackpot variety 174
Open (Pool): said of the table before one of the players has chosen which group of balls to play 232
Open Misère (Solo Whist): see Misère Ouverte 144
Opening Moves (Chess) 25, 32; (Chinese Chess) 46; (Shogi) 95
Opening Plays (Backgammon) 16
Opposing Cannons openings (Chinese Chess) 47
Order Up (Euchre): a declaration by an opponent of the dealer accepting the turned-up suit as trumps 131
Orthogonal move: in board games, a move along a file or rank (as opposed to a diagonal move)
Oudlers (Tarot): the 21 and 1 of trumps and the Fool 149
Oware (Mancala Game) 53

Pack (Patience Games): to arrange cards in order, prior to final moving 102
Pair (Boule) 178; (Roulette) 191: a bet on even numbers
Pair (Casino): to play a card of the same rank as one on the table, thus capturing it 122
Pair (Card Games): two cards of the same rank
Pair Royal (Brag): three cards of the same rank 180
Partie (Piquet): a game, consisting of six deals 138
Pass (Craps): to win (i.e. the shooter) 163
Passe (Roulette): a bet on numbers 19-36 191
Patience Games (Cards) 102
Pawn Promotion (Chess) 22, 32
Peep (Napoleon): a variation whereby each player may look at the top card of the stock 186
Peg (Cribbage): the peg used in scoring on the cribbage board; to score 126
Penalties (Bridge) 113
Peter (Bridge): a signalling play in which the higher of two cards is played first 114
Petit (Tarot): the trump 1 152
Physical Games 205
Picture Card (Card Games): any King, Queen or Jack (also called Court Card or Face Card)
Pig (Dice Game) 81
Ping-Pong (early name for Table Tennis) 243
Pips (Domino and Card Games): the number of spots on a domino and the number of symbols on a playing card (i.e the 3 has a pip count of three)
Pique (Piquet): to score 30 points in hand and play before opponent scores a point 138
Piquet 137
Place bets (Craps): bet that a point number will or will not be rolled before 7 165
Plain Suit (Card Games): a suit other than the trump suit
Plakato: a Greek version of Backgammon 17
Pochen (old version of Poker) 171
Point (Backgammon): positions on the board or table 12
Point (Craps): a roll of any number on the come-out roll other than a natural or craps 163
Point (Piquet): the number of cards held in the longest suit 137
Point (Strung Flowers): a roll of any pair with 2,3,4 or 5 168
Point-count System (Bridge): a method of evaluating a hand 114
Poker 171
Poker Dice 170
Polish Draughts 58
Pone (Piquet): the non-dealer 125
Pool 227
Pool (Gambling Games): the collective amount of players' stakes and penalties, also called Kitty
Pope Joan (forerunner of Newmarket) 187
Pot (Snooker, Billiards, Pool): to cause an object ball to be pocketed
Prial (Brag): three cards of the same rank 180
Prime (Backgammon): six consecutive points made by one player, thereby blocking opponent's men 15
Primero (forerunner of Brag) 180
Prise (Tarot): a bid 149
Prison (Roulette): a method by which a stake on even-money bets, when zero appears, is lost or retained on the result of the next spin 194
Prison (Trente et Quarante): method by which stakes, after a refait, may be lost or retained as the result of the next deal 202
Progressive Jackpots (Poker): a variation in which the requirement to open the betting gets higher with each passed hand 174
Promotion Zones (Shogi) 93
Prop (Solo Whist): see Proposal 144
Proposal (Solo Whist): a bid which seeks a partner in making eight tricks against the other two players, also known as prop 144
Propose (Ecarté): a request by non-dealer that cards in hand be exchanged for cards in the stock 129
Proposition bets (Craps): bets of various kinds made on one roll of the dice 166
Pung (Mah Jong): a set of three tiles of the same kind 85
Punto Banco 188
Push Stroke (Snooker, Billiards): a foul – when the cue remains in contact with the cue ball after it has begun its forward motion, or has made contact with the object ball
Pyramid Spot (Billiards): the spot between the billiards spot and the centre spot, i.e. the pink spot in snooker 218
Pyramids (forerunner of Snooker) 207
Pyramids (Patience Game) 107

Qualify (Dice game) 169
Quart (Piquet): a sequence of four cards 137
Quatorze (Piquet): four cards of the same rank higher than 9 137
Queen of Italy (Patience Game): see Terrace 105
Quinte (Piquet): a sequence of five cards 137

Raise (Poker): to increase the stake 173
Rally (Table Tennis): period during which ball is in play 244
Ranging Rook opening (Shogi): 96
Rank (Chess, Draughts and other games played on a board with squares): a row of squares running from side to side of the board (see also File)
Receiver (Table Tennis): the player to whom the server plays the ball 244
Red Dog 189
Refait (Trente et Quarante): when both rows equal 31, when the casino takes half the stakes 202
Repique (Piquet): to score 30 points in hand alone before opponent scores a point 138
Rest (Snooker, Billiards): implement used to support the cue when the cue ball cannot be reached with a normal bridging hand
Reversi 99
Revoke (Card Games): a failure to follow the rules of the game when playing a card, e.g. failure to play a card of the suit led when able to
Rien ne va plus (Roulette): a call meaning 'no more bets' 191
Right bet (Craps): a bet that the shooter will win 163
Right Bower (Euchre): the jack of the trump suit 131
Robin Post (Patience Game) 106
Rouge (Boule) 178; (Roulette) 191: a bet on red numbers
Rouge (Trente et Quarante): a bet that this will be the winning row 202
Rouge et Noir (alternative name for Trente et Quarante) 201
Roulette 190
Round the Clock (Darts Game) 238
Round-the-corner Straight (Poker): a special hand – a sequence which incudes Ace as high and low 176
Rover Rule (Nine Men's Morris): the rule whereby a player with only three men left may move a man to any vacant point without restriction 60
Royal Abundance (Solo Whist): a declaration to win nine tricks, with the turned-up suit as trumps 144
Royal Casino 124
Rubber (Bridge): the series of three successive games between two sides; winning two of the games 112
Ruff (Card Games): to play a trump card on a trick
Run (Brag): three cards in sequence 181
Running Flush (Brag): a sequence of three cards of the same suit 180
Running game (Backgammon): strategy in which men are advanced as quickly as possible 15
Russian Draughts 58
Ruy Lopez (Chess): a popular series of opening moves 25

Sabot (Card Games): a shoe from which cards are dealt singly
Saint (old name for Piquet) 137
Sand (old name for Piquet) 137
Saratoga (alternative name for Newmarket) 187
Schneider (Skat): the making by declarer of 90 or more card points in his tricks 140
Schwartz (Skat): the making of all the tricks by declarer 140
Scoring (Backgammon) 14; (Bridge) 112; (Mah Jong) 88
Scram (Darts game) 240
Screw (Snooker, Billiards, Pool): a form of spin 216
Seki (Go): a situation in which neither player can occupy a point without being captured 71
Semeai (Go): the situation in which each of two opposing armies can evade capture only by itself capturing the other 70
Sente (Go): the initiative 67
Septième (Piquet): a sequence of seven cards 137
Sequence (Card Games): two or more cards of adjacent ranks
Server (Table Tennis): the player who introduces the ball into play 244
Seven-card Stud: a variation of Poker 176
Shanghai (Darts Game) 238
Shogi 91
Shoot (alternative name for Slippery Sam) 189
Shooter (Craps) 163; (Barbudi) 168: the player who rolls the dice
Shut the Box (Dice Game) 78
Sicilian Defence (Chess): a series of opening moves 26
Side (Snooker, Billiards, Pool): a form of spin 216
Side Suit (Card Games): a suit other than the trump suit
Signora (Patience game): see Terrace 105
Single Knight defence (Chinese Chess) 47
Singleton (Card Games): a holding of only one card in a particular suit
Sink (Piquet): to omit to announce a scoring combination 138
Sixain (Roulette): a bet on six numbers 192
Sixtième (Piquet): a sequence of six cards 137
Skat 140
Skewer (Chess): an attacking move with the object of a capture 27, 32
Skip Straight (Poker): a special hand – a sequence of 'odd' or 'even' cards 176
Slam (Bridge): the winning of 13 tricks (Grand Slam) or 12 tricks (Little Slam) 112
Sleeper (Roulette): a number which has not appeared for a certain number of spins 198
Slippery Anne (Black Maria) 118
Slippery Sam 189
Sniff (Domino Game) 38
Snooker 207
Soda (Faro): the first card dealt, which is discarded 183
Soft Hand (Blackjack): a hand which counts an Ace as eleven 160
Solitaire Games (Cards) 102
Solo (Solo Whist): a declaration to win five tricks 144
Solo Whist 144
Sowing (Mancala): distributing stones from one cup to others 52
Spade Casino 124
Spanish Draughts 57
Spider Rest (Snooker, Billiards): a special rest with a high bridge used if it is necessary to bridge over an intervening ball
Spin (Snooker, Billiards, Pool): applied to the cue ball to govern its behaviour after contact with the object ball 216
Spit in the Ocean: a variation of Poker 176
Split (Blackjack): to take each card of a pair dealt as the first card in two separate hands 160
Spoil Five 146
Staggered Cannons opening (Chinese Chess) 47
Stalemate (Chess) 28, 32; (Chinese Chess) 46
Stand (Blackjack): to decline additional cards 160
Star points (Go): points used in handicapping 63
Starter (Cribbage): the top card of the cut, turned face upwards 125
Static Rook opening (Shogi) 95
Stem (Darts): part of dart which usually screws into barrel and holds the flight 236
Step (Halma): a move to an adjacent vacant square 40
Stock (Card Games): the undealt part of the pack
Stones (Go): the men or counters used in play 64
Stops (alternative name for Newmarket) 187
Straddle (Poker): a compulsory bet of twice the ante made before the cards are dealt 172
Straight (Poker): five cards in sequence 172
Straight Draw Poker 171
Straight Flush (Poker): a sequence of five cards of the same suit 171
Straight Poker 171
Stringing (Billiards): method of deciding first break 218
Strung Flowers (Dice Game) 168
Stud Poker 176
Stun (Snooker, Billiards, Pool): a form of spin 216
Suicide Rule (Go): a rule forbidding a player to play a stone which would leave his army without liberties 66
Sweep (Casino): to take all the cards in the layout 123

Table Games 9
Table Tennis 243
Tableau des Voisons (Roulette): a chart showing each number in relation to its neighbours 196
Tables: early name for Backgammon 11
Take the Chalks (Darts): to score 238
Talon (Piquet): cards placed aside after the deal for later use 137
Tarocchi, Tarock, Tarokk: alternative names for Tarot 148
Tarot 148
Terrace (Patience Game) 105
Thirteen Grades of Imperial Treasure (Mah Jong): a special hand 87
Three Blind Mice (Patience Game) 103
Three Great Scholars (Mah Jong): a special hand 87
Three-stake Brag 180
Tierce (Piquet): a sequence of three cards 137
Trail (Casino): to play a card from hand face up to the table layout 122
Transversale plein (Roulette): a bet on three numbers 191
Transversale simple (Roulette): a bet on six numbers 192
Trente et Quarante 201
Trick (Ecarté): the making of three or more tricks 129
Trio (Piquet): three cards of the same rank higher than 9 137
Turkish Draughts 58
Turn-up (Card Games): a card faced after the deal to determine the trump suit
Twenty-six (Dice game) 169

Undercut (Gin Rummy): to achieve a lower count than knocker 137
Upcard (Gin Rummy): the card turned up after the hands are dealt 134

Value of Pieces (Chess) 24
Void (Card Games): holding no cards of a particular suit
Vole (Ecarté): the making of all five tricks 129
Vulnerable (Bridge): describes a side which has won a game towards a rubber and is thus subject to higher penalties and bonuses 112

Wellington (Napoleon): a bid to make five tricks at double stakes 186
Whisky Poker: a variation of Poker 176
Whist 153
Widow (Card Games): an extra hand dealt to the table
Wild Card (Card games): a card that its holder may specify as representing any card (often a Joker or a 2)
Winning Hazard (Billiards): a pot of an object ball 220
Wriggly Snake (Mah Jong): a special hand 87
Wrong bet (Craps): a bet that the shooter will lose 163

Xiangqi (Chinese Chess) 43

Yacht (Dice game) 76
Younger (Card games): the dealer in two-handed games